D0387418

Why cant U teach me 2 read?

Why cant U teach me 2 read?

THREE STUDENTS AND A MAYOR PUT OUR SCHOOLS TO THE TEST

BETH FERTIG

Farrar, Straus and Giroux

New York

Farrar, Straus and Giroux
18 West 18th Street, New York 10011

Distributed in Canada by D&M Publishers, Inc.
Printed in the United States of America
First edition, 2009

Library of Congress Cataloging-in-Publication Data
Fertig, Beth, 1966–
Why cant U teach me 2 read? : three students and a mayor put our schools to the test / Beth Fertig. — 1st ed.
p. cm.
Includes bibliographical references.
ISBN: 978-0-374-29905-7 (hardcover : alk. paper)
1. Reading—Remedial teaching—New York (State)—New York—Case studies. 2. Reading disability—New York (State)—New York—Case studies. 3. Children with disabilities—Education—New York (State)—New York—Case studies. 4. New York (N.Y.). Board of Education. I. Title. II. Title: Why can't you teach me to read?

LB1050.5.F46 2009
372.4309747'1—dc22

2009011520

Designed by Jonathan D. Lippincott

www.fsgbooks.com

1 3 5 7 9 10 8 6 4 2

Contents

Spring: Inputs and Outcomes

Why cant U teach me 2 read?

Prologue: Lost

Yamilka was just trying to take the subway home from school. It was a Monday evening in July 2006, a few weeks after her twenty-third birthday. She left her class on the Upper East Side of Manhattan at around 5:30 and went to exercise at a gym a block away on Eighty-sixth Street, using a guest pass her teacher had given her. She then walked another block to the subway on Lexington Avenue and caught the number 4 train to the Bronx. Yamilka lived with her parents and three siblings in an apartment in Morris Heights. It was a ten-minute walk from the Mount Eden Avenue station, three stops north of Yankee Stadium. The train ride normally took about half an hour.

Everything seemed normal when Yamilka got on board during the evening rush. But then the train zipped past her stop because of some track work and kept on going. Yamilka was frozen with terror and a feeling of helplessness.

Yamilka was illiterate, and she was taking classes at the Manhattan branch of Huntington Learning Center, a national tutoring chain, so she could finally learn how to read. Not knowing what to do, she got off the train a few stops later. But unable to determine the name of the station or read a subway map, she had no clue how far she was from her home. She figured the sun would be setting soon and she didn't want to linger. "I didn't want to walk from there; it was too late, I was scared of walking by myself," she said. So she took a train back downtown, hoping to find her way.

Again the train passed the stop near her house. In her confusion she stayed on board and kept going until she passed the familiar Eighty-sixth Street stop near her school. She got off the train a stop or two later, somewhere in Midtown.

It would be difficult making sense of this story if you didn't know Yamilka very well. She moved to New York from the Dominican Republic at the age of ten, and her English is bumpy. She often mixes up her tenses and gets things out of order. But she was very clear about how frightening and disorienting the event was for her.

"I got off the train and I take the bus," she told me, when recalling how she wound up in a mysterious part of Manhattan. "I was just walking, walking around. I wasn't able to do anything. I didn't know nothing." Yamilka hopped on the first city bus she saw. She was tired and frightened of the train and just wanted to get back to the Bronx. But she didn't ask where the bus was going. "I didn't want to bother the driver," she explained. "I was thinking, the bus maybe take me around my house."

When the bus got to the end of the line, Yamilka wasn't anywhere near her home. She didn't even know what part of town she was in. All she remembered was seeing a lot of white people wearing suits. From her description of the buildings and bus route, it seemed as though she wound up near Wall Street, but this didn't mean anything to her. She didn't know that Wall Street is at the southern tip of Manhattan, eleven miles south of her apartment building. Her world was extremely limited by her inability to read, restricted to the few bus and subway stops that she could visually recognize or determine by street numbers.

Yamilka said she got on another bus hoping it would go uptown, and she knew she ended up in Harlem, which is closer to the Bronx. At one point she was the only woman on the bus. "I was feeling so nervous, I couldn't think clear what was going on in my mind," she said, explaining why—once again—she didn't ask anyone for help. "You know like when you're on a roller coaster and you go around and around and you stop, and your head is still spinning? I was so tired taking trains and taking buses and not feeling safe."

Yamilka got off the bus and tried to call home, but the pay phone ate her quarter. She had used up all the rides on her Metrocard and needed to hang on to as many quarters as she could for more bus rides, so she gave up on calling her family and got on another bus. This time she decided to ask for help. "I said I want to go to 174th Street," but the driver gave her a "nasty attitude." She got off the bus when it pulled up at a subway and she took another train. She eventually recognized where she was and got off at a familiar stop in the Bronx where she knew she could take a bus back home. But it was late and she was frightened while waiting at the bus stop, surrounded by men. Yamilka was overweight and extremely self-conscious about her body and any male attention. "My stomach was going crazy. My heart, it was going so fast that I was thinking I was going to pass out. I was the only girl waiting for the bus," she said. She relaxed a little when another woman joined her. But a taxi driver approached and made some comments that got her upset. "He was talking to me, he was going around looking at me. He was telling me things like 'You pretty,' and that moment I was not feeling comfortable again. I was like, What am I supposed to do in this moment? I'm putting my life in danger only to go home?"

When Yamilka finally arrived home, it was after midnight. The whole trip had taken about six hours. Her family had been so worried that her parents, a sister, and her brother had even taken a taxi to East Eighty-sixth Street, hoping to find her near the tutoring center, while her other sister waited at home by the phone. Despite the trauma, Yamilka found something oddly funny about the whole thing. When she had left for school that morning, she told one of her sisters something like "Goodbye, I'll see you tomorrow!" It was an obvious joke. Yamilka never went anywhere except to school. "We were joking around, you know, like sisters always do," she recalled. "And this is what happened to me. I got lost. It was amazing, sometimes you joke about something and it comes true."

Unfortunately, laughing about the situation didn't make it any easier. Yamilka didn't go back to Huntington Learning Center the next day or the next. She was too shaken up, so she stayed home watching television. It was about a week before she returned to the private tutoring center. Her teachers tried to make her feel better about the whole experience. "Everyone gets lost," they said. "You just have to ask for help." Yamilka admitted that she was afraid to ask for a simple reason: she didn't want to reveal that she was illiterate. "I didn't want to put my life in more danger," she said. "It would be more easy if I tell somebody that I didn't know . . . But I didn't want people to take advantage of me. I didn't want to put my life in more danger than it already was. For what I'm going to be telling people about my life?"

Her tutors encouraged her to ask basic questions that didn't have to reveal she couldn't read. "You can try asking, 'Can you tell me where this bus stops?'" suggested Anthony Liberatoscioli, an assistant director and teacher Yamilka adored. She had jokingly dubbed him "Crazy Italian Boy." Liberatoscioli also reassured her that bus drivers are used to meeting people who can't read. But Yamilka didn't take comfort in that. She was twenty-three years old, and didn't want to be illiterate. "Sometimes I wish I could have a normal life so I don't have to worry about absolutely anything," she told me later, in a tired deadpan voice.

"Sometimes I feel like so . . . it's getting old. I feel like I don't got enough strength to keep fighting. I wish it could get a little more easy. I get so frustrated; I get so mad. Why everything have to take so long? I feel like sometimes I'm not going to be able to do anything."

A few days later she stopped going to Huntington altogether.

Yamilka does not want to reveal her full name, in order to protect her privacy, and the names of her family members have all been changed. But she gave me full access to her records. Her tutoring at Huntington Learning Center was funded by the New York City public school system—at a total cost to city taxpayers of up to $120,000. Her lawyers believe she won the biggest one-time settlement ever awarded for "compensatory education," which is basically the city's admission of educational neglect for not having given her appropriate help for her learning disabilities. In 2005 a hearing officer granted Yamilka 1,500 hours of tutoring at Huntington, at eighty dollars an hour. She had two years to use those hours.

Yamilka wasn't the only student in this situation. In the summer of 2006, the director of the Manhattan branch of Huntington Learning Center, Carrie Meyers, said she had about ten students in her program who were awarded educational services at the city's expense. Several of them were reading at low elementary levels. But Yamilka's reading level was the worst Meyers had ever seen for a student her age. "When Yamilka began her instruction here, we did an assessment of her skills," said Meyers. "Yamilka knew eight letters of the alphabet in terms of identifying letters."

Shockingly, Yamilka was a high school graduate. She had attended public schools ever since she had arrived in the Bronx in 1993, at the age of ten. She started off in English as a Second Language classes and was eventually assigned to special education classes in middle school. Later, she attended special ed classes at Norman Thomas High School in Manhattan, a conventional high school with two thousand students. After one semester the administration concluded that she didn't belong there because she still couldn't read, and she was transferred to a career-development high school in the South Bronx with about five hundred students. Schools like these are intended for students with disabilities who have fallen off, or been steered away from, the academic track. They are part of a separate network in New York City called District 75, for students with serious academic, emotional, and physical disabilities. Students at the career-development schools take some reading and math classes, but the focus is on work-study jobs, not academics. Bonnie Brown, who headed District 75 in 2006, bluntly told WNYC Radio, "There are some children who will never learn how to read."[1] She went on to explain that career-development high schools in District 75 taught their students enough basic life skills to get a job and live independently.

But they rarely get full diplomas. The nonprofit legal group Advocates for Children of New York released a study in 2005 finding that less than 1 percent of the students in District 75 earned regular diplomas. The vast majority of its graduates left with special education diplomas like Yamilka's. These certificates merely state that the student has completed whatever was expected based on his or her Individualized Educational Program, or IEP, a document required by federal law for all students with disabilities. IEP diplomas do not have the same value as traditional diplomas, because the students don't have to pass statewide tests. When Yamilka earned her IEP diploma in 2004, right after turning twenty-one, she was so embarrassed about how little she'd learned that she didn't bother to attend her own graduation. "It was not meaningful for me," she said, pausing to find the right words. "One cannot pretend to be around other kids, to be laughing and having a good time. See, I knew in my heart that it had no meaning. That they didn't help me. For why was I going to waste my time? For why was I going to waste twenty bucks on cap and gown?"

A year after her graduation, Yamilka's younger brother, Alejandro, discovered that their family could challenge the school system. He, too, had gotten to high school without learning to read. The move from the Dominican Republic would have been a tough adjustment for any child. But it was especially difficult for Alejandro and Yamilka, both of whom have learning disabilities. "I was a shy kid," said Alejandro. "I had a lot of problems because I was picked [on] a lot when I was a kid, and you know, a quiet kid. I really didn't talk to nobody." Alejandro is short and sensitive, and said he was beaten up a few times in middle school. By the time he went to Theodore Roosevelt High School in the Bronx, he was still in special education classes and was terrified that his teacher would call on him, exposing his inability to read. He came to dread going to school and started missing classes. "The situation got so, so bad that he would miss months, weeks," said his older sister Elizabeth. "He wouldn't go at all to classes because he was afraid of taking the [city] bus."

The city transferred Alejandro from his large comprehensive high school to a program where he was supposed to earn a GED, or general equivalency diploma.* Elizabeth knew something wasn't right. She had earned a full diploma from Jacqueline Kennedy Onassis High School in Manhattan a few years earlier, and was horrified when she went to visit him in school. "He was taking classes in a basement with boxes."

Alejandro asked to speak to a guidance counselor and was told he could get a new special education evaluation to make sure he was in the right kind of school. He was given the name of the Kennedy Child Study Center in Manhattan, where his visit was covered by his mother's health insurance. Not many families know they have a legal right to an independent evaluation at places like Kennedy, which aren't part of the school system, or that they have a right to a free attorney provided by groups like Advocates for Children and Legal Services.

Alejandro and Elizabeth learned more about their rights at the Kennedy Center and were steered to Advocates for Children. Elizabeth began gathering her brother's paperwork, and they filed for an impartial hearing at the Department of Education.

At the age of nineteen, Alejandro won an initial 480 hours of tutoring because of the city's failure to address his learning disability, a right guaranteed by federal law. He eventually won more than 1,900 hours in total. Soon afterward, he began a rigorous program at Lindamood-Bell Learning Processes, another private tutoring chain with a Manhattan branch that charges $94 an hour. Within a year he was able to read at a fourth-grade level. His tutors saw so much progress that they were hoping he could take the GED after finishing their program in late 2007, at a total cost to the city of almost $160,000.

Alejandro is obviously bright, but he said written language never

*Officially, "GED" stands for General Educational Development (tests).

made sense to him in either English or Spanish. He couldn't see how individual letters were part of a bigger word. "It's like if somebody had never seen a dog before, you tell them this word and that [animal] are the same thing," he tried to explain. "Can you really comprehend that in the beginning? If you see the word 'dog' and see a picture of the dog, you wouldn't comprehend it . . . I don't know, the whole idea of putting letters together to create words is like a weird concept to me."

Alejandro didn't know there was a word for his reading problem: dyslexia. He just knew his problem connecting letters to words didn't stop him from absorbing information through other channels: specifically the History Channel, the Discovery Channel, and CNN. The television was Alejandro's link to the world outside. He watched everything from Charlie Rose and *Frontline* to the smart science fiction series *Battlestar Galactica* and Saturday morning cartoons, which he'd loved ever since he was a child. Alejandro's entire education seems to have come through television. He even learned to speak English by watching TV.

When Alejandro won his case against the Department of Education, he told his lawyers about his older sister Yamilka. She had been staying home, depressed, ever since graduating from high school the previous year, and he wanted to know if there was a way to help her, too. She was grateful for getting a second chance to learn how to read and considered it a "gift" that her brother led her to the lawyers who eventually won her the 1,500 hours of tutoring. But it was a gift she wished she didn't need. At twenty-three, she felt too old to be learning the sounds of the alphabet—especially while her younger brother was quickly progressing to chapter books in his reading program. "It's not easy living life without knowing anything," she said. "Sometimes I feel like I live in a prison and I don't know how to get out."

But Yamilka didn't have time to waste if she was going to get out of her prison. She had a two-year deadline to use the 1,500 hours of tutoring she'd won from the city, and she was only halfway there.

As a civil rights lawyer, Jim Liebman has spent more than half his life working to change big institutions from the outside. At the age of fifty-four, Liebman was working for change from deep within one of the nation's largest and most bureaucratic institutions: the New York City public school system. Ensconced in a cubicle in Lower Manhattan, he was far away from his comfort zone. In 2006 he took a partial leave of absence from his job as a tenured law professor at Columbia University uptown to put his theories about school reform into practice.

With 1,035,000 students and more than a hundred thousand teachers, principals, and staffers, the city school system was at a turning point. Mayor Michael Bloomberg and his chancellor, Joel Klein, had introduced a new curriculum and a management structure modeled after a corporate flowchart. Both were outsiders who were resented by the teachers and principals. Bloomberg was a billionaire who had created a financial media empire. Klein had been a deputy counsel to President Bill Clinton, and an assistant U.S. attorney general in charge of the Justice Department's antitrust division. He was best known for leading the department's fight to break up Microsoft. After leaving the Clinton administration, he was chairman and chief executive officer of the media company Bertelsmann, Inc. Now the two men were set on reforming the nation's largest public school system by creating a new data framework that would be used to track precisely how many students in each school were passing their math and reading tests, and to grade schools based on student progress. Liebman was in charge of this accountability system.

Pressure to raise student achievement had been building ever since the No Child Left Behind Act had been signed into law by President George W. Bush in 2002. It required states receiving federal funds to ensure that all students reach academic proficiency by 2014. The schools had to hire "highly qualified teachers" and measure student achievement with annual subject tests starting in third grade. To live up to NCLB's title, states were also required to disaggregate their data and show how many black, white, Hispanic, Asian, Native American, special education, English Language Learner, and low-income children were meeting the proficiency targets, instead of just reporting an overall total that masked the performance of these subgroups. Schools and districts that didn't reach "proficiency" would be identified as needing improvement—even if just one of the nine subgroups fell short—with the possibility of losing their federal funds or being restructured if they didn't improve.

The challenges were enormous, given the dismal reading scores of U.S. students. ACT, which produces college admissions tests, reported that half of high school graduates in 2005 didn't have the reading skills they needed to succeed in college.[2] Only 33 percent of fourth-graders were reading at or above "proficient" (at grade level) on the 2007 National Assessment of Educational Progress (NAEP), which is also called the Nation's Report Card. And about a quarter of eighth-graders were reading below the "basic" level, meaning they couldn't read for information or identify the main idea of a short passage. There was also a persistent achievement gap. Seventy-eight percent of white fourth-graders were reading at or above the basic level, compared to 46 percent of blacks and 50 percent of Hispanics.

English Language Learners and students with special needs were performing even worse on these national reading tests. That might be expected for students who are still learning the language, or children with severe impairments. But fewer than 2 percent of the nation's 6.6 million students who were receiving special education services in 2004 were classified as mentally retarded, according to the U.S. Department of Education's National Center for Education Statistics (2006). Almost half of all students with special needs had learning disabilities. And the vast majority of them—up to 80 percent, according to many experts—had conditions that affected their ability to read. Although children with learning disabilities are given more time on their exams, they are much less likely to graduate from high school and find good jobs. They're also more likely to wind up in prison. One study suggests more than a *third* of all juvenile offenders qualify for special education services.[3]

Special education students and new arrivals to the United States aren't the only ones struggling to read. A Connecticut study by researchers at Yale found that as many as one out of five children could suffer some kind of reading impairment.[4] There are mixed opinions about whether these students have real neurological problems, such as dyslexia, because a child's readiness to read is also a product of his or her family environment. Children from middle-class families whose parents read to them at an early age, and who attend good preschools, are much more likely to be academically successful than students like Yamilka and Alejandro. But regardless of cause, reading problems are so widespread that teachers refer to slow readers without specific disabilities as having "garden variety" reading problems, as though they're weeds that crop up in every classroom.

Much has been written about the state of American literacy and the declining popularity of books in the Internet age. While the Internet may contribute to shorter attention spans, people *are* reading when they surf the Web. And national reading scores have actually been rising overall, even if the progress is slim. It's also true that if you look at various agencies that track international literacy, the United States is at or above 99 percent—the same level as Denmark, Finland, Japan, and the United Kingdom.

But those numbers don't tell the whole story. When you examine the quality of literacy in the United States, it is often below that of other developed nations. The International Adult Literacy Survey interviewed and tested adults in twenty-two developed countries between 1994 and 1998. It found about 21 percent of Americans between the ages of sixteen and sixty-five were reading at the lowest of five levels. That was about the same percentage as the United Kingdom and Ireland, but it meant the United States had many more poor readers than Sweden, Denmark, Canada, or Germany. This lower level of reading was defined as about the same as a high school dropout's—not illiterate, but also not a reading level sufficient for a technologically sophisticated economy. Only half the U.S. adult population had a reading level considered proficient enough for the current labor market, as defined by several national and state organizations. And among foreign-born adults, reading scores in the United States ranked sixteenth out of seventeen wealthy nations.[5] A smaller Adult Literacy and Lifeskills study of six developed nations in 2003 found the United States did better than Italy in literacy and numeracy, but was outperformed by Bermuda, Canada, Norway, and Switzerland in both skill areas. Once again, even the lowest-performing readers in other countries scored higher than those in the United States.[6]

In a global economy that relies on computer skills, educators and business leaders all agree on the pressing need for twenty-first-century American students to become much more literate than previous generations. This was a big shift from just a few decades ago, when high school students could earn vocational degrees that weren't considered academically challenging.

Joel Klein grew up in that era. Born in 1946, he attended his local public schools in Queens. His father was a high school dropout who worked as a postman. Klein says his father read tons of books—but he didn't need to be so highly literate to become a postman. There were plenty of blue-collar jobs back then, many that paid enough to support a family. "When my father grew up, it was a very different world than the twenty-first century," he says. But as Klein looks at the list of countries that are competing with the United States, he says technology is much more dominant, and in that setting, "if you can't read, you can't play."

Like other urban areas, New York City had seen its manufacturing base shrink dramatically. And its students had more challenges to overcome if they were going to become highly literate adults who were ready for the new economy. The poverty rate had fallen slightly during the boom years of the early twenty-first century. But almost three quarters of the city's 1,035,000 students qualified for free or reduced lunch in 2007, based on a sliding scale that allowed a family of four, for example, to earn between $26,845 and $38,203. Seventy-two percent of the city's students were black or Hispanic. And at least 13 percent were still learning English. The city's test scores had arguably been improving over the past decade, but just over half its high school students were graduating in four years in 2007, according to the state's methodology.

While many school systems found the new testing mandates onerous, the Bloomberg administration embraced much of NCLB. By forcing schools to demonstrate annual progress, the law gave the mayor and his chancellor more leverage over the powerful teachers union and other players they perceived as roadblocks to reform. Klein and Bloomberg thought New Yorkers had a right to demand more for their money. The city's public schools have an annual budget of more than $20 billion, including state and federal funds. Those finances cover school meals, guidance counselors, busing, and medical care in addition to teaching. Bloomberg made improving public education a top priority in his 2001 mayoral campaign. In a speech that June, before an audience of business leaders and philanthropists involved in the schools, he pledged: "As mayor, I would do for public education what Rudy Giuliani did for public safety. I would be the school system's strongest champion and its strictest monitor." Giuliani's police department created a program called CompStat in which precinct captains monitored crime data on computers, and then sent extra forces to any trouble spots. By 2007 Mayor Bloomberg's administration was considering a similar approach to public education, using test scores to spot schools in trouble.

At first glance, Jim Liebman wouldn't seem like an obvious choice to lead such an ambitious new initiative. He's a short, soft-spoken man who wears wire-rim glasses and loves to talk about philosophy. Klein hired him in 2006. Liebman's two children were attending the city's public schools. His daughter went to a respected middle school on the Upper West Side and his son was at the Beacon School near Lincoln Center. When his son applied to public high schools, he had wanted to go to the prestigious Stuyvesant High School in Lower Manhattan. Liebman brought him downtown to take the admissions exam on a weekend morning, and they ran into a group of black students from Brooklyn who were asking how to find the school. They were lost and running late for the test—putting them at an obvious disadvantage. "It was a minor tragedy," recalled Liebman, who had long been concerned about issues of equity in education as a desegregation lawyer. He had been assistant counsel for the NAACP Legal Defense and Educational Fund during the early 1980s. The incident prompted Liebman to send Klein an e-mail expressing concerns about the high school admissions process. As a lawyer, Klein knew about Liebman's work and said he had "enormous respect for his intelligence, integrity, and commitment to educational equity." Klein invited him to a meeting and became convinced this was the person who could help lead the system through its next wave of reform, to reduce the achievement gap.

Liebman wasn't an educator. His title was chief accountability officer, though he was often referred to as "the Architect." He was tasked with building an online data system for tracking almost everything one could possibly know about the city's million-plus students, its 1,453 schools, and its ninety thousand pedagogical staffers and other employees. Student test scores, social security numbers, addresses, family information, native languages, and immunization records would all be included, as would human resources data for the teachers and principals.

Liebman was excited about this data system because he'd long been intrigued by the question of how to change big institutions. At Columbia he researched death penalty cases, arguing that too many innocent people had likely been convicted. His work before that with the NAACP also influenced his thinking. "My view of desegregation, the extent to which it worked was because it was an organizational reform," he said. "It turned out to work in places where it served as political reforms and structural reforms." In other words, desegregation worked only when it was part of a larger effort to make the schools better for all students; it couldn't just be a mandate from above.

That view of change as something that needs to trickle up from the bottom might sound like the exact opposite of the approach of a big-city school system led by a mayor and a chancellor. But it was something that intrigued Klein. He'd already given a couple of hundred principals more control over their buildings and their budgets in exchange for meeting strict performance targets. By 2007 he was planning to take that philosophy citywide by adding another kind of performance target.

The federal No Child Left Behind law requires districts to count the percentage of students in each grade meeting state standards. That means comparing this year's fourth-grade test scores, for example, to last year's fourth-grade results. But those are two different groups of students. The Bloomberg administration wanted to see if a class of third-graders did better on their fourth-grade tests. Under Klein and Liebman's new standard, schools would be judged by this measure of progress. Florida had already been measuring how much progress students were making in its schools, and Chicago was about to embark on a similar "value added" assessment, based on scores.

This bottom-line emphasis on testing rubbed many teachers and principals the wrong way, because they didn't believe tests were a real gauge of learning and critical thinking. Schools weren't factories. Educators had been complaining about the nation's overreliance on test scores ever since the passage of NCLB. They thought politicians were taking the easy way out by mandating standards instead of looking for real solutions to improve the schools.

But others thought testing could be used to help find those real solutions. NCLB had forced states to give annual exams in almost every grade. To get ahead of the curve, states started collecting more information about their students through data management systems and periodic tests to predict which children were most in danger of failing, and therefore in need of more help. Teachers have always given quizzes to stay on top of their students. But the Internet age made it possible to collect this data in "real time" and capture it on websites, allowing teachers and principals to look for trends and tailor their instruction to help struggling students well before they got lost in the cracks like Yamilka. Jim Liebman believed this "data-driven instruction" was key to reforming New York City's schools from the bottom up.

Other districts, from Corpus Christi, Texas, to Philadelphia, were involved in similar activities. By 2009, President Barack Obama's administration was offering extra stimulus aid to states that improved their student data systems. Education secretary Arne Duncan stated during a visit to New York that frequent assessments could help teachers understand how children are doing over time. "We should be able to look every second-grader in the eye and say, 'You're on track to being able to go to a good college' or 'You're not.'"

In the fall of 2007, Liebman and his staffers were getting ready to unveil a massive data system called ARIS: the Achievement Reporting and Innovation System. This $80 million Web-based network, managed by IBM, would merge all the student and school information records in a way that could be used to gauge both performance and progress. Liebman laid out the goals during a press conference earlier that year, when IBM was awarded the five-year contract for ARIS. "Every day in many of our schools in the city, there's a student who tragically fails to learn for a reason that's entirely knowable, solvable if only we could figure out what's blocking that student," he said. "That pattern is not visible to us today and that keeps us from figuring out that problem, [and] that tragically slows down that student. And every day in our city, a teacher in a school figures out exactly how to solve that problem." Liebman believed that if the city schools could use a Web-based computer system to track each student, they'd have a better idea of how to help more children succeed.

Liebman was finally getting his chance to make the organizational reforms he had studied as a law school professor. As chief accountability officer for the New York City schools, his desk was in a room full of cubicles orbiting Chancellor Klein's desk. Liebman sat near a window facing the rear of City Hall—a constant reminder of his new, politically sensitive position. He didn't have much time to put his theories into practice. The whole ARIS system was scheduled to be up and running before the term-limited Mayor Bloomberg left office in 2009. (When he decided to challenge that law in 2008 so he could run for a third term, Bloomberg argued that during the economic downturn the city needed his financial stewardship, as well as the technocratic approach that was emblematic of his school reforms.) The launch of ARIS during the 2007/08 school year would be Liebman's chance to leave a lasting mark on public education, and to be held accountable for the results.

• • •

While Jim Liebman was figuring out the lay of the land downtown in the Tweed Courthouse during the fall of 2007, eighteen-year-old Antonio* was hanging out on the familiar streets of Washington Heights in Upper Manhattan.

Antonio hadn't gotten a haircut in a while and he was also growing his facial hair. He looked a little fuzzier than usual, with thick, curly hair, a trim beard, and long sideburns. He wanted to resemble the comic book character Wolverine and was hoping that would become his new nickname. But on a mild night in early November, the name didn't seem to be catching on just yet. He saw a kid he knew sitting on top of a car outside the Subway sandwich shop on 164th and Broadway and asked, "What do you call me?"

"Seven-thirty," said Joey, using the hip-hop slang for a crazy person. It was Antonio's street name in Washington Heights. The term comes from section 730 of the New York State legal code, which can be used to find a person mentally unfit for trial. But Antonio was hoping Joey would start using the new nickname, and he asked him once more what he was called. "Anthony?" Joey responded, not knowing what else to say. Most people do call him Anthony.

"No," said Antonio, pointing to his hair and making a hand motion that looked like a claw. He really wanted Joey to say "Wolverine." Finally he came right out and asked Joey if he was starting to look like Wolverine and got a friendly laugh. Antonio smiled, said goodnight, and walked into the sandwich shop.

Nobody remembers when Antonio became known as 730. It just seemed to fit, said twenty-four-year-old Juan, another acquaintance from the neighborhood. "He really doesn't like it. He doesn't like it at all," Juan said. "I mean, when they first gave him the name, he was okay with it. But as you grow up you start not liking it."

Juan had been hanging out with Antonio because he was helping him write some lyrics. Antonio had posted a bulletin on MySpace saying he was writing a song and needed advice, and Juan wrote back when he recognized who had posted the request. Juan was looking sharp that Friday night. He wore a purple leather jacket, a bright green-and-black-checkered newsboy cap, jeans, and matching green-and-purple sneak-

*His full name is Antonio Rocha. Most of the people in his life asked me to use first names only, or else pseudonyms, and I have complied.

ers. He was also wearing a black T-shirt that said "Fresh" in bright pink letters, and round earrings with little red stars in the middle. Juan said that he shopped in SoHo and knew a friend in the fashion business. He said he was going to Monroe College and wanted to be a medical technician. He also considered himself something of an expert on the subject of dating, which was why he was helping Antonio write his song.

"I told him a relationship is like a game," Juan said, on his advice to Antonio about how to handle women. "If you treat them too nice, they're not going to appreciate it. And it's not just women, it's in general. It's true."

As if to prove his point, Juan's phone rang a few minutes later with "I Get Money" by 50 Cent. "Who is this?" he asked. "What's your name? It's Juan. I'm gonna call you back." Juan wasn't exactly sure who it was, but he thought it was one of the two girls he was dating.

Antonio was impressed by Juan's way with women because he'd never had a girlfriend before. Though he's tall and attractive, with light brown skin and deep-set eyes, he is also a bit of an outsider. He'd been in love several times and he wanted to write about his feelings, but the words didn't come easily. Antonio has dyslexia and he never learned to read in the city's public schools. Like Alejandro and Yamilka, he also won private tutoring by getting a lawyer from the nonprofit group Advocates for Children to prove that the city schools had failed to provide him with the free and appropriate education he was entitled to under federal law as a student with learning disabilities.

Antonio was born in New York. Like Yamilka and Alejandro, he is the child of a Dominican immigrant with little formal education. When he was first identified in second grade as needing special education services, his mother was hopeful the schools would help him. But he was transferred again and again and was still unable to read when he got to high school. After winning his settlement, he attended the same tutoring center as Alejandro for about six months while going to the High School of Graphic Communication Arts (also known as Graphics) in Midtown. His reading improved substantially, but he was still very self-conscious about his writing—which was why he reached out to Juan for help with his song.

Antonio had recently had a falling-out with a girl, Theresa, he'd had a crush on for almost three years. They only shared two short kisses. But Antonio could still recall when they happened (November 28, 2005, and January 5, 2006) and how her green eyes looked when he got down on his knees and asked her to be his girlfriend. Though they never really dated, they did hang out when he was a student at Graphics. They had argued in September 2007. Antonio said that he had tried apologizing, but it was too late. She wouldn't accept it. He wanted to write her a letter, but he was too insecure about his writing. Then he dropped out of high school, frustrated in large part because his reading hadn't progressed enough for him to pass his classes. He wanted to find a job.

Antonio was trying to pour his feelings about Theresa into a song. At the Subway sandwich shop in Washington Heights, he and Juan were sitting near a young couple with a toddler. Antonio looked at the mother and said, "God bless." She thanked him and smiled. Antonio is habitually friendly to strangers, sharing his cigarettes, holding doors, or striking up conversations with merchants in a way that might seem either odd or endearing to some go-it-alone New Yorkers. He would also love to join the army. He was carrying a National Guard folder that night with a few pages of lyrics he'd handwritten on lined paper. He pulled out two of them, each of which was titled "Ideal for a Song." Antonio meant "idea," but he thought there was an *l* at the end of the word.

Yeal this song goes out to all ya special ladys that got hurt by us assholes that we are some time
But we are sweethearts deep inside
So yeal I knew a girl that stopped my heart the moment I lade my eyes on her for the very first time that makes me go to hevan just to be with her
I remember how her lips feels sawf a strawerry flavor that made me catch feelings for her until one day I sed something stupid that I would like to take back but it already too late for that

It sounded like it was about Theresa, but Antonio said it was about another girl he knew from the neighborhood. He knew a few of the words weren't spelled correctly, but said he was writing quickly because he wanted to get it all out. His other song was about Theresa.

When I think it's okay or even close to it
I hurt the one girl that I thought I was in love with but I got to live with the things that I did

I wich that I could take it all bach but it's too late for that I wich that life wasn't so hard

Antonio read it aloud like he was rapping to a hip-hop beat, but he didn't get too far. That was all he wrote, he said, explaining that he ran out of steam. Still, he posted these lyrics on his MySpace profile. He wanted people to see he felt bad about hurting a girl.

Juan described Antonio as "a good kid. Real good. Has a good heart." He knew Antonio had a hard time in school. But he didn't know it was so bad that Antonio had been almost illiterate a year ago. "He likes school; the way he talks about school, he talks about it with so much pride," said Juan. "'I'm going to school, I'm going to be this when I get older,' like he wants to be successful. But I think there's a lot of obstacles in his life that keep him from doing what he wants to." Juan could sort of relate. He had gone to a rough high school on the West Side of Manhattan and dropped out. He eventually got his GED and enrolled in Monroe College.

Antonio wished he could get a GED, but he was nowhere near that level of literacy. The tutoring program had changed his life, and he had gotten to about a fourth-grade level in less than a year. After using up that initial award in late January, he applied for and won a few hundred more hours he could use at another tutoring center. But he stopped going after a couple of sessions for a variety of reasons. Part of it was the stress of combining high school with intensive tutoring every afternoon. He was also frustrated that the second tutoring center he attended started him off with material he thought he'd already covered. And he was eager to get a job so he could make some money to supplement his small allowance. By mid-September he stopped going to high school. His lawyers and his principal agreed Graphics couldn't serve his needs, anyway, because it didn't have any specialized programs for students with such a low reading level.

So as the fall wore on, Antonio was drifting. He had problems getting the right paperwork for a state ID card, which made it tough to find work. And he didn't want to go back to school. "I don't want to be another year in high school," he sighed. "I was supposed to graduate last year." He was going to be nineteen in January and was still technically a freshman. The prospect of enduring three more years of high school was overwhelming.

But it was time to make some hard choices. The tutoring hours he had fought so hard to win were set to expire in seven months. He knew he had to find some way of moving ahead with his life. He just didn't know if that meant getting a job or returning to class.

I met Antonio, Yamilka, and her brother in 2006 as a reporter for WNYC Radio. I was investigating the very low percentage of special education students who were earning diplomas in New York City. The group Advocates for Children of New York had alerted me to the problem.

Advocates for Children introduced me to Yamilka and Antonio when I asked if they knew of any special education students who had had trouble graduating from high school. Despite having spent more than a decade covering the public schools for WNYC, I had never met anyone like Yamilka. We sat together in the family's Bronx apartment with her sister Elizabeth and her brother, Alejandro, as she told me about the shame she felt in being illiterate. She had barely left the house except to attend her tutoring classes at Huntington Learning Center. She said it was the first place that ever treated her like a person. Yamilka's broken English made it difficult to understand her words at times. But there was no way to misunderstand her feelings. The clarity of her emotions and her desire to learn to read were extremely powerful.

When the radio series aired that June, Yamilka called me at home to tell me how happy she was to finally share her story. She was excited, but she had also been enraged to hear the school official I had interviewed, Bonnie Brown, state that some children cannot learn how to read. Yamilka said she wanted to prove that person wrong. We talked at length, and as Yamilka revealed more about her life, we decided that there should be a book about students who can't read.

Unless they know someone with dyslexia or another reading disability, most educated people presume that learning to read is a simple process. They might not even remember how it happened for them because it seemed so natural. If you grow up in a household with books and newspapers, you're constantly surrounded by printed words. Your parents read you bedtime stories and give you alphabet blocks. In kindergarten and first grade, those letters become words and sentences. By fourth grade, students have ideally progressed from learning to read to reading to learn. They're given science and social studies books along with literature and written math problems. Middle schools and high schools amp up the reading levels even higher as students are expected to process more and more information through written language. But too many students get stuck along the way. Yamilka is an extreme example even among special education students. But there are millions of other students—in general and special education classes—who are nowhere near what the United States considers proficient. The fact that a third of fourth-graders and a quarter of eighth-graders read well below grade level, according to the National Assessment of Educational Progress, is a ringing alarm bell. So is the glaring achievement gap between white students and blacks and Hispanics.

Our public schools have historically been considered the great equalizer, where all children can make the most of their potential—regardless of race, class, or ability. The No Child Left Behind law, with its strict proficiency targets and sanctions for schools that aren't performing, was supposed to ensure that all children are held to the same high standards. But the standardized tests that can help schools identify any struggling children can also become a distraction from learning. Teachers often feel as though they are teaching to the tests, not the subject matter, and that the intense focus on math and reading has left less time to engage students through art and music. They wonder if the current trend in using data to identify lagging students will increase efficiency or just eat up more of their precious time.

This book is an exploration of what it takes to teach every child to read, at a time when literacy is essential. A century ago, most people didn't need to read as much as we do today. Farmers and factory workers could get by with basic skills. But our text-based Internet culture demands higher literacy skills. How much higher, though? What does it mean to be fully literate?

The National Assessment of Adult Literacy uses two definitions. One, which was used in the 1992 and 2003 assessments, is "task-based" literacy. This is defined as "the ability to use printed and written information to function in society, to achieve one's goals, and to develop one's knowledge and potential." In 2003 the NAAL broke this down further by adding a "skills-based" component. It said that "the successful use of printed material is a product of two classes of skills: word-level reading skills and higher-level literacy skills," or critical thinking.[7]

Yamilka, Antonio, and Alejandro expected that higher level of reading when they went to school. They wouldn't have used a phrase like "develop one's knowledge and potential." But Yamilka wanted "to get a really good education like other kids" and maybe take a cooking class after graduating. Antonio wanted to join the army. Alejandro wanted to learn about history and go to college.

These three students were joined together by bad luck and difficult circumstances. They were born with learning disabilities; their families' income levels forced them to rely on the public schools; and their classrooms never gave them all the help they needed. They also happen to be the children of Dominican immigrants. It was a coincidence that I chose to write about three Dominican students. But in a city where 13 percent of public school students don't speak English, these three are part of the ever-evolving story of New York. Their parents are no different than previous generations of immigrants hoping to earn a good living and provide more opportunities for their children—opportunities rooted in the ability to speak, read, and write English.

Each of these students has a story to share about his or her own extraordinary challenges in learning to read. As the nation's largest school system, New York City also has something to teach us about students who struggle with reading. Every principal knows a child like Yamilka, Antonio, or Alejandro. They are the heartbreakers, the students who are stuck. Then there's a much larger category of students who are performing below proficiency but well enough to get promoted. They often struggle with reading comprehension and can't write coherent essays. The Bloomberg administration was counting on frequent assessments, coupled with a sophisticated data-tracking system, to identify those students and help them read better.

The Bloomberg years were also a critical time for urban schools. The ambitious mayor who flirted with a bid for the U.S. presidency brought a more corporate mind-set to public education with his focus on data and accountability. He also benefited from a good economy prior to 2008, and a landmark lawsuit that resulted in more funds for the public schools. His reforms (and his highly effective public relations experts) inspired superintendents in other cities, including Washington, D.C. With 1,453 schools in 2007, New York City became the nation's largest public education laboratory.

What happened in New York City's classrooms toward the end of Bloomberg's second term, and the challenges faced by Yamilka, Antonio, and Alejandro, can tell us something about what it takes to get all children reading. And those lessons could prevent other children from having to fight a legal battle in order to accomplish the most basic thing they expect from our schools: learning to read.

FALL

Three Students, a City, and the Quest to Read

I want I can open a book and I can have emotions and understand everything that the book is giving me in the moment. I want to feel, I want to cry, I want to get sad when I read the book. I want to have the feeling normal people have when they're reading a book.

—Yamilka

Yamilka, Alejandro, and Antonio all had serious learning disabilities that weren't identified promptly or adequately by their public schools. Yamilka and her brother languished in English as a Second Language classes for years before their teachers even noticed they couldn't read. Antonio's problems were identified in second grade, but he was transferred from school to school without learning. A wealthier or more educated family might have caught on to these problems sooner and argued for more services. But their families were poor immigrants from the Dominican Republic who didn't speak any English and didn't have enough education to know what to do when their children ran into trouble. This section is about each of their stories. It also introduces the New York City school system at a critical juncture, when a technocratic mayor and his chancellor planned to overhaul existing systems for tracking and measuring academic progress. These efforts would be costly and controversial at times as the city altered its definition of a successful school, challenging long-held presumptions.

ONE

Yamilka's Journey

Yamilka returned to her reading classes at Huntington and continued going until July 2007, when she reached the deadline for using her 1,500 hours. She typically had three hours a day of classes, five days a week, with certified teachers who taught her basic phonics: the sounds of each letter and how to blend those sounds into words. "Fuh-reh-Fred," she would say, in what teachers call decoding. It was a painfully slow process; she knew she stood out in a place where most of the pupils were much younger.

Yamilka is about five foot two and chubby. She dresses casually, often in jeans and a denim jacket, but it's clear that she takes time putting herself together. She has smooth brown skin and typically wears a little bit of carefully applied eye makeup and a hint of lip gloss. Her curly hair is usually pulled back into a ponytail, revealing a few silver earrings on each ear. And she always has beautifully manicured nails. Sometimes she would sit inside a semiprivate conference room at Huntington with her tutors, who would alternate every hour when she switched activities. But many times she was placed at tables in the center's big open room, among the teenagers and younger children. She slowly read picture books, including *Goodnight Moon*, *Love You Forever*, and the "Bob" series. Sometimes she'd listen to a tutor read short words such as "man," "well," and "jet," and would write them on a page. Then she would practice using these words by writing brief sentences such as "The man likes to fly a jet." As her skills increased, she was given worksheets with illustrations to help her read short paragraphs. One showed a couple loading groceries into their station wagon. The text read: "Mother and Father went to the store. They were surprised when they came home Jill had cut the grass. Mother and Father said, 'Thank you, Jill.'"

Her tutors used a variety of different reading exercises to customize their approach for an older student, but they still had to concentrate on the basics. Yamilka learned how putting the letter *e* at the end of a word makes a vowel "say its name," as when the *e* in "make" prevents the word from being pronounced like "mack." She also learned addition and subtraction and how to tell time with a clock. She had always relied on a digital watch.

Yamilka didn't use all 1,500 hours of tutoring she was awarded by the city because she skipped a few weeks of instruction. And when she finally finished her program in July 2007, she was still reading at a low elementary level.

That a twenty-one-year-old woman could win more than a hundred thousand dollars' worth of tutoring to learn how to read—all at taxpayer expense—would have been unthinkable a century ago, or even a few decades ago. Yamilka's struggle to learn at Huntington, and the steps she would take after leaving, wouldn't have been possible without the development of the very concept of public education that culminated in the civil rights movement.

There is no federally protected right to an education in the U.S. Constitution. The word "education" isn't even mentioned in the document. Although the nation's founders were intellectuals who valued book learning, the war they'd fought against British rule also left them wary about consolidating too much power in their nascent federal government.

Education was therefore left to the states—as in colonial times—and it was heavily influenced by Protestantism. Some churches created charity schools for the poor, while parents with means sent their children to grammar schools. The most common textbook was *The New England Primer*, which was used to teach reading and the Protestant catechism.[1] By the time of the Revolutionary War, most adult Americans were educated just enough to read the newspaper and the Bible and to figure their taxes.[2] But public schools as we know them didn't exist. Massachusetts and New Hampshire had enacted laws requiring towns to support local schools with taxes and fees. But there was little support for taxpayer-funded education outside of New England. Plans for a national school system were rejected by Congress in the late 1790s.[3] Thomas Jefferson's efforts as a Virginia state legislator to guarantee three years of public schooling for all (white) children was defeated three times. "People have more feeling for canals and roads than for education," he declared in frustration.[4]

But things began to change by the nineteenth century, thanks to the industrial revolution and the growth of newspapers. Horace Mann, the Massachusetts secretary of education, traveled throughout his state promoting a taxpayer-funded public education system to ensure a minimal level of quality. Though he was rebuffed, his reformist ideas made an impact, and by the 1840s there was growing support for "common schools." New immigrants were arriving from Europe, mainly Ireland; they were poor and had little if any education. Social reformers saw the schools as a means of "Americanizing" the children of these new arrivals. Nearly half of New York City's residents were foreign-born in 1840.[5] While laborers didn't need high literacy skills to work in the factories, the poor and the immigrants wanted a better life for their children. So did the settlers who were moving to western states, and the slaves who were freed after the Civil War. To encourage this western expansion, Congress began requiring the new states to set aside land for free, nonsectarian schools.[6] Public school enrollments increased from 7.6 million in 1870 to 12.7 million in 1890—out of a total population of about 69 million. The United States provided more public schooling to more children than any other nation.[7]

But public education still wasn't widely available past the elementary level. Many children left school at the age of fourteen to work in factories or on farms. That gradually began to change as public high schools sprung up throughout the country. In 1900, 10 percent of teens between the ages of fourteen and seventeen were attending high schools; by 1920 that number had tripled to 31 percent.[8] Yet there were debates about whether all young people really needed twelve years of schooling. Immigration had swelled, with many children arriving from poor countries in Southern and Eastern Europe. Progressive educators argued that a classical education grounded in Latin and literature was no longer relevant to these masses. They persuaded schools to make their lessons more practical, and to "track" less academically inclined children into vocational programs. The public schools taught reading, writing, and arithmetic, but the goal was employment.

The debate about public education shifted again in the 1950s. The Soviet Union had launched the *Sputnik* satellite, and industrial work was getting more and more technical. Americans feared their schools weren't competitive, and the government directed more money toward science, math, and higher education. Meanwhile, a book called *Why Johnny Can't Read*, by Rudolf Flesch, had become a bestseller in 1955 by fueling another insecurity about the nation's schools. It argued that teachers were neglecting the basics of reading. But the ensuing debates about the best ways of teaching children how to read were driven by philosophy and practice. Education was clearly valued, but it wasn't considered a fundamental right.

That all changed in the years after the Supreme Court's 1954 decision in *Brown v. Board of Education*. This ruling struck down a common practice in seventeen states of racially segregating white and black students. *Brown* held that all students were entitled to the same education, under the Fourteenth Amendment's guarantee that no state shall deny to any person the equal protection of its laws. The court found "separate educational facilities are inherently unequal." This ruling ushered in the civil rights era, as blacks marched and protested for equality in the schools, in voting booths, and in the workplace. *Brown* also empowered other minority groups to fight for their own educational rights, including students whose disabilities made it difficult for them to learn. Education wasn't a constitutional right, strictly speaking. But the nation's highest court had ruled that everyone was entitled to the same services, including the public schools.

Students with disabilities had a long way to go to achieve such equality. For most of the twentieth century, they were treated as second-class citizens. Children with physical or mental handicaps were warehoused in institutions, or segregated from other students when they were allowed in the public schools. The court's finding in *Brown* that all students were entitled to the same education gave these children and their advocates a powerful weapon. By the early 1970s, mentally retarded students in Pennsylvania and Washington, D.C., had won landmark victories, as courts ruled that children with handicaps were entitled to attend the same public schools as other students. That right to a seat in the schoolhouse was secured in 1975, when Congress passed the Education for All Handicapped Children Act. This legislation was later renamed the Individuals with Disabilities Education Act, or IDEA.

The basic tenet of IDEA was revolutionary: that children with disabilities are entitled to a "free and appropriate" public education. It also required that schools provide these children with any services they needed to meet their individual disabilities. These services could include audio recordings for the blind, speech therapy for a child who has trouble with spoken language, or physical accommodations for children in wheelchairs. Schools have to evaluate these students at regular intervals and make sure the parents are involved in all decisions.

Because of IDEA, districts had to hire specialized teachers and counselors. They had to provide smaller classes for students with special needs. The law required the federal government to offset 40 percent of these extra costs, but that commitment was never fully honored. Though many students with disabilities got what they needed and went on to higher education, the vast majority of them continued to perform well below their nondisabled peers. A gap is to be expected given their extra needs, but that gap is enormous. Nationally, a little more than half of all students with disabilities earn high school diplomas—about twenty percentage points below the average. In Georgia and Louisiana, graduation rates among students with disabilities are forty percentage points lower than for the high school population as a whole.*[9]

The Bush administration considered its No Child Left Behind law another step forward in making education a civil right. This law aimed to close the achievement gaps between children of different races, abilities, and income groups by requiring states and school districts that receive federal dollars to meet annual performance targets. It's no longer acceptable to merely report the overall number of children passing a statewide test. Schools have to show how well their Hispanics, blacks, English Language Learners, and children with disabilities are performing, as well as the five other subgroups. All these students are held to the same standards. They can't be shuffled off to vocational schools or institutions as they were just a few decades ago.

*It's hard to make state-to-state comparisons, however, because each state has its own way of calculating its rates and some don't separate alternative diplomas, like Yamilka's, from regular full diplomas.

But despite these laws, and the threat that schools will lose federal funds if scores don't improve, there are still many students like Yamilka who claim they haven't gotten the education they're entitled to from the public schools. Students with special needs rely on attorneys to persuade local school districts to provide their services. Education advocates have used the courts to fight for state funding to ensure that all students receive an adequate education. Though public education was never mentioned in the Constitution, our society now clearly considers it a fundamental right.

In her own small way, Yamilka was challenging America's commitment to teach every child. Her rights as a learning-disabled student had been violated. The city's agreement to provide her with 1,500 hours of private tutoring was meant to rectify that wrong. She finally had her chance to find out whether she could learn to read.

Yamilka's case was extraordinary because of the size of her settlement. But it's not unusual for a school district to pay for extra services, or even full tuition at a private school, when a student with a disability is able to prove they can't get the education they're entitled to in the public schools. During the 2007/08 school year, the New York City Department of Education says 4,368 students won taxpayer-funded tuition at private schools. The city spent $89 million on private school tuition that year, an increase of more than 50 percent over the previous year. The Department of Education's chief attorney, Michael Best, said that was partly due to a backlog of cases. The city had settled a class action lawsuit charging it was taking too long to pay for students to attend private schools.

In late 2007 *The New York Times* reported on how the Department of Education was trying to rein in these costs by doubling the size of its legal team to fight these cases—at the suggestion of an outside consultant.[10] Five lawyers and a dozen paralegals were added, with the goal of saving $25 million on private tuition and expediting the backlog. It was that same year that "Tom F" became Exhibit A in the city's argument that some students were abusing the system as they sought a taxpayer-funded private education.

The plaintiff in the case was Tom Freston, a former Viacom chief executive whose son attended a private school from the age of eight through high school because, he claimed, the city schools couldn't adequately address his reading disability. Freston had reportedly left Viacom with a golden parachute worth $85 million.[11] He had already been reimbursed for about $50,000—two years' worth of tuition—for his son's attendance at the Stephen Gaynor School on the Upper West Side. He wanted the city to pay for the rest of his son's education. Freston's lawyers argued the case wasn't about his individual wealth, but about preserving the rights of all students with disabilities to have the city pay for their services. To support that point, the attorney Neal Rosenberg said Freston donated the $50,000 in reimbursements he had received from the city to underwrite an after-school reading program at Gaynor to be used by public school students from the neighborhood. He said Freston also gave the program an extra $100,000 of his own money. But New York City argued that Freston's son had had a good option at a downtown public school and that he should have been required to try it before seeking permission to attend a private school at taxpayer expense. The city fought the case all the way up to the U.S. Supreme Court, which issued a split decision in the fall of 2007, letting a lower court's ruling stand. Freston won.

The case was closely watched across the country because special education is so expensive. In the fall of 2007, there were more than 66,600 students nationwide whose parents placed them in private schools at public expense, according to the U.S. Department of Education's Office of Special Education Programs. Overall, however, the number of such placements remains relatively small—just 1 percent of the country's 6.6 million special education students. But private school tuition is a great expense for districts. Washington, D.C., was reportedly spending $118 million in 2005 for 2,283 of its special education students to attend private facilities. That was about one out of every five of its special education pupils. In financial terms, that amounted to 15 percent of the city's education budget for just 4 percent of its pupils, and the costs were growing every year.[12]

Special education is so expensive because the children require many mandated services and more individualized attention (more teachers) than general education students. In New York City, special education students made up roughly 12 percent of total enrollment in the 2007/08 school year. But the city's Department of Education was spending about $4 billion—roughly 20 percent of its budget—on services and classes tailored to their physical, emotional, and learning disabilities. Approximately sixty thousand special education students were eligible for yellow bus service because they couldn't travel alone to their school or program—at a cost of $640 million, including the salary of the driver and matron on each bus.

In a system with finite resources and seemingly endless needs, one could rationally argue that the schools can't do everything—especially when it comes to older students. If a student gets to the age of twenty-one and still isn't reading, is it time to give up?

When the supervisor for District 75—New York City's program for the neediest special education students—stated, "There are some children who will never learn how to read," she was speaking from experience. Bonnie Brown had been in the school system for about thirty years as a teacher, assistant principal, and principal. She said there are thousands of high school students who are overage and undercredited. Those who don't progress academically are often referred to the high schools in District 75. Yamilka attended District 75's Jeffrey M. Rapport School for Career Development in the Bronx, where the goal was to teach pupils basic life skills: functional math and functional reading, such as counting change, balancing a checkbook, and being able to read subway and bus signs.

"Those children are basically reading at second to fifth grade," Brown said. "They will never qualify for a GED or be able to pass, and they will never get a Regents diploma," which requires students to pass state exams. She said students in these "career schools" usually leave with a portfolio of three job experiences, for example, in food service, building maintenance, or messenger mail. The school system also helps them find employment after they earn a diploma stating they've met the goals of their Individualized Education Program. In very rare cases the students earn regular diplomas.

Brown wouldn't talk about Yamilka directly, because of legal concerns. But she suggested that in a case *like* hers, in which a student is still illiterate in high school, the city might not have been able to do very much. It had spent at least $120,000 educating her already.* "Our goal was not to

*This is an estimate, but Yamilka attended special education classes from 1998 to 2004, when the average cost per pupil was between $15,000 and $20,000 per year, after four years in general education classes with some English as a Second Language instruction.

get her to read at a second-grade [level] and maybe if we're lucky get her to fourth grade," Brown said, again speaking hypothetically. "It was to get her trained so that she can reach her full potential and live independently, to teach her some kind of skill so that she can be a contributing member of society and an independent member. And I don't think our goal is to look at raising her from no reading to grade two or grade four. By any standard in the United States that is not being literate."[13]

But Yamilka wasn't some freakish exception. Most special education students who graduate from high school in New York City leave with meaningless diplomas like the one Yamilka earned, diplomas that don't require basic levels of math and reading. Only a quarter of the city's special education students graduate with regular, state-approved diplomas. Many educators believe this number could be even higher if the students had more support services—noting that a third of special education students drop out of school.

Yamilka's lawyers at the nonprofit group Advocates for Children believe the city should never give up on any student so long as that student is eligible for schooling. "The point I always make to people is, well, if she's reading on a kindergarten level and you can bring her up to a first- or second-grade [level] and she can read some subway stops or whatever, that's going to make a huge difference in her life," said the group's deputy director, Matthew Lenaghan. "For all of us who are sitting around as college-educated, graduate-schooled people, we might in the first instance say that's not such a big jump." But, he added, "it's very significant."

However, Yamilka hadn't even learned basic life skills at her career school. She rode the subway to a few familiar stations, but she couldn't read the maps. She did not think she could handle a job. She couldn't even count change. But while her attorneys blamed the schools, one of her former teachers, Janet Gardella, said Yamilka and her family bore some responsibility as well. Gardella taught a short reading class each morning at Montefiore Hospital, which was among several locations where Bronx career development students were assigned to gain work experience. The twelve students in her class were assigned to work in either the child-care center or some other department in the hospital. Gardella said Yamilka couldn't keep up with the responsibilities. "To tell you the truth, she really wasn't emotionally ready to concentrate on anything," she recalled. "She was very upset with her weight. Social things . . .

all the things that go along with being an adolescent. She wasn't a mature eighteen-year-old." Gardella said Yamilka—like most of her students—was often absent or wandered in late. And she frequently resorted to excuses like "I'm tired" or "I can't."

Gardella retired in 2004 after twenty-five years as a special education teacher in New York City. She said Yamilka was not an unusual student, either socially or academically. Very few of her students from the career development school could read. By the time they got there, it was too late. "They criticize teachers," Gardella said, her voice rising with frustration. "It is an extraordinarily difficult population. Somebody once described it like getting a cancer patient in the end stages."

Yamilka's attorney, Matthew Lenaghan, began collecting documents in his effort to prove she could have been taught to read before reaching that critical stage. Her high school placement was the culmination of a long, sad history of educational struggle after she arrived in New York in 1993. She sat through years of classes taught in Spanish and English without picking up a thing, while her sisters tried to help her at home. It wasn't until 1998, when Yamilka was in the seventh grade and fourteen years of age, that a special education evaluator filled out a form stating Yamilka's teacher "feels that she needs one-to-one guidance, which he is unable to provide due to a large class size and lack of assistance in his classroom. [The teacher] did pair Yamilka with a student partner and he does give her one-to-one help whenever possible. However, he insists that Yamilka needs more being that, at present, she is unable to read or write."

An impartial hearing was held—a formal proceeding for families who wish to challenge their child's special education placement or services. A representative from the city's Department of Education argued that it had already made every attempt to educate Yamilka and that her family had been properly informed about their rights. But the hearing officer, Susan Marcus, wrote that the department demonstrated "bad faith or worse" by not providing her the services she needed when it was clear she wasn't learning, and by not including her family in the evaluation process. Marcus concluded that the family members were never informed about their rights to outside evaluations and attorneys. "The Department never placed Yamilka in a program where she would learn to read and write and the result that she cannot, at the age of 22, read or write constitutes a harm to her," Marcus wrote.

• • •

While the city and its schools were ultimately held responsible, teachers are right when they say there are other factors outside the classroom that keep students from learning to read. The city and its schools weren't the only ones who let Yamilka down.

Yamilka arrived in New York in 1993, in the middle of the school year. She remembers seeing snow for the first time and briefly wishing she could return to the Dominican Republic. But she was thrilled to be reunited with her parents and sisters—and not just because she missed them terribly. Her life in the Dominican Republic had come to resemble that of an indentured servant.

Yamilka's father, Pablo, was the first member of the immediate family to move to New York, during the late 1980s. He soon got a job as a contractor and made enough money so his wife and two eldest daughters could join him. Yamilka and her younger brother, Alejandro, stayed behind with a relative until the family could afford to bring them along, too. It was a common pattern of migration.

Yamilka was seven when her mother, Isabel, and sisters left, and Alejandro was just four. She has fond memories of her childhood before then. The family lived in a small village with coconut palms. Yamilka remembers they had little pigs in their backyard and her brother had a bicycle, which she taught herself to ride by taking off the training wheels. Her mom discouraged the kids from sucking their thumbs by smearing chicken poop or spice on their fingers because she wanted them to have straight teeth. The children walked to a public school nearby and their parents paid for uniforms and supplies. Yamilka recalls getting to first grade and learning the Spanish alphabet.

This idyllic childhood ended when her parents left for New York. Their father's aunt was entrusted with caring for Yamilka and Alejandro, but she had very little interest in the two young children. Even though the parents sent money for the kids' school supplies, the aunt—or "Tanta," as Yamilka called her—took the cash and kept them both at home, turning the young children into her servants. Yamilka remembers being woken at dawn on many mornings and forced to walk down a path to bring back buckets of water. The house had plumbing but it wasn't very reliable. She was scared, cold, and often hungry as she carried the big bucket of water in her arms or on top of her head—trying not to drop the heavy load.

"Step by step, I used to put it down, pick it up again, keep walking," she said wearily. Alejandro was defiant and would lie in bed and pretend to be asleep in the morning, refusing to do the housework. Yamilka covered for him.

There were no books for the children to read at Tanta's house. Yamilka asked why she couldn't go back to school with other kids. Sometimes Tanta told her she didn't have enough money. Other times she said there was no reason for Yamilka to go to school, because she was stupid and would never amount to anything. Yamilka's parents would often call to speak to their children. But Yamilka couldn't tell them what was really happening because Tanta always stood by the phone. "I had to stay quiet," she said. "I was a kid." She was also afraid things would only get worse if she told the truth. A man who was living in the house beat her with his belt because she refused to get him anything to eat and he thought her dress showed too much skin. She was only seven or eight. One day her mother's brother paid a visit and noticed that the kids were hanging around the house during school hours. He told his sister in New York. Isabel felt terrible but said she had to keep working to save money to bring her children to New York.

Once they finally rejoined their family, Alejandro and Yamilka went to a local elementary school in the Bronx and later to Community Intermediate School 82 for grades five to eight. The school was just up the hill on Macombs Road, near the Cross Bronx Expressway. Like many other newcomers, the siblings were enrolled in English as a Second Language classes. Their neighborhood is largely populated by immigrants from the Dominican Republic. But neither Yamilka nor Alejandro could read even Spanish, putting them behind in two languages.

Isabel said she went to the school and complained. She had very little formal education because she had started working at the age of five, helping her mother clean the house of a wealthy family. She can read in Spanish but she knew nothing about special education or evaluations, let alone her right to an attorney. She just knew her children were having a hard time and asked the teachers at CIS 82 about sending them to lower-level classes. But she said they told her everything was fine.

While Yamilka was in middle school, about three years after her arrival in New York, Isabel got a call one day from the principal's office, asking if her daughter knew how to dress herself. Isabel was confused and said of course. This led to a discussion of special education services. Yamilka was finally evaluated at her family's request in 1998. By then she was fourteen years old. A team of bilingual experts classified her as learning disabled and filled out a form stating that she should go to classes with no more than fifteen students to one teacher. They also recommended weekly counseling. One of the evaluators noted that she was overweight and was being teased by her peers, and that she was angry about having missed three years of formal schooling when she was young.

Isabel now believed her daughter would finally get the help she needed, and she expected Yamilka would soon learn to read. "They told me there was no problem," she said in Spanish. "They lied." Even after being assigned to special education classes and to the career-development school in District 75, Yamilka was still illiterate when she finished high school. Isabel was so angry that she fantasized about going to the graduation ceremony so she could stand onstage and tell everyone the truth: her daughter still couldn't read.

"I remember I was in high school and a girl said, 'You're so pretty, I want to be like you.' I said, 'You don't want to be like me. How can you be in my shoes? Why does it come to you that my life is so perfect?'"

Yamilka couldn't believe that anybody would want to trade places with her when she was in high school. She was in a school for special education students and she was the lonely kid, pretty but overweight, who sat in the back of the class trying to avoid the students who made cruel remarks, like the boy who called her "Free Willy," after the whale movie. Sometimes she fought back—literally. If another kid touched her, she admits, she would "kick their butt." She once got suspended for pulling the hair of a girl who told a substitute teacher that Yamilka didn't know how to read. The girl said it in front of the rest of the class, and Yamilka was so livid she started a fight at the end of the period. But she remembers the one student who saw her in a different light.

"She said, 'I always see you dressed so nice, you pull yourself together so perfect.' I was like, 'The clothes don't make a person.'"

Yamilka still wonders about this girl. "I was thinking like, 'What's wrong with this girl? Why she want to be like me? You don't want to be like me at all . . . I think you would kill yourself.'"

• • •

After graduating from high school, Yamilka spent a year sitting home watching television. She said there was nothing else to do. She couldn't read. She couldn't do math well enough to handle a cash register, like her sister Gabriella, and—to be honest—she didn't want to apply for low-level work cleaning dishes or houses. Her mom made a living cleaning smelly hospital sheets and towels. Isabel wanted a better life for her children and so did they. "Not like I'm putting my mom down," Yamilka explained, describing why she didn't look for a job like her mother's. "But I want something bigger for myself." Yamilka loved the cooking shows *Lidia's Italian-American Kitchen* and *Thirty-Minute Meals with Rachael Ray* and wished she could become a cook or open a café.

Her parents were troubled by her idleness, but they did not pressure her to work. The family of six is extremely close-knit. They rent a ground-floor apartment in a low-rise building on a busy street in the Morris Heights area of the Bronx. The unit has four small bedrooms. Lacy curtains are hung over the doors, and the sofas are covered with plastic. "I think they're waiting for the pope to visit," says Alejandro. There's a big TV with cable against the living room wall and each bedroom also has a television. This cozy setting is a haven from the world outside. Because it's a ground-floor apartment, the windows are barred. The apartment is next to the building's entrance, and neither the front door nor the vestibule door has a working lock. The family hears the constant traffic of neighbors, drug dealers, and occasionally violent criminals.

"You walk into the smell of marijuana," says Elizabeth, describing what it's like to come home to her lobby. Elizabeth is twenty-seven and she's the most outgoing person in the family, with long curly hair and a bright giggle. She was attending the Borough of Manhattan Community College, about an hour downtown by train.

Isabel wakes up at 4:45, five mornings a week, to ride a shared van to her job at the laundry service. It's in Fairfield County, Connecticut, about an hour and twenty minutes away. The wages are low but it's a union job and she will eventually get a pension. When Alejandro sought his city-funded private tutoring in 2005, Elizabeth testified that their mother made less than $20,000 a year, and that their family's combined income was about $42,000, including her father's disability payments. Pablo injured his arm, back, and jaw very badly a few years earlier when he fell while working as a contractor. "The doctors thought he wouldn't walk again," says Alejandro.

Pablo always worked as a manual laborer. He never learned how to read and his children say he has dyslexia. Yamilka and Alejandro's oldest sister, twenty-eight-year-old Gabriella, also struggled with reading. "School didn't seem to work for me," she tells me, thinking back on her first experience in a classroom in the Dominican Republic. She would look at the letters on a page and feel like she "didn't get it." She still couldn't read when she moved to the United States and attended a Manhattan middle school that assigned her to special education classes. But she says her reading finally improved when a high school teacher worked with her one-on-one. She graduated with a special education diploma and went to work part-time in the gift shop of a hospital in Washington Heights. She is thinking of going back to school to get her GED so she can get a better job, and she wants to become a U.S. citizen.

Isabel and Pablo wish all their kids could be working, but they want them to continue school. "The worst jobs are for people without an education," Isabel told me in Spanish. So in September 2007, at the age of twenty-four, Yamilka found herself going back to school yet again.

The Fisher Landau Center for the Treatment of Learning Disabilities is located in the Bronx neighborhood of Morris Park, and specializes in working with adults as well as children. The directors of Huntington Learning Center, Dawn Helene and Carrie Meyers, thought it would be a good match for Yamilka, especially since it's not too far from her home and takes Medicaid. She was done with her city-funded tutoring but she could still get help there. She qualified for Medicaid because she wasn't earning any income.

On September 7, 2007, Yamilka and Gabriella made their first visit to the Fisher Landau Center. It was the week after Labor Day, when a million students were heading back to the city's public schools. It was more than three years after Yamilka had graduated from high school without learning to read, and two months after she'd finished her city-funded tutoring at Huntington. Unlike Huntington and other private tutoring chains, such as Sylvan, which charge hourly rates, the Fisher Landau Center is a public clinic. It's affiliated with the Children's Evaluation and Rehabilitation Center (CERC) at the Albert Einstein College of

Medicine of Yeshiva University. CERC was at the forefront of the movement to distinguish learning disabilities from mental retardation in the 1970s, back when students with serious academic problems were all lumped together.

Morris Park is a middle-class Italian neighborhood that looks upscale compared to where Yamilka and Gabriella live. There's a Citibank on the corner and a modest commercial strip with bakeries, a nail salon, and a yoga studio. The signs are all in English, unlike the Spanish-speaking places in Morris Heights, where even the Chinese restaurants serve yellow rice.

The two sisters rode the elevator up to the second floor of the small office building and sat in a clean, large waiting room with a few children and adults. When Yamilka's name was called, she and Gabriella met with the center's director, Dr. Mary Kelly, in her office. Kelly asked about Yamilka's education history. Yamilka said she arrived in the United States at the age of thirteen in 1997. "That's not true," said Gabriella, pointing out that she had actually been ten years old. "It was ninety-three." They then went over the different schools Yamilka had attended and the special hearing she had won, which led to her tutoring classes at Huntington. Kelly explained that at Fisher Landau, Yamilka qualified for two private reading sessions a week for up to a year. Because it's a clinic, she could use her Medicaid card and get reimbursed for mass transit to and from the sessions.

Kelly gave Yamilka a brief reading test and remarked that she was having a little trouble with her eyesight. She encouraged her to get a new pair of glasses before her first session, which wasn't scheduled until November because the center had a waiting list. But, Kelly assured her, "Once we have you here, we'll keep you here. We really stick with you."

Yamilka was disappointed she couldn't start classes sooner. As they left, she told her sister, "I hate waiting."

TWO

Education, Inc.

While Yamilka was waiting for a chance to continue her education, New York City's Department of Education was celebrating a high-profile achievement. In September the city was awarded the prestigious Broad Prize for Urban Education. The annual prize is given to the U.S. school system that has demonstrated the greatest progress in raising academic performance while also narrowing the achievement gap between ethnic groups, and between high- and low-income students. New York City had been a finalist two years in a row. The financial reward—$500,000 in college scholarships—was insignificant for a school system with an annual budget of nearly $20 billion. But the award's stamp of approval was invaluable good publicity. The Broad Foundation praised the city for outperforming other systems in the state serving students with similar income levels, such as Rochester and Buffalo, and for gains among black and Hispanic students that outpaced those of their white counterparts.

This boost was timely because it came just as the city's Department of Education was about to put its schools through another round of changes. Five years after asserting "mayoral control" over the nation's largest public school system, Michael Bloomberg and his administration were about to embark on a plan to measure the performance of all 1,453 schools by quantifying their progress in raising student achievement. The schools wouldn't be measured based simply on how many students were *passing* the state exams from one year to the next, which was the standard approach. They would also be scrutinized for signs of individual student *progress*. Scholars call this a "growth model," because it follows the same cohort of pupils from year to year—rather than measuring one class against the class from the year before. For example, instead of looking at third-grade reading scores from 2006 to 2007, the city would try to see whether those third-graders from 2006 did better, as a group, as fourth-graders in 2007.

Despite the gains cited by the Broad Prize, a plethora of good neighborhood schools, and several selective, world-class schools such as Stuyvesant High School, New York City still had lots of room for improvement. Just over half its high school students were graduating in four years. When the prize was given in 2007, 56 percent of New York City students in grades three through five were reading at their grade level. That was better than Los Angeles, Philadelphia, and Detroit, but about the same percentage as Chicago. And the scores went down after sixth grade, with just 42 percent of eighth-graders in New York City reading at the proficient level, compared to 67 percent statewide. This "middle school slump" was a phenomenon troubling educators all around the United States. And in New York, as in other districts, blacks and Latinos had lower scores than whites. Still, there were signs of progress. The proportion of students scoring on the lowest level of state reading tests had declined to less than one out of ten. And overall, the scores had been rising since Mayor Bloomberg took control of the school system—although they dipped slightly in 2007, after the federal government required New York to test all English Language Learners who had been in the United States for a year or more. (These students had previously been given more time before taking the English exams.) This aspect of No Child Left Behind was considered especially onerous for New York City because 13 percent of its public school students (140,000 students) were still learning English. More than 150 languages are spoken in the city, the most common being Spanish, Chinese dialects, Bengali, Arabic, Haitian Creole, Russian, Urdu, French, Korean, Albanian, Polish, and Punjabi.

Among large urban school systems, the schools of New York City are also exceptionally diverse in quality. New York is home to some of the most selective and prestigious public high schools in the country, including the aforementioned Stuyvesant High and the Bronx High School of Science, where students rack up Westinghouse Science Awards the way students in other schools win sports championships. There are a few hundred good, solid elementary schools that inspire passion (and waiting lists) among local parents. These schools are usually clustered in middle-

and upper-class neighborhoods like Park Slope, Brooklyn; Douglaston, Queens; and the Upper West Side of Manhattan. But there are also dozens of schools considered so bad that the state is in the process of shutting them down, and hundreds more where fewer than half of the children are reading at grade level. After NCLB was passed, there were about four hundred New York City schools each year considered "in need of improvement" because they weren't meeting proficiency standards for blacks, Hispanics, English Language Learners, special ed pupils, or low income students (the different categories schools have to disaggregate).

Mayor Bloomberg undertook a new round of education reforms in 2007, amid speculation that he was considering a bid for the presidency the following year. That June, he was featured on the cover of *Time* alongside California governor Arnold Schwarzenegger[1] with the headline "The New Action Heroes." The article referred to "the Hollywood brute" and "the Wall Street mogul" as "the oddest couple since 'Twins,'" but went on to describe how the two socially liberal Republicans were challenging their party by taking on climate change and stem cell research. The piece also mentioned Bloomberg's "hostile takeover" of the city schools, and their gradually improving test scores. Days later, Bloomberg left the Republican party and registered as an Independent.

Politically, Bloomberg was an unknown quantity when he was elected in November 2001, just two months after the devastating attacks on the World Trade Center. He had become a billionaire through his financial media empire. The then-fifty-nine-year-old was also a fixture of the society columns because of his generous philanthropy and his homes in London, Bermuda, and upstate New York. But he had little previous involvement in politics. When he ran for mayor, he switched his party registration from Democratic to Republican mainly so he wouldn't have to face as much competition in the heavily Democratic city's primary contest. Bloomberg's wealth allowed him to buy lots of advertisements. He easily conquered the weak Republican field and became his party's nominee. Yet he was still considered a long shot because he was up against a better-known Democrat, Mark Green—the city's elected public advocate, who had been a frequent, and very visible, critic of Mayor Rudolph Giuliani's administration.

The city's mind-set changed, however, after the Twin Towers were destroyed by Islamic terrorists. New Yorkers became obsessed with security, and the outgoing Republican mayor Giuliani's endorsement of Bloomberg became a seal of approval for a nervous city. By then, Giuliani was "America's Mayor," who pulled the city together after 9/11, and New Yorkers were bombarded with television ads featuring Giuliani praising Bloomberg as his logical successor. The Republican businessman narrowly won the election that November, to the surprise of political veterans. He had spent more than $70 million of his own money on the successful race.

Upon taking office in early 2002, Bloomberg vowed to use his business experience to make government more efficient and high tech, starting with the schools. The man who made his fortune selling a new type of information terminal to Wall Street firms wanted to apply the expertise and competition of the private sector to city government.

The New York City Board of Education, as it was known back then, was a vast and infamous bureaucracy. Headquartered across the East River in downtown Brooklyn, the school system was technically independent of City Hall. It was run by seven board members, only two of whom were appointed by the mayor. The five others were appointed by the political heads of the city's five boroughs: Manhattan, the Bronx, Brooklyn, Staten Island, and Queens. This meant all decisions—from where to build new schools to condom distribution in schools to choosing a new chancellor—were made by political horse-trading. Former board members admitted as much. This frustrated mayor after mayor, and Giuliani even declared that the whole school system should be "blown up," a rhetorical flourish that wasn't appreciated by the city's teachers union.

To other critics of the system, the Board of Education often resembled a series of Soviet satellite states. It was "decentralized" into thirty-two community school districts in the late 1960s after an especially explosive chapter in city race relations. The predominantly black Brooklyn neighborhood of Ocean Hill–Brownsville had been part of an experiment to give parents more say over their schools. When the local board dismissed a handful of white, mostly Jewish teachers and administrators in order to bring in more minority educators, the move triggered a series of teachers' strikes. Afterward, the state (and the union) agreed to a new structure in which local school districts were created throughout the city to provide more community involvement at the elementary and junior high school levels. Each district had an elected board with the power to hire superintendents and other personnel. But while some boards were respected by their communities, others were accused of acting like fiefdoms, rife with corruption and patronage. Being on a school board was a voluntary position, but if you worked it right, you could get all kinds of graft. Some board members were arrested for misusing their offices by taking trips to Hawaii at taxpayer expense, or for taking bribes in exchange for hiring certain people to work in the schools. After a wave of scandals during the 1990s, the state legislature stripped the school boards of most of their power. The public didn't fight back. Voter turnout in school board elections had been less than 5 percent.

These problems, and the city's lackluster achievement scores compared to the surrounding suburbs, led to a renewed push for mayoral control by the time Michael Bloomberg was elected. In his 2002 inauguration speech, on January 1, Bloomberg declared, "We will improve our public schools." But, he said, "the real test is that of political resolve, the test of ourselves. The need is real. The time is now. Without authority there is no accountability. The public, through the mayor, must control the school system."[2] With an annual budget of about $13 billion back then, he argued, the schools should be doing better.

By June of that year, Bloomberg had successfully made his case with the state legislature. Unlike his antagonistic predecessor Giuliani, Bloomberg had a (publicly) low-key, pragmatic approach that helped him persuade the normally territorial and risk-averse lawmakers to put him in charge. The law was rewritten to give the mayor sole control over the school system until 2009, when the state legislature could decide whether to renew it. The mayor would have the power to choose the chancellor, who would report directly to him. That chancellor would select all superintendents and make any curricular decisions. Bloomberg announced the historic agreement outside a school in Harlem, where he promised that the reform of school governance "will give the school system the one thing it fundamentally needs, accountability."

The mayor made public education a top priority in his new administration. He renamed the Board of Education the Department of Education and moved its headquarters from Brooklyn to the Tweed Courthouse, right behind City Hall, in Lower Manhattan. The Tweed, as it's known, is a nineteenth-century landmark with a huge Corinthian portico surrounded on either side by imposing wings. The building is named for the infamous William "Boss" Tweed, who led the city's Democratic machine in the late 1800s. Tweed lined his pockets (and those of his cronies) by making the courthouse the most expensive project in city history, and he was sent to prison before its completion. The glorious building has marble tiles and a dome with glass windows, allowing sunlight to drench all four floors of the building's rotunda. Former mayor Rudolph Giuliani dedicated $90 million of city funds to repurpose the courthouse as a museum. Bloomberg's decision to make the building into the Department of Education instead was highly symbolic of the importance he was according the public schools—and a bit of a warning, perhaps, given the Tweed legacy of corruption.

The mayor's next move was to pick a chancellor with no experience running a school system. That July Bloomberg called a press conference in the Tweed Courthouse, where he announced his selection of Joel Klein. The education reporters covering the event either had never heard of Klein, or didn't connect him to the government's case against Microsoft. Many confused him with Joe Klein—the political reporter who anonymously wrote the book *Primary Colors*, a biting parody of Bill Clinton's presidential campaign. The slim, balding man who took the lectern after Bloomberg's introductory remarks that day recalled his own experience attending public schools in Queens, but he acknowledged that his own daughter had gone to a private school, the Potomac School, just outside Washington, D.C., when he had worked for the Clinton administration. His second wife, Nicole Seligman, was general counsel for Sony. He had known Bloomberg socially before his appointment. That day, Bloomberg praised Klein's background, which he said would allow Klein to take a fresh look at intractable problems plaguing the school system. He called him "a true leader who never shies away from the tough and sometimes controversial decisions that are necessary to implement change."

"Change" was the buzzword as Klein and Bloomberg set about remaking the public schools. By 2003 they sought to do away with the thirty-two community school districts and replace them with a scheme dividing the schools into ten larger regions. New acronyms entered the vocabulary as the mayor and the chancellor created a management system with local instructional supervisors (LISs) and regional operations centers (ROCs) for supplies. Bloomberg and Klein called the new reforms Children First.

They also sought consistency, or at least the appearance of it. The Department of Education adopted a so-called universal math curriculum and a controversial approach to reading instruction called "balanced literacy." Students sat in clusters instead of rows. Teachers gave "mini-lessons" of just ten or fifteen minutes, after which the students split up into groups for different reading and writing activities. Some teachers were already using this approach, but others found it an unwanted and intrusive departure from traditional lessons, or "talk and chalk."

The Bloomberg-Klein reforms were greeted with mixed reactions, as one would expect in a system with more than 1,400 schools and 79,000 full-time teachers. "Balanced literacy" would become the latest chapter in almost a century's worth of battles over the best way to teach children to read. Some critics thought the city's approach didn't put enough emphasis on phonics for early readers. Meanwhile, teachers and principals—who were already absorbing the impact of the federal No Child Left Behind law—had to comply with another new management system. They complained that too many outsiders with Ivy League degrees were running the Tweed instead of experienced educators. Many teachers also felt like they were under too much scrutiny, as supervisors roamed through their classrooms, checking to see if they were spending the right amount of time on each reading and writing activity during their ninety-minute balanced literacy blocks. A common cry at protest rallies during those early years was "Let teachers teach." The teachers did, however, get a 15 percent raise in 2005 in exchange for agreeing to provide struggling students additional instruction and test prep for one extra period at the beginning or end of the school day, from Monday through Thursday.

Bloomberg and Klein encouraged partnerships with outside reform groups. The Open Society, the Carnegie Foundation, and the Bill & Melinda Gates Foundation contributed $100 million toward the creation of small new schools. Failing high schools were phased out so that three or four smaller schools could replace them in the same buildings. The small schools offered "personalized" environments and had themes to keep students engaged, such as law and social justice, communications, aviation, and business. But they were criticized for not taking a fair share of special education students and English Language Learners. These needy children were disproportionately enrolled in large, violent, and failing high schools.[3] And the sprawling system was still a big and ineffective bureaucracy. When the balanced literacy program went into effect during the 2003/04 school year, elementary teachers were required to gather their children onto "reading rugs" for part of the class time. But the *Daily News* ran a series of reports about how the rugs had become so filthy by midyear that students were getting allergic reactions. When principals and teachers complained, the custodians union said cleaning the rugs wasn't part of its contract.[4]

There were other snafus. The city hired a new parent coordinator at every school to lighten the load for principals and give parents a more direct point of contact. But many parent groups felt pushed to the sidelines, no longer having local school boards in their neighborhoods or monthly Board of Education meetings where they were able to speak out on issues affecting the schools. Klein and Bloomberg enacted a controversial plan to stop promoting elementary children to the next grade if they didn't pass the statewide tests, reversing a policy known as social promotion. Many parents and education advocates feared the change would encourage more students to drop out. When members of an educational policy panel objected, the mayor fired them.

Parents and education advocates complained that Klein hired too many vendors without competitive bidding and wasted money on expensive consultants. The city paid $15.8 million to the consulting firm Alvarez & Marsal to come up with cost savings. It changed the entire school bus route network in the middle of winter, a disaster that left children stranded on street corners and caused days of embarrassing headlines. Klein's management team was also criticized for including several highly paid "chief officers" who made more than $160,000 a year. Klein's own salary was $250,000—the highest of any city official (Bloomberg declined a salary and opted for a symbolic payment of a dollar a year).

Meanwhile, some critics were wondering how all these changes would actually put children first. Diane Ravitch, a former U.S. assistant secretary of education and an education historian, wrote several stinging critiques of the Bloomberg administration's balanced literacy curriculum. The city was boasting that scores on state tests had gone up. But Ravitch and other education experts argued that the National Assessment of Educational Progress is a more consistent measurement of proficiency than state exams, since states were allowed to define proficiency however they wanted—resulting in huge discrepancies. Most students in Mississippi, for example, passed their state exams while failing the NAEP. When Ravitch looked at New York City, she noted that NAEP reading scores went up four points between 2003 and 2005, and stayed at that level in 2007. The gains had been greater under the previous chancellor, Harold Levy. "The biggest score increase was 2002/03," Ravitch said—right before Bloomberg's Children First initiative went into effect. The percentage of city fourth-grade students reading well below grade level declined from 53 to 47 percent that year; put another way, that's a reading gain of six percentage points compared to the four-point increase under Bloomberg. Ravitch argued that these results proved the new literacy program wasn't working. The city's schools were doing better than many large urban districts, but Boston, Washington, D.C., and Atlanta were making greater progress. Meanwhile, the city's math scores on the NAEP increased more than reading and were even approaching the national average for fourth-graders in 2007.

The pressure on public education was relentless. Administrators in big-city districts were asking tough questions as they tried to raise test scores for all students, but especially the black and Hispanic pupils most likely to attend low-performing schools. Should they give parents vouchers to send their children to private and religious schools, as Cleveland had tried? Were charter schools the answer? Klein and Bloomberg intended to open one hundred charter schools by September 2009, and they were well on their way. Charters were publicly financed but free of most school district policies, including requirements to hire union teachers. New York City even embarked on a hotly debated experiment to pay students for passing their tests. Fourth- and seventh-graders in a handful of schools could make a few hundred dollars if they aced all their exams, in a small program that was privately funded.

So when Klein announced that he would be embarking on another round of management reforms in 2007, the move added fuel to a simmering debate over how to improve the city schools. Between the spring and fall of that year, the ten regions that Klein and Bloomberg had created were completely eliminated, without public input. Schools would no longer report to some geographic office; instead, their principals would elect to join networks of like-minded administrators. The principals would also get more freedom over how to allocate their budgets. Other school systems have embraced a similar form of site-based management, with the goal of reducing bureaucracy and becoming more cost-effective. Chancellor Klein and his team admired Edmonton, Canada, which boasted that 94 percent of its education budget went straight to its schools, rather than to layers of administrators, under a site-based system. Klein wanted to do something similar in New York City. But in exchange for more authority, principals would have to prove their students were learning.

That's where ARIS came into play. Klein's team created the Achievement Reporting and Innovation System. Launched in 2007, ARIS was considered a Web-based network for managing every conceivable form of data about the public schools and their students. IBM won an $80 million contract through competitive bidding to build the system over a five-year period. The goal was to eventually merge all student records that were previously in aging and separate systems and to add new sources of data. Other states and districts were designing their own information management systems or buying them off the shelf from software companies. They were also buying new assessments from testing companies such as Kaplan and Princeton Review. The clumsy phrases "data-driven instruction" and "data-driven decision-making" joined the jargon of edu-speak.

New York City was one of the biggest prospective customers when it started shopping for a new data system. It was also flush with cash. In 2007 the Department of Education received an extra $700 million from the state following a protracted lawsuit in which education advocates successfully proved the city's public schools—with their high number of immigrants and children in poverty—had been shortchanged by the state. The city itself was also kicking in a few hundred million dollars more to match the additional funds from Albany.

Soon after selecting IBM to design ARIS, the city's Department of Education awarded another big contract in its push for greater accountability. It selected the publishing company CTB/McGraw-Hill to design assessments to be given several times over the school year in math and reading. Of course, this meant even more training for everyone. The new ARIS system required principals and data specialists at every school to learn how to look at years of test scores. They needed to "drill down" so they could see the results for each child and sort out the subgroups required under No Child Left Behind: students from high-poverty families, blacks, Hispanics, Asians, whites, Native Americans, English Language Learners, and special education students. The individual teachers wouldn't have to use these sorting tools yet, but they would have to use the assessments. The goal was to raise scores and close achievement gaps.

Altogether, the city would have to train up to ninety thousand teachers, coaches, and principals over the coming year—people whose daily jobs, as professional educators, required them to spend very little time in front of computers. It would be a massive task. When Starbucks decided to retrain all 135,000 of its baristas, it shut down its 7,100 stores in February 2008 for several hours. The New York City schools would have no such luxury. Though some teachers and principals had gotten pilot training the previous year, or gone to seminars over the summer, they'd have to learn on the job—with occasional workshops and training sessions—while continuing to educate more than a million children without losing sight of those who were struggling.

THREE

Renaissance Man

Unlike most young adults, Alejandro wasn't interested in the Internet. His family had gotten a desktop computer about a decade earlier, but the modem broke, so he'd never been on the Web. However, in September 2007, at the age of twenty-two, Alejandro found himself suddenly interested in Facebook.

His sister Gabriella would often bring home magazines from the hospital gift shop where she worked, and Alejandro was intrigued by an issue of *Newsweek* with a cover story about the twenty-three-year-old Facebook founder Mark Zuckerberg. It was tough to read for someone who didn't know about the online world, because it was filled with references to the "social graph" and "third party applications." But Alejandro pushed himself to read most of the story without any help, figuring out words he didn't know from the context and getting the general drift. He couldn't imagine himself wanting to send messages to strangers through a website. Still, just reading the article was a huge accomplishment for Alejandro. Less than three years earlier, he had decided to take on the city's Department of Education for failing to teach him to read, the case that ultimately inspired his sister Yamilka's victory as well.

Alejandro was frequently picked on when he was a kid. But this small, compact young man with a round face and soft brown eyes also has a fiercely stubborn streak, and a temper, too. His mother, Isabel, recalled how back in the Dominican Republic he would stand on the porch giving a "concert" whenever he was angry or frustrated. She'd let him yell until he was ready to calm down.

When Isabel and her two older daughters joined Pablo in New York, leaving Alejandro and Yamilka with their father's aunt, Alejandro decided to resist Tanta in little ways. "I remember one incident, I asked [Tanta] for money to buy a sandwich," he said. "She gave me five pesos . . . she tell me, 'Go buy a piece of bread with butter and bring me the rest.' I went to the store and got a sandwich with *everything*. She was pissed!"

Alejandro laughed with his sisters about this in their kitchen while the family ate a hearty Dominican stew called *sancocho*. He's about five foot six, the tallest in the family. Alejandro and his sister Elizabeth are both considered headstrong. "Maybe we got the ability to see stupidity in people," Alejandro mused, "how weak they are."

It probably wasn't a surprise, then, that Elizabeth and Alejandro were the ones who eventually fought the school system. Alejandro was in high school and he still wasn't able to read, despite being in special education classes. He decided to go see a guidance counselor to talk about his reading problems and says he was told that he could get an independent evaluation at the city's expense. At the evaluation, he and Elizabeth learned for the first time that they could get free legal assistance and try to force the Department of Education to give Alejandro better services. Because he was a student with a learning disability, the city had to comply with whatever was written on his Individualized Education Program, and the family was allowed to legally challenge the city for noncompliance. Elizabeth was given a list of references and called the first name she saw: Advocates for Children. They met with Deputy Director Matthew Lenaghan.

It was early 2005 and Alejandro was nineteen years old. He went into the office on West Thirtieth Street with Elizabeth. Lenaghan recalls he was mature and articulate but very shy, admitting he was afraid to go out on his own. "He was uncomfortable with buses, he was uncomfortable about being in school, and I think he was also very embarrassed," he said. Alejandro's high school placement made no sense to the attorneys. He'd been transferred from a regular high school to a GED program for three periods a day, where students study to earn their high school equivalency degrees. Lenaghan wondered how the school system expected a kid who couldn't read to take the GED. "He's a perfect example of a child who, for lack of a better cliché, slipped through the cracks, and the system was just waiting for him to go away."

Lenaghan had trouble retrieving Alejandro's records. It was widely reported that special education records were a big mess at the time because of Mayor Bloomberg's recent reorganization of the city school system. Many files never made it from one office to another. Elizabeth wound up tracking down the paperwork by going to different offices around the city, playing paralegal for Lenaghan and his fellow attorneys. Meanwhile, Lenaghan talked to Alejandro about his possibilities. He was too old to get into a private special education school at the city's expense—the typical recourse for younger students with disabilities who cannot get the free and appropriate education in a public program that they're entitled to under federal law. Lenaghan also told Alejandro he should drop any hope of accumulating the number of credits he'd need to graduate from high school. It was too late for that. Instead, he suggested an intensive, private tutoring program that could teach him to read and open other opportunities. They filed for an impartial hearing against the New York City Department of Education, seeking compensatory education services.

The hearing was held in a conference room in downtown Brooklyn, with Elizabeth, Alejandro, Lenaghan, and a representative from the Department of Education (who wasn't a lawyer) all making their arguments to an impartial hearing officer. Alejandro wore a black suit and a blue shirt he'd bought for the occasion to show respect. The Department of Education's representative barely defended her agency. According to the transcript, she merely stated that the Department of Education "maintains that the program we offered to Alejandro was an appropriate program, given the information that we had at the time." Alejandro testified that he had never gotten any help for his reading problems. By high school, he said, he was pulling teachers aside and asking them not to call on him during class because he couldn't read or write in either English or Spanish. He also said he wasn't going to school because the situation was causing him so much stress. His sister Elizabeth said his personality had changed and that he had become depressed and withdrawn. She also testified that she attended school meetings about his Individualized Education Program but that she was never told about the family's right to obtain a lawyer and challenge Alejandro's placement.

The hearing officer, Mary Margaret Kinery, initially awarded Alejandro 480 hours of compensatory education services in the form of private tutoring. Later, Advocates for Children went back and won him another 1,440 hours, enough to take him past his twenty-first birthday, the age at which a student is no longer entitled to public education. Lenaghan said Alejandro's demeanor especially impressed the hearing officer. When Kinery asked him what he saw himself doing in the future, he said, "Something in science and computer. I would like to study also history, Renaissance art, and philosophy."

Alejandro started his classes at Lindamood-Bell Learning Processes. Founded in 1986 by the educators Nanci Bell, Pat Lindamood, and Phyllis Lindamood, the program specializes in treating dyslexia, autism, and various other learning disabilities. The private company has forty offices around the United States and one in London. At the time of Alejandro's first visit, the New York office was located in Greenwich Village—way downtown from Alejandro's neighborhood. The funky clothing stores and upscale restaurants couldn't have been a more drastic change from the run-down apartment buildings, auto shops, and bodegas of the Bronx. Alejandro was eager to enroll, but he had to get over his fear of mass transit. Elizabeth showed him which bus and trains to take into Manhattan. The trip took him forty-five minutes to an hour. He often took a CD player along to block out the sounds of all the people. He liked rock music by the bands Linkin Park and Audioslave, and also brought along a classical string quartet CD a friend had given him.

Alejandro recognized just seven printed English words when he was first evaluated at Lindamood-Bell in January 2005. Advocates for Children had requested this evaluation when they took his case so they'd know what to ask of the city. Like Huntington Learning Center, Lindamood-Bell is among a handful of private tutoring centers that are willing to accept students who win compensatory services from the city. Lindamood-Bell estimated that 25 to 30 percent of its students were enrolled at the city's expense in 2007; the rest were students who needed additional help in school and whose families could afford the services, which typically last for just six to eight weeks. Tutoring at the time Alejandro started was ninety-four dollars an hour—a little less than what individual tutors charged for private services. Alejandro's award would cost the city more than $160,000 if he used all his hours and student transit passes.

Lindamood-Bell has a "multisensory" reading program. Students concentrate on the sound and feel of words in their mouths, and even draw letters in the air with their fingers. The point is to stimulate the brain to process language properly, a technique researchers have found especially effective with dyslexics such as Alejandro. The neuropsychiatrist Samuel Torrey Orton and the educator Anna Gillingham pioneered this technique in the early twentieth century. Their methods were highly respected, and today the Academy of Orton-Gillingham Practitioners and Educators certifies programs that adopt its step-by-step approach to reading. Lindamood-Bell has its own research-based program, as do many education services that work with dyslexics and other students who have great difficulty learning to read.

Contrary to popular belief, dyslexics aren't seeing backward letters when they read. They have no problem seeing. But they can't instinctively judge whether what they perceive matches what they see on the page—leaving them unable to figure out when they've made a spelling or reading error. That's why the International Dyslexia Association and a slew of researchers call it a "language-based learning disability," a weakness in the brain's language system that makes it difficult to identify the separate speech sounds (phonemes) within a word. It's a neurological condition, though it's not always formally diagnosed, and it often runs in families—which could explain why Alejandro, Yamilka, and their father all had problems learning to read in Spanish and in English. Sally Shaywitz, a professor of pediatrics at the Yale Center for the Study of Learning and Attention and the author of the book *Overcoming Dyslexia*, predicts that between a quarter and half of children born to dyslexic parents will also be dyslexic.[1] But there's growing evidence that children and even adults with dyslexia can carve out new "neural passageways" and learn to read when given the right kind of multisensory program that can get them to understand the sounds and structures of words. A Carnegie Mellon University brain imaging study of fifth-graders with dyslexia and other reading problems found that after a hundred hours of instruction, there were measurable changes in the parietotemporal area of the brain, which is responsible for decoding the sounds of written language and assembling them into words.[2] Their brains adapted to the instruction.

Lindamood-Bell focuses on three key areas of reading. First, there are phonemes, the different sounds within a given word, such as the "ih" and the "tuh" within "fit." This is what teachers mean when they refer to "phonemic awareness" as a building block for reading. Young children are taught to read through rhymes so they'll recognize how a tiny change can turn "fit" into "fat." But those with poor phonemic awareness can't automatically hear the different sounds within each word. They'll look at a word such as "steam" and immediately reach for a word with similar sounds, such as "stream," says Jennifer Egan, who heads the New York office for Lindamood-Bell. "They're not able to track all the sounds in that word," she explains. "Maybe they get the 'st' and they go 'stream,' and they don't hear that they just added a sound in there." Egan says students in her program also often confuse "imagination" with "immigration." "They get the beginning, they get the end, they see a bunch of *m*'s and *g*'s, and they can't take all those parts and bring it to a whole."

Many struggling readers also have trouble with "symbol imagery." For example, most of us can picture the letter *i* when we hear the nonsense word "frip," but a dyslexic can't see that image. This is what Egan and her colleagues call "weak symbol imagery." People with this problem might spell a word phonetically, but they can't remember what the word is supposed to look like. They aren't getting the visual pattern, the orthography, of a word like "seize" or "right" that doesn't follow the usual phonetic rules. Reading teachers call these words that don't "play fair." Eventually they become "sight words," words we recognize without having to phonetically master and sound them out each time. Poor readers may also have trouble with "concept imagery," or putting together different pieces of information into a whole they can visualize. They have to read and reread information multiple times. Lindamood-Bell's approach is to strengthen reading comprehension by helping students visualize a story line or directions.

This is where the multisensory technique comes into play. Lindamood-Bell relies on the "dual-coding" theory to help struggling readers like Alejandro. Dual-coding is attributed to Allan Paivio, a psychology professor at the University of Western Ontario, who's written about how the brain processes verbal and nonverbal information through different channels. "The two parts of the brain that we're stimulating and getting to work in concert are the part of the brain that deals with language and the part of the brain that deals with, in this case, imagery," says Egan. With Alejandro, she explains, "he's saying the letter and visualizing the letter at the same time" to help develop this dual-coding strength.

Alejandro's reading teachers started by getting him to learn the sounds of each letter, and then gradually taught him to blend these sounds together. They would read words to him from flash cards and ask him to spell them, encouraging him to imagine the different letters and draw them in the air several times, committing them to motor memory. When he read a sentence or paragraph, he would use his pencil to isolate the different sounds or phonemes within a written word. If he wrote a word, such as "want," he would stop and concentrate on whether the vowel should be an *o* or an *a*. Alejandro was almost twenty years old when he started the program, but he tried not to think about how far behind he was. "I knew I had nothing to be ashamed about," he said, referring to the city's failure to teach him to read.

One day about a year and a half into his instruction, Alejandro sat with a young tutor named James Bocchicchio going over a novel called *Tomorrow Men*, which is about the comic book characters Iron Man, Captain America, and Thor. They easily could have been mistaken for two friends in their twenties hanging out in a college library. James had a scruffy beard and wore khaki pants, a plaid shirt, and wire-rim glasses. Alejandro wore a black shirt over a white T and jeans. One of them had brought along a bottle of Vitaminwater. There were two boxes on the table labeled with Alejandro's name. They held hundreds of word cards, some he had mastered and others he was still in the process of learning.

Alejandro started reading aloud from a page in *Tomorrow Men* about Captain America. "'Making his way east toward rows of offi—offices . . .'" He had trouble with that last word. James told him to look at the word after the one he was struggling with, which was "buildings." "Is it one or two?" he asked Alejandro. "Office buildings," he read aloud, correcting himself. Then he came to the word "light" and stopped again. James pulled a pencil out from behind his ear and asked Alejandro to read the word "sight." He then showed him how putting the *s* before "light" created "slight," helping Alejandro make the connection between the "ight" sound in each word. After a few more sentences, he asked Alejandro to read the next paragraph on his own, circling any problem words. Alejandro read slowly and stopped at the words "antique" and "emerald." James conceded that the "-que" ending is tough and showed him how it's pronounced. Then he said the word "emerald" and asked Alejandro to picture the object. "Green jewelry," Alejandro replied.

"Okay, I'm going to give you some sentences to write," said James, switching gears to their next activity. It was time for Alejandro to practice using some of the words he'd learned so he could self-edit and make corrections based on both phonetic spelling and sight memory. He read Alejandro his first sentence: "I don't want to hurt my friend."

Alejandro wrote "wont" instead of "want" and "frien" instead of "friend." "You're trying to do it by sound," said James. "How does 'want' *look*? Not how does it *sound*. I know you don't remember how it looks, but that's the only thing you've got to work with."

Alejandro erased and began writing "wh," but James stopped him. "There are other words that have 'wh,' like 'when' and 'where.' But 'want' plays fair. That means what vowel?" Alejandro fixed the word by erasing the *h* and writing the letter *a*. James then told him that he had left off the ending of "friend" and he fixed that word, too, adding the *d*.

James thought Alejandro was reading well, but generating a word on his own from visual memory was tough. "Spelling is always the thing that comes last with building visual memory," he explained of dyslexics. "It's definitely the hardest part."

James had been working with Alejandro from the very beginning, when he first started learning the sounds of the letters. After a year of what he considered "remarkable" progress, he helped Alejandro choose his very first real book, *A Wrinkle in Time* by Madeleine L'Engle. He thought it would appeal to Alejandro because he liked comic books and science fiction. The classic children's book is about a sister and brother who travel through space and time to rescue their scientist father from a bleak planet where everyone has succumbed to conformity and follows the rules of a giant brain called It. The imaginative story was written in 1962, and it also has a political message about the dangers of totalitarianism.

It was a difficult first book, but James wanted to push his student to decode more unfamiliar words as he learned how to navigate written language. As a native Spanish speaker, Alejandro also had to significantly expand his English vocabulary. "Once we got Alejandro reading, we wanted to make sure he was challenged and motivated to continue," he said. James and the other tutors—who are called clinicians—had trouble finding a book at Alejandro's level. He was too sophisticated for most of the books at the center, which are targeted for younger readers. *A Wrinkle in Time* was at a middle school level. James figured Alejandro would have no problem with comprehension. "He had a natural proclivity to see the irony, to see the twist," he said. His goal was to get Alejandro more confident with reading.

Alejandro read a few pages of the book during every day's session, with James or another clinician. They would spend just a few minutes on the book and then move on to other lessons because Alejandro was still learning how to become a better reader, and he was also starting to learn basic math. But *A Wrinkle in Time* was difficult. The book's vocabulary is fairly rich, with words such as "perturbed," "ineffable," and "wafted" that aren't commonly used in spoken English. There's a character who stutters and another who speaks in quotations by writers, including Shakespeare and Cervantes. At one point there's a discussion of iambic pentameter. And when the characters travel, they "tesseract."

It took Alejandro more than six months to finish *A Wrinkle in Time*. James said he sometimes engaged in "avoidance behavior," diverting his tutors by talking about movies or television shows because he was so exhausted from reading. There were also days when he didn't come to class—because he was tired, intimidated by mass transit, or both. "Four hours a day was tough on every day," James recalled. "At the end of a day, sometimes he was just speechless, he was just burnt."

Months later, Alejandro said he liked the book. He could recall the plot about three kids going to another planet, and compared it to the movie *The Stepford Wives*. But he couldn't remember too many other details. "I think at the time since it was one of the first books I read, I was concentrating on every word," he said. But James was correct that Alejandro's reading confidence did grow over time.

By the fall of 2007, Alejandro had made enough progress to get through the *Newsweek* article about the Facebook founder. Reading was still hard, but, he said, "I'm living with it." His program would end in January 2008, when he was scheduled to complete the last of his 1,920 hours. His lawyers and the program director of Lindamood-Bell were encouraging him to apply for a GED preparation program. He was too old to go back to high school, so he'd have to shoot for an equivalency degree. But he would have a lot of material to cover. The test consists of five portions: math, history, science, reading, and writing. It would be a huge challenge for someone who, in effect, had missed out on his entire formal education. Alejandro was determined to take the GED, but now that the end of his tutoring was drawing near, he was afraid of failure. He would return home from Lindamood-Bell each afternoon exhausted by stress, skipping his regular exercise routine on the treadmill he keeps in his bedroom. He also had trouble sleeping.

"It's a lot of work to do," he said, referring to the GED. "I don't know if I'm confident enough now. We'll see later next year."

FOUR

Breakthrough Moment

Every child has a distinctive way of learning, but not every teacher knows how to make the "breakthrough" needed to tap into a student's individual learning style. That's the core argument of a 2006 book called *Breakthrough*, by three educators who strongly believe in "data-driven instruction." The phrase describes teachers who use all the information they can glean about a student's academic history and learning styles to individually tailor instruction. The book's authors—Michael Fullan, Peter Hill, and Carmel Crévola—argue for a new form of teaching in which classroom teaching follows the student, instead of a room full of students following their teacher. They explain: "Rather than beginning with instruction and ending with measuring student progress, instruction would begin with measuring what students know and are able to do; instruction would be designed on the basis of this information. In other words, the logic would be reversed."[1]

In an age when compact disc sales were plummeting because so many music fans were shopping for individual songs on iTunes, and when network television had to compete with hundreds of niche cable channels, education was also becoming more customized through technology.

The authors of *Breakthrough* called for schools and districts to build new information systems that could provide classroom teachers with the latest data about their students; professional development to help them understand this data; and on-site experts who would be responsible for making sure the teachers don't get overwhelmed.

The first computer-based systems for tracking student achievement were created in the 1980s, after the National Commission on Excellence in Education released "A Nation at Risk." This was the damning 1983 report that concluded that America's lead in commerce, industry, science, and technology was being overtaken due to international competitors such as Japan, and that the quality of our education system was to blame. In the fury following this report, Florida and Texas both created "data warehouses" so they could measure progress. Florida merged student records from its schools with information from its child welfare agency and records of which families were receiving food stamps. Texas included information about its teachers' degrees and class sizes.

With the passage of the No Child Left Behind law, states had even greater incentives to track their students on the quest to "proficiency." Nancy Smith, a former Texas state education researcher and deputy director of the Data Quality Campaign, said that in 2005 there were thirty-six states with the capability of tracking a student from grade to grade and from district to district by a unique identification number. In 2008 that number jumped to forty-eight. And all fifty states are able to collect annual records on individual high school graduates and dropouts. The Data Quality Campaign was launched in 2005 with funding from the Bill & Melinda Gates Foundation. It partners with education and business groups around the country to improve the collection, availability, and use of education data that states can use to boost student achievement. It's a field that's in constant motion now as vendors come up with new information management systems.

But just keeping all this data on the desktops of state education officials wouldn't help an individual student succeed. Teachers would need to see performance trends on annual and semiannual tests, too, if they were going to help their pupils with "data-driven instruction." In 2003 Jeff Wayman made a presentation about this concept to a technology-in-education conference at Harvard University. Wayman was a researcher at Johns Hopkins. He and a fellow researcher argued that teachers could use some of this new data to tailor—or "differentiate"—their instruction according to the strengths and weaknesses of each student. But they were greeted with skepticism about whether teachers would, or even could, use the data without misinterpreting so many numbers and test scores. "We didn't get chased out of town with burning torches," Wayman joked, in his Texas accent. "But I remember a couple of people who were like, 'You shouldn't even be talking about this'" because it was considered so difficult.

That attitude changed quickly as school districts felt greater pressure to raise their test scores and wondered what the numbers could tell them. Now an assistant education professor at the University of Texas–Austin, Wayman has since studied districts from Wyoming to Michigan that have been using data to improve their instruction. But he acknowledges it really isn't easy. Teachers need to wade through the "hard data" of annual test scores and practice tests, while also relying on the "soft data" of their own classroom observations—such as which students have trouble concentrating or reading aloud. "My message started out as 'Hey, this is easier than you think,'" he said. "Now it's 'Hey, this is harder than you think!'"

Wayman said he got a call from Jim Liebman as New York City began planning its new Web-based network, ARIS. He was never paid to serve as a consultant to the system, nor was he asked to. He said he just listened and supported Liebman's idea of using periodic assessments, created by testing companies or teachers, throughout the school year to help teachers improve their instruction. "They got the idea that these assessments needed to be about learning," he said of New York. "That we need to put technology in teachers' hands that makes stuff easy for them."

Despite being a relative outsider in the world of public education, Jim Liebman had long been drawn to this technocratic kind of inquiry. The Columbia Law professor was greatly influenced by the writings of the educator and philosopher John Dewey (1859–1952). Dewey was a pragmatist who believed that human beings learn best from experience and constant challenges. He founded the Lab School at the University of Chicago and became a leader in the progressive education movement, stating that "the only true education comes through the stimulation of the child's powers by the demands of the social situations in which he finds himself."[2] In Dewey's world, teachers and principals weren't presumed to know all the answers. They were encouraged to give their students lessons that drew from real-world experiences, such as sewing and farming, and to make the classroom a learning experience for everyone. Dewey saw education as something that happens from the bottom up, not from top-down assumptions about what students should know. He believed that the school was the primary vehicle of social progress and reform.

Because he was a follower of Dewey, it was a natural progression, then, for Liebman to shift his attention from civil rights to Dewey's own passion: school reform. Liebman's focus on data-driven assessments might sound at odds with Dewey, who wrote, "Examinations are of use only so far as they test the child's fitness for social life and reveal the place in which he can be of the most service and where he can receive the most help."[3] But Liebman interpreted that as an attempt to individualize education. Dewey, he argued, "was reacting to a very, very one-size-fits-all approach which assumed there was a key set of knowledge that we wanted everybody to learn." In Liebman's eyes, Dewey wanted teachers to find out how children learn and then "teach them in context of how they learn. Well, data is just data about how kids learn." In other words, standardized tests were bad if they were used solely to make every child learn the same thing. But they could be useful tools for figuring out how to help every child reach his or her potential, and to close the achievement gap.

A few years before he went to work for the city's Department of Education, Liebman coauthored a long scholarly essay titled "A Public Laboratory Dewey Barely Imagined." He and his cowriter, Charles F. Sabel at Columbia, looked at new models for school governance by drawing on examples in New York City, Texas, and Kentucky in the 1980s and '90s. Each system was finding its own way of holding schools accountable for results—whether by professional development, community oversight, or tougher standards and more frequent testing. Like Jeff Wayman, they concluded that the federal government's No Child Left Behind law presented schools with a ripe opportunity for giving the public more information about school performance and for identifying children at risk. If done right, it was a chance for school districts to adopt some of the best practices from the districts they studied, driving changes from both the top and the bottom.

Popular culture frequently portrays school reform as something driven by one great leader, like the demanding principal portrayed by Morgan Freeman in *Lean on Me*, or a passionate teacher who inspires hardened students to write from the heart. But Liebman and his accountability team viewed change as the product of thousands of moving parts. And despite its emphasis on standardized tests, Liebman insisted the Department of Education didn't want to impose a one-size-fits-all model. He and the chancellor said principals could choose whatever interventions they felt would make the biggest difference with struggling students—whether that meant expensive new computer programs to build vocabulary and bolster spelling skills or buying more books. This was Dewey's laboratory, as Liebman argued: to try new things, to share information, and to be held up for scrutiny. But there were no guarantees that any given school would actually be able to help a student like Alejandro or Yamilka. Just the promise that if it didn't, its leadership would be scrutinized and possibly replaced.

FIVE

Like a Regular Kid

Eighteen-year-old Antonio didn't go to any of his classes on the first day of school in September 2007. He was still enrolled at the High School of Graphic Communication Arts in Midtown, where he'd been a student at various points over the past few years. But he was feeling enormous pressure that fall to get a job and make some money. So on the first day of school, he went to the Department of Motor Vehicles to apply for a new state ID card. School wasn't going so well, anyway. Despite his age, he didn't even have enough credits to be considered a sophomore.

Like Yamilka and Alejandro, Antonio was barely literate when he got to high school. But his problems had been identified much earlier.

Antonio was first evaluated for special education services in second grade because he was clearly falling behind academically. His records indicate he had behavioral and academic troubles. Over the years, he was given speech therapy and counseling, and he was placed in separate special education classes. At various times he was labeled emotionally disturbed, learning disabled, speech-impaired, and even mentally retarded for two years of middle school. That classification was later changed back to learning disabled when an evaluator conceded it was a mistake. But Antonio's reading never progressed beyond a first-grade level, even though he and his mother say they often asked for more help.

"I've been in public school my whole life and the Board of Education people never done nothing right," he says, his voice revealing a mixture of pain, anger, and self-pity.

Antonio's mother, Noelia, moved to New York from the Dominican Republic in the late 1980s. She grew up in a large family near Puerta

Plata, and says she attended school only through third grade because her parents couldn't afford class supplies and clothes for her and their nine other children. Noelia doesn't speak any English. Sitting on the couch in her apartment in Washington Heights, she counted the number of public schools Antonio had attended on her fingers and stopped at eleven. "They told me he was a slow learner and he was lazy," she said in Spanish, sighing in exasperation. She has a round face and long hair, which has been lightened and pulled back into a ponytail. A Spanish-language soap opera was on the television, and Antonio's older sister sat at the corner desk using her computer. She had graduated from high school and worked as a medical assistant. Antonio was always the one with the problems in school.

Antonio grew up in Washington Heights, in this one-bedroom apartment divided into two bedrooms. He and his sister shared the smaller bedroom, sleeping on two twin beds squeezed into the tiny space. Their stepfather, Hector, painted the hallways bright green, with cheerful stencils of trees, grass, and red flowers that seemed to come alive whenever the family parakeet flew from room to room. Hector is an artist who used to work in a professional photographer's studio, and now sells cameras. Noelia is a home-care attendant. They met in the 1990s while she was working at a restaurant in Chelsea across the street from a photo studio where he was working. They both work full-time and they own a house upstate with an apartment they rent out to tenants.

Hector said he tried to help his wife navigate the complicated education system. He's a compact, lively man with shiny black hair who moved here from El Salvador when he was a teenager, and he speaks fluent English. "My wife is a brilliant woman," he said, defending Noelia. Hector said he had attended Newtown High School in Queens briefly but didn't finish, earning a GED instead. They were both baffled by the explanations and paperwork they encountered whenever they inquired about Antonio's lack of progress.

"I wanted him in smaller classes, but it was always more, sometimes fifteen students," explained Noelia, who was distraught that her son wasn't reading. She thought the special education classes were still too big for Antonio to learn. She cries when she recalls how her son would eagerly await the delivery of the day's mail. "He would ask, 'Mommy, is that for me?'" He couldn't even read the names on an envelope. Hector and Noelia put a blackboard up on the living room wall and wrote numbers and words for Antonio to practice. But they said the child had trouble concentrating.

A crazy routine developed. Every year Noelia would go to the Board of Education's district office in Washington Heights and plead for help because Antonio wasn't progressing. She would push them to re-evaluate her son. Each time, she said, she heard the same promise: things would improve at a different school with a better program. Then he'd be transferred midyear. By seventh grade, after another evaluation, Antonio was classified as mentally retarded. Noelia couldn't believe this. But when she went to Intermediate School 143 to complain, she was told this classification was best for him because he was assigned to smaller classes where he would learn more. "A bus came to pick him up with all the retarded children," Hector recalled of the start of that miserable school year. Special education students were usually the only students taking yellow buses to junior high, because most students walked or took public transportation. Antonio went on the bus just once. Noelia said a child spat at him, and they decided he wouldn't ride it again.

Antonio and his mom have a tense relationship. One night in September 2003 they got into a terrible fight. He grabbed a kitchen knife, and when she ran into her bedroom he stabbed the door several times. Noelia called 911 and the police arrested Antonio, despite his parents' refusal to press charges. The arresting officer wrote that Antonio's mother "states she had an argument with her son because he didn't go to school and her son started to push her." Antonio was charged with criminal mischief for allegedly damaging property (the door). His attorney at Legal Aid's Juvenile Rights Division, Karen Yazmajian, said he spent a few weeks in a home for juvenile offenders because he didn't comply with the terms of his parole, which included counseling and going back to high school. After his release, she said, he did everything expected of him. Hector agreed he was much more mature

Noelia blames herself for Antonio's problems. If she knew how to speak English and fight for her rights, she said, things might be different. At times, Antonio blames his mother for his problems in school but at other times he is very protective of her, and defends her efforts to help him. He believes the city's education department is the real culprit. "They always been trying to refer me to another school," he said. "It's like they keep me there for this year and then they put me in another school, put me there a certain amount of time. It's like they're just trying to hide their garbage."

More than anything, Antonio wanted to be a normal kid, taking normal classes. In ninth grade, after special education evaluators conceded he was not mentally retarded and changed his classification back to learning disabled, he was sent to Humanities High School in Chelsea, a regular comprehensive high school. He later transferred to the High School of Graphic Communication Arts, known as Graphics. The school is a huge, 1950s-era complex west of Midtown with about two thousand students. Antonio was still assigned to special education classes, with a student-teacher ratio of fifteen to one. But he loved the freedom of being in a big high school and meeting new people.

While Yamilka and Alejandro became introverted and afraid of school after years of feeling like failures, Antonio is much more social and sought out friends. His two front teeth are big and a little crooked, giving his smile a sweet quality. He enjoyed high school—maybe a little too much. At the first high school he attended, he says, he met some students who introduced him to marijuana and cocaine. He had never tried drugs before and admits he got high often over the next couple of years. But he says he quit drugs completely after falling out with those friends, and he's been sober ever since. His performance in school didn't improve, though, because he still wasn't able to read.

When Antonio transferred to Graphics at the age of fifteen, his reading was barely at a first-grade level. His math was at about third grade. "From the beginning he was really out of place," recalled the school's assistant principal for special education, John Harnett. "It was not his fault because he was really [given] an inappropriate placement." Hartnett wondered if a more intensive special education program could help Antonio.

The special education program at Graphics is supposedly for students who are several grades behind their peers academically, but who still have the potential to earn a basic diploma. Whether they actually do is another matter. Graphics was on the state's list of schools in need of improvement while Antonio was there because its test scores and other indicators didn't go up enough under the No Child Left Behind law. Just about 35 percent of its students were graduating on time with diplomas, and only 8 percent of its special education students. Those rates were low even compared to other large New York high schools—but the school still maintained an aura of standards. Graphics is a vocational school, but its students are held to the same standards as those in other high schools. "Students who are sent to us, the assumption is they are going to follow the New York State curriculum," said Hartnett. Special education students are given more time on their exams but they are still expected to master the same material as everyone else.

Hartnett has worked in special education for more than twenty-five years. He's a husky man with a long gray ponytail, and he sat at a broad wooden desk in his tiny office during a visit in 2007, with stacks of paper covering almost every surface. He said he typically had more than three hundred special education students each year to worry about, and he was clearly tired of dealing with Antonio. Hartnett said the teen had become a fixture in the assistant principal's office. He would skip class to hang out there and try to talk to his guidance counselor. Hartnett thought Antonio was seeking the adult attention he couldn't get in his classes. He was too far behind academically to keep up with the other students and he couldn't do any of the work, even in a special education class. But Antonio couldn't spend his school days in the office. Nobody had the time or patience. Hartnett recommended that Antonio transfer to a special ed high school like the one Yamilka attended.

Again, the school system was trying to cut its losses. What do you do with a sixteen-year-old student who still isn't reading? Antonio had earned only one credit at Graphics. The city's solution was to teach him a trade at a career-development school, where it was hoped he could learn basic math and reading while also acquiring life skills.

The Manhattan Career Development School is in an old, narrow walk-up building in the East Village. It's a small school—about three hundred students—but it seems even smaller most of the time, because its students are at work sites for part of the day. Some work at New York University, learning food preparation in a cafeteria. Later they'll spend a forty-five-minute period with an instructor who teaches them how to open a checking account with practice documents.

"We work on filling out applications, we work on functional materials they'll need," the school's principal, Jeff Rothschild, told me, during a visit before he retired in 2007. "Reading ads to rent an apartment, how to read employment ads … We make sure they know how to travel independently, read a train map." Students do take math and reading classes as well, but the academic level is much lower than at a regular high school. Some of the students are mentally retarded. Others have a combination of learning and emotional problems. Rothschild said most are reading at around the equivalent of fourth grade. Antonio wasn't even at that level. And the school couldn't offer him one-to-one tutoring services.

Despite their low academic levels, some students accomplish a great deal at Manhattan Career Development. A handful of students renovated the Lexington Avenue Armory, painstakingly restoring the wooden floors of the elegant old officer's club and repairing a neglected bathroom. I met a student named Esther* who was hanging out with the male students in the Armory, learning how to use a table saw. She was tough and proud, confessing that she couldn't read very well and that she'd had "anger management" problems all her life. But she was happy working with her hands and she wanted a job in building maintenance. She thought the school had really helped her get things under control and taught her enough to find a good career.

Rothschild pointed to statistics showing most students who complete his program do get jobs, and there are letters from grateful alumni posted in one of the hallways. Students can also earn professional certificates while they're attending the school. But many students drop out along the way. Antonio was one of those kids. Rothschild said Antonio didn't really give the program a chance, because he barely attended. But Antonio claims he refused to go to a school that awarded only IEP, or special education, diplomas. He knew that wouldn't get him into the army.

Antonio remembers becoming fascinated by the military when he was about eight years old. His older cousin had signed up for the army and Antonio decided to follow in his footsteps. As he got older, he enjoyed movies like *Rambo* and *Full Metal Jacket*, anything with guns blazing and girls to save. But his motivation to serve his country was crystallized on September 11, 2001. He says he was playing hooky that day, hanging out in Lower Manhattan with a friend who lives downtown. He was twelve

*The names of students I met in classrooms throughout my reporting for this book were either changed or provided without last names, except for those whose families gave permission to use first and last names and those old enough to give consent to use their full names.

years old and had just started seventh grade at a middle school, after being labeled mentally retarded by the Board of Education. He would rather have been anywhere than in school, he says.

On September 11, Antonio says, he and his friend were hanging out three blocks north of the World Trade Center, just as the airplanes struck. "I was eating a hot dog," he says. "Everybody's like looking up, everybody hears something, and the ground was shaking 'cause the plane was so low you could hear it.

"The guy selling the hot dog said, 'Please tell me this thing's not going to hit.' I'm like, 'I hope not.' Then all of a sudden it hit," he says, his voice rising with excitement. "The explosion was so loud, it was like the biggest stereo that you could have and you could not hear one thing out of a person's mouth."

Antonio says he and his friend saw one of the towers fall and then walked all the way home while the cloud of concrete dust, ash, and human remains settled over downtown. It was a two-hundred-block walk for Antonio.

Antonio decided he wanted to fight the people who had attacked his city. He went to youth cadet corps programs in East Harlem and the Bronx where young people practice giving and responding to marching orders in uniform. The adult volunteers are called generals. Students who have good attendance rise through the ranks from private to private first class to sergeant. They wear khaki uniforms and black combat boots and learn about military time and orders. They can also go to after-school tutoring and field-training sessions. On Saturday mornings Antonio could sometimes be found at Junior High 45 in East Harlem, wearing a uniform and marching with the other teens and younger children in the cadets. For a while his cell phone had an outgoing message that said, "This is Private Rocha of the ROTC." The cadet program actually has no affiliation with the Reserve Officers' Training Corps, but in Antonio's mind it's all connected.

Antonio has big goals. "I want to be a Navy SEAL, a marine," he would say with confidence. Though Antonio's parents are Dominican, he was born in New York and considers himself American. One could easily dismiss his military ambitions as some unrealistic desire to be a hero. He didn't even follow the news about the war in Iraq. He also spoke about wanting to become a firefighter, a police officer, or a paramedic. "I want to do the same thing as many men and women [who] died," he said, referring to 9/11. "They went to the building like, 'So be it, we got to save some people.'"

But those people who ran to the rescue knew how to read.

One day when Antonio was enrolled at the career-development school, he argued with school administrators about his placement. "I want to see your boss," he remembers asking them. But he says they kept ignoring him. Finally, he blurted out, "I want a lawyer!" It was as though he had spoken the secret code. He recalls a man who worked in the office taking him aside and handing him a list of attorneys. He circled Advocates for Children, the same nonprofit law firm that helped Yamilka and Alejandro.

When Antonio eventually met with an attorney, he said he needed to get a real high school diploma so he could join the military. He knew the armed services wouldn't take an IEP diploma. In fact, most branches of the military take only a small percentage of applicants with GEDs. Antonio insisted on transferring out of the career school and returning to Graphics, his last regular high school. Because Advocates for Children sees so many teens who can't read, the nonprofit had developed relationships with private tutoring programs, including the ones Yamilka and Alejandro attended. Deputy Director Matthew Lenaghan recalled that Antonio was upset with the Department of Education, but eloquent about his desire to get a diploma so he could serve in Iraq. The attorneys advised him he would have a better chance of learning to read at a private tutoring program than in the schools that had failed him, and referred him for neuropsychological testing to determine the extent of his learning disabilities. The city's own evaluators certainly hadn't been able to agree on what was wrong with him, since his classification had changed so many times. A professional evaluation by someone outside the school system could help Advocates make the case that Antonio's rights had been violated.

Antonio saw Dr. Michele Shackelford, a neuropsychologist and director of the Center for Attention and Learning Disorders at Lenox Hill Hospital. She gave him a series of tests over a period of days. These were much more intensive than any evaluations done by the city schools, and

Advocates for Children intended on having the city pay the bill (and its own legal fees) if Antonio won his case. Shackelford determined that Antonio had average intelligence and suspected he had been diagnosed as mentally retarded years ago because he didn't bother answering basic questions, possibly because he was angry or frustrated with the test format. She also found he had attention deficit disorder and dyslexia.

When Shackelford told Antonio he had dyslexia, he was shaken. "I felt kind of depressed, really sad," he said. Shackelford said he was confused by the term "dyslexia." "He had never heard that word in his life," she said. "And at first I think it was very, very difficult for him because it meant that there was something wrong with him and not what he thought—because any kid with a learning disability thinks they're dumb. They think they're stupid.

"He blamed the Department of Ed for everything," she continued. "And while he's correct that the Department of Ed failed him miserably, it's also true that he has a neurological disorder [dyslexia] that requires very, very specific remedial instruction."

Shackelford has seen countless educational evaluations over the years that she's been asked to revisit by dyslexic students and their attorneys seeking more appropriate services. The word "dyslexia" is actually never used on an Individualized Education Program. The city schools use the broader category of "learning disabled." School officials say that's because dyslexia isn't one of the thirteen specific categories of handicap covered by special education laws. These include learning disability, deafness, blindness, autism, emotional disturbance, and mental retardation. The phrase "learning disability" is defined by New York State as a "disorder in one or more of the basic psychological processes involved in understanding or in using language, spoken or written, which manifests itself in an imperfect ability to listen, think, speak, read, write, spell, or to do mathematical calculations." There's generally a discrepancy between a learning disabled student's inherent intelligence and his or her academic performance. Dyslexia is one type of learning disability. Shackelford and others suspect the state is trying to avoid being held accountable by keeping the evaluations so vague. But Linda Wernikoff, the head of special education services for New York City, argued the label shouldn't matter as long as the child gets the right services. "It's about good teaching," she explained, adding that good teachers should be able to discern which form of instruction works best for students with disabilities, regardless of whether they're formally diagnosed as having dyslexia. But even with a "learning disability," Shackelford said, the city failed to give Antonio the right kind of individualized instruction.

Antonio worked with Lenaghan and a young lawyer at Advocates for Children who found him a spot at Lindamood-Bell, because it had a good reputation for working with these kinds of language problems. Antonio liked the idea but he insisted that he wanted to return to high school so he could get a real diploma and join the military. The attorneys were impressed by his insistence, even if it wasn't entirely realistic. His hearing was held on April 11, 2006. He sat at a conference table with both his lawyers, a representative from the Department of Education who wasn't an attorney, and an impartial hearing officer. His mother joined in by cell phone. She could not get any time off from her job as a home-care attendant, so she called while she was out running errands for her job. As everyone at the table listened by speakerphone, an interpreter helped Noelia when it was her turn to answer questions about Antonio's educational history.

"They have offered me everything but they have not given me anything," she said, according to a transcript. It was difficult to hear Noelia's voice because her cell phone kept breaking up and there was a lot of noisy traffic. The hearing officer had to stop the proceeding several times.

The city's case was fairly simple. Because Antonio *was* offered so many services, the education department argued that it had not broken the law. A representative went through Antonio's paperwork, going through his various placements. "Antonio has never been denied access to school," she stated. "He's been continuously attending special education programs since 1997." She also argued that at no time was Antonio ever "knowingly" classified inappropriately, when confronted with his multiple and sometimes conflicting evaluations, especially the one that found him mentally retarded. And she argued that Antonio had chosen to give up on his own education by becoming a truant both at Graphics and the career-development school. Returning Antonio to Graphics as a remedy "would be inappropriate." John Hartnett, assistant principal at Graphics, was called to testify, also by phone, and he agreed his school would not be the right environment because Antonio's skills were so far below those of his other special education students. "It would be like me sitting in a class that was being taught in Greek," he said. He also described Antonio as a loner who didn't appear to have any real friends.

But when the hearing officer asked the Department of Education to suggest a more appropriate setting for Antonio, the representative couldn't come up with an alternative. "I am not sure," she said. "It could be another comprehensive high school with a small class, or it could mean remaining for the school year at [Manhattan] Career Development where he might get some job skills."

Antonio got to testify on his own. He seemed eager to have someone in an official capacity finally listening. When the hearing officer asked him what kinds of things he liked to do in his spare time, he sounded like any other seventeen-year-old. "I like to talk and hang out with my friends," he said. He pulled out his cell phone to contradict the assistant principal's claim that he didn't have any friends, showing the long list of names in the contacts list. Antonio also described how he'd been treated by the Department of Education. "They put me in a school, um, in a class with kids with Down syndrome," he said, referring to the two years in which he was classified as mentally retarded, which he resented terribly. Antonio was asked on direct examination if he ever told the teacher he didn't think he was in the right place. "I kept on and on and on, as I always been doing. All my life. And they only, they only pretend. They pretended like they care. But they don't."

Antonio also explained why he had stopped going to the career-development school. "That school is unprofessional," he said, adding that it "sucks." When his lawyer asked him if he had ever sought help for his reading there, he said he did but the school didn't have that type of tutoring. Then he got emotional. "I'm about to be eighteen years old in seven months and, what, twenty-something days?" he said. "And I don't want to turn eighteen years old and not learn how to read. By eighteen—I'm supposed to graduate high school. I'm supposed to go to the military. Where am I now? Where am I now?

"I want a high school diploma because I want to become a U.S. Navy SEAL," he told the hearing officer. "The U.S. Navy, the military, they will not allow an IEP diploma."

When asked if he was willing to go to reading classes at Lindamood-Bell, Antonio said yes and promised to do so if given the chance. "That would be my responsibility to go over there every day," he said. He also said he would go to Graphics if he was allowed back for a half-day program, adding—on a lighter note—"I miss the girls there."

The Department of Education's representative pressed Antonio about his reason for going back to high school.

"I want a regular life, you know? I want like everybody else. Everybody goes to high school, everybody has a lot of girlfriends in high school, everybody have fun in high school. Everybody have friends in high school. And that's something I want. That's something, you know, you can't take away from me, you know?"

By the end of the hearing, the city seemed to stop fighting Antonio's request for one-on-one tutoring services, but it was adamant that Antonio did not belong in a regular high school. Without any alternative, however, the hearing officer granted Antonio both the tutoring and a half-day program at Graphics. He also won the right to apply for additional services until the age of twenty-three, giving him two extra years of school if he needed it. But he'd first have to use his initial 480 hours of tutoring at the city's expense, at a cost of about $48,000.

Antonio was very happy at Lindamood-Bell. The program had moved uptown by the time he arrived. The office was in a town house on Sixty-fourth Street and Madison Avenue, near famous designer stores, including Chanel, Hermès, and Furla. But he wasn't intimidated at all by the expensive neighborhood. The grassy median strip a block away on Park Avenue reminded him of Broadway in Washington Heights. And he barely noticed the white-gloved doormen in uniforms just inside the apartment buildings. He felt completely at ease, bumming a cigarette off a man sweeping outside the Fifty-ninth Street subway stop as he left class one day. At Lindamood-Bell, he would visit the receptionist when her young son stopped by after school, teaching the child how to organize his wallet so the lower bills were in front and the bigger ones were tucked in back.

During his initial assessment, in March 2006, Liz Craynon—who was the center's director at the time—said he scored at a first-grade level on the "word attack" test measuring his ability to read a word by breaking it down into sounds. He started going to classes that spring for four hours a day, and by the end of the summer he had progressed to a fourth-grade level. He'd also gained a whole year's worth of vocabulary, putting him at the level of an eleven-year-old.

One day in the early fall of 2006, Antonio sat in a cubicle with his tutor learning how the letters "tion" sound like "shun" at the end of words such as "lotion" and "potion." He was also practicing words that end in "tive," like "native" and "festive." His tutor, Becky Herman, was going over the rules of spelling with him for words that "play fair" (because they follow predictable rules) and words that don't. To test him, she'd read a word aloud to see if he could spell it correctly. He'd take his time to sound out the different letters and divide the word up by syllables, getting many of the answers correct. Antonio sometimes got frustrated that he wasn't learning fast enough. He would often talk about wanting to graduate from high school so he could join the military. His attendance, which had been generally good—though he was often late—began to lag. He seemed to have a hard time juggling high school and tutoring. One staffer at Lindamood-Bell said he sometimes seemed more interested in socializing and had trouble with comprehension even as his reading skills improved. Craynon said he also frequently complained of headaches after a difficult session, scrunching up his face in physical pain. This could have been a symptom of his attention deficit disorder, or maybe a result of the sheer difficulty of learning to read. Eventually he stopped showing up. He was also skipping classes at high school—even though he had fought so hard to attend both programs.

At the High School of Graphic Communication Arts, four students sat in a math class in a narrow room facing West Forty-ninth Street. Antonio was supposed to be among them. But the teacher, Sharon Levine, said he rarely came to class. She looked at her attendance register, which had a row of *A*'s for absent next to his name. It was November 2006, and she counted only five days since September in which he'd been present.

Levine's math class was for special education students, and they were preparing for a statewide test called the Regents Competency. It's a lower-level exam than the regular Regents and it was being phased out by the state. Levine wore glasses, a brown newsboy cap with sunglasses perched on top, and a long T-shirt over her khaki pants. She had the attitude of the funky older aunt who enjoys being with teenagers. "Here, babes," she said, handing out a page of practice questions. She kept a bag of candy in her desk to reward them for their efforts toward the end of class.

The students were working on integers. In one example they figured out how many degrees the temperature changed if it started out at –2 and rose to 15 degrees above zero by late afternoon. Levine drew a line on the blackboard and showed them how to count the value below and above zero. The students, who were all tenth- and eleventh-grade boys, with no girls in attendance that day, followed along pretty well and gave their answers. A paraprofessional worked with any who needed extra help. Levine said this material was probably at a sixth-grade level and involved a lot of word problems. Antonio couldn't have done it even if he had come to school. But just in case he did show for class, Levine had prepared some basic addition and subtraction problems for him on a lined sheet of paper to help him keep the answers straight.

Levine said Antonio's behavior in class was fine on the few days when he did attend, but he was easily distracted. Her other students had attention deficit problems, too, but she said they had better social skills in class—probably because they'd developed a routine. "The problem with him is you can't get any consistency. Because if he would come every day, you would be able to prepare and prepare and prepare and prepare and gradually take him up. But when he comes once every two weeks . . ." Her voice trailed off.

If Levine was frustrated, Assistant Principal John Hartnett was furious. After losing the special hearing and being forced to readmit Antonio, Hartnett had scheduled him for math, photography, history, and a reading class. He said these were the lowest-level classes in special education for a student of Antonio's age.

"I have three hundred fifty students in special education I'm responsible for," Hartnett said that fall. "And when you have to spend an inordinate amount of time on one youngster who clearly does not benefit from this school and this placement—as we have stated many times—and he's placed here anyway because he verbalizes that he wants to be here, and then when he's placed here he doesn't come, he doesn't work, he doesn't benefit from the placement, it takes away from the time that could be spent doing things for other students."

A few minutes after Levine's math class ended that morning, Antonio showed up in the waiting area outside Hartnett's office. He was neatly dressed in a long-sleeved T-shirt and jeans. He looked serious and carried a large knapsack. He said hello to the staff members and ran into one he knew named Julio Torres, who pulled him aside to talk about time management. Torres was a young, lanky teaching assistant assigned to Antonio's reading class. He had noticed significant progress since Antonio started going to the tutoring classes at Lindamood-Bell—at least on the days he came to high school.

Antonio looked down and seemed embarrassed when Torres confronted him about his frequent absences. "I can't find it in myself," he said. "I can't do what I'm trying to, like, what I want to, like going to school early like I'm supposed to."

"It's more about managing your time and prioritizing," said Torres, who'd known Antonio since he had started at Graphics. "You need to write it down on a piece of paper: 'I'm going to do this today,' you do it hour by hour. It's going to help you focus." It wasn't clear how Antonio could do that, given his limited reading skills.

As we stood in the hall, Antonio was briefly distracted by two girls he knew. One of them, Theresa, was in the Junior ROTC program. She wore her dark navy uniform. Antonio had had a crush on her for years; she's the girl he kissed two times. He approached her awkwardly and said something to her about his plans to enter the army, speaking quickly. He was clearly trying to impress her but he seemed nervous just to be in her graceful presence.

Torres suggested Antonio might need a different school, a smaller one that could give him more focus. "There's no other school has that," said Antonio wearily, recalling his bad experience at the career-development school. Torres said vocational studies could be good for him. "You can learn something and go out and start making a living and that might be a good thing for you, you can learn something that you might be really good at." Antonio wasn't convinced.

"You shouldn't shun it," Torres told him. "You can always pursue a high school diploma while you're learning a trade." He suggested getting a GED later on, after he learned how to read. Antonio again insisted that he wanted to go into the military. But he also admitted that he wasn't taking anything seriously. "I just gave up on myself," he told me.

Assistant Principal Hartnett had his own theories about why Antonio had been sleeping late and not coming to school. "He sees he's almost an adult male and these little kids coming in from junior high school are beyond him academically, socially, emotionally."

Matthew Lenaghan acknowledged the difficulty of the situation, but he still lamented the result. He wondered how far Antonio really was behind the other special ed students at Graphics, given the school's low graduation rates. He also pointed out that in the time since Antonio had won his case, the city had declared its intent to stop schools from getting rid of students who are difficult to educate. After all, said Lenaghan, it is the school system's job to either provide an appropriate education or find a student like Antonio a more appropriate school. Antonio hadn't been offered any alternative to the regular special ed classes at Graphics or the career-development school, which he'd already rejected because it wouldn't provide him with enough academics.

"This is where the system really breaks down," said Lenaghan, noting that the Individuals with Disabilities Education Act guarantees every student a free appropriate education. "It is unacceptable to tell a student, 'It's too late, we can't educate you,'" said Lenaghan. "What the system is effectively saying in such a case is 'After years of failing you, we have now lowered our expectations of you,' and 'If you don't accept our lowered expectations and the offer that comes with it, you are out of luck.'"

The city had transfer schools where older teens without enough credits could earn a diploma, but Antonio's reading ability wasn't high enough. Lenaghan thought the city should have tried to create new programs for students like Antonio, or modified existing programs. "Otherwise, we are stuck in a situation where no principal wants the student who can't read and may drag down a school's numbers. Given the pressure on schools, most will be unwilling to hire the new staff and put the effort into overhauling unsuccessful programs for the students who are most in need. The result will be pushing the problem onto somebody else, or more likely, out of the school system."

A few weeks later, Antonio started showing up again at Lindamood-Bell. He was reluctant, saying he didn't feel ready for the commitment. But Craynon and his lawyer both told him he was running out of time. He only had until the end of January 2007 to complete the initial 480 hours of tutoring he was awarded by the special hearing officer, and it was already the end of November. When Antonio first returned, Craynon said he tried to leave an hour early. "I was tough love Liz and told him that's not how this works," she wrote the next day in an e-mail. "He told me he wasn't ready. I told him he didn't have time not to be ready. So we went back upstairs and got him back to work. At the end of the day he was happy."

Antonio finished his hours in January. On the last day of class, Liz Craynon and the staff planned a surprise for him during the afternoon break. They brought out a plate full of brownies and homemade chocolate-covered pretzels for Antonio and gave him a book signed by everyone on the staff. It was a biography of John F. Kennedy. They knew he was interested in the Vietnam War and Kennedy because of his military ambitions. The pocket book was written at about a fourth-grade level, and the staffers had scribbled notes inside the covers. "I hope that you are as proud of yourself as we are. Your hard work has paid off greatly and it can only get better and better. Stay as cool as you are," wrote one of his tutors. Antonio stood to give a speech in the conference room as the other students clustered around, picking out sweets.

"I want to thank everybody that supported me and, um, cared for me during the whole six months that I've been here," he said, naming staffers who had helped him "when I was not responsibly getting here on time." He looked at Liz Craynon and thanked her for giving him so many chances, even when he screwed up. The staff and students applauded and hugged him when he finished speaking, and congratulated him on his accomplishment. A nineteen-year-old boy named Anthony, who also had dyslexia, looked on with admiration. He told me he considered Antonio a role model.

As he left for the day, walking out onto Madison Avenue, Antonio said he felt like a new person. "It feels different; this is the first time I can breathe," he exclaimed. He had thought he would still feel like a failure because he still wasn't reading at a high school level, but upon finishing the program he was buoyant. "It's like, a lot of stress or sadness is like lifted up, it just got out of me . . . I feel like I succeeded at something for the first time. Tonight I'll probably drink a beer to myself and probably cry a tear."

Antonio clutched the Kennedy book and reread the personal notes, laughing at a joke someone had written and signed "Private Snowball." It's a *Full Metal Jacket* reference. He was still grinning as he got on the subway. Evening rush hour had begun and the train was crowded, but Antonio was oblivious, happily floating in his own world. He took one of the open seats and began reading the back cover summary of the book aloud: "'John F. Kennedy grew up in a family where nobody had to worry about money but everyone was expected to make a—to make a difference in society. After providing—proving his courage in World War Two, Kennedy took to politics. He became the thirty-fifth president of the United States and changed the world's idea of what a young nation and a—a young president can accomplish.'"

Just like that, he finished the paragraph. He seemed stunned by what he'd just read and struggled to describe his feelings. "It hurts. But it hurts like in a good happiness," he said of his new ability to read. "I feel like a regular kid now."

A week later, Antonio met with Craynon for the results of his final evaluation. She used a big whiteboard to write down his scores. She told him that he had jumped ahead two to three grade levels in his vocabulary and ability to recognize words. His overall reading level was just below fifth grade. But he still had trouble making sense of unfamiliar words and understanding longer sections of text. Craynon told Antonio that his brain was like a muscle and he needed to keep practicing his reading. They talked about the Kennedy biography he had been given on his final day. He'd only gotten to page thirteen, out of maybe sixty pages. Craynon said she knew the book would be a little bit above his level, but said it was important to keep trying and looking up any words he didn't know. She also told him to stop blaming the Department of Education for his problems, because he'd never get ahead if he couldn't move past his anger. She urged him to see a therapist. But he didn't have health insurance.

Antonio could have immediately started another round of tutoring, because the original ruling preserved that option until he was twenty-three years old. However, he didn't want to keep going to Lindamood-Bell. He felt like he'd graduated from the program and wanted to try something new. So as he waited for his lawyers to act on his request, he continued going to high school. His attendance was a little better, though still spotty. He persuaded the school's Junior ROTC class to admit him, even though he didn't have the academics to attend. The ROTC sessions were held during lunch and after school. The retired navy lieutenant who ran the class said Antonio had trouble with the reading materials, but "he tries so hard."

In June, Antonio finished the school year, passing two academic classes: a global history course with a photography emphasis and a media class involving the computer lab. In the section for comments, his teachers wrote that he was "excessively absent" and noted his "poor work habits." One said he "has the ability to do better." But the computer teacher, who gave him his highest grade—a 70—wrote that he was "highly motivated and cooperative," and made "excellent progress."

Antonio was especially interested in the computer design class. The teacher, Vito Licciardi, had been at Graphics for twenty-one years, mostly as a general education teacher, but he said he loved the challenge of working with special ed students. The computer lab was bright and cheerful, except for a bored-looking paraprofessional who sat by the windows clipping her fingernails. Licciardi wanted to make the class as practical as possible, so he showed the students how to make websites and design their own business cards. He didn't want to be too easy on the teens, but he did believe in giving the ones who were often late or absent, like Antonio, multiple opportunities to turn in their work. He worried that automatically failing these at-risk students wouldn't give them any incentives to keep coming to school. It's better to teach a student like Antonio "twenty or thirty things he didn't know before and are useful in everyday life," he said. Licciardi showed Antonio how to use the website Ask.com, and how to write a mock letter to Sony about a defect in his PlayStation game. He encouraged him to go to extra Saturday classes at the school next fall.

But Antonio didn't make it back to school, or to his tutoring classes. Even though Advocates for Children eventually won him another two hundred hours for tutoring at Huntington Learning Center, Antonio declined to use them. He went for a couple of sessions in the spring and decided the work was too similar to what he had already done at Lindamood-Bell. "I just want to know how to take notes and learn how to react in a class on my own," he explained. "And how to do math problems." Antonio was also intent on getting a summer job and wasn't sure how that would fit into a tutoring schedule. He got a couple of jobs making deliveries for a few days at a time, but he wasn't able to find any work as a messenger or a dishwasher because he never got all of his paperwork together for a state ID.

Antonio's lawyer told him not to give up on schooling. He'd won the right to apply for more tutoring hours until he turned twenty-three. But Antonio was exasperated by the thought of spending so much time learning to read. Sometimes he wondered why the school system couldn't just award him a diploma, or cash, as compensation for his trouble. He knew he wasn't really able to earn a diploma but he also knew that without one, he'd only make minimum wage. "Seeing other kids being successful in class and everything makes me jealous," he admitted.

Antonio's life had also become more complicated. His parents moved to a house in suburban New Jersey in 2007. It's just a half-hour bus ride away from Washington Heights. But going back to Manhattan for high school or tutoring would be more difficult logistically, on top of the emotional hurdles and pent-up feelings of failure. His parents gave him twenty dollars a week in allowance, but he needed more money than that to get around. He continued looking for work.

Antonio stopped going to high school in the fall of 2007. He told the other students that he was leaving to study for a GED. It wasn't true, but it sounded like a good excuse—much better than admitting he didn't know what to do with himself.

SIX

A School in Need of Improvement

New York has always been a city of immigrants, and their experiences have long been shaped by the public schools. Likewise, the schools have often had to adjust to the needs of their new arrivals.

In the nineteenth century, Irish immigration helped the city's population grow from 120,000 in 1820 to more than 300,000 in 1840. By 1855 more than half the city's residents were foreign born, and more than half the foreign born were Irish.[1] The Irish shared the same experiences as later waves of immigrants from poor agricultural regions—whether in the Dominican Republic or elsewhere. They were uneducated; they lived in crowded slums and were looked down upon by other New Yorkers. But relatively few of the Irish arrivals in the nineteenth century enrolled their children in the public, or "common," schools, in part because they feared the Protestant influence. They preferred Catholic schools and fought for the right to support them with taxpayer dollars. When they lost that quest in New York and in other cities, the Catholic church developed its own school system in the 1880s and decreed that every parish should have a parochial school. However, Irish Catholic leaders soon amassed enough political clout to influence state legislation creating a new structure for New York City's public schools—with a guarantee of religious neutrality. After that, the schools enrolled more and more immigrants—and not just the Irish.

Prior to the U.S. restriction on immigration in 1924, several million poor and uneducated newcomers from Southern and Eastern Europe arrived in New York in the early twentieth century. Between 1900 and 1915, the historian Diane Ravitch found, the city's average annual school register nearly doubled, rising to almost 800,000 pupils.[2] Schools were crowded and lower grades were packed with overage pupils. But—unlike the Irish—these immigrants arrived speaking little or no English. Jews from Russia and Poland and Italians were the dominant groups. Schools were seen as a force for Americanizing the new arrivals and providing an opportunity to all.

It's easy to look back on these early years of the twentieth century as some kind of golden age of assimilation. Immigrant adults worked in factories; their youngsters went to school and then went on to get good jobs or pursue higher education. Jews, in particular, often excelled in academics because they had their own Hebrew schools in their native countries. Ravitch writes that Jews made up more than half the city's doctors, lawyers, dentists, and public school teachers by the 1930s.[3] City College, which was tuition-free, became the poor man's Harvard. But not everyone was a scholar. Students could leave high school as teenagers and find decent jobs. There are estimates that three quarters of young people during the 1920s were high school dropouts.[4] These earlier immigrants owed their success to the economy, not just the schools. "The curriculum was rigid and irrelevant to children's lives, the classes were overcrowded, and the teachers (many of them second- or third-generation Irish or Germans) had no special affection for the immigrant children or for their parents' strange culture," writes Ravitch.[5]

But when jobs grew scarce after the Great Depression, high school attendance rates began to rise. Immigration had slowed down and enrollment fell, putting less pressure on the public schools. Graduation rates continued rising throughout the 1950s as the growing postwar economy demanded more education skills. The struggling newcomers who arrived in those years (largely from Puerto Rico), and the black migrants from the South, could still find work in the 1950s and '60s. But the fiscal crisis of the 1970s drove the economy to a halt. The economist and urban planner Emanuel Tobier called it the worst period ever for the city schools. The middle class pulled out, reversing decades of steady improvements in the economic well-being of the city's public school students.[6] Poverty rates went up—especially for blacks and Latinos, whose children formed the majority in the public schools. The budget cuts to the schools had a lasting effect even after the economy improved in the 1980s. Families with means continued moving to the suburbs or choosing private or Catholic schools.

While the city's overall poverty rate was 20 percent in the 1980s, the poverty rate among public school children was about 35 percent.[7] Tobier cited the increasing proportion of children being raised by single women, and the fall in real earnings of less skilled, low-paid workers. The jobs that had sustained previous generations of uneducated immigrants and native-born Americans just weren't there. This change in the economy occurred as new immigrants were arriving from China, Russia, South America, and the Caribbean. By 2000 New York City's foreign-born population hit 2.87 million—an all-time high—with Dominicans making up the largest share (13 percent), according to the city's Department of Planning.[8] The Dominican Republic had experienced political upheaval in the 1960s after the brutal regime of Rafael Trujillo came to a violent end, followed by economic hardships, prompting a huge migration to New York. Foreign-born students now account for about 17 percent of the city's student population. The U.S. Census estimated that in 2007, 37 percent of New Yorkers were born abroad. In the Bronx, 51 percent of the population is Hispanic.[9]

This latest wave of immigrants has had some great success stories. As a group, Asian elementary and middle school students often have the highest test scores in the city. At Gregorio Luperon High School for Science and Mathematics, in the heavily Dominican neighborhood of Washington Heights, 72 percent of students graduate in four years. That might not sound impressive until you realize more than 60 percent of them are English Language Learners. The demanding Mott Hall middle school in Harlem is also almost entirely Hispanic, and more than 96 percent of its students met or exceeded state standards on their English Language Arts exams in 2008.

But today's immigrants also experience tremendous hardships. Those without much education have found it harder and harder to support their families. Yamilka's and Antonio's mothers are living proof of this trend. They took low-paying jobs in a laundry service and as a home-care attendant because there was little else they could do. When their children ran into trouble in school because of learning disabilities, language and cultural barriers made it difficult for these parents to understand what was happening and to help their children. And while the city was growing more diverse and income levels were going up prior to the economic collapse of 2008, the Bronx neighborhood where Yamilka's family resided—

Morris Heights—was the only one in the city to see its poverty rate go up, though by less than one percentage point.[10]

Poverty and struggling schools were a constant in Morris Heights, which is located in the poorest congressional district in the country.* The neighborhood middle school Yamilka and Alejandro attended was considered such a failure that it was shut down by the state shortly after they graduated. Community Intermediate School 82 reopened in 2001 with a new name, Middle School 232, but little else seemed to change. The school went through five principals in five years. In 2007 just 25 percent of its 550 students were reading at grade level. However, that was an improvement over the previous year, when only 20 percent were meeting the mark.

The five-story redbrick building on Macombs Road got off to a promising start. It was built in 1924, at a time when the city was investing in grand public schools to accommodate its growing immigrant population. The original name, Public School 82, is still carved in stone over the entrance columns. One flight up, a plaque honors the graduates and faculty who served in World War II. Two other schools—another middle school and a small new high school—also share the building, each with its own floor.

At 8:15 on an October morning, Raedyn Rivera is already frustrated. She's the school's literacy coach, and she's just seen the results from September's reading comprehension test. The school gives its own reading test every month, and even though Rivera tried to make it simple yet challenging for all the students in grades six to eight, she's disappointed with the results because they're wildly inconsistent. In some classes, students scored anywhere from 3 to 28 percent, while others earned 96 percent. The teachers all used different ways of grading their students. And the reading passage Rivera selected didn't help matters. The two-page story is called "The Day I Threw the Trivia Bowl." Unfortunately, the students took the "bowl" in the title literally. "They didn't know it was a contest," says Rivera, explaining how that misunderstanding was enough to mess up an entire test.

*In New York's Sixteenth Congressional District, 37.7 percent of residents live in poverty, according to the 2007 American Community Survey of the U.S. Census.

Rivera is a thirty-two-year-old dynamo who's been a Bronx teacher and staff developer for ten years. She's a fast-talking Puerto Rican woman with a wild mane of long brown curly hair and light brown eyes. She says the teachers have a hard time keeping up with her energy and her demanding standards. It's her second year at MS 232, and even though she's supposed to be giving the staff tips for planning lessons and working with students, she spends most of her time teaching the teachers how to teach. Seven of the school's twenty-one literacy teachers are new and some have never taught before.

Rivera's office is on the second floor. The shelves by the window are filled with thick, old basal reading anthologies that were used before the city switched to its new curriculum. Instead of following scripted lessons with reading passages chosen by a publisher, the teachers now have to plan their own ninety-minute classes to fit the city's balanced literacy approach. But Rivera says many of them aren't experienced enough. "I say, 'I need a short story with a great character that changes over time,'" for example. Rivera can immediately think of two stories that fit the bill: one called "The Circuit" and another called "The Mustache." But she says her teachers don't yet know enough material to come up with their own ideas. So Rivera winds up doing it for them.

"I'm a constant resource," she says, pointing to the monthly lesson plans she's written. The list of aims for October includes "characters in fiction and nonfiction." Rivera has suggested a few resources for the teachers, such as the short stories of Edgar Allan Poe. But she says they often don't know how to use these stories for teaching different reading skills. At the teachers' request, Rivera wrote a pacing calendar with suggested daily lesson plans. So far, she's only gotten up to October 18.

"They see the words 'narrative nonfiction' and they turn to me," she sighs. "They won't look it up. I say, 'What do you do with a *child* who says, "I don't know?"' You *teach them* to be independent thinkers!" Lately, she's been telling the teachers to use Google to look up terms before they ask her a question. She also holds weekly meetings every Monday after school for them to share their experiences. But then, two days ago, Rivera observed a teacher who was doing so little to involve the students in a classroom exercise that she walked out in disgust. "I feel like I'm banging my head against the wall," she says.

This week Rivera is scheduled to observe nine teachers and give three demonstration lessons. On this Thursday morning, she stops by Anna Maley's eighth-grade classroom. Because the school has had so many discipline problems, the students are all on "lockdown." They don't change classes every period like other middle school students. At MS 232, the pupils stay in the same classroom all day like elementary students, and different subject teachers come to them.

With five years of teaching under her belt, Maley is one of the school's more experienced English Language Arts teachers. She's thirty-nine years old, and previously worked in a law firm while raising a family before deciding to get a master's degree. She's hung big yellow sheets of paper from the overhead fluorescent lights, just as she's supposed to, with instructional reminders such as "Read aloud, listen carefully, use textual evidence." The class seems attentive as Maley passes around a handout about a boy who fakes being allergic to broccoli. The story is followed by a few brief questions. This activity takes up half the class time, which bothers Rivera. Ideally, the students should also have time for individual reading, so the teacher can move around the room to see what books they've chosen and whether they're encountering any problems. Maley has been working with one girl who is reading below grade level. She encourages her to draw a diagram comparing two different characters from either the broccoli story or anything else the girl has read in class, but she can't recall a single character.

This is one of the school's higher-performing eighth-grade classes. The New York State exams are scored according to levels 1–4, with 1 being well below grade level and 2 meaning slightly below but still at risk. Most of the students at MS 232 are at level 2, and Maley's students tend to be at the higher end. She even has a level 4 student in this class, the only one in the eighth grade. The girl sits in the front of the room, raising her hand with enthusiasm whenever Maley asks the class a question. Later, Rivera describes Maley as "old school" because she's had trouble adapting to the new balanced literacy approach of moving quickly from one task to the other while also focusing on individual students. Her class is functioning, though.

Rivera's next classroom observation doesn't go as well. A new seventh-grade teacher named John McDonald is shouting "Excuse me" to a room of nineteen students. Several students are absent but the classroom is still out of control. "Guys, I need you to settle down," he says a few times.

McDonald is white, with short brown hair, and he's attempting to lead a writing workshop on character development. The pupils are asked to compare and contrast the characters they've been reading about in recent stories by drawing charts. They're also supposed to come up with their own characters and provide a list of traits such as physical appearance and likes and dislikes. McDonald gives them twenty minutes and Rivera takes a seat among a cluster of students and begins looking over their black-and-white marble notebooks. A girl shows her a first draft she's written. Her character is a tenth-grade cheerleader who is "happy, sad and heartbroken." Rivera asks the girl why the character is feeling this way, encouraging her to dig deeper. Meanwhile, McDonald paces around the room trying to keep the students from talking. Two girls pass notes to each other but ignore the assignment. McDonald approaches one to ask her about her character. Then, before she can answer him, he walks away to attend to another student. Chaos is building. He makes a dramatic gesture and turns out the lights, counting backward: "Five, four, three, two, one, zero!"

Rivera looks up but doesn't say anything. She's immersed in her own work with the students. She moves on to a boy who's been placed alone in a corner to keep his attention from wandering. He's holding a book called *From Pieces to Weight*, a biography of the rapper 50 Cent. He hasn't written about his own character, so Rivera asks him what he liked about the biography. The boy rattles off a list of things 50 Cent has done in his life, but he's silent when Rivera asks him to recall a particular scene or "vignette," a word the students learned last year. "I know you like the thug literature," she tells him. The boy is quiet. She can't get him to relate to the literature, to talk about any specific scenes or moments that he identified with. During this brief meeting, McDonald turns the lights off three more times to silence the students. A girl yells, "Shut up," and he thanks her.

Without classroom management, Rivera says, it's impossible to teach. "It can't happen between commercial breaks," she says. And without good teaching, the school will never be able to help every one of its struggling students. The boy with the 50 Cent book was held back after failing seventh grade last year. Rivera gave him part of the same state reading test this fall to see if he was able to improve after summer school, but he only got a grade of 46, well below the basic 65 needed to pass. She says this confirms that he has comprehension problems. "He's not trying to connect with the reading," she says. And a new teacher doesn't have enough time to spend with a student like this while also trying to manage the class.

In the last school year, seventy-four students at MS 232 scored a 1 on their reading tests. A teacher at the school says they have problems with comprehension and fluency, which is what's keeping them well behind grade level. Fluency is a combination of speed and accuracy. She also estimates that four seventh-graders are reading at a kindergarten level. She gives them what the teachers call "skill and drill" lessons from various workbooks to improve their reading. But she says, "The kids we're working with at level 1, it's not helping them." She didn't want to be identified because she was concerned about appearing to criticize the leadership. Rivera confirms there was no intensive intervention last year for the lowest-performing students. The teacher who was assigned to help them got pulled away to focus on scoring tests—which has taken on greater importance under Klein's reforms.

The current principal of MS 232 has had a lot on his plate since taking the job in March 2006. Neifi Acosta, a trim Dominican immigrant with a mustache, came to New York City while in college. He's been teaching math and running schools as a principal or assistant principal for almost twenty years. His small office has white-and-yellow walls (to match the linoleum tiles), leather chairs, and an old glass-and-wood bookcase in the reception area topped with several athletic awards. He believes things are slowly improving at MS 232. "The school was in bad shape," he says bluntly, recalling what it was like when he first arrived. "The kids were running the school, there wasn't much instruction." Students were assaulting teachers and there was gang activity.

Acosta imposed a new disciplinary system, creating separate entrances and exits with staggered dismissal times to reduce fights outside. He also required students to wear school uniforms: yellow or white golf shirts for sixth- and seventh-graders, blue or white for eighth-graders. Many educators believe the middle grades are the toughest to teach, because the students are surging with hormones and easily distracted at a time when the workload also surges. But Acosta has been working with this age group for his entire professional life and says he loves the challenge. He's also spent most of his career in this local Bronx school district, which has long been troubled by low scores. It also used to have a community school board that was so corrupt its elected members were suspended twice by two different chancellors in the 1980s and '90s. They were accused of pocketing and misusing district funds for car insurance, phone bills, attorney's fees, and even sexually explicit cable pay-per-view programming on an office television.

In his quest to bring order to MS 232, Acosta also focused on his staff. He hired Rivera to improve literacy instruction and he began getting rid of the "dead weight." The principal discovered that 90 percent of his teachers were teaching outside of their license areas. Yamilka's old math teacher, for example, was licensed to teach math—but not to special education students. Acosta eventually removed a total of twenty teachers and says he's looking to get rid of five more. Principals and the teachers often resent each other's union rules, and they've each found ways to use the system to their advantage. Teachers rely on their tenure. But principals still manage to force out the ones they don't like by assigning them to different classes, or by offering to write a favorable recommendation if they leave (and implying they'll get a dreaded unsatisfactory rating if they stay).

Acosta has focused heavily on results. Soon after he started, he required teachers to give weekly quizzes in math and reading as well as monthly ninety-minute tests. He searches around his office and pulls out colored charts Rivera made with a simple spreadsheet. The charts are encased in plastic binders. We look at sixth-grade performance for September 2006. The bottom of the chart shows the name of every sixth-grade teacher, matched with vertical columns to show the percentage of students who passed their monthly exam. Among the six reading teachers, the scores vary tremendously—from a high of 76 percent passing the test to a low of 6 percent. That low score was not from a special ed classroom, he says. "That's someone who found greener pastures," clarifies his assistant principal for sixth grade, Desiree Martinez, referring to the classroom teacher. She gives a knowing laugh. Acosta says the staff needed real professional development, which is why he brought in Rivera as the literacy coach and Martinez for her background in literacy.

Acosta sees signs of progress. He's already reduced his number of level 1 students from 20 percent in 2006 to 13 percent in 2007. Most of his students are now at level 2—which is usually good enough to be promoted but still below grade level. Acosta wants his teachers to focus on comprehension and fluency because these are the most common reading problems in middle school. Most students (unlike Alejandro and Yamilka) can sound out the words. Rivera credits Acosta with improving the tone of the school, which should allow more time for teaching now that staffers aren't so worried about safety. He also won high marks in a quality review, conducted by outside educators, for using data to track the performance of each class. And he's just hired a family counselor to visit homes and crack down on truancy. The student body is almost entirely black and Hispanic and very poor. Attendance is generally below 90 percent, a few points below the citywide average of 91 percent for middle schools.

Acosta's homemade data chart is a low-tech version of the new math and reading assessments that all elementary and middle schools will begin using this year. Teachers will be able to look at the results online and search for trends. The Department of Education has also asked principals to create "inquiry teams" of about five staffers at each school to identify a group of low-performing students and try new interventions with them. Teachers and staffers on the inquiry teams are paid to work a few extra hours each week. Schools single out the low-performing students by crunching data from ARIS, the new Web-based computer network, and their inquiry teams are told to focus on either math or English Language Arts. Acosta directed his team to concentrate on math. Just a quarter of the school's students are meeting state standards for reading, but the state has put MS 232 on the list of schools in need of improvement because of its math scores, which, while equally grim, were even worse the previous year.

Rivera says it's just as well that she's not on the inquiry team, because her English teachers need so much attention. "Maybe it's not fast enough for me. I'm pushing too hard," she frets. But it's October, and the state's English Language Arts exam is in January. Rivera takes her work very personally. She grew up in the Bronx and attended the local Catholic schools. She moved away for college, studying anthropology and civilization at Brown University, but then returned to the neighborhood. "My mother threatened me to come back to the Bronx" (to be near home), she says, laughing. "I come from a strict Puerto Rican household." She earned two more degrees in education and administration while working in the public schools. She's tried to become an assistant principal, but says she lost out to other applicants who were better connected.

"I'm just like these kids," she says flatly. "The Bronx is like a drug. You get stuck here." A colleague from an outside education group who's working with Rivera on professional development challenges the young reading coach when she hears that statement. "You *want* to work here," she says. Rivera concedes the point, blaming her bad attitude on not being an assistant principal and feeling like "a failure."

But there's no time to dwell on the past. Rivera has to order Magic Markers, glue, and crayons for the teachers. She also has to come up with a word of the day for the rest of the year. Today's word is "haughty." And Friday she'll be holding her weekly sessions with the teachers to go over their progress. In her view, she's on a mission to bring up the scores. "I have to keep hitting them with good instruction," she says of the teachers. But even so, she knows a few students are bound to fall through the cracks, the way Yamilka and Antonio did a decade ago. "It's okay if we lose five," she says, in a teacher's version of triage. "I'm worried about losing masses."

SEVEN

"Double Whammy"

Mary Kelly was surprised by Yamilka's very limited reading skills. Her quick diagnostic test at the Fisher Landau Center, in September 2007, put Yamilka at a first-grade level. Kelly wondered how much the young woman had really learned at Huntington. But, she conceded, "I don't know where she started." Sometimes with adults, she said, "you can push and make nice gains, but with others it's really difficult to get the information in." She needed more data about Yamilka's cognitive processing abilities—meaning how quickly she could solve basic problems.

Kelly earned a Ph.D. in educational psychology at Teachers College, and has a master's degree in reading. She grew up in the New York area and went to Boston College, majoring in special education and graduating in 1972. "I'm a big reader," she said. "I'm also a little politically oriented. So I put these two interests together to go into reading—in that I felt like if people could read, then they could be good citizens and they could vote and you can't fool them."

Yamilka's appointment for the cognitive test was at the end of November. It was a gray, rainy day and her sister Gabriella joined her, just as she had in September. She left her sister in the empty waiting room when she was called into Kelly's office for her evaluation. It was about 1:30 in the afternoon—before the younger students would arrive after school—and Gabriella had taken along a copy of the magazine *Real Simple* so she could read the holiday recipes. Yamilka hurried into Kelly's office. She was a few minutes late and tense with excitement. But she smiled shyly and calmly took a seat across from Kelly's desk. She wore a black long-sleeved sweater and jeans, and her hair was curled up in a bun. She could have passed for the mother of one of the younger students who would arrive later. Facing her was a wall full of books about disabilities: *How to Increase Reading Ability*, *Dyslexia*, and *Reading Reflex*. Two bobblehead dolls, of Sigmund Freud and Albert Einstein, stood watch on the shelves. Kelly, who has short brown hair and an informal manner, wore a casual blue sweater and glasses.

She immediately noticed Yamilka's new pair of rectangular glasses and complimented her on the style. Back in September, she had given Yamilka a quick eye exam and suggested it was time for a new prescription. Yamilka and one of her sisters had gone to an optometrist who accepted Medicaid.

Kelly asked Yamilka what she'd been reading since their first meeting two months ago, and Yamilka told her she had continued going through her word cards from Huntington, the ABC's, and sounds of the letters. She had also done some math in a workbook given to her by a former tutor. She said her sisters checked to see if her answers were correct. "Do you have a calculator?" Kelly asked. "That way you could check yourself." Yamilka said she didn't have one and didn't know how to use one, either.

"We're going to do a lot of work, okay?" Kelly smiled and pulled out a big book. "The first bunch of things we're going to do will not seem like reading or math. I want to see what kind of information is easy for you to work with and what gives you trouble. I'm going to show you some pictures. I want you to tell me what's missing."

Yamilka nodded her head and watched as Kelly flipped to the first page of the book. There was a drawing of a door. Yamilka instantly noticed that it was missing a handle. Then she turned the page to a drawing of a face wearing an incomplete pair of glasses. Again, no problem. But she was stumped by the next drawing. There was a jug full of water tilted from above and a glass of water beneath it. Yamilka stared at the page, unable to figure out that the water should have been flowing into the glass. "I don't know," she said softly. Kelly told her that was fine and they moved on to other images. Then they began with words.

"Now, tell me what these words mean," asked Kelly. "Bed?"

"Something you sleep," Yamilka answered.

"Ship?"

"It's an animal."

"You're telling me about a sheep. A ship."

"It's a boat."

They continued with the words "penny," "repair," "assemble," and "winter." Gradually the words became less familiar. Yamilka didn't recognize "terminate," "confide," "remorse," or "sanctuary." But she said a colony "is like these people that live in this little prairie town and have to wear this little funny outfit." She laughed and so did Kelly.

"If I ask you these words in Spanish, would that be easier?" Kelly asked her. "Maybe," said Yamilka. "But I have never heard these words in my life."

The next section involved words that were alike and dissimilar. Yamilka knew that socks and shoes go together because you wear them; that bananas and oranges are both fruits; and that work and play are opposites. This section seemed easy for her until, again, the words became less familiar. "Democracy and monarchy?" asked Kelly. Yamilka had no answer. They continued with words for a few more minutes.

Then Kelly pulled out a set of red and white blocks. Some sides had single colors. Others were split, diagonally, into red and white triangles. Kelly put four of them together in a square. The two bottom blocks were red, the top left block was white, and the top right block had both colors. She asked Yamilka to replicate her pattern.

Yamilka looked at the blocks and began moving them into a square of her own. But it was the opposite pattern of Kelly's square. Kelly wondered if Yamilka had deliberately made a mirror image. "Don't make it for me," she said. "Make it for you."

Yamilka thought about it and switched the two red blocks to the bottom, so they were positioned just like Kelly's. She then correctly put the white block in the top left corner. But she flipped the pattern on the red and white block. She looked at it again and determined something was wrong. Slowly, she moved the blocks around. "Are you happy with that?" asked Kelly. "Yes," Yamilka said.

They went through a few more block patterns. Some involved following a book of pictures. Yamilka struggled to reproduce them. She tried holding the blocks over the page to see if that made it easier to create the same image. This helped her get one combination but not the rest. Kelly timed each attempt with a stopwatch and wrote in her notebook. "Let's call it a day on these," she said gently.

"I like how you work," she told Yamilka, in what seemed like an effort to put her at ease. "You have excellent attention and concentration, perseverance. You stick with it." They moved on to other exercises involving patterns of colors and shapes. Then Kelly tested her memory. When she said two numbers, Yamilka could repeat them back. But if she said three or more numbers, such as four, one, five, Yamilka would often forget the order and might say five, four, one.

Kelly also tested her knowledge of the world around her with a few questions about objects and places. Yamilka knew what a thermometer is used for, and the shape of a ball. But she said there were seven months in a year, and thirty weeks. She might have been thinking about the number of days in a week and a month. She drew a blank when asked what continent Brazil is in, and who was president during the Civil War. She guessed that the capital of Italy is France and didn't know who wrote *Hamlet*. But she knew that Martin Luther King, Jr., was a "leader of the blacks." And even though she didn't know where the Olympics originated, she told Kelly that her favorite sports were swimming and skating and named a few of the male athletes. "You like the cute boys!" said Kelly. Yamilka laughed, then sighed, "My brother would get all of these questions."

Kelly handed her a page full of math problems, which appeared to be at a second- or third-grade level. Yamilka could do a few of the addition and subtraction problems, though she needed to draw tally marks as she counted along. She could not do any of the multiplication or division problems involving one- and two-digit numbers. Kelly stopped her after a long period of time and asked if she would like to move on to spelling. Yamilka seemed relieved to be rid of the math.

The spelling questions started with simple words such as "hi," "in," and "six." But Yamilka had difficulty remembering how the letters were supposed to join forces. When she heard the word "was," she sounded out the "wah" and "ah," erasing each attempt to match the sounds to letters because she knew she was wrong. When she heard "house," she wrote "home," and "rain" became "rine." Kelly tried to help her by saying the words very slowly, breaking them down into sounds and syllables. "Table," she said, repeating herself. "Tay. Tay. What says buh?" Yamilka wrote down "ta" and the letter *b*. "Now it has to end." Yamilka thought for a moment and wrote down "le."

The potential for frustration was enormous. Here was a twenty-four-year-old woman struggling to finish simple words, many of which she had already learned at her previous reading program. And yet Yamilka never got angry with herself or asked when the test would be over. "You are really a terrific person," said Kelly. "It's unbelievable how hard you work." She asked Yamilka if she wanted a break and again Yamilka declined. She wanted to keep on going.

Kelly tested her comprehension by reading and showing her written sentences and asking Yamilka to fill in the blanks. She could finish a few of the simpler ones, such as "There is no milk in the refrigerator. We need to get more at the [blank]." She correctly answered, "Store." But she couldn't finish many of the others. She had an easier time when Kelly read her very short stories, with two or three sentences, then asked her which word was missing. She listened carefully and thought hard before answering.

The test lasted almost two hours. Yamilka declined a few more offers to take a break. Her final exercise involved drawing shapes she saw on a page. They were made with dots and lines, and she completed each one very slowly.

"You are an exceptionally terrific worker," said Kelly. "I've rarely met someone who works as hard as you and sticks with it." Yamilka looked down at her fingernails, which had French tips from a recent trip to the salon. Kelly told her it would take about two weeks to complete her report and plan Yamilka's lessons. "You're going to be a pleasure to work with," she said as Yamilka got up to leave. "Me, too," said Yamilka. "I'm tired of being at home."

Yamilka found Gabriella in the waiting room, now filled with children. It was four p.m. Every seat was taken. Gabriella couldn't believe the test had taken so long; she said she had fallen asleep waiting. They asked the receptionist about which buses would get them back home, and walked down the block to a bus stop. "Look around and remember this," said Gabriella, pointing to the Citibank at the intersection. She wanted Yamilka to be able to get home by herself next time. Yamilka was happy, relieved that the test was over. She told Gabriella that it had been pretty easy except for the math.

"To be really frank, she's more impaired than most people that I see and reading on a far lower level than most people that I see," said Kelly two days later.

Yamilka's reading was stuck at a first-grade level. That's what Huntington had found as well. Kelly expected this based on her initial evaluation of Yamilka in September. But the block patterns and pictures she had given her in November were measuring intellectual or cognitive skills, some of which had nothing to do with written language. "She really had really big struggles on the nonverbal side as well," said Kelly. "And that was a little bit, to me, unexpected."

The IQ test Kelly had given her was considered a "snapshot" of her cognitive capabilities. But she cautioned that it would not be a reliable predictor of her potential. That's an important difference. Yamilka's IQ score was technically in the range for mental retardation. But Kelly said this did *not* mean she was retarded, because the definition is no longer based solely on scores. Educators once used IQ scores of 70 to 85 to designate which children were "educable," or only mildly retarded, compared to those in the lower range, who were "trainable."[1] Today, the American Association on Intellectual and Developmental Disabilities (formerly the American Association on Mental Retardation) doesn't just rely on IQ. It now defines the disability as being characterized by "significant limitations both in intellectual functioning and in adaptive behavior." This latter part is key, because it includes the ability to function as an adult. There are mentally retarded people who can read better than Yamilka, but Kelly says they cannot function as adults and their comprehension is limited.

This is why Kelly said Yamilka's scores were misleading. She was obviously able to take care of herself, cook, clean, talk about things going on in the world, and crack jokes. But Kelly said she had cognitive problems in "being able to perceive visually and verbally, and being able to solve problems in both of those realms." In other words, she had great difficulty taking in information and using language to express herself clearly. Kelly says these "processing disabilities" have made it difficult for her to learn how to read. "This is not to say she cannot learn—I may as well not be here," she explained. "I would never say that. But I do perceive she would have—and has had—extreme difficulty learning new information."

In some ways, learning to read is like learning to speak. "You have to be able to process sound, you have to be able to remember what you hear," said Kelly. "Your vocabulary has to grow, you have to develop a sense of grammar." But unlike speech, which has always distinguished human behavior, reading isn't so natural. The written word has been around for only a few thousand years. Reading was an evolution, one that the Tufts University professor Maryanne Wolf has described as something that actually caused the brain to physically change. In her book *Proust and the Squid*, Wolf has written how each person's brain must learn to make new circuits by connecting older regions originally designed and genetically programmed for other functions, such as recognizing objects and retrieving their names.[2] Reading development therefore involves three main functions: rearranging these brain regions to make new learning circuits; the capacity for these groups of neurons to specialize in storing different types of information; and their ability to retrieve and connect that information automatically. And experts have found that brain activity actually changes as these reading skills develop.

Dr. Sally Shaywitz, co-director of the Yale Center for the Study of Learning and Attention, has also written extensively about how the reading circuitry consists of brain regions dedicated to different functions. Some regions process the visual features—the lines and curves that make up letters—and others transform those shapes into the sounds of language and the meanings of words.[3] Early readers have to spend time breaking apart and analyzing new words. But as they become more skilled, they can instantly recognize familiar words and connect them to sounds and meanings. In that sense, the brain is like a muscle that gets stronger as it learns a new exercise. Neural pathways are formed and they adapt to their new strength.

Studies with functional magnetic resonance imaging have shown how reading activity normally takes place in the back left side of the brain. Dyslexic readers have trouble activating these neural pathways for putting together visual representations (letters) and sounds (words). The MRIs revealed how they're actually relying more heavily on the front of their brains as they read, compensating with higher verbal abilities—such as saying the words aloud and memorizing what they hear. That's why educators have had success at overcoming dyslexia with multisensory programs such as Orton-Gillingham. The sounds and feelings of different letter combinations stimulate brain circuits, much like physical therapists' work with weakened limbs. Research has shown that students who are exposed to these programs on a regular basis actually build new brain circuits. That's why Alejandro and Antonio could improve their reading skills when they attended the Lindamood-Bell program regularly.

But Kelly said Yamilka's other processing skills weren't strong enough to help her compensate for her problems with reading. She couldn't use her memory the way Antonio can, when he rattles off the first day he kissed a girl, or the addresses and phone numbers of his school friends. She couldn't recall odd facts and figures the way her brother, Alejandro, can after watching a nature documentary on cuttlefish. When Kelly read Yamilka a series of numbers during the IQ test and asked her to repeat them, she could only recall sets of two and three numbers. The average adult can remember up to seven digits—the rationale for our system of phone numbers.

Those are examples of auditory memory, or storing what we hear. Kelly was also able to pinpoint another memory problem. It revealed itself during the very first part of Yamilka's test. "I showed her pictures with things missing and she really struggled—and she didn't have to label, she just had to point. So it's not a language thing," said Kelly. "She really did poorly on that. That suggests to me there is some visual memory issue, she can't look and remember what might not be there." The red and white blocks were another example of Yamilka's weaknesses with visual and spatial processing that had nothing to do with language per se.

An untrained observer might have confused Yamilka's backward version of the block pattern with dyslexia—especially since Yamilka had a tendency to make some of the same mistakes as dyslexics in the writing portion of the test, such as flipping her *b*'s and *d*'s. But Kelly said dyslexics often excel at design problems because they're not reliant on language. Some people who study learning disabilities believe Albert Einstein and Thomas Edison had dyslexia. Block tests are examples of "spatial nonverbal reading." Yamilka missed most of the patterns. She couldn't even make her blocks form the same square shape as the ones on the page. They wandered across the desk as she tried in vain to make the red and white pieces conform to the stripes and triangles she saw within the model. Kelly said this revealed how Yamilka had difficulty perceiving, organizing, and using information in both the verbal and visual realms. She called it a "double whammy."

Kelly concluded that Yamilka's two different paths for learning—the visual and the auditory—were both very weak, resulting in a double deficit. These serious learning disabilities would explain why her problems absorbing information weren't just limited to reading. Kelly pointed to

Yamilka's low score on the general knowledge portions of the test. Lots of her clients at the clinic don't know the capital of France or the definition of a monarchy because of their poor education. But Yamilka had trouble explaining much more basic concepts that she did understand. She knew that work and play were opposites, but when pressed she could only say that "play is 'something you do in the park, work is inside.'" She knew that winter was "snow" and that a bed was "something you sleep." But those are not the complete definitions one would expect from a twenty-four-year-old woman, even one for whom English is a second language. Kelly called that a problem with expressive language and memory. "It's effortful for her; the words did not come out easily.

"A big part of the cuing system in reading is grammar," Kelly continued. "And she doesn't have a good feel for that, so she's got fewer and fewer things she can depend on to help build her reading skills." Yamilka performed at her best when Kelly read her the very short stories and asked her to figure out which word was missing. She didn't have to struggle with looking at the words and trying to break them apart. Her other strength was in drawing multisided shapes. Her angles were slightly off, and she took longer than average, but overall Kelly said they were "beautiful."

Not surprisingly, math was also a disaster because of the same weaknesses in processing information and remembering things. Yamilka lost track of herself as she added and subtracted simple equations, such as seventeen minus five, drawing tally marks and then *numbering* them as she went along. Kelly said she had never seen anyone number their lines as they counted. This was obviously Yamilka's way of making up for her memory problems.

Kelly said it was no wonder, then, that Yamilka had absorbed so little at Huntington Learning Center. Her understanding of phonics was terribly stunted, despite almost two years of direct instruction. Kelly could see how Yamilka tried, very hard, to put her phonetic skills to work. When asked to spell the word "was," she wrote "wouis." Kelly said this meant she knew the right letters for the beginning and end of the word, but she had no idea what vowel to put in between. She spelled the word "under" as "norb." It made no sense at first, but Kelly said if you considered the sound of "un," you could see how Yamilka wound up with the letter *n*. The "orb" was a backward version of "der," with a dyslexic's classic substitution of *b* for *d*. Kelly asked Yamilka to spell a few nonsense words just to test her ability to blend sounds, and to use her decoding skills. She couldn't do very many.

"I did like 'dright,'" said Kelly, referring to one of the nonsense words she asked Yamilka to spell. Her answer was very revealing because she confused the *b* and the *d*. "She said, 'Buh-itch.' I bet that's a deep dyslexia error!"

Yamilka's learning disabilities *were* a bitch, so to speak. Her difficulty tackling verbal and nonverbal problems that most people can solve intuitively was only compounded by her awful luck. This was a woman who had missed out on the formative years of schooling. When she finally did go to school, she was taught in another language and then didn't get the interventions she had needed all along. It wasn't a hopeless case. But it would need a completely different approach. And that's what troubled Kelly, who said, "This is a girl who should have been in speech and language therapy in school." Kelly said any evaluator should have seen that Yamilka needed help learning how to listen for information and to express herself clearly. These techniques would help her strengthen the language skills she needed for reading because they're in the same part of the brain.

"This is not a subtle problem," she stated, repeating herself for emphasis. "I did not give her one test that is not sitting in every public school. I gave her a standard battery of measures; they are very common measures. Every psychologist is aware of them.

"If someone really listened to her for a while it would be clear it's not just a reading problem. I would not even call her dyslexic. I think she has a more global learning disability that would include not just the verbal aspects and the reading parts but that's also affected her nonverbal functioning."

The public schools never addressed the complexity of Yamilka's learning problems. She was ten years old when she first started attending elementary school in the Bronx. But it wasn't until she had started seventh grade, at the age of fourteen, that her parents requested an evaluation because she still couldn't read or write. The middle school didn't come to them earlier with that suggestion. This long delay could have had something to do with her being an English Language Learner. "We as a school system are not allowed to refer bilingual children immediately for special education because we have to demonstrate that we've addressed their bilingual needs before assessing them [as] handicapped children," said Peter McNally, executive director of the New York City Council of School Supervisors and Administrators—which represents the principals. McNally said this requirement prevents many needy children from being referred promptly for services. As an elementary principal in Queens, he admitted he once bent the rules for a Chinese newcomer who was physically and mentally handicapped because he didn't think the child could afford to wait.

When Yamilka finally was evaluated, the tests administered by the school psychologist were similar to the ones given by Mary Kelly at Fisher Landau. Whoever filled out her paperwork wrote:

"Both the verbal and performance scales were in the intellectually deficient range. No significant differences were noted. In the verbal scale a better-developed skill was displayed on a task involving social judgement. Weaknesses were noted on tasks involving general fund of knowledge, abstract verbal reasoning, numerical reasoning, and word knowledge. Weaknesses were noted across the non-verbal scale."

Yamilka's middle school psychologist had discovered the same weaknesses with language processing that Kelly diagnosed almost ten years later. The evaluation also said she could not write the alphabet, just a few uppercase letters, and that she couldn't read in Spanish. Yet her Individualized Education Program did not recommend any speech and language classes to help her learn how to read. It merely called for weekly counseling sessions in Spanish and special ed classes with a student-teacher ratio of fifteen to one. This was insufficient. Four years later, the schools missed another opportunity to intervene when Yamilka was still unable to read in high school. Her family requested a new evaluation, and a diagnostic center in Brooklyn reached a similar grim conclusion. Yamilka's sister Elizabeth went along with her for that meeting and was furious. "They was like, 'Oh, she's mentally retarded.' I was like, 'You cannot say that!' It's a horrible feeling!"

It's possible that the school system gave up on teaching Yamilka to read because of her low scores. Her brother, Alejandro, tested in the "borderline" range and also got no reading interventions. But Kelly was shocked that the schools ignored the central findings of the evaluations. This was a student with obvious language disabilities. Special ed classes alone would do nothing to help her without extra speech and language classes. Young children are sent to these types of classes when they have trouble talking or getting the sounds of letters. Almost every public school has a speech teacher.

Two weeks after her test that November, Yamilka returned to Fisher Landau with Gabriella to get her results. The two sisters sat down with Kelly, who explained how the test results were consistent with the evaluations Yamilka had gotten in the public schools. Yamilka was immediately troubled by that word.

"It's not good for me to be consistent every time?" she asked, concerned that she had made no progress.

"You made growth as a person," Kelly explained. "This means you're growing." She told her how some adults have problems that get worse over time, so consistency was good in Yamilka's case. But Yamilka sounded a little surprised that her reading level wasn't higher. She told Kelly that she thought she was reading at maybe an eight-year-old's level. Kelly said it was more like that of a five- or six-year-old's.

Kelly then explained the root of Yamilka's learning problems. She told her that she had difficulty processing information. "When the information comes in visually, it's not always stable," she said, trying to stay away from too many clinical terms. "Understanding words and visually getting that information through your eyes is sometimes mushy." Yamilka seemed to catch on, telling Kelly how she confuses the letters *b* and *d*. Kelly nodded.

"When you read information through the eyes, it's processed in the brain. When you're talking, the information comes in through the ears but it comes through the same language center in your brain. I feel it will help you if it comes in through the ears," she said, going on to describe how she wanted Yamilka to begin with speech and language therapy. She said this would better prepare the language part of her brain for reading. Yamilka was intrigued, saying, "That's so cool!"

As the meeting wrapped up, Yamilka asked Kelly point-blank if these new classes would help her. "I think you're really motivated, you're a hard worker, and all of those things contribute to making progress," Kelly told her. "I can't promise you a hundred percent," she said, but "I feel like we can help you or I wouldn't invite you into our programs."

Yamilka left the office feeling very comfortable with Kelly. She liked the fact that she didn't make any promises, unlike some of her teachers in middle school who she said made "phony" assurances like "Don't worry, everything takes time, maybe next year you'll be able to keep up with the other students." Kelly "wasn't bullshitting me," said Yamilka. "I can say she was not lying to me, she was being real. She said I have to [do] my part, I have to work."

But she admitted feeling a little bit down because her reading hadn't improved as much as she had hoped.

Kelly was disappointed with Yamilka's progress at Huntington. Shortly after the evaluation, she called Dawn Helene, the program's assistant director, to find out more about Yamilka's history there. Kelly said she had no doubt about Helene's sincerity. And she agreed that Yamilka's first year of multisensory instruction with phonics and decoding was probably an appropriate plan in order to introduce her to the basic concepts of reading. But she said it sounded as though Huntington repeated the same type of work during Yamilka's second year when she still wasn't catching on, and that should have been a warning. Even though Yamilka didn't even know the alphabet when she started her tutoring in 2005, Kelly still concluded, "Kindergarten to first grade is not much growth over two years."

Kelly readily concedes she is not a fan of private tutoring centers like Huntington. She believes they often aren't worth the steep price. At eighty dollars per hour, New York City paid close to $100,000 for Yamilka's instruction. Kelly wondered whether that money would have been better spent sending Yamilka to a language specialist. She questioned why Yamilka's lawyers hadn't pushed for a different placement.

But Advocates for Children didn't have many options. When they first learned of Yamilka through her brother, she was three weeks shy of her twenty-second birthday—the cutoff point for filing a case. Their primary concern was making sure they had a case and finding a tutoring center that would accept her on short notice. An extra evaluation by outside experts would have taken too long. Advocates for Children works only with tutoring centers and service providers that they believe provide quality services and that are willing to take students from the city schools. Not everyone wants to deal with the system's bureaucracy and the problems associated with its students. Deputy Director Matthew Lenaghan said Advocates took Yamilka for a visit to a cooking program, but she was not accepted and couldn't attend because she couldn't read, and state-funded vocational programs don't offer reading services.

At Huntington, Dawn Helene said her clinicians wouldn't have been able to evaluate whether Yamilka needed speech therapy. "We're not really in a position to pick up anything like that; we're not psychologists," she said. Helene declared herself pleased with Yamilka's progress. On her last day of tutoring in 2007, Helene looked over the change from Yamilka's first reading evaluation in 2005. "Sight word testing on the first testing session was only three words of twenty on a primer list," she said. "Today, in addition to seventeen of those, she was able to identify fourteen of twenty first-grade words and eight of twenty second-grade words. So she's done a little bit more than two grade levels of progress." Yamilka had also done that with just fifteen hours a week of instruction, three hours each day, rather than the recommended twenty hours, because she had trouble with the intensity. Helene noted that public school students have at least thirty hours a week of instruction.

There were also personal issues. Yamilka stopped attending for two long stretches of time when she got upset and frustrated—once after getting lost on the subway, and the other time after a favorite instructor left. Helene says she assigned her most upbeat staff members to the struggling young woman. By the time Yamilka left in 2007, she knew all her letters and sounds and could write a few very simple sentences with assistance. She also learned how to tell time, and the basics of addition and subtraction. Her workbooks showed that she successfully completed many simple math problems. Helene thought a first-grade reading level was considerable progress given her enormous deficits and the struggle it took getting her to come to class each day. "We were too busy trying to keep our eye on the ball and do the best we could," she said.

But when Kelly evaluated Yamilka at Fisher Landau later that year, and saw the results of her IQ test, she could only conclude that her progress had stalled at first grade because of her more "global" learning disabilities. That's why Kelly was determined to use a different program. Speech and language therapy would lay the groundwork for developing her reading brain. But since learning the rules of written language were so difficult, she wanted Yamilka to learn what she called "functional sight words." It wouldn't be the "Dick and Jane" type of stuff for little children, with repetitive sentences like "See Dick run." She said her materials were more interesting for adults because they used words they would see in their daily lives. In a way, Kelly was drawing the same conclusion the city's education department reached when it sent Yamilka to a non-academic high school. There, too, the goal was "functional literacy"—which the city defined as knowing how to read subway maps and bathroom signs. But Yamilka wasn't able to learn in that environment, and her evaluations were ignored—otherwise she would have gotten the speech therapy to develop her communication skills.

Kelly didn't consider this giving up on reading. She said she was trying to be more realistic, by strengthening Yamilka's weaknesses and recognizing the limits she has right now. Medicaid would pay for only a year of services. Kelly couldn't predict whether Yamilka would have more success with reading by combining the two approaches. But she was more than eager to try.

EIGHT

The Architect Meets the Public

Mayor Bloomberg and Chancellor Klein actively promoted and defended their school reforms. But the architect of ARIS, the school system's new computer network, was much less visible. At least until November 2007.

That was when ARIS generated A through F letter grades for every school, based largely on how much progress individual students had made in the past year on their annual state exams.

When the first-ever progress reports were released in November, they were full of surprises. "Topsy Turvy—Shock Marks in New Report Cards" was the headline in the *New York Post*.[1] "City: Make the Grade or Else!"[2] cried the *Daily News*. The papers went on to list schools with good reputations that had been branded with low grades. In Lower Manhattan, IS 289 made headlines when it was given a D—even though more than 80 percent of its students were performing at or above the state standards on their math and English tests. The school had even earned a "blue ribbon" mark of achievement under the federal No Child Left Behind Act. Parents were furious and so was the principal, Ellen Foote, who told *The New York Times*, "It is just so demoralizing to have a number or grade assigned that is just sort of trivializing things. It doesn't reflect, I think, the valuable work and the very complicated work that we do here."[3]

The outrage extended throughout the city, wherever beloved schools were given low marks because of the complicated formula. Park Slope's renowned PS 321 earned a B, which shocked local parents, who believed it deserved an A. In Queens one longtime educator who didn't want to be identified said her school's administration was in "a tailspin" because it was given a D, even though about half of its mostly low-income population was reading at grade level. She said people feared losing their jobs and that the principal had been visiting classrooms, micromanaging the teachers. In Carroll Gardens, Brooklyn, PS 58 also got a D. "The grade does not reflect who we are," the school's principal told the *News*.[4] In Staten Island, one parent told the *Post* that the F given to their child's school must have been a mistake. More than 86 percent of the students at PS 35 were meeting or exceeding the state standards in English, and 98 percent were making the marks in math.

The progress reports were full of other inconsistencies. Nine schools that had been considered failures by the state's education department were awarded A's or B's. They included two junior highs where more than three quarters of the students were performing below grade level. They were on a state watch list of schools in danger of being closed. "State Sez F, but City Sez A!" crowed the *News*,[5] pointing out the obvious disparities. Even schools that were characterized as "persistently dangerous" by the state were given high marks. Dan Brown of *The Huffington Post* asked, "Whom do you trust?" Referring to a South Bronx middle school, he wrote: "Should you listen to the 'Persistently Dangerous' headlines, which beg you to transfer your child out as fast a humanly possible, or do you cheer the 'A' that the Department of Education just awarded the school? The same confusion sweeps across the city. Parents are rightly asking, 'Can I trust these report cards?'" The answer, he wrote, was "not really."[6]

The blogosphere was abuzz. Angry teachers vented by writing haiku on the website Eduwonkette. Most of the posts were anonymous, such as these:[7]

Who would have thunk it?
A system that is worse than
No Child Left Behind

Bloomberg, Klein, Liebman
Masters of the universe
Have you ever taught?

The principals union was also disturbed, though its leadership chose not to be as vocal as the teachers. In letters to Liebman, the Council of School Supervisors and Administrators (CSA) complained that its members weren't properly trained in "cleansing" the data that would be used for the progress reports. Union officials claimed some schools lost a grade because of attendance-taking measures, or because state and city records didn't always match up. CSA president Ernest Logan said he supported the goal of the progress reports but that these inaccuracies unfairly penalized his members. "If there's garbage going into the system you're going to get garbage coming out."

The next month, the Department of Education announced that several schools would be closed at the end of June, based on their low marks. Those schools had been considered obvious failures before the new progress reports were released. No principals were fired based on the grades. That only added to the confusion over how much weight the grades would carry. New Yorkers had a hard time absorbing a grading system that seemed to turn around most of their long-held assumptions about what defined a successful school—and at the same time, to suggest that no one would really be held accountable.

Jim Liebman and his accountability team tried to prepare the city's press corps to put a favorable spin on the news. The week before the progress reports were unveiled, Liebman and Chancellor Klein held a briefing with reporters in a conference room at the Tweed where they explained their new system for crunching data.

"This is a no-excuses system," Liebman declared.

"Obviously we understand the power of grades," said Klein. "But I also think a critical aspect that has to be emphasized is the power of this information to change what's happening."

Klein and Liebman sat at a long table next to Rajeev Bajav, a Northwestern University graduate who had previously worked for Microsoft in technology marketing. He'd been inspired to join the public sector after reading *There Are No Children Here* by Alex Kotlowitz. All three wore dark suits and ties. Bajav was in charge of a laptop computer connected to an overhead projector. It showed a sample progress report featuring a fictional school.

Liebman explained how progress reports were the very first "accountability tool" created by the ARIS system for measuring the effectiveness of teachers and principals. A similar A–F grading system for schools had been used in Florida. Liebman pointed to the mock report on the overhead of a school that got a B. The grade was determined by three main factors: school environment, student performance, and student progress. Environment was determined by surveys given to parents, teachers, and students and counted for 15 percent of the grade. Student performance on the statewide tests counted for 30 percent, and progress on those same exams counted for 55 percent. The sample school wasn't doing much better than average on its test scores. Fewer than 60 percent of students were meeting the standards. But its students had made big gains compared to the previous year—which is why it earned such a good grade. With great precision, Liebman then explained the concept behind giving so much weight to progress.

"The basic strategy here, the thing that makes this different from other accountability systems, is to say [to the] school: These children arrived at your doorstep. Wherever they were performing, whatever they could do at that point, your job is to get them to move forward. If they're already at a level three, move them to a level four. If they're scoring at a level one, move them to a level two and keep it going from there."

For years, the city's test scores had really been lumped into two groups: students who scored a level 3 or above and those who scored below a 3, meaning below grade level. Schools with a high percentage of students at or above a level 3 were branded successful when the scores were published in the local media. Those with a high percentage of students scoring below grade level were considered failures. But Liebman's new system shook up this premise. By looking at how many students moved from 1 to 2, a school with a lot of students below grade level could still be considered successful for making progress.

The progress reports also awarded schools extra credit for "closing the achievement gap," meaning they had raised test scores among special education students, English Language Learners, minorities, and low-income children. Some schools had made great progress with these groups even if their overall scores didn't change very much, and Liebman wanted them to be recognized. He also believed in making fair comparisons. A school filled with low-income immigrants who didn't speak English, for example, shouldn't be expected to do as well on reading tests as a school in a wealthy white neighborhood. But it also shouldn't be let off the hook. So Liebman's team designed two different ways of measuring progress. Each school was compared to a peer group of forty schools with similar demographics. It was also compared to the citywide average, which included the best schools. This way, the city would know if that elementary school with a high percentage of low-income immigrants had done worse than a similar school. The city would also know if a school with excellent marks could have done even better, if a similar school was able to make *greater* progress.

"In the past schools have been able to say, well, you're comparing me to suburban schools and I'm in a very urban setting, it's very different, I've got kids that are different, it's not fair to compare me," Liebman explained. "If another school has done better and you haven't, that's because the instruction has failed, not because the kids at the school have failed."

That's why the progress reports weren't just about rewards and punishments. The grades, Klein and Liebman argued, were ultimately supposed to help drive instruction, the way Giuliani's CompStat program in the police department revealed which neighborhoods needed more protection. Liebman and Bajav demonstrated how ARIS could be used to help a principal sort out which students in a particular grade had the lowest scores. They used the scale scores from the state exams to see where each child fell within the four different testing levels. "Every bit of data that you want to know about how well your school is doing, how it's evaluated, is there at the click of your mouse," said Liebman, describing how principals and teachers will eventually be able to "drill down" and see which students are falling behind. At the sample school, they showed how students "got better" by a tenth of a proficiency level on math—moving from an average of 2.0 to 2.1 on their statewide tests. Bajav then clicked and sorted the scores. Suddenly, they were displayed in order from the lowest marks to the highest. He showed how the principal could then click on each mark to see a student profile with all the relevant records for that individual child. Contact information for the parents, attendance, and school enrollment history were accessible in the same place for the first time—sparing principals from having to comb through different computer systems that were never before compatible.

It was a lot to absorb in an hour-long presentation. The reporters were confused by the different formulas, and had many questions about how the schools would be scored and compared to one another. Was it fair to compare a small school to a big school? A school with small classes to one whose classrooms were overcrowded? And why let test scores determine 85 percent of a school's overall mark? Many parents thought the schools were already placing too much emphasis on annual scores.

As for the parents, Klein urged them to keep in mind that this was just the first year. "What I would say to people is, this is the beginning of a process. We put this in place, we got to start somewhere," he said. "And I, at least, would focus on how you use the information to move people forward. So in a school that people think . . . is a good school because it has level threes and level fours, which is the way you measure, that tells you about the students at the school. It doesn't tell you what the school does for students."

But that new measurement wasn't going down so well with the public, or with some educators.

Middle School 232 in the Bronx got a C on its progress report. That might sound pretty good for a school where only 25 percent of the students were reading at grade level. But Principal Neifi Acosta didn't think the grade was an accurate reflection of the school's improvement. His team had reduced the number of level 1 students—those with the lowest reading levels—from 21 percent to about 13 percent, and he thought the school would have earned a B if he'd gotten more support from his teachers.

The school's environment counted for 15 percent of its grade, but it earned only one out of those fifteen points. The environment survey consisted of multiple-choice forms that were filled out by teachers, students, and parents. Only nine teachers bothered to respond—just 17 percent of the staff. When asked if their principal was "an effective manager who makes the school run smoothly," all nine teachers said they "strongly disagree" with that statement. They also checked off boxes saying they didn't trust him, and didn't think he placed the needs of children ahead of other interests.

Principal Acosta and his allies believe those low marks were a retaliatory strike. He had gotten rid of at least twenty teachers in his brief year and a half at MS 232. "It was totally wrong," says the eighth-grade literacy teacher Anna Maley. "A lot of teachers [sent] text messages all day; they didn't care about kids. Mr. Acosta said the kids need to learn."

City parents were also anxious about the new scoring system. Their questions were simple: How could good schools with solid reputations get C's and D's? And how could failing schools earn A's and B's? MS 232 was in danger of being shut down by the state, and it still earned a passable C. The concept of "progress" wasn't easy to explain. Principals at struggling schools that got good marks were delighted to see their efforts vindicated under the new definition of progress. But many parents at high-performing schools didn't think it was fair. They thought the system penalized schools where there arguably wasn't much room for improvement. In some neighborhoods, people even worried that low grades could have an impact on real estate prices.

One night a few days after Thanksgiving, Liebman personally took the heat when he appeared before the Community Education Council for District 2 in Manhattan. District 2 had long been known for having some of the best schools in the city. Liebman had even praised its innovation in his essay about the "public laboratory Dewey barely imagined." The district's neighborhoods include the wealthy Upper East Side as well as the more fashionable TriBeCa in Lower Manhattan—home to the now infamous IS 289, the high-scoring school that earned a D. Liebman came equipped with a slide show similar to the one he had presented to the reporters a few weeks earlier. Like a lawyer preparing for court, he also made sure to include a breakdown of the scores for IS 289 and a comparable middle school.

About thirty parents, most of them white, attended the meeting near Gramercy Park. It was in the auditorium of a small high school called the School of the Future—which had gotten a B. The council members sat onstage at a long table. They have no real authority but they do serve as something like a local sounding board, and on this evening they were getting an earful.

One panel member, Michael Markowitz, told Liebman that he was concerned that the city had created a "muddle of speed and acceleration." He said the formula for the progress reports penalized schools that had big gains one year that weren't replicated the next. "We have a high percentage of schools where the kids are doing well," he said. "But if they did a little bit better last year, they're getting creamed" on the progress reports, he stated. The audience applauded with enthusiasm.

Liebman, who is about five foot four, paced quietly while listening to the argument. Then he took the microphone and stood in front of the auditorium. "There's a lot I actually agree with," he said, in a concession to his opponent. "But I don't agree with the 'muddle.'" He then proceeded to explain how the system would eventually include three years' worth of data on every school, so the risk of big fluctuations from one year to the next wouldn't be such a problem. Then, just like a law professor, Liebman told Markowitz why "the main point you got an applause on was not correct."

He asked his assistant to pull out the charts for IS 289 in TriBeCa and MS 243, on West Seventieth Street in another upscale neighborhood. Both schools had earned a D even though between 80 and 90 percent of their students were performing at or above the state standards. These figures were displayed on a green row labeled "student performance." Liebman pointed to the next section for student progress to highlight the problem. Only 40 percent of the students at IS 289 had made a year's worth of progress on literacy and just 42 percent had gone up a year in math. The percentages were even lower at the uptown middle school, where just about two thirds of students were making a year's worth of progress in literacy. These schools were both doing a poor job compared to others, said Liebman. "You can look and see other schools with fifty, sixty percent or as many as seventy percent making a year's progress in math," he told the parents. "What that shows, among other things, is there is no ceiling." Even at good schools like these, he argued, there is still a lot of room for every child to make improvements.

Then Liebman pointed to the numbers he considered even more important: the scores for children who were performing in the lowest third. At IS 289, the average child in that category actually lost ground in math and reading by a measurable tenth of a percentage point when the city broke down the state's scoring system. In comparable schools, the average scores were going up. "Finally," Liebman said, clearing his throat as he got to his summary, "most parents would like their kids to go to schools where other kids are doing really well." He told the audience that most of them could probably identify four or five schools in their district that are good. But with this new rating system, they'd be able to see which of those schools were moving children forward and which were not.

The parents were respectful but several raised their hands to speak. They weren't buying it. Two women with children at PS 150 in TriBeCa took the microphone. They described how between 91 and 98 percent of the elementary school's students were meeting or exceeding the math and reading standards, and yet their school only earned a C. "We're an extremely small school," one said, with fewer than two hundred students. They didn't think there were enough low-performing or special education students for the school to earn extra credit by lifting their scores. Did that wind up penalizing the school? "We're vibrant and inclusive," one said, but the letter grade was "demoralizing and dispiriting." Another parent from PS 150, Mitchell Cohen, asked Liebman if the city was "trying to be sensational" by giving good schools low marks.

Liebman encouraged the parents to view the progress reports as a success because they had generated so much discussion. "The purpose of the progress reports is to get parents and other people around schools to ask, 'Why did this school get this grade?'" he said. Maybe they would see some strengths and weaknesses, or groups of students who were benefiting while others remained stagnant. He then shifted gears, acknowledging that the real question on the minds of many was "Why grade schools?" He called that a fair question and one the Department of Education had thought about very hard. But he concluded that grades could serve as an agent for change. To those who saw the progress reports as a cynical tool for pitting schools against one another, Liebman said they should think about those children "who are performing in the lowest third when other schools are moving those children forward.

"From my perspective the idea is to really put those children first, those children who don't have parents like you," he told the auditorium.

But the parents still had concerns about the validity of putting so much weight on test scores. The principal of the high school hosting this community forum was bubbling over with frustration. With 85 percent of a school's grade determined solely by math and reading tests, Stacy Goldstein worried that instruction would become entirely test-focused with no real room for learning. And she said students in the twenty-first century needed a variety of skills that weren't all measured by these statewide exams. "I'm very scared about what will happen to the New York City schools," she exclaimed, to another round of applause. Liebman urged her to see her own school as a sign of success, because the School of the Future raised performance levels among its lowest third without sacrificing its values. But he insisted that standardized tests were the only way to consistently measure performance, adding, "Don't let the perfect be the enemy of the good."

After about an hour of questioning, Liebman and his assistant, Phil Vaccaro, packed up their equipment and walked out of the auditorium. Liebman zipped a lightweight winter jacket over his shirt and tie, and then pushed the puffy sleeves into his suit jacket. Vaccaro stood watching as Liebman continued fielding questions from parents who had followed him into the hallway. Like many of the members of Liebman's accountability team, Vaccaro had an Ivy League degree and a commitment to public education. He had graduated from Harvard and then worked in banking before becoming a high school math teacher in the Bronx. He was impressed at the way his boss handled the parents with the same respect and patience he had shown inside the auditorium.

As they left, Liebman admitted it was a tough crowd. In other districts, he said, parents who were unhappy about the public education system wanted to know why more schools didn't get an F. But here, they were outraged over getting C's and D's even though their schools were high performing. The conversation he wanted to generate about public education's commitment to every child had clearly begun. Had a child like Yamilka arrived in the United States in 2007 instead of in 1993, he argued, she might have gotten more help because her lack of progress would contribute to her school's grade—giving her principal an incentive to make sure she got the special services she needed to learn how to read.

NINE

Dropping Out

The High School of Graphic Communication Arts, where Antonio was enrolled, earned a C on its progress report. Less than a third of its students were graduating in four years and its attendance rate was 72.5 percent. The school had gotten extra points for raising the scores of students in the bottom third, but it hadn't done very much to help its special ed scores or those of its English Language Learners.

In a grading system like this, students such as Antonio are a principal's biggest headache. Technically, he hadn't officially dropped out or transferred. He just stopped coming to class, hurting the school's attendance record. He racked up only a few credits. And he hadn't taken his Regents exams last year. However, he still had a right to attend the school because he was under the age of twenty-one. And the school was obligated to try to help him—if he bothered to show up.

But Antonio spent the fall much as he had spent the summer. He hung out at home, surfing the Internet. The computer class he took at Graphics got him acquainted with websites, which he was able to read after progressing to a fourth-grade level through his tutoring at Lindamood-Bell. Soon he figured out how to become "friends" on MySpace with rock bands he liked, and with kids from Washington Heights. Antonio tried to express himself by writing. Not all his rap songs were about heartbreak, like the one he had written after consulting his friend Juan. Something else was on his mind lately. This song is called "Immigrants":

I am the young voice of the blacks and Spanish people
Let me tell you a story about a place called Washington Heights
So people hear my words out carefully

I am not black but this still goes out to them
People come to America to work hard for some day their kids won't work that hard
And hope they buy them a house to retired
Some are immigrents some are not, we see them all the time in fast food places working 50 dollars a day a nine hour shift
They just dying to get home and hit that bed is the only thing every one of them have in commen
Some don't complane about their slavery because some thinks is worthed some day

Antonio said he worked on the song for about a day. There were only five spelling errors (not counting misused words) on the sheet of notebook paper he showed me. He took his time writing and then rewriting it to get everything correct. Some of it came from personal experience. He once worked as a dishwasher in a Latin restaurant on Broadway near 166th Street, where he saw immigrants making fifty dollars for nine-hour shifts. He didn't want to wind up like them. The song is also an homage to one of Antonio's favorite rock stars, Mike Shinoda of the bands Linkin Park and Fort Minor. Shinoda wrote a rap called "Kenji" about his grandfather's experience during World War II, as a Japanese-American who was sent to an internment camp and lost everything. Antonio loved Shinoda's reimagining of what the injustice must have been like. His lyrics to "Immigrants" follow the same beat, and he said he wanted to write a few lines imagining his own grandfather's life in the Dominican Republic. He has hazy memories of visiting as a child, and recalls seeing the young shoeshine boys scrounging for cash, knocking on the door of his grandfather's house looking for food. His family in New York certainly wasn't wealthy, but that trip was his first taste of real poverty.

Antonio knew it was tough out there for immigrants. He'd seen Hispanic day laborers near his parents' house in New Jersey and felt that he could relate to them because his parents also had come here for a better life, but "the system failed," he said, referring to what happened to him in school. Antonio had been looking for work as a messenger or a dishwasher during the fall but he still didn't have a state ID card. There was some disagreement between Antonio and his mom over who had which paperwork.

Despite his sympathies with immigrants, Antonio refuses to identify as Dominican. He feels no affinity with the Dominican Republic. When asked to describe himself, he'll say he's Dominican, Puerto Rican, and Italian—a reference to the mixed blood on his father's side. "My parents are Dominican," he said. "I'm American." As far as he's concerned, he grew up at his aunt's old restaurant downtown on West Seventeenth Street—not Washington Heights. His mother worked at the restaurant when he was little and brought him there on a regular basis. He heard English and Spanish but said he didn't want to be speaking Spanish. And even though he was placed in bilingual classes as a child, he insisted, "I would only speak Spanish to get by, to communicate with people."

When his friend Juan heard Antonio say that he wasn't Dominican, Juan told him that was messed up. "I think you should be proud of what you are," he said. Juan is also the son of Dominican immigrants.

"I was raised on Seventeenth Street in English," Antonio tried to explain to Juan. "I'm not like—I don't know how to dance."

"I learned how to dance at a late age," Juan retorted. "And I learned how to speak Spanish at a late age. Now I'm proud of being what I am."

"It's just like all the things I went through, all the things I been through," Antonio said, pausing. "Like I wish I was white," he finally confessed. "I was trying to be white, you know. I was trying to be American. Like I was trying to, you know like, always trying to get into . . . get by. I was always trying to beat the system, try to overcome it."

Juan cut him off. "You're never going to beat the system," he said. Antonio tried to jump back in with a retort. "No, you're not," Juan warned him. "You could be white, black, you're not going to beat the system."

Antonio's aunt Sely now runs another restaurant in Chelsea, not too far from her old one on Seventeenth Street, which closed. Soon after Thanksgiving, she hired Antonio to make deliveries and wash dishes. He got a ride into Manhattan with his parents each morning and evening. Sometimes he took the bus if he was running late.

The Latin American restaurant on West Twenty-sixth Street is like a home away from home for Antonio. Sely watches over her staff like a den mother in a big green apron and a hairnet. She has fond memories of Antonio as a child; her outgoing little nephew would talk to strangers at her old restaurant and ask to help out in the kitchen. She says he was probably around three years old when he first started learning how to peel potatoes and carrots.

Sely is the fifth of ten children—nine daughters and a son who died when he was young. One of her older sisters moved to New York from Santo Domingo and started another Latin restaurant in Chelsea. Sely followed and so did Antonio's mother. Eight of the sisters wound up living in New York.

When Sely first arrived, she was a single mother with a young daughter. She came for the American Dream, she said, and got an apartment in Washington Heights, where she worked in a restaurant. She took English classes for two years and saved up her money until she was able to buy her own restaurant on West Seventeenth Street. Later, when the landlord sold the building, she bought the place on Twenty-sixth Street and she's been in business ever since, serving meat and chicken with rice and beans, and tropical drinks. Late in 2007, Antonio stopped by to ask for a job. She said yes because she wanted him to "stay out of trouble." Sely knew about Antonio's reading problems. She said his mother, Noelia, had dyslexia, too, and didn't learn how to read in school. Nobody knew how to help her at their small school in the countryside. Noelia said she eventually started reading when she went to visit a sister in Caracas and took a class.

At the restaurant, Sely said she'd seen a difference in Antonio's reading since he finished the tutoring program at Lindamood-Bell. "He can do more deliveries, make more money," she explained. There wasn't a lot of reading involved in the deliveries. Just slips of paper with numbers and cross streets, sometimes abbreviated with a B for Broadway. But Antonio could make them out quickly and earned about twenty-five or thirty dollars a day in tips.

Sely's younger daughter, fifteen-year-old Ashley, stopped by the restaurant after school one day and sat down to do her homework. Antonio calls her "the brain." She wore a navy blue Catholic school uniform with a pleated skirt and vest. Antonio got a delivery order and rushed out, clutching a brown paper bag. "Anthony's like a big baby," said Sely, smiling. "He's a big teddy bear," added Ashley.

Ashley calls herself the "surprise" in the family. Her older half sister is fourteen years older and living on her own. Ashley and her mom and stepfather live in New Jersey not far from Antonio's family. Her Catholic school is in Manhattan and she joins her parents every morning on their drive to work. Ashley works hard and earns good grades. She used to help Antonio with his reading when he was in school. She noticed that he was mixing up the letters *b* and *d*, so she would switch them around. "I'd put in a *b* so he would say it right," she said, explaining how she would write the word "side" like "sibe." "I'm not that hard at noticing things!"

But Ashley knew she couldn't help her older cousin very much and felt strange about it, too. "Can you imagine an eight- or ten-year-old helping a twelve-year-old?"

Like her mother, Ashley also noticed a recent improvement in Antonio's reading. She said he was "transformed" and no longer had dyslexia. But she tested her theory that day by writing the word "photosynthesis" on a piece of paper when Antonio returned from his delivery. She asked him to say it.

"Photo . . . sen . . ." he said. He got the first half but struggled with the latter half of the word. "Photo-sensis? Ugh!"

"You see? It's not dyslexia anymore," Ashley proclaimed. "He has problems with big words." Ashley wrote down "synthesis" on a piece of paper and asked her cousin to say it. Antonio said something that sounded like "synsesis," and then tried again with "sin-the-ness."

Ashley said she wished she could make him look at words under a microscope, to see if that made any difference. "You can go on the Internet at Ask.com," Antonio told her.

He pulled out his knapsack to show Ashley what he'd been reading lately. There were four books from the Japanese comic series *Cowboy Bebop*, about a group of intergalactic bounty hunters. He checked the comic books out from the library near Graphics when a friend showed him how to become a member. The drawings are in the manga style—eyes all wide and women with big breasts. Ashley called them sexist. "Why do you read these books?" she asked, noticing how they read from right to left. "They go the wrong way."

Antonio said the books are really cool. He's a fan of the cartoon show on which the comics are based and he said he read them every night and got confused only when he couldn't connect the word bubbles to the right characters. In truth, some of the words were also a little difficult. They referred to space terms and places that don't exist. But Antonio said he was able to follow the stories partly because they are similar to the cartoon versions he's seen and the *Cowboy Bebop* movie. He had a hard time reading the summary on the back of one book that described the upcoming adventure facing the characters:

"Now with more scruples than the rest of their ilk, the gang often find themselves without the cash, and consequently without food on their plates."

Antonio struggled to read this aloud, stumbling on the words "scruples," "ilk," and "consequently." He didn't know what they meant, and Ashley said she'd also never seen the word "ilk."

By working in the restaurant, Antonio said, he was also trying to hide from his past, just like some of the characters in the comic book. He wanted to forget about school, about tutoring, about his problems with the city schools. He'd rather work here for a while, save money, and try being responsible, even though he had no desire to work at a restaurant full-time. "I'm not made for this," he said, stepping out for a cigarette. Again he talked about his dream of going to Iraq, or maybe working in computers, or selling things for a company. He wanted a "real" job. He wanted to pay income taxes.

There was another big reason why Antonio wanted to be responsible. He had recently started dating a girl he knew from high school named Amy. They had become friends the previous spring and kept in touch over the summer by phone and MySpace after she switched to a different school. Antonio wanted to impress her by having a job, since he wasn't going to school. He'd saved up $130 in the past week and a half—though he said it was actually $170 before he blew $40 on meals with Amy.

In the city schools, progress may be something you can measure in test scores and school report cards. But for Antonio, progress was just about reading enough to understand the gist of some Japanese comic books, making a few bucks, and getting a girl to like him. "I feel young," he said. "I know how to kiss now."

WINTER

Learning to Read and Reading to Learn

My son will read and open books, and my son will write and will know writing. And my son will make numbers, and these things will make us free because he will know—he will know and through him we will know. —Kino, *The Pearl* by John Steinbeck

I am sure we missed a couple of Einsteins and Da Vincis out there, a lot of smart kids get lost and never get to show what they're made of. I'm sure we missed a lot of good people. —Alejandro, on the New York City schools

How do we learn to read? It's a simple question, but there are no simple answers. While most people easily learn how to associate those twenty-six letters of the English alphabet with sounds and words, a significant minority is confounded by the squiggles and lines they see on a page and require more intensive help learning to read.

It's often said that students spend their early years learning to read while the rest of their lives are spent reading to learn. That's why the early years are so critical. Educators have spent the past century debating the best methods for teaching children to read.

In this section, we'll see how teachers in New York City's public schools use a reading program called "balanced literacy"—plus various interventions to help struggling students. At the same time, we'll see how those teachers and their principals—already straining under the weight of No Child Left Behind and the standards movement—cope with the Bloomberg administration's efforts to track student achievement with more frequent assessments. We'll also watch as Yamilka, Alejandro, and Antonio each take steps toward becoming more literate and learn more about what's holding them back.

TEN

Behind the Scenes

In the 2007 movie *Freedom Writers*, Hilary Swank plays a young and idealistic (and glamorous) high school teacher named Erin Gruwell who transforms a class of low achievers into successful graduates.

Freedom Writers fits perfectly into the genre of Hollywood movies that portray the teacher as a charismatic agent of change. We know Swank's character is going to succeed from the outset because she's so darn determined. She shows up on the first day of school at Wilson High in downscale Long Beach, California, wearing her huge smile, a classy skirt suit, and a pearl necklace, ignoring an assistant principal who warned her the pearls would be stolen. She learns that some of her ninth-graders are reading at a fifth-grade level. But she insists on teaching them the *Odyssey*—explaining to her supervisor that she chose to become a teacher instead of a lawyer so she could avoid having to represent kids like these later on, after they're arrested.

Of course, Swank's character finds her optimism challenged at every step. There's a boy who doesn't want to be in her class because he knows "it's the dumb class." When she tries to teach the students about Homer, another boy asks her if she's talking about Homer Simpson. There are also deep racial divisions. This is Southern California in 1994—just a few years after the Rodney King verdict and subsequent riots—and Swank's black, Asian, and Hispanic students are embroiled in gang warfare and won't talk to one another. There's a critical scene when Swank discovers that a Hispanic boy is passing around a drawing of a black classmate. His sketch has exaggerated the African-American student's lips and nose. Swank halts her lesson to lecture her students on how the biggest gang in the world did something similar: the Nazis. But as she explains anti-Semitism in Hitler's Germany, she's shocked to realize her students have never heard about the Holocaust.

Newly energized with the mission to teach, she marches to the school library looking for books about the Holocaust. Her cynical supervisor tells her not to bother because the students won't be able to read them, adding, "You can't make someone want an education." Her fellow English teachers ridicule Swank's character again when she decides to teach her students about the Holocaust through *Anne Frank: The Diary of a Young Girl*. She uses the Holocaust to engage her students in a class dialogue about gangs and hatred. She asks them to form two lines facing each other, and for each kid who's lost a friend to step forward. In a dramatic moment, almost every teen takes a step. Swank's character then decides to buy journals for her students to write about their experiences, promising she'll keep the diaries locked in a cabinet and not share them with anyone else. The students gradually start writing essays about their family problems and life on the streets. By writing about their lives and by reading about someone they can relate to—the teenage Anne Frank—the students come to care about school. Swank's character proves her supervisors wrong. She works round the clock, at the expense of her marriage, dedicating herself to the pupils. In the end, they all graduate from high school.

Getting a class of high school students who can read only at a fifth-grade level to finish *Anne Frank* was a big accomplishment. And yet we never saw them learning to read—struggling with the actual words on the page. How did they get through Frank's diary? How did they write their own diaries? And what about the other books and essays required for them to graduate?

Freedom Writers is based on *The Freedom Writers Diary: How a Teacher and 150 Teens Used Writing to Change Themselves and the World Around Them* by Erin Gruwell. I called Gruwell in California, where she now runs the Freedom Writers Foundation, which describes itself as promoting "acceptance and innovative teaching methods" in classrooms all around the United States.

Gruwell is proud of the movie, but she's quick to state, "I didn't write the screenplay," saying that there's only so much one can do in a two-hour film. Given that time limit, she says, the film was bound to simplify how hard it was for her students to master the nuts and bolts of reading and writing. As with most movies about a teacher, we saw Gruwell working with only one class. But she was actually teaching five English classes each semester, with a total of 150 students. Some spoke only Spanish or Cambodian and they were all in trouble academically.

"They were in my class specifically because they weren't at grade level—they scored on the lowest rung of the standardized tests," she explains. She also had some children with special needs and others who she believes should have been placed in special education classes. At least two of her students had dyslexia.

As a new teacher, Gruwell was immediately overwhelmed. "I was there sometimes till eleven at night," she says, working with students individually after school and then going over their work. She divided her students into small groups and practiced what teachers call "cooperative learning and collaboration" to keep them engaged. This involved pairing stronger students with weaker ones and letting them work together, reading each other's papers.

With 150 students, each with his or her own particular problems, Gruwell applied something else she had learned in her teaching courses: she reached out for help. Before taking the job at Wilson High School, Gruwell had gotten her master's in education at California State University in Long Beach, where she had taken a course with Professor Mary-Ellen Vogt on how to work with students who have reading disabilities. "What I tried to get these young teachers to understand was that we have a whole slew of techniques," Vogt explains. For example, teachers can highlight key vocabulary words or topic sentences to keep their students focused while reading, and to improve their comprehension. They can teach students to graphically organize their thoughts before writing a paper. "So if you're teaching the causes leading up to the Civil War, you provide a cause-and-effect organizer, with cause-and-effect boxes," says Vogt, adding that there are now myriad resources like these available on the Web.

Sue Ellen Alpizar came to Gruwell's class during her junior year in high school, after Gruwell had been teaching at Wilson for two years. Her story didn't make it into the movie. She describes herself as a kid who "always tried to be like an A student but I never quite got there." She says she had problems with reading comprehension and spelling and got some speech therapy in elementary school. Her parents both emigrated from Costa Rica, and her mother had very little formal education. One day, her mom spotted a magazine article about dyslexia. Sue Ellen took it to her seventh-grade teacher. "I was like, 'I think this is what I have.' And he looked at it and he was like, 'No, you don't have dyslexia. You don't have a language problem. You're just lazy.'"

In tenth grade, Sue Ellen had some friends at Wilson High who were taking "Ms. G's" English class. They encouraged Sue Ellen to sign up for Gruwell's class the next fall, and she prepared herself for yet another disappointing year, dreading her first writing assignment. "I had this fear of turning it in to her," she recalls. "I was expecting the red pen marks and everything else."

But Ms. G read the paper and didn't criticize it. "Instead she looked up and she was like, 'Do you know what dyslexia is?' I was like, 'I've heard of it, yeah.' She was like, 'I think you might have it.' She was explaining it more. I was like, okay, I'm not freaking crazy. It was this sense of relief."

Gruwell got computers donated to her classroom and let Sue Ellen use a spell-check program when writing. She also made sure Sue Ellen got involved in the class by coming up with creative activities. "I would play silly music, music from *Forrest Gump*. I'd say, 'Write, students, write,'" Gruwell recalls, echoing the movie's "Run, Forrest, run." After these writing exercises, she took special care in breaking her students up into groups so Sue Ellen could benefit. "I'd get students she trusted to sit down with her and ask, 'What were you trying to say?' to take away the fear factor."

Sue Ellen remembers other classroom activities that helped her get over her fears. "A lot of times if we were reading stuff as a group we were 'popcorning,'" she says, using a phrase for taking turns reading aloud quickly. Some educators frown upon this method because it can put struggling kids under huge emotional pressure and set bad models when the other students hear their poor pronunciation and phrasing. But Sue Ellen says, "It helped me follow along and understand comprehension because I could understand the words being read to me, it helped me follow along. Even though it would overwhelm me looking at words on the page. I would use a bookmark or isolate segments to help me out."

Maria Reyes recalls another favorite activity from her former English teacher's class: Froot Loop bingo. Gruwell gave each student a card with vocabulary words and a pile of Froot Loops they were supposed to use if the word she called matched the one on their card. "She would play *Mis-*

sion: Impossible music," says Maria. "She knew all of us were competitive. She'd say, 'Darius has three different bingo boards and you just have one.'" If Gruwell called out the word "confidante," "all of a sudden I'd have to look on one board, the second, and the third," Maria recalls. "I'd just gone over it three different times. This whole time I'm thinking I'm outdoing Darius . . . We always felt we were getting away with mischief and not learning, and all of a sudden these words became part of our vocabulary."

In the movie version of Gruwell's class, the character Eva is based on Maria. She's a tough girl from a gang who comes to school with an ankle monitor for her probation officer. Gruwell says that was all true, but the movie didn't reveal that Eva, or rather Maria, read only at a fourth-grade level. Maria acknowledges she had no interest in school, and didn't do well with authority figures. She'd seen gang violence at an early age and "didn't feel I could learn anything from literature," she explains. "I grew up feeling I'm never going to find myself in books." That was until she read *Anne Frank* in Gruwell's class.

Maria resisted the book at first when it was assigned to the class. She thought she would have nothing in common with a white Jewish girl who loved her father and had a seemingly perfect life in a country so far away. She began reading the book one night just to prove it was a ridiculous assignment. "I was under house arrest, the electricity was turned off like normal. I struggled through every word," she says, because her reading skills had never developed due to her lack of engagement. "I knew that I was not going to be able to relate to this book. And I think that's honestly what pushed me, I struggled through every page. When we went back to class, everything I didn't understand—the whole class went over it. The whole class became that attic, World War II."

It took the class a few months to finish the book. They worked together, learning about history and getting inside the head of each character. Maria remembers the turning point, when she finally related to Anne Frank. "Right before she went into hiding, she has to wear the yellow star, nobody can take it off. It gave me chills when I read that." Maria recalls wondering why she had such a reaction. "I'm not an emotional person. I had to be numb, a lot of us had to be numb to see what we endure each day," as students who were no strangers to crime and violence.

"I connected this yellow star of being the color of my skin, my neighborhood . . . it was things I couldn't help just like she couldn't help being Jewish, that was a big connection for me. She makes this comparison to a bird and how she feels like this bird in a cage and she wishes she could fly away . . . It's from that moment on I felt like, 'Oh, this is my girl.' She lived fifty years before I was even born . . . Ms. G gave us this book and this book was mine and this girl was writing everything for me."

In the movie, Eva angrily confronts Gruwell when she gets to the end of the book and learns of Anne's horrible death. She's so emotional that it seems scripted, hard to believe, like it was made for Hollywood. I asked Maria if the confrontation on-screen was true to life, and she said that it was. "I was devastated, I was like, why would anyone give a book like this . . . I wanted to shake Ms. G. I'd been to so many funerals for family members and my own friends, I never cried [because of] this sense of being tough." But Maria says she cried at the end of that book when Anne writes that she still believes people are good, despite what she's been through.

"Here's a little girl who had every right to hate everyone and be bitter," Maria explains. "I struggle with it so much. The fact that she doesn't make it made it so [much] worse. I cried like I never cried before. I think it connected me to something that died in me. It was that emotion, the value of human life, something I think I had lost before I even read the book."

Maria says finishing the book gave her a new outlook on literature and "the beauty of the English language, and of writing something down. From that book I wanted to read something else. It became this sense of what else haven't I read . . . I wanted to read everything that I didn't read growing up."

Maria and Sue Ellen both graduated from high school and went on to Long Beach Community College. Maria eventually earned an English degree from California State University in Long Beach. During college she worked at a bookstore. She likes the sardonic writer David Sedaris and considers *The Catcher in the Rye* another of her favorite books. She now wants to get a Ph.D. Sue Ellen is still finishing college after what she calls "a long trek," which included taking time off to work. It wasn't until college that she was finally tested and classified as having a learning disability. Both women also now work at Gruwell's Freedom Writers Foundation.

Gruwell left Wilson High School long ago to write her book and to start her foundation. She made an unsuccessful run for Congress, and put together a guide for how to reach struggling students by choosing material they can relate to and encouraging them to write. Teachers from all around the country take part in her Freedom Writers Institute each year, hoping to replicate her success.

Jim Liebman watched the movie *Freedom Writers* during a flight. He knew that being an inspirational and successful teacher isn't as easy as it looks in the movies. With the ARIS network, and more frequent assessments, Liebman believed he was helping New York City's teachers by giving them the ability to collect and monitor more academic data about their students. "In a sense, we're trying to break down the idea that you can only succeed if you happen to be a really gifted, intuitive, inspiring person," he said, quickly adding that he's grateful for teachers like that. "If such teachers come along, what we want to do is find out how to use their know-how and make it explicit enough that they can help other teachers do the same thing. And also break down the idea that teaching and success in the classroom is a very sort of singular, lonely almost, experience where it's an individual with a class. And so it's really—it's about teachers working together to solve problems in schools, organizing themselves around that idea and then collaborating as well.

"All of those movies are about a single individual coming into a situation and making a big difference, and I am quite certain that that happens and it's inspiring, but we want to find ways that the schools allow their teachers to get in that direction."

That winter, as Yamilka, Alejandro, and Antonio all continued working to become more literate, the city's teachers and principals would see whether Liebman's reforms made any difference as they tried to prevent other children from falling through the cracks.

ELEVEN

An Art and a Science

"Teaching Reading Is Rocket Science." That's the title of a 1999 report for the American Federation of Teachers by Dr. Louisa Cook Moats, a consultant on reading interventions and a project director for the National Institute of Child Health and Human Development. Moats concluded: "Although reading is the cornerstone of academic success, a single course in reading methods is often all that is offered most prospective teachers" when they go to college or graduate school.[1] She said the consequences have been disastrous because low reading achievement is often the cause of chronically low-performing schools.

The teaching of reading is often described as both an art and a science. Children have to learn what the researcher and scientist Marilyn Jager Adams called "an abstract and complicated code" of the alphabet "without losing sight of the purpose of reading: comprehension."[2] Those twenty-six figures composed of squiggles and straight lines each correspond to a total of forty-four sounds in the English language, and the words they form may have multiple meanings. Adams described how in Colonial times, the reading materials children encountered in school typically included the Bible or patriotic essays. But as the country's democratic ideals evolved, and printed materials became more widely available, reading took on a broader social value and educators began debating how to teach it.

The mid-nineteenth-century school reformer Horace Mann, who was secretary of the influential Massachusetts Board of Education, believed children should be taught to read whole, meaningful words. He "condemned the alphabet," in the words of the education historian Diane

Ravitch, "claiming it was repulsive and soul-deadening to children."[3] Mann famously described the letters of the alphabet as "skeleton-shaped, bloodless, ghostly apparitions." Other reformers agreed that children should not waste so much of their time learning letters instead of words. That's why twentieth-century reading programs focused heavily on comprehension, or the "look-say" method, as children would look at the words, learn their meanings, and recall them by sight. The "Dick and Jane" books were typical of this approach because early readers were exposed to short, familiar, and repetitive words. Teachers would encourage students to "sound it out," but the books didn't have a well-organized approach to decoding and phonics.

Experts argued over whether the look-say method could work for everyone. Some children are visual learners who have no trouble picking up letter patterns, but others need to hear the different sounds in a word and benefit more from decoding. In 1955, the publication of *Why Johnny Can't Read* by Rudolph Flesch created a sense of crisis that U.S. achievement was lagging because it didn't rely enough on phonics. In her book *Left Back: A Century of Battles Over School Reform*, Diane Ravitch wrote that "Flesch's polemic set off a national debate over literacy," and that several publishers reacted immediately by issuing new reading textbooks that featured phonics.[4] But some reading educators warned that teaching the ABC's would mark a return to rote memorization, and would only bore and alienate children.

In 1961 Jeanne Chall of the Harvard Graduate School of Education was hired by the Carnegie Corporation of New York to settle the raging debate. The United States was caught up in the Cold War, and afraid of losing its educational edge to the Soviet Union. Chall marveled at how the teaching of reading had been widely studied yet remained mysterious and controversial. She hoped to soothe the hysteria over the competing schools of thought with a dispassionate analysis of reading programs. Chall visited schools in the United States, England, and Scotland and discovered that basal readers, or anthology-style textbooks, were considered the norm. She found most U.S. children were being taught to read in a way that emphasized what words looked like and what they meant, as opposed to decoding, or breaking them down into letters and sounds. But contrary to the popular conception, phonics was being taught in a variety of ways. Some schools were even experimenting with an "Initial Teaching

Alphabet," with forty-four characters that corresponded more closely with spoken English, to prepare young children for the real thing. Pupils would begin to read by spelling words completely phonetically, with no capital letters, reading sentences such as "cum on, paul. hit the baull, sed ted."[5] After visiting about three hundred classrooms between 1962 and 1965 and studying countless reports on different types of instruction, Chall wrote in her crisp and clinical tone: "That task was not an easy one. The joys were great, but the frustrations were even greater. The overriding impression was one of strong emotional involvement on the part of authors, reading specialists, teachers, administrators, and, unfortunately, even researchers. Their language was often more characteristic of religion and politics than of science and learning."[6]

Chall's research concluded that phonics, or a code-based emphasis, does produce better reading results—at least until the end of third grade. This early emphasis on learning the shapes and sounds of the letters did give children an edge. But she also said it was a waste of time to keep drilling phonics once a child has learned to recognize in print the words he or she already knows, and Chall was disturbed to see schools using reading materials that still gave basic decoding exercises for upper elementary and even older children.

Chall's commonsense conclusions were generally applauded and the reading wars died down until the 1980s. That was when schools began adopting the "whole language" approach, which was attributed to the educators Frank Smith, of the University of Victoria in British Columbia, and Kenneth Goodman, at the University of Arizona. Whole language is grounded in the belief that children will get excited about reading if they're given creative and stimulating books, as opposed to mind-numbing drills in basic phonics. Students read from whole books instead of the sections of literature found in traditional textbooks. Because little children in whole language classes often make up their own spelling as they figure out how to express themselves, critics assailed the program for having low standards and not putting enough emphasis on phonics.

The approach was common in the 1980s. California adopted whole language throughout its schools, and so did New York City. Esther Friedman, a veteran of the city schools and director of academic intervention services under Chancellor Klein, recalled that teachers were discouraged from using the word "phonics" during the 1980s. "You were called a phonicator," she said archly. Friedman thought whole language had some nice features but it didn't include enough emphasis on one of the main pillars of reading: decoding, which enables students to become automatic readers. Too many children weren't naturally good readers and got stuck trying to break down a word. The creative books and writing projects that made whole language so celebrated were useless if the child didn't master these basics.

In the 1990s, the state of California abruptly abandoned whole language after its test scores went down. In New York City, then-chancellor Rudy Crew introduced a back-to-basics program called Success for All in a few dozen failing schools. Teachers used color-coded lesson plans, and broke their classes down into groups according to reading ability. Some even used egg timers to follow the scripted program and make sure they didn't spend too long on a particular task. Reading scores went up in these schools. But the city never had a unified curriculum. More than a thousand schools were trying many different things, depending on the philosophy of their principal or local district superintendent. In Antonio's school district in Washington Heights, some educators went out on a limb and promoted phonics for classes of struggling readers. Ironically, however, a former educator at Antonio's old middle school says he wouldn't have been exposed to the program because it wasn't offered to children like him who were classified (correctly or incorrectly) as mentally retarded.

So why did the reading wars persist as the debate shifted to whole language versus phonics? Why do so many scholars continue to feud with the religious fervor Chall described? The answer undoubtedly lies in the enormous trust, and funding, we place in our public schools. If we're going to spend billions of dollars on something, we want to make sure our money is well spent. And if we're going to experiment on our children, that experiment had better work out to their benefit.

But the debate is also grounded in the simple fact that not every child learns the same way. Many experts believe that up to 75 to 80 percent of children will learn how to read no matter what kind of teaching method is used in their schools. But that leaves some 20 to 25 percent who won't. Most of those students will have "garden variety reading problems." They might have different learning styles that don't respond well to whatever reading program their teacher uses, or mild learning disabilities. The University of Michigan education professor Karen Wixson is among many experts who suspect that fewer than 5 percent of children have "hard-wiring problems where it's extremely difficult to learn how to read." Yamilka, Alejandro, and Antonio are probably all in that group.

These experts are convinced that almost every child *can* learn to read in a regular classroom with appropriate instruction. But fifty years after Chall's book was published, we still haven't figured out how to teach them. Twenty-six percent of eighth-graders and a third of fourth-graders were reading at the lowest levels on the National Assessment of Educational Progress in 2007, putting them way below grade level. Our children's reading levels lag behind those of developed nations in Europe and Asia. The Russian Federation, Singapore, and Bulgaria had greater percentages of students performing at the highest achievement level on the 2006 Progress in International Reading Literacy Survey, which looked at fourth-grade reading performance in forty countries. Nineteen percent of students in those three countries read at the "advanced" level, compared with 12 percent of U.S. children. Forty-seven percent of U.S. fourth-graders met the survey's next-highest reading level, but that was several points below Canada, Denmark, and Germany, and it was a decline since the survey taken four years earlier. Those results might not be as grim as they look, cautions Michael Feuer, executive director of the Division of Behavioral and Social Sciences and Education of the National Research Council of the National Academy of Sciences. That's because the United States uses the National Assessment of Educational Progress, which educators and testing experts consider especially rigorous.

"I don't think any of us have a very good sense, proportionally, of how reading is taught," says Professor Wixson of the University of Michigan. Wixson and UM's education school have been contracted by the International Reading Association to participate in the first comprehensive survey since Chall's groundbreaking book of how reading is taught. Unlike Chall, their "Description of Reading Instruction Study" is aiming for a nationally representative sample. But Wixson can't really answer the question "How is reading taught in the United States?" Schools "pick and choose among a variety of methods and materials, those things they think will help kids do better on tests," she says. However, she believes most big cities do choose a core curriculum with an anthology and other materials from one main publisher. Urban districts often prefer this consistency because they have lots of new teachers who need help with their craft, and because their students frequently move.

Undoubtedly, the greatest influence on reading curricula in the past decade was the No Child Left Behind law. It was enacted soon after an influential 2000 report by the National Reading Panel. This panel was commissioned by Congress during the Clinton administration to look at the latest reading research and the effectiveness of different instructional methods. Its report concluded that phonemic awareness—or teaching children to focus on and manipulate the different sounds in words—significantly improves their reading more than instruction without phonics. It also found that teaching phonics, systematically, to students in kindergarten through sixth grade had a "positive and significant effect" on the skills of disabled readers. And phonics helped older children with their decoding and spelling, though it didn't significantly improve their reading comprehension.[7]

By 2002 President George W. Bush's administration had made scientifically based reading instruction a condition of federal funding in the No Child Left Behind Act. A new program called Reading First gave states grants to help struggling students, so long as they incorporated recommendations of the National Reading Panel. This meant choosing reading programs that emphasized five pillars: phonemic awareness, phonics, fluency, vocabulary, and comprehension. Schools and districts in Illinois, Kentucky, Massachusetts, Maine, and New Jersey whose programs didn't stress these elements enough were either rejected for grants or pressured to change their methods to qualify for Reading First grants.[8] News reports soon disclosed that districts were pressured to use certain textbook publishers that had actually paid consultants to the federal government to push their products, an obvious conflict of interest. Madison, Wisconsin, refused to accept the federally sponsored textbooks.

This is why New York City was seen as going out on a limb in 2003. Although about fifty of the city's Reading First schools accepted textbooks favored by the federal government, hundreds of other schools risked losing their Title 1 funds, which are given to schools with high concentrations of students in poverty, because the city didn't choose a reading program based on the government's definition of scientific research. Some former school officials acknowledge there was tremendous pressure by the state to use a program called Open Court, which was used in Los Angeles. Open Court is among a number of tightly scripted reading programs with daily pacing plans for classroom reading and phonics instruction. Some educators prefer it because it's easy to teach, or "teacherproof." But the Bloomberg administration had its own ideas. Chancellor Klein and his then–deputy chancellor for instruction, Diana Lam, were impressed by the reading scores of schools in Manhattan and parts of Brooklyn that were using an approach called balanced literacy.

Balanced literacy isn't a curriculum but a way of teaching that was developed in the 1990s following the reading wars between whole language and phonics.* The approach gets its name because it encourages teachers to use phonics in the early grades, while also using "authentic literature" (whole books) instead of selections from anthologies. Classes are conducted in a "workshop model," with a short "mini-lesson" on a particular reading strategy followed by several activities. These include reading together in a big group, guided reading—in which the teacher models a technique for a small group—and independent reading and writing. Making time for independent reading is an essential component to encourage a love of reading and to improve fluency. "A premise of our work is matching kids to books they can read," explains Lucy Calkins, a balanced literacy proponent and professor of children's literature at Columbia University's Teachers College. "They might not do that in middle school. They'll read *The Catcher in the Rye* whether they can do it or not." Students still read these classics and other books as a whole class. But they also read books that are matched to their own levels, so their eyes won't glaze over if the material is too difficult or boring. The program is considered "assessment-driven" because teachers are continually tracking their students' progress.

Teachers College, or TC, is a prominent vendor of balanced literacy materials in New York City. About three hundred city schools (and hundreds more around the United States) buy their professional development and lesson plans from TC, including PS 19 in Manhattan's East Village. PS 19 is a pre-kindergarten to fifth grade school located geographically and psychologically between the housing projects of Alphabet

*Balanced literacy is widely seen as being based on the principles of the New Zealand educator Marie Clay, who founded the Reading Recovery intervention program for young children. Clay is also considered a proponent of the whole language approach.

City, a few blocks east, and the middle-income apartment buildings of Stuyvesant Town, a few blocks north.

Alphabet City, like much of the Lower East Side and the East Village, was once populated by a mixture of low-income Puerto Ricans, blacks, whites, drug dealers, college students, artists, and ordinary middle-class people. Squatters took over abandoned buildings and creatively installed electricity, gas, and plumbing during the 1970s and early 1980s. Their bohemian lifestyle, and the spread of AIDS, inspired the Broadway musical *Rent*. But the entire area had already changed by the time *Rent* first opened Off-Broadway in 1996. The drop in crime, the real estate boom, and the development-friendly policies of mayors Giuliani and Bloomberg led to waves of gentrification that altered the look of the city. Glassy condominiums and a Whole Foods supermarket sprang up on blocks that had been littered with intravenous needles. In late 2006, Stuyvesant Town—the gigantic middle-class complex that was originally built for returning World War II veterans—was sold for $5.4 billion to the real estate giant Tishman Speyer, in a deal brokered by Mayor Bloomberg himself. Rents soon were raised to more than three thousand dollars for one-bedroom units. It was a fatal blow to a vibrant, largely middle-class community.

All of this new wealth, though, didn't rub off on PS 19. Almost two thirds of the students were poor enough to qualify for free or reduced lunch in the 2007/08 school year. Most were black, Hispanic, or Asian, with a declining proportion of white children, who accounted for 6 percent of the student body. The school didn't have a strong enough reputation to attract the upper-middle-class families who had moved to the neighborhood. And some were wary because the building also housed a middle school. One teacher at PS 19 described how obviously prosperous parents visit the school, take a look at the classes, and tell her they don't want their child to be the only white kid. For their part, some parents have said they called the school again and again and never heard back.

With middle-class parents pursuing other options and rising rents forcing out many low-income families, the population of PS 19 shrank to 334 students. Principal Ivan Kushner says that's half as many as when he started running the school in 1991. Though Chancellor Klein was recruiting and training new principals with a privately funded Leadership Academy, and lots of principals were taking new roles in the Bloomberg era's ever-shifting Department of Education, there were still some veterans like Kushner who'd stayed at their schools—either by choice or because they were passed over for promotion. In November 2007, Kushner was thrilled when the chancellor and the mayor chose PS 19 as the site for a major press conference announcing the new school report cards. PS 19 earned a B, which was seen as a coup for the little school, since a lackluster 56 percent of its students were meeting state reading standards, while 72 percent were hitting the marks for math. Kushner keeps a giant cardboard version of the report card from that press conference on the wall of his office.

Kushner started teaching in the 1970s and remembers what things were like before the Bloomberg administration discouraged the basal reading textbooks. "For the most part it was one-size-fits-all," he says. "They'd all read the same book and kids who didn't get it had a hard time, while others were way ahead and bored. Those in the midlevel did well." When children did read whole books such as *Charlie and the Chocolate Factory*, he says not every child was ready. Kushner prefers balanced literacy, and says he enjoys working with Teachers College.

In mid-January 2008, the TC staff developer Christine Holley came to check on the school's reading teachers. Holley has been with TC for five years; she was previously a first-grade teacher in Chinatown. She helps schools from Seattle to Milwaukee to Boston to Florida use TC's balanced literacy materials, and says teachers have similar problems wherever she goes. "They all feel frustrated with kids coming in far below [grade level]. They don't know what to do to meet their needs, they're overwhelmed."

Holley helps teachers figure out how to pinpoint what every child needs to become a better reader. She's blond and friendly, and comes across as a straight shooter. She's been to PS 19 many times before. On this day she meets with the literacy coach Corinne Nieves to observe a handful of classes following the Teachers College approach. They walk through the halls and pass a pre-kindergarten classroom where a teacher says her students are now identifying letters and learning basic concepts about print. Letters of the alphabet are posted and students have been pointing to pictures and words in their early reader books. The children are encouraged to make their own stories by drawing pictures and adding a few letters whenever possible. One child drew a picture of a mother and wrote some random letters on the page. This pre-kindergarten class's work is displayed in the hallway with a sign that reads "I am an author."

The kindergarten teacher Stefanie Della Rocca's students are further along. They just started using early reading books that tell stories with pictures. They also practice writing short sentences by copying models their teacher has written on a big pad of paper on an easel. Della Rocca wrote the words "I like to eat pizza" for her students to riff from. A boy wrote "I like to et pic." Della Rocca says spelling errors are expected at this age and constant corrections would get in the way. She does teach the students proper spelling when they work as a group.

There are sixteen students sitting on Della Rocca's carpet when Holley enters to give her own mini-lesson. The class reflects the nonwhite population of this multiethnic neighborhood: mostly black, Hispanic, and Asian students. Some poke at each other and squirm. Two girls are comparing necklaces and a couple of boys in the front row clap. Holley sits down in a chair next to the teacher and says, "You know what, readers? This is such an exciting time. You're starting to read words in your books!" In balanced literacy, students are often referred to as "readers."

Holley tells the kindergarten class about how they'll sometimes come to words they don't know. One way to deal with this, she says, is to check the picture on the page to get a clue about what it means. She shows them a big book called *I Love My Family*. It has a picture of a family at a wedding. Holley tells the students to think about the people in the pictures. "Who are they?" The students make their guesses and shout out "mother," "father," and "grandmother." Holley opens the book to a page with a drawing of a man with a mustache. The caption reads "I love my father," but she covers the word "father" with a Post-it note. She asks the students to think about who this man could be, and what makes sense. After they guess, she reveals that it's the father.

She does the same with another page that shows a woman at a piano. "Who do you think it is?" she asks. The students yell out "mother" and "grandmother." "Okay, readers," she says. "Some of you said you thought it was the mother. If it's the mother, what letter do we see in the beginning?" A few students shout "m." She asks what they'll see if it's the grandmother. A couple of students say "r." Holley tells them that they'll actually see the letters *g* and *r*, and pulls off a Post-it note to reveal "mother." One kid yells out "mommy" and Holley gently corrects her, saying "mother."

Children have to learn to read before they can read to learn. Balanced literacy doesn't see a stark dividing line, however. Exercises like these emphasize the meaning of words and stories in addition to the breaking of the code. The shared instruction time with Holley is followed by an activity. The students take seats on the floor or at desks, each with a reading partner. The Teachers College approach is among many programs that use a classroom library with a leveling system in which books are grouped according to letters of the alphabet. Books classed as A's and B's and other letters closer to the beginning of the alphabet are easier to read than those near the end.* Teachers track their students' progress by noting what books they're reading. Even kindergarten children are at all different stages, with some reading many words, or recognizing them by sight, while others are still sounding out the letters. In this class, each child has a plastic bag of books labeled with his or her name, which are used for today's activity.

Two kindergarten teachers from other classes have come to observe Holley's teaching lesson, and she gives them a worksheet showing what she looks for during a reading exercise. The list includes early reading steps, such as reading from left to right, using illustrations for information, using letters, and automatically reading some known words. Holley uses this checklist as she approaches a boy and a girl on the rug closest to the front of the room. The girl has a book called *Where's Tim?* It's about a boy whose family is looking for him in the house, and it's got drawings of every room. Holley reads along with the girl: "Is he in the kitchen? Is he under the table?" The girl looks at the pictures of different rooms and puts her finger under each word. The classroom teacher, Della Rocca, comes over to help hold the book as Holley shows the girl how to read with her finger, saying each word as she points instead of just rushing the finger across the page. The girl copies her. "Is he in the bathroom? No. Is he under the stairs?" Holley tells the girl to check the picture to make sure that what she's reading makes sense. The character Tim is shown on the last page sleeping in his room. Holley asks the girl to summarize what the book was about. The girl recounts that Tim's father looked for him in the kitchen and bathroom and under the stairs. Holley then asks her to go to a page and show her the words "the" and "is." The girl points to them, mouthing the words. Satisfied that the girl is making good progress with early reading, Holley moves on to another group.

*The leveling system is attributed to the educators Irene Fountas and Gay Su Pinnell, who created a systematic approach to small-group reading instruction in 1996 with their book *Guided Reading: Good First Teaching for All Children* (Portsmouth, N.H.: Heinemann).

She stops at a table where two boys read to each other. One has already been identified as slightly behind where he should be for his age. He's rapidly moving his finger across the words in a book about animals, and it's clear that he's going too fast to actually read anything; his comprehension will surely suffer. Holley asks him what each animal can do. This forces him to stop and look at each page, taking more time. He tells her that camels can run and birds can fly. His kindergarten teacher asks Holley for advice on how to help this child, and Holley tells her to do what she just did: ask him more questions about what's happening in a story. She explains that he needs to understand each word before he can move on to harder books. "He reads all the words perfectly but doesn't think about what he's reading," she tells the teacher. "People get fooled and think they're reading unless you ask them questions."

Mistakes are common as children learn how to read, but they can also be signs of a problem sounding out letters. That's why teachers need to pay attention to every child and provide appropriate help during independent reading time. Schools in the Teachers College program keep formal "running records" of their students' reading progress. Along with checking which books a child is reading, kindergarten and first-grade teachers will track children's knowledge of letters and sounds. And they'll ask questions to determine whether a student has problems with comprehension or fluency. On another visit to PS 19 in January, the fourth-grade teacher Diane Roach sat at her desk, facing a girl with a brown ponytail holding a book called *Mountain Bike Mania*. She took notes while the girl read aloud and then asked her a few key questions, such as what the character saw in a store window.

Teachers College has long had a close relationship with the New York City public schools. It's the nation's oldest and largest graduate school of education. It opened downtown in the late 1880s as the New York School for the Training of Teachers. The philosopher Nicholas Murray Butler and the philanthropist Grace Hoadley Dodge wanted to provide a new kind of schooling for teachers of poor city children, what TC's website calls "one that combined a humanitarian concern to help others with a scientific approach to human development." It eventually moved to Columbia University, where it became a leader in the progressive education movement. John Dewey joined the faculty, and an aphorism of his is painted on the wall of the main entrance: "I believe that education is the fundamental method of social progress and reform." Today, TC's five-thousand-plus graduate students come from all over the world and work as student teachers throughout the metropolitan area, mostly in the New York City public schools. The city requires its teachers to obtain a master's degree within five years of taking a job, in addition to state certification, so many new teachers enroll in Teachers College and other graduate schools for education such as Bank Street College or the City University of New York.

Teachers College students attend classes in a separate campus of stately redbrick buildings on the northern edge of Columbia's main campus. Because they work in schools during the day, they often attend early evening classes. One of the college's most well-known and respected professors is Lucy Calkins, the founder of the Reading and Writing Project. She's a petite, impassioned speaker who can command a classroom of graduate students while perched on a desk. "You do need to be someone who models a passionate love of literacy and who is so incredibly excited about reading, and you can't imagine the kids don't feel the same way," she tells her young teachers. "It's to be the inspirational leader that rallies people to a cause that's huge, that's important. The cause in the teaching of reading is falling in love with books."

Calkins's own classroom resembles a balanced literacy class. Her twenty-three graduate students, all women, sit in clusters at black tables, not rows. Calkins has chin-length blond hair, which is pushed back by the glasses atop her head. She wears a white shirt with a red V-neck sweater and a black vest over black pants. She leads the class in a Socratic give-and-take, asking them questions about the lessons they've designed as student teachers.

Lauren Korsh, who was teaching sixth-graders on Long Island, describes how she got her class to focus on realistic fiction by using the metaphor of the journey. She thought middle school students would be able to relate to this type of literature. "It's a really critical year in terms of students figuring out what they want to be and where they fit into the school population: what kind of friends they want, what kind of student they want to be. With literature you can effect change. That's how I came up with the idea of internal and external journeys for characters; it provided an opportunity for readers as sixth-graders to think about their own journeys." Korsh hands out a paper describing a "social issues book club" and the read-alouds, or mini-lessons, a teacher could do with each class from books including *The Black Snowman* by Phil Mendez and *Freedom Summer* by Deborah Wiles. There are samples of student writing.

Calkins encourages frequent revising and rewriting. She believes children will become better readers if they learn to write, and take ownership of their work. And the only way to improve is through practice. She tells her class of teachers that in order for children to make a year's worth of progress, they need to read two hours a day. "I still don't know if it's possible, but that's what the research says," she says, warning her graduate students that fancy lessons don't matter if the children don't have time to read in class.

The Teachers College Reading and Writing Program receives several million dollars a year from the city for its staff development and books. It's one of many providers of balanced literacy services that are used in New York and throughout the nation. Another is AUSSIE, the Australian United States Services in Education program. Australia ranks very high on international surveys of literacy, and the nation has a long tradition of using the reading and writing techniques associated with whole language. Balanced literacy programs are found throughout the country, in Tucson, Arizona; Austin, Texas; and South Orange-Maplewood, New Jersey, as well as in Kentucky, Florida, and Missouri. Nonetheless, Calkins's prominence made her a lightning rod when the Bloomberg administration chose balanced literacy as its primary approach to reading in early 2003. Sol Stern, a senior fellow at the economically conservative think tank the Manhattan Institute, wrote an article predicting Calkins's growing influence over the schools:

"Her 'writing-process' approach to teaching writing in elementary and middle schools is based on the romantic idea that all young children are 'natural writers' and should be encouraged to start scribbling in journals and rewriting composition drafts without worrying (or being taught much) about formal grammar or spelling. 'Writing process' encompasses two of progressive education's key commandments—that teachers must not 'drill and kill' and that children can 'construct their own knowledge.' The underlying assumption, inspired by theorists going back as far as Rousseau, is that traditional schooling is an oppressive institution, suffocating the natural talents and expressiveness of children."[9]

Stern is one of several critics who believe children need much more explicit instruction when learning to read, such as the Success for All program used by former chancellor Rudy Crew.

Chancellor Klein's team had hoped to quell the debate over balanced literacy by selecting a separate program called Month-by-Month Phonics for elementary schools. But that, too, came under attack when a researcher at the National Institute of Child Health and Human Development claimed there was no scientific evidence that Month-by-Month Phonics is effective with students who struggle academically.[10] The Bloomberg administration was apparently rattled enough to give schools an *additional* phonics program to ensure the city's receipt of federal funding.

Balanced literacy still has its foes. The reading expert Louisa Cook Moats has stated that it's just another term for whole language, which she sees as especially harmful for "those children who depend the most on valid and effective instruction in school, including minority, low-income, immigrant, and inner city children."[11] She later singled out New York City and other districts, including Denver, describing how the workshops and short lessons of balanced literacy don't provide enough instruction in grammar and phonics.

Many teachers have also complained about feeling restricted by the short mini-lessons of balanced literacy. My friend Jen Goldsmith found the approach way too limiting when she taught fourth grade in Boston's low-income neighborhood of Mission Hill. She said her students needed more instructional time because they were so far behind in their reading levels. She recalls being scolded for spending fifteen minutes instead of ten on a grammar lesson, even though she deliberately let the lesson go overtime because the students enjoyed correcting written mistakes. Spelling lessons were discouraged. And she found the forty-five-minute reading and writing blocks were tilted too heavily toward personal essays and fiction. "Even the approach to nonfiction was of this strange self-absorbed method," she said. "Write what you know—don't try to learn anything. Examples I was given: writing about braiding hair or taking care of siblings. No room for curiosity or expanding knowledge . . . This felt like the Tuskegee experiments to me. Deny black and Hispanic kids the chance to learn as if they didn't deserve it, and pretend this was giving them the best education they do deserve." Meanwhile, third-graders at her sons' public school in the wealthy neighborhood of Brookline, just a few miles away, wrote poems, travel brochures, songs, personal stories, and letters to the U.S. president.

This is why debates about reading are often really about the best ways to help children overcome poverty and the legacy of racism. When researchers call for more direct instruction in urban classrooms, they're often referring to the huge gap in school readiness between wealthy children and those from lower-income households. Poor students generally don't get the same boost in early literacy as middle-class students. Well-educated parents read to their children often and engage them in conversations about books, their community, and where their food comes from. They obsess about how well their children read. The development psychologists Betty Hart and Todd Risley conducted a famous study of the differences in how poor and upper-class parents speak to babies and toddlers. They made home visits to forty-two Kansas City families during the 1980s. They discovered the professional, more educated families spoke to their children a lot more than the poor and working-class families and also used a much more complex vocabulary. They concluded that by the age of three, the average child on welfare was hearing 616 words per hour, *half* as many as the average working-class child. Children from professional families heard even more words—an average of 2,153 words per hour, which was more than three times as many as the poor children.[12] This led Hart and Risley to conclude that wealthy children were exposed to thirty million words by the age of three—or twenty million more than kids from low-income families. It was a small sample of families and the precise numbers of words could easily be debated, but the overall conclusions matched what teachers see every day. The researchers also determined that professionals use more words of praise or affirmation than less educated families. The low-income families had more basic child-rearing interactions with their kids, such as "Say please" or "Don't do that."

In the past decade there's been a renewed focus on the power of words in boosting early-childhood literacy. Brain researchers have been telling parents that it's never too early to read to their babies, even in the womb. School districts have also tried to overcome the gap in school readiness with longer days and year-round schooling so students have more time for instruction. Urban charter schools, such as those in the Knowledge Is Power Program (KIPP), are also known for having longer school days and for teaching on weekends to give low-income children a boost.

Chancellor Klein embraced all these innovations. But he opposed the notion that closing the achievement gap meant poor urban children couldn't handle balanced literacy and needed rote instruction. He believed they should be exposed to the same engaging books as middle-class kids. It was hard to judge whether his approach was making a big difference. NAEP scores had hardly budged since Klein was appointed chancellor in 2002. And while elementary reading scores on state exams had been gradually improving, fewer than 60 percent of students met state standards in 2007. But Klein believed the schools were making steady progress, with an increase of about ten points in five years. "It seems to me this is one of those silly arguments which academics keep wanting to have which is between, on the one hand, should you do these phonics-based curriculums that you're saying are teacherproof? Or should you be doing whole language? And the answer is you've got to do both of these things."

Klein also argued that while some scripted reading programs, such as Success for All and Open Court, may get better results in the early grades, those gains drop off quickly when the students get older and need to rely more on comprehension skills. And proponents of balanced literacy can point to schools in New York City that have made substantial gains with the program.

But balanced literacy is a challenging program. Teachers have to constantly assess their pupils and keep track of their reading progress. Schools such as PS 321 in Park Slope, where almost 90 percent of the students were reading at or above grade level, had a lot of experience with the program. Even first-grade math lessons involved reading and writing exercises, with one class graphing "yes" and "no" responses to the question "Would you like to live in space or in the ocean?" Other schools such as PS 19 in the East Village were coming along. But Calkins wasn't sure that was happening everywhere. "New York adopted balanced literacy but did not talk about how that adoption becomes reality," she said, explaining that teachers needed a lot of staff development to master the ninety-minute literacy blocks, which require a lot of juggling between group and individual activities. Some district superintendents were known for doing a better job than others in getting them up to speed. Teachers and administrators thought this inconsistency was a by-product of having a school system run by a businessman and a lawyer, instead of by educators who understood the real demands of teaching. But Klein said professional development was often a waste of time if the teachers weren't high quality to begin with. He was about to engage in a battle with the teachers union over a proposal to raise teacher quality by linking tenure to student performance. Klein believed test scores could show which teachers were most effective with similar populations, but the union staunchly opposed his plan.

Principal Ivan Kushner at PS 19 in the East Village saw these arguments as just another sign of the times. Kushner's father had come to the United States from Russia as a child and left school in sixth grade. As a city principal in 2008, Kushner knew the students at his school were facing an entirely different world. They needed to be prepared for a workforce that would require more literacy skills than ever before. PS 19 had received a B on its first report card for raising test scores about three points in reading over the previous year. And almost 20 percent of its students receive special education services. Kushner wanted even higher gains in that school year. But with the latest round of reforms, he acknowledged that classroom teachers "have the hardest jobs in the system," because they are under so much pressure. He expected new principals, especially, would pressure teachers to get higher grades out of their students. And he knew the tests weren't always an accurate measurement of student learning.

"I was walking around yesterday to observe test prep, it was very literal," he said, noting that with balanced literacy his students focus on characters and other critical thinking skills when they read. But the third-graders he observed who were prepping for the January exam were encountering unfamiliar territory. "A quote like 'willows on a tree' was a metaphor for snow," he said, struggling to recall the exact phrasing of the question. "They thought it was literally cotton on a tree."

TWELVE

Alejandro's Progress (Genius or Dumb-ass?)

Alejandro always hated math. But his reading had come far enough along that his tutors at Lindamood-Bell were slowly moving him along in math, too, by teaching him addition, subtraction, and multiplication. They wanted him to get an elementary-level foundation in math before he finished the program in January 2008 and started his GED preparation class.

On a rainy day shortly before the end of his city-funded tutoring at Lindamood-Bell, he practiced adding and subtracting fractions. He sat in a corner cubicle with an African-American clinician named Veronica Washington, who wore glasses, a blue hoodie, and a black skirt. She watched him staring at the equation 6/2 + 9/3 = ? and asked him what he had to do first. "Multiply," he said. He wrote 18/6 + 18/6 to get the same denominators, then reduced the total to 36/6. "So how many times six goes into thirty-six?" he asked himself aloud, trying to recall the multiplication table.

The tutor offered a clue. "How many times does one go into six?" "Six," he replied. "So if your answer is going to be one goes into six *six* times, how many whole pies would you have?" Alejandro's tutors often used drawings of pies to help him visualize the numbers. He liked to think of them as pizza pies. "Six pies," he responded. "So what is your answer?" He figured out that six goes into thirty-six six times, but wasn't sure if he was supposed to multiply the top numbers or add them. He looked down at his paper and erased each attempt at completing the problem. He was still having trouble, so it was a relief when his next tutor, Rachel Lamson, stopped by at the end of the hour to work with him on literacy.

Alejandro was reading from *The Pearl* by John Steinbeck during his sessions. His tutors had him read aloud for a few minutes between other exercises. He'd gotten to page 32, and Lamson, a young white woman with a gray sweater and a ponytail, asked him to review the plot. Alejandro told her that it was about a guy who found a pearl and everyone in the neighborhood was talking about it. He picked up the book and began slowly reading aloud, using his finger to guide his eyes. His voice was flat as he concentrated on the words, and he corrected himself whenever he made a mistake.

"'Then he went to a box by the wall, and from it he brought a piece of rod—rag. He wrapped the pearl in the rag, then went to the corner of the brush house and dug a little hole with his fingers in the dirt fluh—in the dirt floor, and he put the pearl in the hole and covered it up and concealed the place. And then he went to the fire where Juana was squatting, watching the baby's face.'"

Just like an elementary teacher at PS 19 conducting a running record, Lamson asked Alejandro a few questions to test his comprehension. He had gotten through the decoding stage of learning to read and was now reading to learn. In Steinbeck's book, the main character, Kino, has found a huge pearl, which can be sold to lift his family out of poverty. But he's worried about jealous neighbors and a doctor who may take advantage of him because his child is ill. "Is this the first time he let go of the pearl?" Lamson asked. Alejandro said yes and told her that Kino was putting the pearl in the corner of the house to bury it. He continued reading.

"'The neighbors showed one another . . .'" He had trouble with the sound of "showed," pronouncing it like "ow" instead of "oh." Lamson stopped him and he fixed his mistake. "'Showed one another with their thumbs how big the pearl was, and they made little car-EE-sing gestures to show how lovely it was.'"

Alejandro's Spanish pronunciation affects the way he says a few words, but he knows what they mean. He continued reading a description of the Gulf at night. The next paragraph contained a challenging word: "Out in the estuary a tight woven school of small fishes glittered and broke water to escape a school of great fishes that drove in to eat them." Alejandro worked out the pronunciation for "estuary" and they discussed what it means. The word had come up before in the book. In the next sentence, there's a reference to big fish that "slaughter" smaller ones, and

Alejandro was able to pronounce this other difficult word, which requires a good foundation in the bizarre rules of English spelling.

Jennifer Egan, the director of Lindamood-Bell's New York office, stopped by to observe for a moment. She considered Alejandro's progress "dramatic." He couldn't read a single word when he started here in 2005, and *The Pearl* is at high school level. But he was still very weak in math and had problems with his reading speed, accuracy, and intonation—which are the main components of fluency. He also had big problems with spelling and was prone to leaving out words or mixing up tenses. He was supposed to write sentences in his workbook using certain nouns and came up with this for the word "letter":

"I wrote a letter about her life England. I send her a letter from the war each week."

He had left out "in" before "England" and he intended to write "sent" for the past tense of "send." His tutor corrected him and he understood the errors.

Egan was planning to give Alejandro a full assessment after his final class at the end of the month. She expected these problems to crop up. But by making him more aware of how letters sound and look, she said, her program strengthened his phonemic awareness as well as his symbol imagery—the ability to picture what he's reading. "Now that the underlying sensory processing is developed, the reading can develop," she said, explaining that dyslexics have a very difficult time picturing or imaging letters of the alphabet. "When we originally tested Alejandro, he couldn't hear a word like 'slip' and visualize all the letters," she said. "He couldn't tell you it's made of suh-luh-ih-puh."

"We taught him to be able to perceive sounds within words, to hear their number and their order, and how to be able to picture letters." This ability to image letters is a sign of the brain's plasticity, to find new neural pathways that weren't working because of dyslexia. He reads with his finger under each word, Egan said, because it's still difficult for his mind to turn the letters into words; using a finger gives him guidance and prevents him from moving too quickly. Some dyslexics have an easier time with math, but she said Alejandro was still building his symbol imagery for visualizing numbers; he also had to learn basic math facts he never learned in his twelve years of school. There's a similar challenge with his "concept knowledge." He had absorbed a lot of information through television, and can tell you that George Washington was the first U.S. president and other facts of American history. But he has a hard time visualizing a time line and remembering which events happened on which dates. With no formal education, he never gained a proper sense of historical time periods.

Alejandro took a placement test last month for a GED program at Hostos Community College in the Bronx. One of his lawyers at Advocates for Children researched all the free GED courses in the city, and he liked the one at Hostos because it's only a few subway stops south of his neighborhood. On the day of the test, Alejandro says, he was uncomfortable entering a classroom full of students. He'd been attending private one-to-one classes for the past two and a half years and he only had negative memories of being in school. Part of him wanted to leave, but he said, "I told myself to focus on the test."

Alejandro got through only the reading portion of the exam before he ran out of time. He says he was the last to leave, getting home late that night. He made an appointment to return to complete the math section on another day. He remembers the reading section had long stories followed by multiple-choice questions. One was about a festival, and he had to reread it several times. He used the imagery lessons from Lindamood-Bell to get through the test. "There's stuff you learn and put in the back of your mind like sounds, rules, how to break words apart," he explained. "Literally, I have to remember whole words. As soon as I say a word I remember how it looks."

There was one short essay question that left him stumped. It asked why he wanted to get his GED. For someone who fought the city in order to learn how to read, one might think the answer would come easily: to further his education. But he didn't know what to say. He couldn't express himself in writing. "I didn't know what the heck to do," he muttered sheepishly. "I said I want to be a toy maker." There was some truth to it, he said. His career goals are still uncertain. "I did what I could."

Alejandro's last day of tutoring was January 17, 2008. The staff brought in lasagna and they ate lunch together with Alejandro at a table. The tutors gave him a copy of the book *Fast Food Nation*, a history of the cultural and economic impact of fast food, because they thought it would appeal to his sense of justice. Alejandro didn't want to make a big deal out of his leaving, and summed up the lunch with his typical dry understatement. "We managed to keep it together," he said, adding that nobody cried. "It's not goodbye." He said he expected to stay in touch with the tutors. However, he admitted he was proud of accomplishing what he set out to do when he first contacted his attorneys about finding a way for the city to teach him to read. "I definitely knew I was going to finish," he said. "I knew that's what I wanted."

After his last tutoring session, Alejandro completed a final evaluation to measure his progress. Jen Egan compared the results to his initial testing in 2005 and was impressed.

When Alejandro was first evaluated, his vocabulary was in the thirty-seventh percentile for a person his age. It was now at the fiftieth. The particular test Egan used was designed for both children and adults and also gives an age equivalency. Alejandro's was twenty-one years and ten months—less than a year behind his actual age. "So he knows the meaning of a lot of words," she said. "When he's reading, when he's listening, he has adequate knowledge of words in isolation."

But that's not the same as defining a word out of context. "What was still very difficult for him was expressive oral vocabulary," Egan continued. In the next exercises, which are called the Peabody Test and the Detroit Test of Word Opposites, the tester said a word and Alejandro had to give the exact opposite. There were no multiple-choice options; the answers must be very precise. Egan said some of the pairs included "convex/concave" and "nocturnal/diurnal." "This was harder," said Egan. "He was at the ninth percentile." Again, it was measured relative to his age. And it was an improvement over the initial test in 2005, when he was only in the fifth percentile. But Egan said the results meant there was still a big difference between Alejandro's expressive and receptive vocabularies. "The connection between the part of his brain that visualizes and the part of his brain that verbalizes—it still needs strengthening," she explained.

When Egan met with Alejandro about the results, she warned him that some of the percentages wouldn't look as high as he had hoped—especially his reading rate. He had scored at a third-grade level because he read so slowly. But speed is different from accuracy, and Alejandro had gotten to a high school level on that test. Egan reminded him that he had come to Lindamood-Bell as a nineteen-year-old nonreader. "So you basically had to ask your brain to do in two and a half years what most people get nine years to do," she recalled assuring him. "He went to a nine-point-two grade level in accuracy. That's really great; I think he believed that."

But that slowness would make it difficult to get into college, Alejandro's ultimate learning goal. Fluency is determined by rate plus accuracy, putting Alejandro's total reading fluency at about a sixth-grade level. Egan says they talked about this painful reality. "Every homework assignment he has, it's going to take him a lot longer than his classmates. And that's hard. When he does prep for the GED, when he does take college classes, there's a lot of reading." There are some colleges for students with learning disabilities, such as Landmark. And Alejandro could qualify for extra time on the exams. But he'd still need to become a more fluent reader.

Alejandro was worried and Egan recalled telling him, "It's okay. You want what you want; however long it takes to get there, it's okay." She suggested taking half a load of classes when he first started college and pacing himself. She said he should take his GED preparation slowly as well. He couldn't expect to pass the test on the first try.

She also told him that his reading comprehension skills were good because he had gotten to the level of a sixteen-year-old. This meant he was able to get the meaning of a story even when he took a long time to read the words. He'd be able to answer the kinds of questions that come up on standardized tests about the main idea of a text, or drawing inferences. "That's very hopeful for him for his academic future," she said. Alejandro was quiet during their private meeting over the scores. She said he just smiled and nodded his head.

Alejandro's initial reading levels were extremely low for Lindamood-Bell, regardless of his age. Most of the program's students move on after a few months of instruction. And older students can get especially frustrated when they aren't progressing quickly. But Alejandro kept coming back, day after day, for more than two and a half years, using a total of 1,660 hours of compensatory education services he'd won from the city.

"I just keep coming down to courage, really," said Egan, looking over his files. "I mean, my God, to have the courage to say, 'I still think I can do this.'"

Alejandro's lawyer, Matthew Lenaghan of Advocates for Children, saw a bright twenty-two-year-old whose huge potential was tragically altered by the failures of the city schools. He could have easily passed for a college student. And yet, said Lenaghan, "as close as he is to being just like the people you know who have gone to every level of schooling, and have gone to college or past college, he's so far away from being there and achieving the life of those people that you know" because of his lack of formal education.

Alejandro acknowledged there were days when he felt overwhelmed and mentally exhausted from trying so hard to read. But he had his sense of humor. When told that the term GED is an acronym for what's commonly called the general equivalency diploma, he came up with one of his own: Geniuses from Earth who are actually Dumb-asses.

THIRTEEN

The Rollout

The assessment tests Alejandro took at Lindamood-Bell are extremely precise in their measurements of reading rate, accuracy, and vocabulary. They take several hours to administer and they're very expensive, which is why the public schools use them only for special education students.

With general education students, classroom teachers typically rely on weekly and monthly quizzes for grading purposes and for charting their students' progress. Early-elementary teachers also use specially designed programs for testing how many words per minute a child can read aloud and say correctly. My mother's cousin Dr. Nancy Prince-Cohen told me about something called "diagnostic and prescriptive education" used when she taught second grade on the Upper West Side in the 1970s. Classroom teachers would use a weekly test to see if their children were able to blend consonants and decode words. The teacher was then supposed to write an individual plan for every child. But, says Nancy, "it was too overwhelming. You'd spend so much time writing out these lessons and prescriptions every week that the reality of use was really hindered by the amount of time." She says it was helpful for new teachers, though, with less experience.

Today's assessments have a different purpose now that districts are under pressure to meet annual performance goals. They're typically given every few months in math, reading, and other subjects before the annual state exams. Some districts, such as Broward County, Florida, and Wake County, North Carolina, design their own assessments. Others purchase them from publishing companies.

That's what New York City did in 2007, when it contracted with CTB/

McGraw-Hill for math and reading assessments known by the name Acuity, which are widely used in other states. The Department of Education was authorized to spend up to $70 million on assessments through 2010. In keeping with the city's decision to let principals run their buildings, however, schools were also allowed to design their own assessments. A few hundred out of more than 1,400 in total chose a system based on the Teachers College Reading and Writing Workshop.

Initially, the city required the schools to give a total of ten assessments during the 2007/08 year—five in reading and five in math—for students in grades three through eight. The first exam was given in October, and was considered a predictive or mini-version of the state's English Language Arts exam, with similar multiple-choice and written response questions. Schools were also supposed to give "diagnostic" reading assessment to pinpoint their students' areas of weakness before the state reading test in January, followed by more assessments a few months later that would tell them how much progress their students had made and whether they'd be at grade level the following September.

In the age of NCLB, school districts and states were increasingly relying on educational publishing companies to help prepare their students for annual tests. The test-prep and assessment market was growing at a rate of more than 11 percent annually, with $2.6 billion in sales in 2008/09, according to Outsell, Inc. The biggest players were CTB/McGraw-Hill, Pearson, Houghton Mifflin, Harcourt, and Educational Testing Service. Other districts in upstate New York were already using Acuity. But nothing could compare in scope to the rollout under way in New York City.

The seventh-grade teacher Michelle Brier is poring over a fat binder she just received from a training session at Middle School 202 in Ozone Park, Queens. Brier was a print and radio reporter—which is how I know her—before she switched careers to become a teacher in 2002. She's got the reporter's natural instinct to find the story. In this case, the story is in the scores.

Brier teaches three classes, with a total of 101 students. She keeps separate binders for each class, tracking her pupils' work. On this day in early February, she's got an even bigger binder filled with new data: the results of the first Acuity test, which her seventh-graders took in the fall. It was the predictive exam, estimating how they'd perform on the state's English Language Arts exam in January. The assistant principal showed the teachers how to go online to comb through every child's results. Brier wanted to try it, but says the Acuity website keeps crashing.

Nonetheless, she says she's picking up some interesting little stories in her first batch of data. She flips through her new report to search for the results for a child who wrote an essay that's posted on her classroom wall. She loved the boy's use of detail but the essay didn't include any paragraph separations, and it ended with a quote from the Declaration of Independence without any real conclusion by the student. It's one thing for the students to reorganize information from textbooks and the Internet, but they have to pick out what's most important and make a convincing argument. Brier awarded the boy 80 percent on his paper, a level 3 in the lingo of New York State standards. But he's one of her lower-performing students.

Brier grew up in this middle-class slice of eastern Queens and attended MS 202 when she was a teen. When she was offered the chance to teach here, she says, "it was such a strange, exciting feeling. It felt like I'd be going home. Sitting at my first faculty meeting in the auditorium, it felt like I had never left the place. Maybe because the school looks nearly the same as when I was a teenager." Well, almost. When Brier was a kid in the 1970s, the school was a mix of mostly Italians and Jews. Today it's 42 percent Hispanic, with the rest of the population a mix of South Asians, blacks, and whites. A Muslim girl in Brier's late afternoon class wears a headscarf. Almost 55 percent of the school's students were reading at grade level last year—ten to fifteen points better than the citywide average for middle schools, but no reason to rest on its laurels.

Brier explains that some of her students' reading problems aren't immediately apparent. For example, the boy who wrote the essay on her wall has some deeper comprehension problems. She looks in her binder and shows me that he got 56 percent on the Acuity test, putting him above the 50 percent cutoff considered failing. But that score is made up of two different test sections, with vastly different results. On the multiple-choice section, he got 76 percent of the questions correct. But he got only 9 percent right on the written part, which required short answers to questions. Brier doesn't know if that means he wrote a terrible response or simply gave up because he thought it was too hard. Acuity doesn't show in its report what the child wrote. A teacher would have to keep all the original paper copies of the exam for comparison. "The problem is, it leads to more questions," she says of the new assessment. She doesn't think the results are out of whack with what she sees in the classroom, however. She's noticed that the boy often gets the meaning of a story but has trouble with details, preventing him from gaining a deeper understanding. She already offered him and a few others who are having trouble a spot in her "lunch club." She's among a few teachers who give up their lunch breaks to spend more time working with struggling readers. "I feel so responsible for them," she says of her students. One has repeated two grades already. Others have been caught plagiarizing essays from the Internet.

Brier has been teaching for six years and is still enthusiastic about her profession. She's excited about being able to take a closer look at her students' performance through the Acuity assessments. She just knows it's going to take a lot of extra time. When I ask her how much, she dryly states, "Forever."

Her colleagues have mixed opinions, though, about having to give so many more exams. On this afternoon in early February, the math and English teachers are attending a workshop on how to use the Acuity system. (Brier went to yesterday's session.) The teachers are being paid overtime to attend these three-hour classes and the school has ordered pizza for dinner.

Assistant Principal James McKeon leads the session. He has close-cropped hair and a firm, no-nonsense demeanor. He was in the military for twenty-two years before becoming a stock trader and then a science teacher. It's not unusual now to find teachers who changed careers to work in the public schools. About 11 percent of the city's teaching force comes through a fellowship program run by the city that pays for new teachers to attend graduate school while working. Teach for America, the national program that places recent college graduates in under-resourced schools, has contributed another 1.5 to 2 percent.

As McKeon goes over the new assessment program with about twenty teachers, he uses a SMART Board—an overhead projector connected to a laptop—to show them how to retrieve information. He asks if anyone has already used Acuity and only a few hands go up. He warns them that there will be some frustrating moments. The website has been crashing from overuse. And it's hard to parcel out all the details. But this is a new way of looking at test scores, he tells them, instead of waiting for the state exams. "If you look at the data and the scores don't move so much, you shrug your shoulders . . . We want to change our orientation and culture to look at student data all the time."

McKeon uses the SMART Board to show the teachers Acuity data for a sixth-grade class. It's the first math assessment results and the students' names are all listed. He clicks on a kid who scored 91 percent on this predictive test, showing the teachers how to drill down and look at the algebra, geometry, and measurements sections. Then he picks another child, who didn't do so well, and shows the teachers how they can click on the word "assign" to create some homework or quizzes specifically targeted to this student's weaknesses in math. He mentions how this could help a girl who got a level 1, and about half the teachers in the room nod their heads, as if they're not surprised. "She'd do better if she came to school," mutters one teacher.

McKeon warns the teachers to look for cases when every student in a class makes the same type of mistake. "It could be a poorly constructed question," he says. He shows them how to click on the question so they can see for themselves and decide whether the question really was poorly written. "Nice," a few teachers shout out, impressed with this ability to break down the test questions.

But the teachers worry about the city's demand for continued progress. The middle school got a B on its progress report. McKeon shows his teachers a growth chart for every class, with the names of each student followed by their scale scores from 2006/07. Some students who got a level 2 on their exam last year were just a couple of points away from level 3, while others were forty or fifty points away. McKeon then gives each teacher a black binder about one or two inches thick, with printouts of each student's scores from Acuity. They eagerly embrace the new information, scanning the pages and looking for any trends. Most of the teachers appear to be under forty. One sixth-grade English teacher named Lisa, who declined to give her full name, says her students are mainly performing at level 2, with some at level 1. "Data is great if it works and you use it," she says. "But it doesn't work for some kids, they're just so far behind." She says a few of her pupils are new to the United States. An English as a Second Language teacher leans over and agrees, saying, "The kids can only do as much as they can do."

When teachers have three English classes a day plus other scheduled periods, there's also the pressure of time. John Duffy, who teaches eighth-grade English, says he would like to spend quality time with each of his pupils and individually target his instruction. "But with thirty-four kids in the class?" His voice trails off. "She has thirty-six," he says, pointing to one of his colleagues. "The average is thirty-five kids in a class . . . If they really want to make this effective, they should lower the class sizes."

He also wonders if all this time spent on the new assessments will really be worthwhile. "I can spend a week with a kid and tell you the test score before I see it," he says. "I understand the idea behind it," he adds. "But the people behind this don't have a hundred kids [to teach]."

Assistant Principal McKeon shares these concerns. He tried to make the teachers' jobs easier by printing out the scores from the first math and reading assessments for every student. It took twelve thousand pages. He thinks good teachers can actually use these results to maximize their time, because they'll get a better idea of which students are doing well and which ones need more work. He sees the assessments as part of a "knowledge management trend" that he's also encountered in the military and the corporate sector. "This is not going away," he states, though he adds one caveat. "The biggest frustration will be if in a year they change [systems], and it's the flavor of the day."

Antonio's old junior high in Washington Heights is IS 143. It's located in a predominantly Dominican neighborhood that, like much of the city, is feeling the effects of gentrification.

Professionals who can't afford the rising costs of Manhattan south of Harlem have been moving to prewar co-ops with gorgeous views of the Hudson River. A Starbucks opened near the A train station; there's a natural food store and a handful of places with live music. But these signs of upscale expansion are a few blocks west of the school. Walk east along 187th Street and you'll see stores with Spanish names and shops that cater to a different clientele. There's a *mas o menos* ("more or less") 99-cent shop, a man selling empanadas on the street, and an electronics store that advertises *"Envoi puerta a puerta a la Republica Dominicana"* (door to door to the Dominican Republic). A few chain stores have also opened branches, including Payless ShoeSource and Dunkin' Donuts. Rents have been rising in this part of the neighborhood, too. Local principals see more working-class families. And those who can afford a few thousand dollars a year send their children to local Catholic schools. Academically, they aren't dramatically different. Children at the Incarnation School a few blocks away, for example, sit in rows, not clusters. Incarnation's principal, Patricia O'Keefe, says the average class size is thirty pupils. Their teachers use reading textbooks, but they also combine phonics in the early grades with a more individualized approach to instruction. Children with learning disabilities are kept after school for extra instruction instead of being pulled out of their classes. Between 40 and 45 percent of Incarnation's students are meeting the state's standards, about the same as the public schools. But Catholic schools have a reputation for being much safer, and for having higher standards and graduation rates.

When Antonio attended IS 143 in 2001, after he was classified as mentally retarded, Principal Ourianna Pappas says there were 1,100 students. She was the assistant principal then and doesn't remember him. Today there are just 859 pupils. About a third of them are English Language Learners. The intermediate school got a C on its progress report in November. Only a quarter of its students were reading at grade level the previous school year, and 40 percent were on target for math. Nonetheless, many parents are content with the school. They say their children get extra help and they like the teachers. But if you ask them about their children's earlier academic experiences, many say their sons and daughters *did* have trouble reading English in elementary school. *"Tengo una historia que contarte,"* says Lourdes Fernandez, meaning "Have I got a story to tell!" Fernandez has come for a workshop on flower arranging in the parent office, and the other fifteen or so women in the room laugh with recognition at what's apparently a familiar story. They all speak Spanish. Fernandez says her son couldn't read English until third grade and she had to get him a tutor. Another woman adds that her sixth-grade son is doing better at IS 143, but he wasn't motivated in elementary school. Several say the classes were too large for their children to get enough attention in a room with thirty or more other students.

This is why some teachers at IS 143 say it's not fair to blame a middle school for low reading scores when children's problems start much earlier. But after thirty years in the school system, Principal Pappas sees nothing wrong with a greater emphasis on accountability. "We can do better here," she says. "It becomes everyone's responsibility." IS 143 is on the state's list of schools in need of improvement, which may explain why Pappas and her staff are eager for any new tool that can help raise reading scores.

Pappas tapped her math coach, Jose Martinez, to serve as "data specialist" for the new assessments. The forty-something teacher has been in the building for seven years and he volunteered for the position, even though there's no extra pay, because he was excited about the potential for using data to raise achievement scores. On the first day back from winter vacation in January, Martinez sat down at a computer in the school's main office and typed in a code to access the Acuity website.

Martinez clicks on a page called "reports," which takes him to seven different categories of information. He can see the "predictive" test that was given in October. He sees the roster for every single class in the school, divided by grade. Martinez selects his own eighth-grade class and we look at the English results. There are thirty-three pupils and their names are all in blue, indicating hyperlinks so the teachers can find out more information about each student. Next to their names we can see what percentage of answers they got correct on the exam. Those who got 50 percent or fewer correct are highlighted in dark blue so the teacher knows who's at risk. Martinez clicks on a kid we'll call Ricky, to protect his identity. He got 46 percent of the questions correct overall, putting him at risk of failing the state's English Language Arts exam this month.

When Ricky's page opens up, we can see why this score is just the tip of the iceberg. Martinez can drill down and see how Ricky did on each of three different state standards for reading comprehension that were measured by this predictive exam. One standard measures "information and understanding," and Ricky got 43 percent of these questions right. The next standard tests "literary response and expression," and Ricky got 46 percent correct. But the third standard measures "critical analysis and evaluation," and here the student got his lowest score—just 29 percent correct.

Martinez could click on each of these three sections to see which specific multiple-choice questions were asked—and Ricky's answers—in order to figure out where the boy is having a hard time. He might be struggling with using synonyms or getting the main idea of a reading passage. Once he isolates those weaknesses, Martinez can program Acuity to design some extra quizzes for Ricky to give him more practice in these areas. Ideally, a classroom teacher could perform this microanalysis with every single child.

But there's a hitch: the test is linked to grade level. If an eighth-grader is reading at a sixth- or seventh-grade level, extra quizzes probably won't make much of a difference because they'll be too difficult. Thankfully, IS 143 opted to use one of the other assessments, called Scantron, which can more accurately determine a child's grade level in reading. Martinez began playing with the program in the fall. He says there wasn't any training; he just figured it out on his own. After seeing that Ricky's second Acuity test results were also low, Martinez used Scantron to determine that the eighth-grader was reading at a grade level of 5.8, well below where he should be. This information is very important because now Martinez can give Ricky quizzes that are closer to his reading level, and can gradually challenge him instead of making him more frustrated. He demonstrates how to do this by picking a few key reading skills that students are supposed to master—such as drawing an inference or getting the author's main idea. He doesn't want to pick too many at once or the boy will be overwhelmed. The computer program randomly chooses a few multiple-choice questions and prints out a quiz.

The quiz has been customized for a student who reads at a fifth-grade level, but maybe not a city kid. One of the questions it's chosen for Ricky involves a short reading passage about a girl who speaks "defiantly" to her mother. The test then asks the reader to decide whether this means the girl's tone of voice is "sympathetic," "understanding," "angry," or "happy." Martinez thinks this is reasonable. But another reading passage is about a girl who accompanies her father on a trip to "tap" a tree for maple sugar with a "spigot." The test asks the student to figure out whether the girl enjoys helping her father. But what if a child from Washington Heights doesn't know that the words "tap" and "spigot" have anything to do with getting maple syrup?

Erika Dunham is Ricky's literacy teacher. She's twenty-five years old, a graduate of the Teach for America Program who got assigned to IS 143 right after completing TFA four years ago. The principal thought highly enough of her teaching to make her a literacy coach. That's a lot of responsibility riding on her slim shoulders.

Her students are wearing the school uniform of navy vests and white shirts. Ricky is in the front, as usual, sucking on a pen and looking at his classmates. He's a slim boy with short-cropped hair and light brown skin. There are twenty-eight students in class today, sitting in clusters of four or five desks and talking about the book *Speak* by Laurie Halse Anderson. It's about a high school student named Melinda who won't tell anyone that she was raped at a party and becomes very withdrawn. Dunham asks the class to summarize what's happened in the scene they just read. She calls on Ricky. "They were doing, some job," he says tentatively, as he tries to find the right words. He's not very comfortable speaking in class.

"You're skipping ahead," says Dunham. She asks him a more direct question and he gets the right answer. Then she asks a girl to read a line from the book that says, "I have never heard a more eloquent silence." She wants them to think about the word "eloquent." What does it mean? A boy offers "fancy." A girl says "well-spoken."

Dunham's classroom is festooned with signs and posters. The city wants teachers to post "rubrics," or standards for each grade. The white sheets of paper hang from the walls like flags, waving bits of advice and encouragement to the students on how to become good readers. One is about synthesizing information. The students are particularly fond of another that compares a good essay to a hamburger. The introduction and conclusion are drawn as buns surrounding three paragraphs. On the side, there's a picture of a box of FRIES—an acronym for Facts, Reasons, Info, Evidence, and Support. It's got a red-and-yellow *M*, just like a McDonald's logo.

Dunham continues reading from a section of *Speak* about Melinda's terrible Thanksgiving. The character brings a wishbone from her father's burned turkey to her high school art class and makes something that impresses her teacher. Dunham's students take time to discuss this passage. Each student has been assigned a role within his or her group. Some are supposed to explain how images are used in the book; others choose important passages. Ricky's job is "word wizard." He's selected the terms "subjectivity," "carcass," and "thaw" as new vocabulary words from the book. He thinks "subjectivity" means "how you're interested in doing something." He looks it up in the dictionary and doesn't like the definition, which says, "relating to a subject." Dunham stops by and tells him it means "individuality." She asks him about one of his other words, "thaw." "What happens if you put the turkey in hot water?" she asks. His face lights up.

When the class breaks, Ricky stays for a little while to go over his work with the teacher. Dunham says this is a regular occurrence. "He struggles with comprehension," she says. She often keeps him after class, with another boy who was looking distracted today. Ricky also comes in at eight a.m. to talk to her during homeroom, even though she's not his assigned teacher. And he stays after school, too. He was among twenty students she invited to an after-school study session (only six or seven came regularly, she says). She gave them exercises from the Acuity website, which she tailored to each student. But these extra classes were cut midyear; after the state's English Language Arts exam, the city ordered the schools to trim $100 million because of the sudden economic downturn. Still, Dunham says Ricky's reading has improved so much that by March she thinks he's at an eighth-grade level.

But while Dunham believes the new high-tech Acuity program is useful for charting her students' progress, she has mixed feelings about giving so many tests. "It's somewhat of a shame," she says. "It's not coming from us; it's the city and the state and NCLB." She thinks reading real books and writing essays are much more exciting for her students than taking assessments. They've just finished a unit on *Before We Were Free* by Julia Alvarez, which allowed some students to explore their Dominican roots. They interviewed family members about life in the Dominican Republic under the former president and strongman Rafael Leónidas Trujillo Molina, and also read Alvarez's *In the Time of the Butterflies*. "This is where I think the bulk of learning happens," says Dunham.

Principal Pappas concedes the new focus on data and constant assessments requires a new style of teaching. She also acknowledges that tests have become so routine that she now gives her students green "IS 143 Lucky Pencils" to use on the state exam—so they know this is the most important test. But she and her staff believe monitoring student progress is especially important in Washington Heights because so many students come to school with built-in disadvantages. Many live in low-income households where the parents don't speak English, making them less prepared for school on average than students in wealthier parts of Manhattan or in the suburbs.

Martinez, the data coach, says he's constantly reminded that his students have relatively limited life experience. Recently, he took his class to see an IMAX screening near Lincoln Center. They went to the bathroom and thought the soap dispensers were filled with hair mousse because they'd never seen soap that looked like foam. They also went to a Barnes & Noble bookstore while they were in the neighborhood. For most, Martinez says, it was their first time in a bookstore. "This is our next generation," he sighs, asking: "If we don't teach them, who will?"

FOURTEEN

Learning to Rhyme

Yamilka's classes at the Fisher Landau Center for the Treatment of Learning Disabilities in the Bronx started in January, and it wasn't long before her speech therapist made a remarkable discovery.

"She can't hear rhymes very well," said Nancy Tarshis, the center's supervisor of speech and language services. "If you said, 'Ted and Fred—does that rhyme?' her accuracy rate is about sixty or seventy percent."

Tarshis has been at Fisher Landau since she started working on a master's degree in speech therapy at Teachers College in 1991. She previously taught deaf and hearing-impaired students. Her cramped office has a tiny children's table and matching red-and-yellow chairs that look like they came straight from McDonaldland. There are board games and toys piled up on the shelves. Tarshis was working solely with children until Fisher Landau got a new grant, enabling it to serve adults who come for language therapy. This was good timing for Yamilka, and Tarshis is intrigued by her new student.

"She processes sounds poorly. Very poorly," she states. "And when I say 'processes sounds,' I'm actually talking about the sounds. She's language impaired in two languages, I would guess.

"Phonemic awareness is one of the things that underlie reading. The ability to hear rhyme, the ability to recognize the first sound, the last sound, to segment words into syllables."

But Yamilka often can't hear those discrete parts of a word. Tarshis gave her the same type of test she would give a child. She asked her if "cat" and "hat" rhyme and Yamilka said yes. She could hear that "cop" and "book" did not rhyme, and neither did "dog" and "top." But when asked if "cook" and "book" rhyme, Yamilka said no. "So then I got concerned," said Tarshis. "At twenty-four she ought not to get anything wrong. So then I decided to add a couple more. Do 'seat' and 'beat' rhyme? No. Do 'rat' and 'fit' rhyme? No. So she got two wrong. That percentile is not great—she should be at one hundred percent." Tarshis says Yamilka should have been able to hear these similarities and differences regardless of whether she was speaking in English or Spanish.

Yamilka's issue wasn't unusual. Many children have phonological problems. Think of the cartoon character Elmer Fudd saying "vewy" instead of "very" and "wabbit" instead of "rabbit." Some children substitute *t* for *k* (like Eddie Murphy saying "Otay" as he impersonated Buckwheat from the show *Our Gang*). They also say *t* for *s*, as in *toup* for *soup*. Young children make those errors until they get the hang of the sounds, but some still can't hear the mistakes when they're ready for school. Of those students, Tarshis says, about 30 percent eventually improve on their own. Another 30 percent need therapy but get better by kindergarten. And the rest will have lifelong learning issues because their phonemic awareness is so poor.

There are many experts who believe all reading disabilities are fundamentally rooted in language disorders, and that having one of these disabilities makes you more likely to have others. For example, Antonio's neuropsychologist, Michele Shackelford, concluded that he has a separate language disorder that interferes with his ability to understand and to use complex grammar. "Basically, he can understand what's being said to him and he can communicate reasonably well," she explained. "He gets individual words and he can make sense, but it's not all coming in correctly. So if you say something like, 'Charles, who was a great athlete, never thought to go to college,' he may not understand the embedded clause—that it's referring to Charles." This difficulty putting different pieces of information together makes it even more difficult for Antonio to read because he doesn't have other clues to rely on, such as a person's tone of voice, hand gestures, or facial expressions. This language disorder also explains the way Antonio speaks. Like most kids (and many adults), he clutters sentences with the words "like" and "you know." But with Antonio it's more than just a speech pattern. When he says "you know" and "umm" or "howdaya call it," he's pausing to fill in the blanks. He has a lot of trouble organizing his thoughts, so the words pour out in fits and starts as he searches for the ones that he needs.

Yamilka had an especially complicated situation because she had so many problems processing language and expressing herself. She wasn't naturally wired to read. But as we know from stroke victims and studies of dyslexics, human brains can adapt. So Tarshis began working with Yamilka just as she would with a child who had a similar type of language disability: by teaching her to hear rhymes.

"The next words are 'pat' and 'shep.'"

Melanie Leong is sitting near the children's table in Tarshis's office, reading a list of words for Yamilka. She's a graduate student in speech and language pathology at Hunter College who's interning at Fisher Landau during the winter/spring semester. Tarshis sits straight up at her desk, attentively watching Yamilka.

Some of the words Leong reads are real and some are nonsense words. The point of the exercise is to see whether Yamilka can identify which ones rhyme. She's supposed to say yes if they do and no if they don't. Yamilka often asks Leong to repeat the phrases to make sure she's heard the words correctly, especially the ones she doesn't know.

"Pap?" she asks after hearing the words "pat" and "shep." Leong repeats them for her. Yamilka thinks a little and then says no, they don't rhyme.

"Good job," says Leong. "Fork and mord?"

"No," says Yamilka.

"Good job."

"Your ear is getting so much better, do you notice?" asks Tarshis. "Yeah, a little tricky still," says Yamilka. She's sitting on an adult-sized chair in the corner, wearing a soft winter scarf. Her hair is pulled back in a black lace headband.

"Yeah, it is tricky, it requires close listening. But it's so much better," says Tarshis, who wears casual clothes and has short brown hair.

Tarshis has been working with Yamilka like this for almost a month. The hourly sessions are held on Thursdays. Yamilka's reading classes with Dr. Mary Kelly are scheduled on Mondays and Wednesdays. Kelly's been using repetitive exercises to strengthen Yamilka's memory and build her sight-word vocabulary. One lesson involved a list of words including "boy," "girl," "child," and "children" that Yamilka had to read and use in short sentences. Kelly gave her worksheets with partial sentences that she had to complete with words from the list. There were also cartoon drawings of a boy giving a girl flowers so Yamilka could visualize what was happening and write her own short sentence from the list of words. Yamilka had trouble discerning "child" from "children" during this exercise, so Kelly made flash cards and they went over the words several times until Yamilka felt confident that she could spot the difference. "I'm trying to build on the part of language which she does have," she said, reiterating that she's using sight words because Yamilka isn't yet ready to read words phonetically. "She does have whole words which she can work with and which she does understand."

Yamilka had absorbed most of her information and vocabulary from television and from conversing with others. She learned about the Holocaust when she saw Oprah Winfrey talking about Elie Wiesel's book *Night* on her television show. But television is a passive medium and Yamilka's language skills weren't good enough to pick up on proper grammar. Her vocabulary is also limited because she wasn't able to expand it through reading in school. Kelly gave Yamilka a Franklin speak-and-spell machine she could use whenever she came across an unfamiliar word on her homework assignments. You type in the letters and a female voice says the word. Yamilka has trouble making out the words sometimes, because the voice has a strange robotic quality, but she's gotten used to the machine.

When Yamilka goes to her speech sessions, she concentrates and listens closely for rhymes. But like a snorkeler reaching out to touch the fish that are swimming past, she has a hard time catching the words. At times she gets so focused on the beginning or ending sounds that she misses the rhyme. Leong enunciates carefully to help her.

"Cred and wed," she says. Yamilka tries to repeat the words and has trouble with the first one. "Creh?"

"Cred and wed," Leong repeats. Yamilka still can't hear the ending of the first word and says, "Cret."

Leong opens her mouth wide to emphasize each consonant sound, "Creh-duh."

"Cret and weg? No," says Yamilka. Of course, the original words—"cred" and "wed"—did rhyme. But Yamilka heard "weg" instead of "wed," so she's right in this case to think the two words don't sound alike.

"Cheel and steel," Leong continues.

"Cheel and steel, yes," says Yamilka.

Tarshis encourages Yamilka to watch Leong's mouth as she speaks instead of repeating the words. "Don't say them," she tells her. "Just watch her mouth and listen carefully."

"Gat, jat," says Leong.

"Yes," Yamilka replies quickly.

"Good job," says Leong, moving along. "Do, hue."

Yamilka asks her to repeat the words and watches her face. "Again," she asks. Leong says the words "do" and "hue" more slowly. "No," says Yamilka.

"Look at my mouth and see what I'm doing," Leong tells her, pursing her lips as she says the words "do" and "hue" one more time. Yamilka takes a long pause and then asks Leong to repeat the words again. Then she answers yes, they do rhyme.

"Good job," says Leong. "Okay, zep, hep?"

"Yes," says Yamilka, watching her face.

"Drass, crass?"

Yamilka pauses. Leong repeats the words one more time, emphasizing the *s* sound, and Yamilka says yes.

Yamilka appears frustrated by the slow pace. "I know it feels like it's tough still," Tarshis reassures her. "But if we look at the total number and your percentages, every single week you're getting more and more correct. Really, the first time we did this, you got hardly any of them correct. Today you got most of them correct. So that's a change. It's only the third week we've done this."

Tarshis has grown fond of Yamilka over these past few weeks. When she first heard about the new adult student, she didn't know what to expect from the low scores she saw on Kelly's evaluation. But upon meeting Yamilka in January, she remembers, "my first impression was wow, this testing doesn't really reflect who she is.

"You know, there's just a spark to Yamilka. She has a sense of humor. And humor implies a certain tilt on the universe, for lack of a better word, that implies a certain level of intelligence. Because her humor was not slapstick humor. It was really humor of a more intuitive kind."

Tarshis says people with language impairments often have low cognitive test scores. Poor readers generally read less than good readers, and don't acquire as much of the knowledge that's measured by verbal IQ tests.[1] They have limited word recognition and listening comprehension. The Canadian cognitive scientist Keith Stanovich wrote an influential article on the "Matthew effect" in education to describe what happens to students like these. It's named for a line in the Gospel of Matthew that concludes that the rich get richer and the poor get poorer. In the same way, Stanovich concluded that children who fall behind in reading can easily keep falling behind without the right interventions. This is why low-income children are at much greater risk of academic failure. As Hart and Risley found, with their research on the twenty-million-word gap by age three, the vocabulary of a low-income child is often so far behind that of a professional family's child that it's tough for the child to keep up without a lot of extra assistance.

Tarshis saw Yamilka as a young woman with a strong sense of empathy and "emotional intelligence."* But she has so much trouble receiving and expressing information that she needs not only to strengthen her ears but also to improve her memory. So while Kelly worked on expanding her sight-word vocabulary in their reading classes, Tarshis helped Yamilka come up with ways to find the words that often elude her. They played games where Yamilka had to name five to ten items she would take to the beach, or pack for cold weather. Tarshis believes Yamilka will have an easier time finding words if she improves her "categorical knowledge" and learns how to organize her thoughts. "I asked her to name as many pieces of furniture as she could in a minute," she says, describing one of her earlier tests with Yamilka. "She named four . . . She had no strategy for 'How do I think of this?' So then I said, 'Let's try again, this time I'm going to time you but I want you to go through the apartment, start in the living room, walk into your room, your parents' room . . .' She named fifteen. She has no strategies for organizing information."

"The way I explained it to her is her brain is like a file cabinet. It's full. But it's not well organized. She can't pull open a drawer and go ABCD and find what she needs."

One way Tarshis hopes to strengthen these organization skills is by doing something Yamilka enjoys: cooking. She's pulled a couple of simple

*Howard Gardner of Harvard's Graduate School of Education is credited with the term "multiple intelligences," which describes seven types of intelligence: linguistic, logical-mathematical, spatial, bodily-kinesthetic (athletic), musical, interpersonal, and intrapersonal. Subscribers to this theory believe that a curriculum can be developed that plays to a child's strengths.

recipes they can make with the center's microwave oven, like Rice Krispies treats and rice pudding. They'll read over the ingredients and walk through the different steps together. Tarshis is trying to find some healthier recipes now that Yamilka has started seeing the nutritionist at Fisher Landau and lost a few pounds by reducing sugar and eating regular, balanced meals.

Tarshis is also teaching Yamilka circumlocution skills for when she's trying to remember a word. "There's a formula for that: it's category, function, form," she explains, giving an example. "So [if] you can't think of the word 'fork' [you use the formula]. It's a utensil, you eat with it, it's long with prongs at the end." Tarshis says she, personally, often has word retrieval problems and so do many other people—especially as they get older. She says she gets around it by prompting herself with different clues based on a word's function or form.

Yamilka likes Tarshis, and finds her warm and friendly. But when they first met, she admits, she had trouble believing her problems with reading were related to her listening skills. The clinic tested her hearing and it was fine. How could she not hear things the same way as other people? It seemed like such a strange thing to say. And what did that have to do with reading? After a few weeks of classes, though, Yamilka now believes this really is connected to her reading problem. She says she often repeats back the words she hears while watching television to check herself. Recently, she caught herself mixing up rhymes.

She was watching the New York City cable news channel NY1 and saw a report on a construction accident in Midtown. A gigantic crane had collapsed onto an apartment building. Yamilka went into the kitchen and told her older sister Gabriella that a *train* had fallen down on a building. Gabriella was confused and said a train couldn't fall on a building. Yamilka went back to the TV and saw the picture of a crane on top of a flattened apartment building. She was struck by how she had mixed up the two words. She knew it wasn't a train. And yet that's what she thought she had heard the newscaster say. As she told me about the two words "crane" and "train," she got mixed up again and couldn't recall which word starts with which letter combination, because she had trouble visualizing the blends "cr" and "tr."

FIFTEEN

The Toolkit

When he first took charge of the city's school system, Chancellor Joel Klein asked his staffers to probe what made some schools successful with poor and needy students while others were failing them. The city commissioned a study by the Harvard education professor Thomas Hehir, a former director of the U.S. Department of Education's Office of Special Education Programs during the Clinton administration. In comparing New York to other big cities, Hehir stated that too many of its public school children were being referred to segregated special education classes for reading problems that could possibly be addressed in other, less restrictive settings.

Federal law requires districts to offer special education services in a timely manner. But in 1979, a Puerto Rican student with learning disabilities, known as "Jose P.," brought a lawsuit because he still hadn't received any services more than three months after his evaluation. The city signed a consent decree laying out precise time lines for the delivery of special ed services. One former school official believes the disproportionately high percentage of special needs students in segregated classrooms was a by-product of this consent degree, because the city didn't want to be perceived as discouraging special ed placements. After the Hehir report, Klein's team decided to expand early intervention services. The purpose was twofold: if done right, interventions could prevent some children from needing the costlier special education services. They could also give other low-performing students a boost, eventually resulting in higher test scores and graduation rates.

Several studies have found early interventions can reduce special education referrals. One approach is called Response to Intervention. In a study of lower- and middle-class first-graders in the Albany, New York, region, interventions reduced the percentage of children who might have been classified as disabled readers from 9 percent to just 1.5 percent.[1] More and more districts are now experimenting with these strategies.

"The research indicates that there's not much difference in the learning processes of typically developing and special needs learners," says Dolores Perin, an associate professor of psychology and education at Teachers College who runs a master's program for reading specialists. She says these children need explicit instruction, dedicated teachers, and resources to succeed.

The woman in charge of academic intervention services for New York City's Department of Education is Dr. Esther Friedman. Unlike many of the key players on Klein's team, who come from outside the education establishment, Friedman is a twenty-seven-year veteran of the city's public schools with a doctorate in applied psychology and a master's in special education. She had been a staff developer, a director of literacy services for a Manhattan district, and an interim principal. Her career began with teaching emotionally disturbed children and students with learning disabilities at the private Lorge School in Manhattan. When the Bloomberg-Klein team reorganized the system, Friedman moved up the ranks and is now in charge of linking teachers and principals with programs that can help struggling readers.

Friedman knew those kinds of students when she attended junior high in the 1960s on Manhattan's Lower East Side. "I was always into the bad boys," she says, laughing. They were the ones typically steered out of academic classes and into shop classes. Others worked as audio-video monitors. With her tortoiseshell glasses and serious gaze, Friedman has the intense demeanor of an academic, though that's easily cast aside by her irreverent sense of humor. She's about five feet tall, with waist-length brown hair that has a magenta tint. As a professional, Friedman suspects a lot of those "bad boys" she knew in school had learning disabilities. She stayed in touch with them and knows a few who wound up in jail.

For decades, steering students like these out of academic classes was the easiest path for the students and for the teachers. But in the era of higher standards and NCLB, *all* students are expected to become proficient in all their subjects. Friedman gets a few calls each day from desperate administrators who don't know what to do with chronically failing students. While public schools may never be able to afford the intensive, one-on-one attention that Alejandro, Yamilka, and Antonio received in private tutoring sessions, Friedman's job is to prepare teachers to do as much as they can.

Friedman's interventions are called the Toolkit. On paper they resemble a pyramid. The first level—the fat one at the bottom—is what she terms "base development skills," the things students learn in elementary and junior high school. But as children learn to read so they can read to learn, they don't all master their skills at the same pace. "Sometimes kids come into this delayed," says Friedman, pointing to the base of her pyramid.

The interventions that teachers use at this stage of the diagram are considered the least intensive. They're reading boosters that are used in all elementary classes and are meant to keep students from needing special education services. At this basic level, when the students are just starting to slip, most of them have problems with phonics. Friedman's Toolkit includes four different assessments for figuring out precisely why a child is struggling and an equal number of strategies for helping them over the hump. She's also thrown in a couple of programs pupils can use on a computer. "The idea is not to overwhelm people," she says, explaining why her list is so concise. "You want programs that are piloted, that we know and support. I could choose about fifty."

Moving up the pyramid, the interventions she's selected become more intensive. Students who are still struggling are given more direct instruction by their classroom teacher, or pulled out to practice their skills with another teacher. For example, a middle school student who's a slow reader may be given a program to build fluency or reading speed.

Friedman schedules workshops so teachers can learn how to use these interventions. About fifty to sixty teachers and administrators attended a talk in the fall at an Upper West Side Barnes & Noble by a leading expert on literacy named Elfrieda "Freddy" Hiebert. Hiebert researches and develops programs to improve fluency. Her research is premised on data that concluded that most elementary school reading passages contain too many "low frequency words" children haven't mastered yet, and don't see very often. These can be words like "fantasy" or "imagine." Pointing to a graphic on an overhead projector, Hiebert told her audience of city educators that twenty out of every hundred words in a typical first-grade reading text are what she calls "singletons," words that don't show up often enough for some students to absorb them into their everyday reading. Hiebert's solution is a program that gradually introduces the less familiar words and repeats them often in a given reading passage, so the slower readers can steadily pick up their pace. The "Dick and Jane" books were the prime example of texts targeted for early readers. "No new words were introduced," said Hiebert, to her room full of attentive educators. "Its 'run, run, run,' not 'jog' and 'frolic.'" Eventually, they'll also be able to learn a word like "frolic" through repetition and context.

Friedman admires Hiebert so much she considers her "a rock star" in her field. But she says Hiebert's program is too expensive for New York to use en masse, although individual principals could choose to purchase it. So Friedman has chosen similar interventions that also rely on word repetition. She's also selected reading programs for students with comprehension problems. They have catchy names such as From Clunk to Clink, Brain Cogs, and Think Along.

Reading fluency and comprehension are often weak among older students who aren't performing at grade level—usually because they didn't acquire a strong foundation when they were younger. To improve their skills, New York City uses a program called Ramp Up to Literacy for middle and high school students who are two or more years behind. Ramp Up is used in districts in Georgia, Kentucky, Arkansas, and other states. The program presumes that most students are able to read the words but often miss out on the deeper meaning. They need more explicit instruction in the strategies good readers use when they come across a word they don't know, and in the skills they need to write a persuasive essay.

Students like these are the norm in many middle and high schools, including New Dorp on New York City's Staten Island. On the surface, the school looks like High School U.S.A. It's a big building, with 2,300 students, surrounded by a grassy field and a parking lot and across the road from a shopping mall. But the neighborhood's suburban flavor and high concentration of single-family homes mask a very diverse population of working-class whites and immigrants (including many from war-torn regions of Africa). There are also housing projects.

At New Dorp High School, more than 80 percent of entering ninth-graders scored a level 1 or 2 on their eighth-grade reading tests. The state considers level 3 proficient but a 2 is usually good enough to get to the next grade, and even level 1's weren't always held back (the city enacted a new policy against eighth-grade social promotion in 2008). Thirty-eight percent of the students at New Dorp get free lunch. The school's graduation rate of 68 percent in four years is higher than the citywide average but lower than the rates at other Staten Island neighborhood schools.

That figure is impressive, though, given New Dorp's challenges. Principal Deirdre DeAngelis credits a major restructuring, which broke up the school into eight small academies and capped ninth-grade classes at twenty-five students. She believes the Ramp Up to Literacy program also made a difference. Students who score at level 3 or higher follow the state's curriculum at the regular pace. But ninth-graders in English Language Arts classes that use the Ramp Up program look more like a typical middle school or elementary class. There's a vocabulary list, and the students read books together very slowly. Classes last for ninety minutes, or two periods instead of one. Students spend the first half of class on independent reading, choosing books at their own level from a library in the back of the classroom. They also work on writing assignments. Later, they discuss the books they're all reading together as a class.

The teacher Holly Acerra's fifteen ninth-graders are reading the book *Go Ask Alice*. Two were absent during a visit in March 2008. Acerra wrote on the chalkboard: "Aim: What major conflicts is Alice struggling with?" She taped a vocabulary list to the board with definitions for "embalming," "resurrection," and "capacity." She also wrote a character list with traits for each character in the story, to help students keep them straight. On the wall, there are guidelines for "Expected Behaviors for Independent Reading" and "Expected Behaviors for the Read-Aloud." They encourage the students to follow along with the rest. "Every student must have his/her book open to the appropriate page. There is absolutely no talking while the teacher is reading."

Acerra reads aloud from the book the way an elementary teacher would, with a lot of animation in her voice: "'Gramps died during the night . . . it seems unbelievable that I will never see Gramps again. I wonder what has happened to him . . .'" She pauses and asks the students to recall any memories of a wake or a funeral. A former New Dorp student died recently and a white piece of paper saying "RIP Alex" was taped to the door of the school, but nobody in this class had known him. One girl volunteers that she had a friend who died when he was hit by a car. "He looked different," she says, about seeing him at the wake. The teacher uses this example to steer the class back to what the character Alice was experiencing. The aim of the day is "conflict" and the teacher engages her students in a discussion about the central character's mixed feelings and the pressure from her peers to use drugs.

"It's making her feel bad, there's more pressure and the kids are bothering her," says one of the girls. "She's nervous, depressed," adds a white boy with glasses and a shaved head. Acerra's next assignment was for the students to write Dear Abby–style letters from Alice seeking advice. Some had never heard of the newspaper columnist, so she explains who Abigail Van Buren is.

Acerra keeps folders for each student to assess their progress. Most were reading at a fifth- or sixth-grade level upon entering school last fall, and four receive special education services for learning disabilities and emotional problems. One girl's binder includes a reading log of the book *Frindle* by Andrew Clements. She's written the name of the book in lowercase letters, which is typical of her work, and her summary is missing apostrophes and other pieces of punctuation. Her Dear Abby essay from today says:

"I was such a beautiful girl inside and out. but then I began doing many neggative things in life that had many bad conequences." Errors like these are common, but Acerra also says these students have trouble "thinking abstractly." The highly structured nature of Ramp Up and the school's reliance on smaller classes is supposed to help them get to a higher level. New Dorp also encourages its teachers in each academy to work on themes, so history lessons incorporate elements of reading or science classes.

But while the work at New Dorp might sound basic for high school students, a small percentage of students can't even make it that far. For them, New York has chosen what Academic Intervention Services Director Esther Friedman calls the "gold standard": Wilson Reading.

Six third-graders at PS 5 in the Inwood neighborhood of Upper Manhattan are sitting in two trios, facing each other across their desks. A black girl with long cornrows tied in a bun on top of her head gets up and walks to a chart of letters attached to the chalkboard. She holds a pointer and begins a review of the vowels: "A, apple, ah; E, egg, eh; I, itch, ih; O, octopus, oh . . ."

These students aren't in a special education class, but they've all been pulled aside for extra reading help because they have trouble sounding out words.

The program was designed by the New England educator Barbara Wilson, based on her work with adults who have dyslexia. Wilson's system is similar in many ways to the Orton-Gillingham style of "multisensory" reading programs used in private schools for children with learning disabilities. Students can be seen sounding out each letter, tapping the different syllables on their desks, and even writing words in the air with their fingers. Orton-Gillingham programs are distinguished by having a sequence of lessons that never vary. This is supposed to make them user-friendly for both teachers and students. Wilson is widely used now, in Albuquerque; Broward County, Florida; and the suburbs of Denver, in addition to New York.

It's because of its emphasis on systematic instruction that the third-graders in this small Wilson group at PS 5 start every class by reviewing their vowels. Their teacher, Joan Normile, then shifts their focus to consonant blends. "CK, sock, cuh," they say together, reading from a series of cards posted over the chalkboard. "SH, ships, shuh; TH, thumb, thuh; WH, whistle, whuh."

The exercise is intended to build phonemic awareness, much like the speech classes Yamilka is taking to practice rhymes. But speech classes are for children who have been determined to need special education services, and therefore have Individualized Education Programs. The thinking behind Wilson is that if caught early, some students may not need those more intensive services—although there are also special ed classes that use Wilson.

As the third-graders review the consonants, one girl calls the letter *q* a "chicken letter," because it's never alone. It's always matched with the *u*. The students have some cute ways of remembering the rules of language but they know the formal terms as well. "There's a digraph," says another girl. "Two letters make one sound," adds the first girl.

The teacher asks them to "tap out" another example containing two letters that make one sound: "miss." "Muh, mih, miss," they all say together. "How many times do we tap?" asks the teacher. They make three taps with their fingers, representing the separate phonemes in the word. "What do we call the *s*?" "A bonus letter!" says the first girl. Bonus letters include *l*, *f*, and *s* because they're often doubled at the end of a word. There's a list of them posted in the classroom. The students tap out "bill," three taps for the three distinct sounds: "buh, ih, lah." A little girl in a denim jacket asks why there aren't two taps for the two *l*'s and the teacher reminds her that the *l*'s actually form one sound.

Principal Wanda Soto says the girl who didn't understand that two *l*'s make one sound may have dyslexia. She's also an English Language Learner. Soto says the school wanted to determine whether she had a problem switching from Spanish to English before they made a more drastic change and sent her to special ed.

The teacher moves on to more words with bonus letters, asking the students to spell "pill" on magnetic letter boards. The girl in denim gets it correct, as do the others. "You know so much about your bonus letters, I don't think you're getting tricked," says Barbara Wilson. She's been watching from a few feet away with the principal. Wilson is a tall, lanky woman and she's been looking on with great interest. She regularly visits schools that use her program, and she's interested in what New York is doing.

New York City is the biggest Wilson site in the country. About five thousand teachers were trained to use the Wilson Reading program between 2003 and 2007. They take a three-day workshop, get three half-day follow-up classes, and enroll in an online academy. This basic training costs schools $250 per teacher. Teachers who go for more classes and a second level of certification can train others in the Wilson system, which makes the program cost-effective. Linda Wernikoff, the city's head of special education services, believes the investment has contributed to a dramatic decline in the number of students reading at the lowest levels on their state exams. Between 2003 and 2007, the Bloomberg administration cut the proportion of level 1 readers in half—from 17.6 percent to 9 percent.

Wilson's program looks extremely elementary, but it's actually got different levels and can be used for students from second to twelfth grade. Barbara Wilson's tour of PS 5 ends in a colorful classroom where the special ed coordinator Aida Hartmann is working with a small group of fifth-graders—three boys and a girl. They have learning disabilities and come from households where English is not the primary language. Inwood is at the northern edge of Washington Heights, and the school's population is almost entirely Hispanic.

The fifth-graders sit at desks clustered around Hartmann, holding pencils with big erasers attached to the ends. They're going to read a short story called "Fun with Dad." Hartmann tells the students she wants to point out some words they might not know before they begin. One is "tots," which she defines as toddlers or very young children. "One other word I think you should know is 'tire,'" she says. She asks a boy what comes to mind and he says "breathless," and another says "weary." "I love your synonyms," says Hartmann. The first boy, in a sweatshirt, then adds another definition: "melancholy." Hartmann says "tire" is more physical, as in having no energy, and melancholy is more emotional. But she praises the boy for using such a great fifth-grade word. They review the words again and she reads them the story, modeling how it should sound before they'll take turns reading sections aloud.

"'Dad likes to have fun with his children, Ben and Josh. They are just tots. The kids hide from Dad and he has to find them and chase them. This game was lots of fun, but the kids did not tire and Dad did. Then Dad wore a mask and hid. Josh and Ben could not find him. At last, he sprang out to scare them, and they went running to Mom. Dad had to take off the mask so they could see it was fake.'"

It's a simple passage, more suited to beginning readers than fifth-graders. But even a brief reading like this can stump students who have comprehension problems or language issues. They need to see the images in their minds and identify with the characters. Hartmann asks them to draw stick figures for each part of the story. A smaller boy with puffy hair says he sees it happening in a yard. When asked to draw a scene representing how the father tires while chasing his kids, one boy pencils a stick figure of a man staying behind as the children rush ahead. They discuss their drawings when they're done and the students take turns reading the story. Some proceed slowly and with little inflection, but they get it. Hartmann also asks them to retell the story in their own words for one last comprehension check.

"You're doing a terrific job," Barbara Wilson tells Hartmann and the other teachers before leaving the school. A total of ten teachers at PS 5 have been trained in her program. "One of the most challenging things to learn is the pacing. I always say you need to get them moving as quickly as you can and as slowly as you need to."

Hartmann then asks Wilson a difficult question. She wants to know how long it will take a student of average ability, but who has difficulty with literacy, to master her program. "There's no easy answer," says Wilson. "Every student and every group is different." But with small group instruction three or four times a week, totaling ninety minutes, she says the average group can go through four steps in a year, or about a third of the twelve-part program. She cautions that English Language Learners might be slower. She also encourages schools to use a kindergarten-through-first-grade program called Wilson Fundations, which she's been testing as a potential Response to Intervention that can help all students master early reading, and hopefully cut down on special ed referrals.

But there's no doubt that it's harder to achieve the same levels of success with older students. Although Wilson's program is used in junior high and high schools, teenagers who already feel branded as failures are less likely to be enthusiastic about "chicken letters" and "bonus letters." At Antonio's old middle school, the special ed teacher Gerald Lakowski has been working with a small group of pupils since October with the Wilson system, and by March they'd only gotten to the second booklet, which included long vowel sounds. A boy who was pulled out of his regular classes for the Wilson group read a list of words including "bind," "kind," "wild," and "told," but he said "bob" instead of "bold." A large boy who is mentally retarded said "bol" instead of "bold." There's another boy in the class with learning disabilities and the fourth was silent much of the time.

Lakowski didn't study phonics very much when he was in teaching college thirty years ago in Pennsylvania. Having been trained in the Wilson system, he says he sees signs of improvement among his students. "When we give a word they don't know, they can approach it better. They break up the word a lot better. Before they would just [guess] a word or say, 'I don't know.'" But he acknowledges it's hard to make a lot of progress when his class meets for just thirty-five minutes a day. Antonio had four hours a day for learning how to visualize words and sound out letters during his private tutoring. That can't happen in a public school where older students, especially, are required to spend several periods a day in other mandatory courses like science and history. Lakowski thinks he could have moved his students faster if he had more time with them, but he also acknowledges they're each working at their own level and a lot of them have emotional issues that get in the way.

At PS 5, Principal Wanda Soto says reading interventions also have to deal with the reality of students who are still learning English. That's about half her school's population. "We don't have social promotion," she says. "We need programs that address those new arrivals, that target the older child, so this way they can meet some kind of success. Because by the time they get to middle school, and they're not meeting success, that's when your kids drop out of school. It's sad."

Some principals don't think Wilson's program is right for their school, because they don't have enough students with decoding problems to fill a class. Janet Chasin, the academic intervention coordinator for PS 19 in the East Village, thinks the program works but can also get overused. "It's like replacing the retinas of people who are nearsighted," she says. Chasin suggests that children who still aren't getting the basics past a certain age may need to go outside the public school system for help.

There are public schools that have selected more expensive and intensive interventions for exactly that reason. Pueblo, Colorado, has a partnership with Lindamood-Bell—the tutoring program Alejandro and Antonio attended. Since 1997, the program has trained more than 1,500 staffers for a district of 17,000 pupils. Schools that used the full model—with some students getting up to four hours a day of intensive services—reduced their special education referrals by 30 percent. Of course, one could argue that such intensive instruction may not be much different from special education, and the program required an initial investment of $1.3 million for training the teachers. But by 2007, the costs were only $150,000 annually, and 79 percent of the district's third-graders met the proficient and advanced levels for reading on their state exams, which was more than the statewide average of 71 percent. Lindamood-Bell's staff considered that especially impressive because Pueblo has twice as many poor and minority pupils as the rest of the state (it's more than 60 percent Hispanic). But the district's reading scores were not as high in the upper grades; students performed at or below the state average. Lindamood-Bell's program is being used by a few elementary schools on Staten Island. But other schools in New York City aren't willing to spend the money, especially when the Wilson program is so much cheaper.

The city is already paying, though, every time a child with a disability wins the right to attend a private school with special services. The Churchill School on Manhattan's East Side, for example, costs more than $35,000 a year. Churchill's classes resemble an amped-up and more personal version of Wilson, and it even uses some of Wilson's materials. Its four hundred students in grades K–12 get small-group instruction, and there are printed schedules stuck to their individual desks listing each child's schedule for speech/language classes as well as occupational and physical therapy. The school says it receives about five hundred applications a year for about thirty-five slots, on average. Churchill is one of a select group of private schools approved by the state to take students whose needs can't be met in the public schools. New York State picks up most of the tuition, and the city pays for much of the rest. The school says it still has to raise its own money, but Churchill is essentially a government-financed private school.

Barbara Wilson sees her program as an affordable, viable solution for public schools and their challenging populations. "The number of kids that need the instruction is far too many to have people going out to private schools and private clinics, and have all their needs met. It's just impossible. And so the goal, my goal, has been since day one to bring this type of teaching into the public schools."

The fact that so many districts are now using Wilson also says something about the new emphasis on the basics of reading. Esther Friedman says students such as Yamilka and her brother would never have been exposed to anything like these strategies when they were in school. "They would have had no access to a spelling program, much less a real phonics program—and they needed that," she states.

But while New York City's schools may be using more of these programs, they're not required to. The Bloomberg administration's decision to "empower" the principals means they can choose whatever services they want. They might not have the time to send a reading teacher for extra training in the Wilson program, or the budget to hire someone else who can take that teacher's place while he or she is gone. And speech teachers are still stretched very thin. Friedman compares it to a doctor's office, because not all doctors have the same equipment.

"Does your doctor have a CAT scan in-house?" she asks. While state law requires principals to provide services for all students who aren't reading at grade level, it doesn't tell them they have to choose a specific reading program. If they use something outside of Friedman's Toolkit, she's all for it—so long as it works. Like doctors who keep up on the latest medical equipment by reading journals, principals now have to recognize what they need, take advantage of the advice they're given, and make decisions within their financial limits.

But how will they know what's best? The Bloomberg administration's technocratic approach hasn't built in a way of measuring which interventions are more effective than others. It merely looks at which schools are making progress.

SIXTEEN

In the Back of the Bookstore

Alejandro needs a dictionary. He's reading well enough now to sound out almost every word. But his vocabulary is still pretty limited, and he doesn't always recognize words on the page as well as he does in conversation.

Alejandro took home *The Pearl* by John Steinbeck after he finished his tutoring program. He had gotten almost halfway through it at Lindamood-Bell. He can sum up the story of a man named Kino whose son, bitten by a scorpion, the local doctor refused to treat until his fortunes changed. "And then when he went diving and found the pearl," says Alejandro, "the doctor heard about it, he found the pearl, so he went to his house, 'I heard your son was bitten' . . . he made this whole thing up so he could treat him." And yet Alejandro stopped reading soon after, about halfway through, when Kino tries to sell the pearl. He thinks it will be easier to keep reading once he gets a dictionary because he doesn't know what some of the words mean. He needs to buy a dictionary, anyway, for when he eventually starts the GED preparation class at Hostos Community College.

One morning at the end of January 2008, then, he goes to a Barnes & Noble on Lexington Avenue by the Eighty-sixth Street stop of the number 4 train. This excursion would not be a remarkable one for most people, but at the age of twenty-two Alejandro has never bought himself a book. He has been to a bookstore a couple of times. His sister Gabriella took him once. They'd stopped inside the Barnes & Noble near Lincoln Center when going to see a movie at the IMAX theater nearby. But the bookstore didn't make too much of an impression because they were just killing time before the movie.

When he walks into the store, he's surprised to see a long display of CDs and DVDs on a shelf near the checkout counter. He didn't know bookstores also sold music and movies. He stares at the familiar titles of recent movies, such as *Good Luck Chuck*, and the soundtrack to *Juno*. He looks longingly at the new album by Radiohead, a band that he likes from the music videos he sees on cable TV. A little farther into the store, he notices a shelf full of audio books and pauses at the Steven Colbert book, *I Am America*, and laughs. Alejandro is a huge fan of *The Colbert Report* and he has heard about the bestselling book Colbert has written in his trademark parody of a right-wing zealot.

There are other names of writers and celebrities Alejandro knows about through television and pop culture. He stops at a display of cookbooks by Sandra Lee. She's pictured on the cover with long blond hair, holding platters of food. Alejandro sometimes watches her show when he works out at home on his treadmill, and he knows Yamilka adores all the cooking shows. There's a book by the mixed martial arts star Matt Hughes. Alejandro flips through older photos of Hughes looking tough in his wrestling days. He goes to another aisle and sees books with the names of movies he knows, *Atonement* and *No Country for Old Men*. Alejandro didn't know the movies were based on books. He's heard of Shakespeare, and saw Baz Luhrmann's *Romeo + Juliet* with Leonardo DiCaprio and Claire Danes falling in love amid dueling gangs on the freeways of California.

Alejandro had watched the State of the Union speech a few nights earlier, and was interested in the display table at Barnes & Noble filled with political books by and about the Clintons and Barack Obama. Alejandro and his sister Gabriella would both love to become citizens this year so they can vote. But the test is hard and he's got plenty of work on his plate already. He laughs when he sees a book called *Citizenship for Dummies*.

Alejandro finds a red paperback Webster's dictionary on a table of "back to school" items for the winter semester. Then he decides to look into the GED study books. He doesn't have enough money with him, and isn't sure yet which one he needs, but he wants to check anyway. He approaches the customer service desk and asks the clerk. "All the way in back to the left," she says. As he heads toward the correct aisle, he jokes that the store must be "ashamed" of the books, keeping them tucked away in the back.

There are probably five or six shelves of study books for the GED, published by Barrons, Princeton Review, and others, with separate books for the five different parts of the exam: math, science, social studies, reading, and writing. Alejandro stares at the enormous collection. He had no clue there could be so many. Some of them are about two inches thick. Most have CD-ROMs, but Alejandro doesn't have a working computer. Alejandro looks at the math guide and sees a lot of problems he's not familiar with, because the tutoring only got him through the basics of addition, subtraction, multiplication, and division. He thinks the word "geometry" sounds like it could be someone's name. "Geometry!" he exclaims in a hushed voice. "Geometry, come to dinner!" He turns to a social studies book and flips through unfamiliar charts and graphs to the essays about slavery and other historical subjects, which appeal to him.

On his way to the checkout, Alejandro stops by science fiction. There are whole rows devoted to *Star Wars* and *Star Trek*. Alejandro loves the original *Star Wars* trilogy and the *Star Trek: The Next Generation* series. He stops next to the Godslayer Chronicles book *Hinterland*. This is a word he doesn't know. He looks it up in the red dictionary he's clutching, running his fingers slowly through the *h-i* words. When he finds it, he sees two definitions that both refer to an area removed from a coast or a place that's remote. He thinks about the word "hinterland" and figures that makes sense. Then he pays $6.50 plus tax for the dictionary and leaves, with a new tool for making sense of the world.

It took Alejandro more than a month to return to the Barnes & Noble for the GED book. Hostos Community College has a long waiting list for its free test-prep classes. Alejandro is on the list for Adult Basic Education courses, which are like pre-GED classes. They're supposed to give students who have missed a lot of school—or haven't attended classes in years—basic reading, writing, and math instruction to get them ready for a test-prep class.

Meanwhile, he has been staying at home, working on the math and reading exercises his tutors gave him when he left Lindamood-Bell. He prefers to study at home instead of the public library down the street because he doesn't want to be surrounded by other people. He knows he could be doing more to get ready for the class, but he's not sure where to start. One of his lawyers at Advocates for Children finally encouraged him to buy a study guide published by the Princeton Review. She showed it to him in her office, which is what spurred him to eventually return to the Barnes & Noble on the Upper East Side in search of the book.

Alejandro remembers where the test-prep books are located, way in back, and he looks for the one that resembles what he saw in his lawyer's office. He remembers that it had a white cover. He sees rows full of confusing acronyms: MCAT, LSAT, GRE, ACT, and the familiar GED books. Somehow he spots the one with the white cover labeled Princeton Review and takes it over to a table. The book is thick and imposing. Alejandro sets it down, preferring to look at the shelves surrounding his table. He's plopped himself down next to a humor section and his eyes are immediately drawn to an illustration of a man he thinks looks like President Bush. The figure is being tortured or stabbed, but it's not actually Bush—just a white guy in a suit who resembles the president. The book's title is *Final Exits*, and it's billed as "an illustrated encyclopedia of how we die." Alejandro turns it over to read the description aloud on its back cover: "An entertaining and irreverent look at the truth behind kicking the bucket." He laughs quietly; this writer is obviously a kindred soul with a dark sense of humor. He puts the book back on the shelf to his right.

Finally, he opens the GED book. It's called *Cracking the GED* and it's divided into different sections for each part of the exam. Alejandro opens the science section and sees an astronomy quiz. "So many stuff I gotta learn." He sighs. Alejandro has been watching shows about science and space for years on cable television, but that's no substitute for a formal education. He can describe the general concept of string theory as the next step in Einstein's theory of relativity, or the "theory of everything," with vibrating black holes and different dimensions. He adores Stephen Hawking. But he can't do algebra, and he can't name many of the elements in the periodic table. He claims not to remember whether he took a biology class in high school, because everything was such a blur.

He reads the astronomy quiz and notices that the questions have Roman numerals. He's seen those before but he doesn't know how to read them. The first question is, "Which of the following planets has the lowest surface temperature?" There's a chart of the solar system with the eight major planets, now that Pluto has been demoted to a dwarf planet. Alejandro guesses the answer is Neptune because it's farthest from the sun, but he isn't sure. He skips around the science section some more and finds another quiz called "Oceans, Tides, and the Moon Drill." He's confused by the word "drill." He wonders if it's about people mining on the moon. He doesn't know that "drill" can also be a substitute for "quiz."

Every section of the book is followed by drills, which clue him in to the nature of test prep. "I'm going to spend a lot of hours looking at this," he says. He skips ahead to the math portion and finds an arithmetic drill with word problems. He reads one aloud:

"Sheila works in a factory for $14.50 per hour up to 40 hours. After 40 hours she is paid $19 an hour."

The question asks him to figure out how much Sheila will make for working forty-three hours, and to express that as an equation. Alejandro learned similar addition and multiplication problems at Lindamood-Bell, but this one stumps him. It's a multiple-choice question and the choices are all written in unfamiliar ways. He reads right past the correct answer—40(14.50) + 3(19.00)—because he doesn't know the parentheses are a substitute for the × he normally sees in multiplication problems.

He looks at another math question, one illustrated with a pie chart. Alejandro was working with pie charts at the end of his tutoring, and this one shows the percentages of professionals who work with desktop, laptop, and other types of computers. The question under the chart asks how many people prefer mainframes. Alejandro correctly chooses "none of the above" because he notices there's no portion of the pie chart devoted to mainframes, only "other."

Written questions like these are much easier than equations. They just take him longer to process because the skills he learned in tutoring aren't yet automatic: he's still a slow reader. He looks at the beginning of the book, where it explains how to use the process of elimination in multiple-choice questions. The book gives a classification question as an example. It would be familiar to anyone who's ever taken a standardized test, but it's new to Alejandro. The test question describes five different terms: cannibalistic, mimetic, mutualistic, parasitic, and saprophytic. Alejandro reads the definitions for each and then turns the page to the questions, which ask the test-taker to determine which term best applies to different scenarios, such as:

"Jennifer Lopez's personal manager gets 10 percent of all the money her client earns. This kind of behavior is called?"

Alejandro looks over the five terms again and rereads their definitions. He's ruled out "saprophytic," which means living on dead or decaying organic matter, even though he loves that word. He's also sure the relationship isn't cannibalistic, or mimetic, which describes an organism that acts or tries to look like another. This process of elimination leaves him with parasitic and mutualistic. The parasitic relationship is defined as "an organism that lives in or on another, at whose expense it obtains nourishment and shelter."

"I guess that's me," he says, laughing, referring to how he lives off his parents. But he believes the Lopez-manager relationship could also be mutualistic, which is defined as "two or more organisms that live together for mutual benefit." After a bit of debate he decides on "mutualistic" and then reads that the correct answer should actually be "parasitic." He finds this confusing, because both could really apply. The manager is probably helping Jennifer Lopez, so isn't that a mutualistic relationship? he wonders. This process of elimination isn't so easy after all.

Frustrated with the study guide, Alejandro turns his attention again to the books surrounding him. There's a philosophy section, and Alejandro notices a book called *Buffy the Vampire Slayer and Philosophy*. He turns to the back cover and has a little trouble reading it aloud because it's written in the voice of a teenager:

"'She alone will stand against the demons—in the force of darkness she is the slayer. So if you're kid—kind of killing time between the apocalypse or just wondering about that mountain—meaning of life thing, here's some . . .'"

Alejandro pauses at a word he doesn't know. It's "readage," which isn't really a word, just an imitation of Valley Girl speak. Things like these are still tough for him because he takes most words very literally. He can get more nuanced meanings in spoken English than he can when he sees the words on paper. He's been using the dictionary he bought a few weeks ago to help cut through the layers of meanings while reading the superhero novel *Tomorrow Men*. He looked up two new words this week: "furrowing" and "swore." "Sometimes small words get me," he says, citing "phone" as one example. He says he often confuses it with "foam" because "ph" and "f" make the same sound.

Alejandro's lawyer has been encouraging him to read more and so has Jennifer Egan at Lindamood-Bell, who calls him once a week to check in. They want him to stick to a daily reading schedule in these weeks before he starts the GED preparation course. Gabriella brings back magazines from the hospital gift shop, and he's been reading them more often. He picked up *Vanity Fair* for the first time and read an article about an upcoming Hugh Jackman movie. He called the magazine "gossip for rich people." Despite his interest in politics and news, though, Alejandro still won't pick up a newspaper. He claims it's annoying to read about current events. He'd rather watch the television for that, and save books for reading about "the old guys" from history, such as George Washington. Why waste his time reading newspapers when he can get the same information, faster, on CNN or *Good Morning America*? For Alejandro, reading isn't fun because it's still so challenging. The things he really wants to learn about—like the Renaissance, history, and comic books—he doesn't consider himself ready to read about.

Liz Craynon, the former director of Lindamood-Bell, has been staying in touch with Alejandro. She says dyslexics often feel inhibited by their disability. "Nobody likes to expose their personal weaknesses, especially over and over again," she says. With dyslexics, "the attempts to read lessen because of the humiliation surrounding the failure. Think of how many times a parent or teacher says, 'Just try, just sound it out.' But trying doesn't bear any fruit." She says this eventually leads to something called "learned helplessness." Even after someone like Alejandro finally gains the tools to read and problem-solve, she says it's much more comfortable and easy to just give up or say the classic "I don't know."

Craynon's own sixty-three-year-old father has dyslexia and told her about leaving a job at a bank because a manager had asked him to read something aloud he had written. Apparently he had misspelled some words. "This manager reminded him of his second-grade teacher who ridiculed him in front of his class when he misspelled 'girl' as 'gril,'" she wrote me in an e-mail. "As he recounted the shame and ridicule to me, I saw him as a little seven-year-old so proud of his hard work, and then I saw his pain. He was transported back to that moment when he was put on the spot at his job."

That morning at Barnes & Noble, Alejandro bought the GED book. But as winter turned to spring, he admitted he hadn't read any of it.

SEVENTEEN

Like Picking Out Mercury

It's hard to get people to break old patterns. It can be even harder to teach them new ones.

Mike Staunton encountered that problem while working with the literacy teachers at MS 232 in the Bronx. Staunton is a consultant with AUSSIE, the Australian-American literacy program, and he's been at the school three times already this academic year. He's a tall man with a gray beard, glasses, and dark brown hair. He finds MS 232 "extremely well organized" and praises the literacy coach, Raedyn Rivera, for helping her teachers design their lessons. But he calls that "both a strength and a weakness" because they wind up relying on her too much.

Staunton was working with ten to twelve schools in New York City during the 2007/08 year. He found the standards of high school writing "very low" and middle school writing "okay," with MS 232 being typical. He's also deeply familiar with the push for more data-driven instruction. "Jurisdictions all over the world are going down this path," he said, citing England and his native Australia. Staunton was a school review officer for sixty schools in Australia and says educators are still refining their use of data as they become more adept at interpreting the numbers. From what he's seen in New York City so far, the concept of giving frequent assessments is a good one. But, he says, "The way they're doing it is simplistic.

"You can measure the width of a table with a tape measure, that's valid," he said. "Measuring learning is like trying to pick out mercury. It's very slippery." He feared teachers would get so obsessed with test scores—and the promise of merit pay for good scores, and negative consequences if they went down—that they'd forget the point of the data: to figure out how to work with different learning styles, so as to help teach individual students better. It wasn't that test scores weren't useful. Staunton just thought teachers should also spend time on another measurement: student writing. This was the point of his staff development sessions at MS 232.

Reading and writing are highly related. Though some good readers might not be great writers, you'll rarely see a strong writer who isn't also a good reader. Reading provides a model for writing, explains Esther Friedman. In the early stages, writing provides a way of remembering the sounds of the letters *d-o-g*, for example, while spelling out "dog." A child who struggles with decoding will have great difficulty writing. As we get older, and read more challenging texts, books don't just provide examples of good spelling and grammar; they help us learn about style and expression. "You might recognize, 'I'm writing like John Updike,' or a Pinteresque pause," explains Friedman. Likewise, the writing process informs the reading because it requires comprehension skills. A student might read something over and over again, but when they try to write about it in an essay, everything suddenly clicks.

Five teachers and Raedyn Rivera showed up for Staunton's session in March, including John McDonald, the seventh-grade literacy teacher. They sat in a circle of desks. Staunton told them that the goal was to learn how to "conference" with a student, and discuss writing assignments. To demonstrate the process, he asked them to read one student's essay about how she wants to sing on *American Idol*. Then he asked them, like the TV show's panelists, to score the seventh-grade student's essay, which began:

"I have a dream . . . to be a famous singer. That is my dream because ever scince I was about 7 years old I started to sing. So then when I was 10 years old, when I went to my aunt's house my aunt told me to make a show so then I did. Then my aunt told me to pick a song to sing and then she told me to put the volume low, get the microphone and sing."

The handwritten essay filled three pages. "Is it well developed and complete?" Staunton asked the teachers, using one of his measurements.

"It's certainly not clearly organized," said McDonald.

"Why?"

"Each paragraph is similar to the previous," McDonald answered, noting that the girl kept repeating the same information about how she wanted to sing. "She needed to tell me why she wants to be a singer, what people say, how she expects to get there, instead of writing everything over and over." Still, he said, the girl's writing has a "very clear voice."

Staunton asked some of the other teachers for input. An older special education teacher named Sharon Smith agreed that the essay was redundant, and that the girl started too many sentences with the words "and then" or "also," rather than using varied and logical transitions. Staunton suggested having students make line breaks between their paragraphs, instead of just using indentations, so they can visualize each paragraph as a new idea. But the special education teacher said her pupils didn't have any base of knowledge to correct their own writing; they didn't know when something was wrong. Rivera added that many students don't apply what they learn in class: "They fall back on bad habits."

"Mine, too," said McDonald.

"Because they don't have the core knowledge?" asked Staunton.

"It's hard," the special ed teacher said, with a hint of exasperation. Kids write the way they speak, she explained. "I don't want to hurt their feelings, but there's nothing wrong with learning the correct way also." The other teachers complained that e-mail and text messaging have changed how students write, because they've gotten into the habit of using shortcuts from these media. They'll write "g2g" for "got to go," and substitute "nutin" for "nothing."

Staunton explained that a good writing conference could educate both the student and the teacher by providing a window into the students' language skills. He demonstrated by calling the student who wrote the *American Idol* essay into the room. She wore glasses, a braided ponytail, dark jeans, and a red T-shirt with the words "baby phat" emblazoned in gold. She was a tiny girl, and as she sat next to Staunton she looked a little nervous but also happy to be the center of attention.

Staunton began by asking her what she liked about the essay. "I like that I expressed my feelings, like what do you want to do when you grow up," she answered. She mentioned how someone once told her the expression "If at first you don't succeed, try, try again." Staunton praised her for using words like "destiny" in her essay. "It's a nice, strong word," he told her. "I got a pretty good sense of where you are heading." Then he asked her to read a bit from the second paragraph of her essay.

"'So then, I started to sing and my aunt said that when I turn sixteen years old, then that is when she is going to take me to *American Idol* so then I could sing to the three judges,'" she read. Staunton stopped her. "Is there anything that sounds as if it could be said in a smoother way?" he asked. She looked puzzled, so he told her that one good rule of writing is not to use the same word in a sentence more than once. He asked her to rewrite the sentence she had just read. "I could put 'at that time,'" she suggested, instead of "so then." He called that a very good transition.

"'So then I started to sing,'" she continued reading, "'when I turn sixteen years old, at that time she is going to take me to *American Idol* . . .'"

"That was a long sentence," said Staunton gently. "Is it possible to break it up without using any [more] words?"

"I could put a period after *American Idol*," the girl offered. "Excellent," said Staunton. "I think it's better."

They continued for a few more minutes. Staunton wrapped up the exercise by asking her to remember a new rule: Don't use the same word more than once, and if you do, you should use a period. He told her she wrote the essay the way she'd tell a friend, and advised her to be a little more formal because "when you write something it's different from how you speak."

"I look forward to seeing you on *American Idol*," he said. "I'll be voting for you."

After the girl left the classroom, Staunton explained to the teachers that he focused on only one or two main points to avoid overwhelming the student, and that he wanted her to suggest changes so she'd have to participate. He showed the teachers how they can use a chart to track these writing conferences for every student. He also encouraged them to use what they learn from these sessions to adjust their lessons, and teach to their students' weaknesses. That's why he considers writing conferences a type of "formative" assessment. "If you have to tell a kid a hundred times, you're missing the point as a teacher. Who's the slow learner?" he asked, making it clear it was them. "You're not adapting."

McDonald was impressed by the demonstration. "I don't spend enough time doing that," he acknowledged. But there were good reasons.

• • •

McDonald was forty years old that winter and had just switched careers to become a teacher. He had managed bars and restaurants and had worked in advertising, but sought a job with the Department of Education because—like many new teachers—he wanted to make a difference in society. Many new teachers are assigned to difficult schools, because those jobs are tough to fill. In his first year, McDonald was teaching two seventh-grade English classes and a social studies class. At first he was uneasy, but by the winter he felt he had gained confidence and learned to establish order in the classroom. He was eventually able to "conference," or meet, with small groups of students while other students read and wrote independently. "The one thing they all want is help," he said.

The poor quality of their work had surprised McDonald when he first arrived in September. Some students had trouble understanding what they read, and their writing often resembled the work of elementary students rather than young teenagers. During a unit on memoirs, the students were asked to write three or four pages based on a personal experience. But one girl could barely read, let alone write. McDonald pulled out her handwritten memoir. The *i*'s were dotted with circles and the spelling was terrible. It also made no sense whatsoever:

> I like lisining to music and that Regoton end inglesh or Spanish on day may drother top Spanish end I said take that CD of please so he top inglesh music so I was dancesing with my little cousin . . .

Three months into the school year, this student was evaluated for special education services. McDonald said it took that long to convince her family that she needed to be screened for a learning disability. School officials weren't initially convinced, either, because she was new to the state and had no records. The other teachers thought she might have had a bilingual issue. Then McDonald began to notice that she was trying to fool her teachers by copying sentences from books and from her classmates. She'd string them together to make an essay without realizing that the different parts made no sense together. He thinks her memoir began with a piece of someone else's essay.

McDonald has another student whose family resisted getting him evaluated for special education services. He called on the boy one day to read aloud part of a published interview with the basketball star LeBron

James, and discovered that he could barely read. The boy took a long time trying to say each word. McDonald planned to meet with the boy's mother and have him read to her so she would see he's not ready for high school.

All the memoirs were handwritten. Some students in other classes use computers, but the seventh-graders in this class apparently didn't have them at home, or chose not to use the school's computer lab—which was considered small before more computers arrived later that spring. The students wrote on lined paper in carefully penciled words, making their work resemble that of young children writing their first essays. A boy who scored a level 2 on his standardized exam—putting him below grade level but able to pass—wrote a memoir about his little brother. There was barely any punctuation:

> Have you ever been so afraid you think that somebody is watching you? well I think that was a funny story because one time my little brother and me were playing now my grandma was looking at me . . .

McDonald wrote this last boy a note saying the essay wasn't well developed and needed more description and dialogue, as well as some work on organization and the use of paragraphs. The student was sent to after-school workshops. McDonald believes many of them could do better with more help on the basics, such as the use of capital letters and paragraphs. He suspects these skills could be weak because of the influence of text messaging. Of McDonald's two seventh-grade English classes, he says the students in one are able to focus and do their work. The other class is much more challenging.

They look deceptively well behaved when McDonald greets them after the writing session with Mike Staunton. There are only twenty-two students because a few are absent. They discuss the myth of Eros and most seem attentive, though a few have their heads on their desks. "Are you listening?" McDonald asks. He isn't shouting like he was in the fall, though he does occasionally flip the lights to get attention. "What did Kronos do?" he asks a boy. "I read that story," the student says, with hesitation. "He became Zeus, right?"

As the class continued, chaos simmered under the surface. A boy who'd been placed at his own desk in the back of the room, as a form of discipline, couldn't sit still. He'd get up and then McDonald would order him to sit down. Another boy sat by the window putting Scotch tape over his lip like a mustache. A slow buzz began to build in the class as the students talked. McDonald would attempt to quiet them down and focus on a writing project involving a myth, but his efforts weren't always successful. On two occasions he used his cell phone to call for Assistant Principal Anthony Hooks, a very large and very tall man who was able to establish order merely by standing at the classroom door. Hooks removed the boy in the back, who was fussing with a belt, and another troublemaker McDonald later said had "gang issues" and was also "a very bad reader." The majority of the class, he said, had started last fall well below grade level.

With so much drama to handle on a daily basis, McDonald isn't sure how he'd apply what he learned in the writing workshop earlier with the AUSSIE consultant. "I have no idea how I could do that in my class," he says. In the class of twenty-six students—several of whom are absent on any given day—McDonald estimates only five or six would do the work required to make individual writing conferences valuable for them and for him.

Down the hall, the word of the day is posted on the wall for everyone to see. It's "baffle: to foil or frustrate."

The literacy coach Raedyn Rivera says she went to the computer lab at the end of February to look at the results for the school's Acuity assessments. Three had been given so far: a predictive test, to gauge how the students would do on their state exams, and two more diagnostic assessments for teachers to figure out their students' strengths and weaknesses. The last one had been given a few weeks after the state's reading test in January.

Rivera said only one teacher in the entire school had looked at the results online before that January exam: eighth-grade English teacher Anna Maley, who had begun looking at the printouts right away in the fall. Rivera said the rest might have wanted to get online, but couldn't. There were glitches with the website and people had problems getting their access codes. Even Rivera couldn't see all the scores. A consultant who'd been working with the school finally helped her get into the online system by giving her a different password. "He did it in two seconds," she said. She suspected the math teachers might have more access and encouragement to use data because they're part of the school's inquiry team, which is looking at the lowest-performing students in math.

Meanwhile, Assistant Principal Desiree Martinez had been posting data on the walls outside her office for all the teachers to see. The teachers give weekly quizzes, and she graphs out those results as well as the scores from the school's own monthly reading tests. The charts show the results for every classroom teacher, and Martinez can see a few trends. The sixth-grade classes have the lowest test scores overall. In October, when teachers were supposed to be "engaging classes with characters," the top sixth-grade class had a pass rate of 32 percent. The Acuity test in November pointed out similar weaknesses among the sixth-graders: the highest pass rate of any class was 52 percent, compared to 55 percent in one seventh-grade class and 71 percent in the top-scoring eighth-grade class. Martinez suspected this had something to do with the high concentration of new and inexperienced teachers in sixth grade.

Martinez had given each English teacher a printout of their Acuity test scores, so they could see the results even if they didn't go online. But she didn't notice much enthusiasm. With the exception of Maley, "nobody had the reaction of 'that's online, let me go'" and see it. Most either weren't interested or weren't aware of what they could do with the data until a meeting was held in January, when they finally got to learn about Acuity in a formal setting. Martinez took some of the blame for this, acknowledging she could have planned things differently. Ellen Padva, a consultant from the Center for Educational Innovation–Public Education Association who's working with MS 232, thinks the teachers might have had a difficult time absorbing the new assessments while also preparing their students for the state reading and math exams in January and February.

Assistant Principal Martinez remained hopeful that her teachers would use the results from Acuity, and new ideas from the Australian writing coach, to figure out how to group their students so they could work with ones who have similar problems. This was the real goal of using data to shape instruction. But just as she was looking over her monthly charts, a teacher stopped her in the hall with a familiar refrain: "I can't get onto Acuity."

EIGHTEEN

Antonio's Space

Antonio's job at his aunt's restaurant lasted two weeks. He said he was filling in for an employee who then returned to work, so his aunt had to let him go. But he landed on his feet. A couple of months later, he was working at a new dry cleaning business in New Jersey owned by a family friend. He worked part-time sorting all the clothes as they came in and bagging them. It didn't require much reading because he dealt mostly with tag numbers. He made about $150 a week.

Things were slow at the new job, so he brought along his PlayStation Portable with video games. By February, he was itching for a new cell phone that could send e-mails and text messages to friends. He was still seeing Amy and he wanted to be able to stay in touch.

Antonio had become surprisingly adept at e-mail, given that he had barely known how to read two years earlier. Having learned how to navigate websites in his high school computer class, he practiced at home on his stepfather's desktop machine. He joined MySpace when he heard about it at school, and soon began looking for other kids in Washington Heights by typing in the zip code. Sometimes he hung out at the public library near his old high school, the Donnell Library on West Fifty-third Street, across from the Museum of Modern Art (it was closed in 2008 after the site was bought by a developer). The Donnell Library was a pretty ordinary-looking library with a run-down 1960s feeling. But it was very popular with the high school crowd thanks to the second-floor lounge, which was illuminated by a neon light that said "Teen Central," a feature at many public libraries.

One cold winter day, dressed in a red, white, and blue parka his mother had bought him, Antonio stopped by the library to check his e-mail. "Pretty Vacant" by the Sex Pistols was playing over the sound system in Teen Central. The crowd—mostly black and Hispanic boys—sat at round tables while they searched the Internet, laughing and chatting. Some were playing video games. The only books they looked at were comics. A shelf near the staircase was filled with games for Xbox, Wii, and PlayStation. Antonio headed over to the games and saw a skinny kid he knew from school with a crooked smile and a slow gaze. "I want a game!" he told Antonio, looking longingly at *Assassin's Creed* and the others he wanted to try. They talked for a few minutes and the boy showed Antonio his trick for checking out more than his allotment of video games: a key chain filled with electronic library cards all registered to different users. Antonio was impressed and laughed. His own small collection of overdue *Cowboy Bebop* comics was nothing compared to the other kids' scams.

Antonio had come here before to fill out job applications online, but on this day he was more interested in socializing. He signed onto one of the four computers at a round, blue table and logged on to MySpace, covering the keyboard as he typed his password. "You never know when somebody might be looking," he said. There was an e-mail waiting for him from a user pictured as a blond woman with sunglasses. He typed, "do you live in 164?" It's a reference to 164th Street in Washington Heights. Antonio hunts and pecks when he types, but he finds the letters with no problem and corrects himself as he goes. He says it's easier to write on a computer than in longhand because he doesn't get mad about writing slowly. He has more time to look at the letters and to choose the right ones.

He saw that his girlfriend, Amy, was online and clicked on her page. Her banner read, "1 Month Has Gone By and Plenty to Go." It's a reference to her one-month anniversary with Antonio. She had posted a few photos of herself. Some were blurry, but they all showed a slim girl with long brown hair and a big smile. Antonio was her number one friend on MySpace because he was her boyfriend. He went to his own page, which had a photo of himself smiling with a cigarette in his ear. His screen name is Alfie (for his favorite movie) and his eighty-four "friends" include music acts like Fort Minor, Linkin Park, Timbaland, and Mims, as well as people from his neighborhood and Amy. He saw a message that said there were no upcoming birthdays for any of his friends. He had answered a lot of the profile questions so people could learn about his tastes in music and movies. For school, he wrote that he went to Graphics from 2004 to 2008 but answered "N/A" for "degree." For "status" he answered "in a relationship." Next to "books" he wrote "JFK," the title of the book he was given by Lindamood-Bell. And for "TV" he indicated MTV's *The Real World Denver*. Despite the cigarette in his photo, he also checked that he's a nonsmoker (he didn't want Amy's mother to find out about his habit). He wrote in lowercase letters but there were no misspellings, and MySpace doesn't autocorrect.

When Antonio went into his mailbox, he noticed an e-mail from Amy saying that she had gone on a class trip that day. She was online and wanted to chat. He wrote back, "whitch trip," pausing to remove the erroneous letter "t" before hitting send.

Amy wrote back that she went to see Ellis Island. "You immagrant," he replied, sounding it out as he typed. "Go back where you came from." He thought this was hilarious. People write all kinds of "mad crazy things" on MySpace, he said. He knows a lot of their messages aren't spelled right because they're using Internet shorthand, with "n" for "and," and "u" for "you." He's still learning to spell correctly, so he doesn't want to write this way. He usually types whole words in his e-mail messages.

Antonio's able to maneuver his way around the Internet. He was reading almost as well as a fifth-grader when he finished his tutoring at Lindamood-Bell, though he still read slowly because of his dyslexia. He left MySpace for a moment to check his Yahoo account. There was an e-mail from Job Finder, a website he signed up with a while ago. He's decided that it's a scam because every message he receives refers to some school where he can pay to learn a trade. He deleted some old messages. "I could be hooked on this all day," he muttered, and returned to MySpace.

One day in February, Antonio's boss gives him a lift into Harlem, where he owns another dry cleaning store, and drops him off on a busy stretch of West 125th Street.

He goes to a T-Mobile store and looks at the three different models of the Sidekick phone, which has a big keyboard that slides out—easier for text messaging and e-mail. The cheapest one is a yellow, clunky model advertised for $49.99 after a rebate. The other two are priced at $199.99 and $299.99 after rebates. They're sleek black phones with wide screens and keyboards that jut out when fully opened. Antonio calls them "scraminoes" because he says they look like dominoes. He's excited and wants to buy one right away, but he worries about the cost. Should he get the most expensive model, he wonders, or the cheap one?

Antonio looks at the checklist next to each model to figure out the differences, and reads the features aloud: "My faves; text and instant messaging; speaker phone; Bluetooth enabled; camera; memory card slot; music player; voice dialing; real Web browsing." He knows what most of these terms mean. Web browsing is "like MSN," he says, "instant messaging." The less expensive of the two sleeker models has e-mail. The other doesn't have broadband-speed Wi-Fi, which he describes as "high connection." He gravitates toward the cheapest phone—the yellow model that has been out for a while—but then he realizes it doesn't have the camera option.

Antonio understands the different features of the phones but he's stuck on one word: "rebate." He knows it has something to do with getting money back, but he suspects it involves a coupon to spend more money on T-Mobile products. "I don't want to pay," he says, "I just need a phone."

He waits to speak to a clerk. He's wearing a new olive-colored jacket instead of the lined denim jacket he usually wears during winter. He says it was a gift from his boss. He's stuffed his PlayStation Portable into one of the pockets. It's slim and black, loaded with his favorite music and video games. The long line moves quickly and Antonio is soon standing across the desk from a T-Mobile clerk in the store uniform of black pants and a fuchsia shirt. He asks him about the Sidekick. The clerk takes him over to the phones and they discuss the difference between the two more expensive models. Antonio asks him about the rebate and the clerk says he might not have to pay as much as advertised if he's already a T-Mobile customer. Antonio says it's probably in his stepfather's name and the account is located, but the phone can't be ordered without his stepfather's permission. Antonio thanks the man and asks for a card, saying he'll call him later after he speaks to his stepfather.

Antonio is itching to get the phone. But the $150 a week he makes at his job never seems to last very long; he spends much of it on treating

Amy to meals and movies. His family gave him a new video game for his nineteenth birthday in January. But he mastered it quickly and decides that if he can't get the phone right now he'll look at other games, and maybe get himself a new pair of headphones. He walks west on 125th and into a GameStop store to look around. A sign in the aisle says "Cash In on Your Past Conquest." Antonio reads the directions aloud: "Once you've mastered a game, the ultimate truth is selling it back for cash." He missed one critical word: "triumph," not "truth."

Antonio looks at movies and games for the Xbox and Wii systems, which he doesn't own. He sees a game he knows called *Devil May Cry* and reads the back of the box aloud, slowly but carefully, getting almost all the words:

"'Long ago the Dark Knight Sparda rebelled against the dark emperor and waged a one-man war to save humanity. Thousands of years later, a religions organization worships this re-re-known-ed sav-savior and has taken it upon themselves to rid the world of evil. Resid-residing in Fortuna, this organization is known as the "Order of the Sword" and is made up of an elite group of "Holy Knights."'"

Antonio knows this game series well and launches into a whole story about the game's mythology and comic books. He then picks up *Resident Evil 4*, about an agent trying to rescue the president's daughter. The two series share the same Japanese game designer and are popular for their extreme combat sequences adored by teenage and preteen boys. But they also have a great deal of text. You can't advance past certain levels without being able to read the instructions.

As he walks west on 125th Street, a beggar asks for money and Antonio gives him some change. Surprised that someone has actually paid any attention, the man thanks Antonio and the teen wishes him good luck. He seems at home here on the streets, easily talking to strangers. But he says he's also glad to have a routine, a job, and a girlfriend. Antonio is still thinking about getting more tutoring at Huntington Learning Center before the hours his attorneys won for him expire in June. He feels some pressure from Amy's family to continue his education. "She wants the best for me," he says, adding that she knows he didn't learn to read until recently but she doesn't know all the details. Antonio seems more concerned about Amy's mother. "She told me on Christmas Eve, 'You know my family comes from a hardworking family, everybody works, nobody's lazy, everybody's a professional.' She wants to know when am I starting a GED program. She doesn't want her daughter going out with a bum."

Antonio's stepfather, Hector, also wishes he would go back to school but says, "We cannot do anything." After all, Antonio is nineteen. "At least he learns how to write, read," says Hector, adding that he can always improve with practice. He's planning to buy his stepson a laptop because he knows the computer has improved his literacy. And he's very happy that Antonio is working steadily.

Antonio doesn't seem to be in a rush to go back to Lindamood-Bell or Huntington Learning Center. His boss told him he could leave early on some days for tutoring. But he doesn't quite know how to reconcile his conflicting desires for a paycheck and for more education. His reading has improved enough for him to communicate by text messaging. He's been working for more than a month, which feels like a great accomplishment. Maybe it's a holding pattern. But for now, it's holding together.

NINETEEN

Reality Bytes

New York City's campaign to encourage its teachers and principals to track student achievement with a new computer network was happening at the same time as a much bigger campaign: the 2008 presidential race. While school officials huddled around printouts of practice tests to see which students had passed, aides to Mayor Bloomberg studied ballot rules in all fifty states as their boss considered an independent bid for the White House. He traveled around the country giving speeches on issues of national importance—organizing a group of mayors against illegal handguns and speaking out on the need to address climate change. Bloomberg kept the media asking "Will he or won't he?" up until the end of February. By then, Republicans were rallying around John McCain as their likely nominee and Democrats were captivated by the fierce nominating contest between senators Hillary Clinton and Barack Obama.

On February 28, 2008, Bloomberg wrote an editorial in *The New York Times* with the headline "I'm Not Running for President, But . . ." Though he declined to run as an independent, he urged the divided country to embrace bipartisan solutions: "I have watched this campaign unfold, and I am hopeful that the current campaigns can rise to the challenge by offering truly independent leadership. The most productive role that I can serve is to push them forward, by using the means at my disposal to promote a real and honest debate."

Bloomberg certainly had the means. As mayor of the nation's largest city, and a billionaire beholden to neither party, he could use both the bully pulpit and his own finances to try to sway public opinion. Bloomberg cited the economy, immigration policy, and school reform among the issues that demanded new approaches. He wrote that the presidential candidates must know "that we can't fix our schools without holding teachers, principals and parents accountable for results."

But as Bloomberg called on national leaders to challenge the status quo in public education, his own efforts back home in New York City were running into a few roadblocks. He and his team blamed some of their problems on the so-called orthodoxy of unions and special interest groups. There was an obvious culture clash between Bloomberg's incentive-oriented, private sector approach and the school system, which like any government bureaucracy had developed a mentality in which jobs were seen as a cross between public service and an entitlement. But critics also blamed a combination of hubris, as Bloomberg tackled so much at once, and the political ambitions of a man they viewed as more eager to leave his mark on New York City and the nation than to improve the schools in their own right.

One day before Bloomberg declared he wasn't running for president, the *New York Post* reported on new and potentially costly problems in his education department. The tabloid announced that the Achievement Reporting and Innovation System (ARIS) wasn't doing all it had promised: "The school system's new $80 million computer super system to track student performance has been a super debacle, teachers and principals say."[1] The article went on to explain that the city's 79,000 teachers weren't able to log on to ARIS because of glitches and delays.

The problems were actually twofold. Yes, ARIS was turning out to be much harder to access than people expected. And if you asked a teacher if he or she had ever tried using ARIS, the typical answer was "What's that?" But the system's architect, Jim Liebman, said not all of the 79,000 full-time teachers were supposed to be using it during the initial rollout. As Liebman explained, at first ARIS was supposed to be used only by principals and a few teachers in every school, who would turn to it to figure out which students they should study on their inquiry teams. Liebman later acknowledged that people may have gotten a different impression when they heard the system would go online in the 2007/08 school year. He portrayed it as a misunderstanding. "We promised to get ARIS to principals and inquiry teams, we aspired to get it to teachers," he said. "And we probably should not have even acknowledged that aspiration because it was an aggressive aspiration and it did not happen."

But even the superusers were sometimes frustrated. Principals typically appointed a teacher or a staff member with a math or technology background to collect and organize data. At PS 189 in Washington Heights, the go-to guy was the business manager Arnold Lorenzo, chosen because of his knowledge of spreadsheets. One day in March, he logged on to ARIS and gave a tour. It took a long time for the screen to load. Lorenzo wasn't sure if this was the fault of ARIS or his school's own lousy connection. "Budgeting software is faster," he said ironically, referring to another notoriously large data system.

After a wait of several minutes, the ARIS home page was fully loaded, with the school's name at the top of the screen. Lorenzo could click on different tabs for retrieving information on his school's students, classes, and Acuity assessments. However, Acuity's data had not yet been loaded into ARIS, and apparently wasn't supposed to be put there until the end of the year. Teachers and principals were encouraged to use Acuity's own website to see the results of the math and reading assessments. This was why they didn't know about ARIS; they didn't have to deal with it.

Lorenzo clicked on "students and classes" to show what he *could* get from ARIS. He was directed to a list of children's names, along with their transcripts, dates of birth, free meal status, attendance, and whether they were English Language Learners or in need of special education services. All this information is subject to federal privacy protections, so only certain teachers and administrators can gain access. Lorenzo clicked on the "collaborate" tab to demonstrate how he could sort student data and make customized spreadsheets. Again, it took several minutes to load the page. But he was able to see what he needed and sorted it to find the lowest-performing students in math or reading. They were highlighted in dark blue.

Principals found this main function of ARIS very useful because much of its information was previously kept on different systems, but some also discovered its limitations. At PS 59 in Midtown, Assistant Principal Gabriel Feldberg had sorted out twenty-one students who were at the bottom third in either math or reading. Students like these stand out at PS 59, where 84 percent are meeting state standards in reading and 95 percent in math. Despite these high marks, however, the school got a B on its November report card, because not enough students were making a year's worth of progress, by the Department of Education's reckoning. Feldberg had sent an e-mail to Jim Liebman arguing that the grading system punished high-performing schools like his. PS 59 lures many wealthy children whose parents work nearby at the United Nations, but it also has a good number of working-class pupils.

Feldberg's chart showed that a fourth-grade girl came to school in the fall reading at level H (more than a year behind her peers), even though she had gotten as high as level J at the end of the previous school year (closer to third-grade level). Her reading skills had obviously declined over the summer. By January 2008, she was back at level J. This could have given her teacher the false impression that she'd made progress since the fall—even though she was at the same level she had reached at the end of third grade. Feldberg found other children with the same patterns. But when he wanted demographic information about the children, to look for trends such as whether the struggling students were all English Language Learners, he discovered that ARIS didn't have as much of it as the city's existing computer-based record system (called ATS, or Automate the Schools). ARIS imported data from ATS but Feldberg said it didn't have addresses, admission dates, and some other details he wanted to mine for clues. And when he finished his chart, he couldn't upload it back into ARIS. Nor was he able to use ARIS's own spreadsheet because it didn't have enough columns for his purpose. The ARIS spreadsheet also wouldn't continuously update itself when a child left school or started receiving special education services. So the city had spent $80 million on a new computer system that didn't do anything different than what Feldberg could already do with Excel and the existing record systems.

Meanwhile, teachers ran into their own technical problems as they tried to use the new math and reading assessments from Acuity. Several, like those at MS 202 in Queens, found the website jammed with traffic. Others didn't have the time or training to sift through the sudden information overload. Acuity provided much more than a snapshot of how many students in a class got each test question right or wrong. It enabled the teachers to see how each individual child performed, to look at the test questions and answers for trends, and to design homework assignments aimed at strengthening their weaknesses. An elementary classroom teacher may have had twenty-five or thirty students to work with. But middle school subject teachers could have a hundred or more students if they taught three math or English classes a day. Many teachers said the assessments helped them figure out which skills their students needed to practice. A geometry teacher could devote an extra lesson to polygons, for example, and an English teacher could create more homework assignments with synonyms and antonyms. But Lila Teitelbaum, a fifth-grade teacher at PS 59, said the Acuity test didn't tell her anything she didn't already know about her students by monitoring what level of books they were reading. She said she could tell who was at grade level based on comprehension skills and how well they read aloud to her during one-to-one meetings. (In fact, a few hundred schools chose to assess their students this way, with the help of Teachers College, instead of using Acuity.)

New York wasn't the only school system asking itself these questions as teachers' skills were increasingly being outsourced to publishing companies. John W. Hutcheson, a former teacher from Dallas, Texas, told *Education Week* that he decided to work in a private school because he found giving assessments three times a year so meaningless. "We would spend entire afternoons analyzing benchmark results," he told the publication. "The district, every time the kids took the test, would print up a thorough record of how many answers they missed, the answers they put down, a list of sub-skills to be worked on, and a complete analysis of each test." A Philadelphia social studies teacher echoed that sentiment when he complained to *Education Week* in the same article that giving multiple-choice tests every six weeks was taking too much time from instruction.[2] Among some educators, testing often represented an intrusion or, even worse, an opportunity to find someone to blame. But others saw opportunities, and so did the software companies. States such as North Carolina and Utah, as well as individual districts such as that of Philadelphia, were hiring companies, including Pearson, DigitalBridge, and SchoolNet, for tracking student achievement. A study comissioned by Pennsylvania's Department of Education found math and literacy scores had increased in Philadelphia schools using SchoolNet's systems.

Richard Yeh, an assistant professor of evaluation studies at the University of Minnesota, wrote about how data could be an asset to teachers. Yeh studied a curriculum that was used in McKinney, Texas, which combined software aimed at finding a child's appropriate reading level with books to match his or her skills. Through small-group instruction, tutoring, and frequent assessments, the scores went up, and 87 percent of teachers said the program (which was called Reading Assessment) helped them adjust and improve their instruction.[3]

But many observers were wary about drawing any sweeping conclusions about the effectiveness of all this testing and tracking. Michael Casserly, executive director of the Council of the Great City Schools, had no doubt some districts had gotten gains. But, he cautioned, "you want to see a longer trend line." Data management systems were springing up all over the place as districts rushed to buy the latest technology—often without involving their staffers to the degree of the McKinney, Texas, program.

Veteran educators also cautioned that additional assessments would be useless unless teachers believed they were closely tied to the curriculum and therefore legitimate. Long before NCLB, Tennessee created the Value Added Assessment System—which was capable of linking individual teachers to classroom performance, so the state could determine which teachers were "adding value" and raising test scores. Its creator, an agricultural statistician named Dr. William Sanders, determined that students could gain twenty-five percentile points if they had three consecutive years of instruction with the most effective teachers.[4] Doug Wood, a former executive director of the Tennessee State Board of Education, said the data was interesting but also led to more questions. "Superintendents and principals have to carve out enough time and space to really give teachers an opportunity to learn how to interpret data and then to figure out, 'How do I change my instructional practices to address what the data are telling me?' I'm not thoroughly convinced we give teachers enough time and space and support." Wood is now executive director of the National Academy for Excellent Teaching at Teachers College, and he's been working with a coalition of New York City schools.

With the Department of Education having rolled out so many high-tech tools at once, New York City's teachers and principals were obviously going to be overwhelmed. But the people behind the scenes were also feeling the stress of uploading and verifying the records of more than a million students. The makers of ARIS had expected to create a searchable Web-based system for teachers and principals with features similar to those of Facebook and Google. It turned out to be a bigger homework assignment than they had expected.

Larry Berger's corner office has a postcard view of Manhattan. His company, Wireless Generation, is located in the Brooklyn waterfront neighborhood of DUMBO, an acronym for Down Under the Manhattan Bridge Overpass. From his desk, he can see the twinkling lights of the bridge at dusk over a calm and peaceful-looking East River in winter. The educators and administrators at the Tweed are on the other side of the water. Here in DUMBO, a mini Silicon Alley has taken root. Tech companies, furniture stores, and wealthy professionals had followed and often displaced the artists who had originally reclaimed the spacious buildings abandoned long ago by manufacturers.

Wireless Generation was cofounded in 2000 by Berger after he saw early elementary school teachers using handwritten sheets for keeping track of their students' reading levels. Wireless created a product called mCLASS. It's a software platform that takes the very same early reading and math assessments teachers were already using and puts them into an easy-to-read format for measuring progress on handheld devices. The company claims its product is used by more than a hundred thousand teachers across the United States. More than two hundred schools in New York City use the handhelds. At PS 112 in East Harlem, teachers can be seen carrying PalmPilots in fat silver cases. The reading assessments are easy to give and take just a few minutes. A teacher can pull a student aside in the hallway and have her read from a booklet while following along on the handheld, tapping the screen every time the child makes an error. The computer then calculates how many words the child reads per minute and compares that to the previous assessment. This lets the teacher see whether the child is hitting established reading goals, or benchmarks, for different times in the school year. The children who aren't meeting these benchmarks are coded in red, and Principal Eileen Reiter steers them to extra intervention services.

It was this experience in making educational software relatively accessible that led IBM to partner with Wireless Generation on ARIS. IBM hired Wireless as the subcontractor. Its task was to make all student and class summaries easy to navigate whenever teachers log in to ARIS. It was also charged with making the Web 2.0 features that would give the New York City Department of Education something akin to Facebook—a portal where teachers could communicate with one another and share successful techniques. Access to confidential records would be limited, because of federal privacy laws. If teachers, principals, and even parents could get all the information they were able to obtain about student performance in one place, and then communicate with one another about trends, ARIS would provide the dynamic, John Dewey–type of laboratory for learning that Jim Liebman had envisioned when he joined the chancellor's team. Or that was his theory, anyway.

But it was a huge challenge. In 2007 most school systems were still gathering their test scores and other data in what was called Web 1.0: a stagnant, read-only format. Some districts let parents and students go to a website to check out the latest homework assignments. But Berger said most districts didn't know how to make their student information useful and relevant. "They are generally data mausoleums. You dress up the data nicely one last time before you bury it away." By switching to a Web 2.0 format, with real-time data that's continuously added, updated, and shared, Berger and the rest of the ARIS team hoped to make their system more user-friendly, enabling educators to stay on top of the latest achievement data and share what they've learned with other teachers about how to improve instruction—whether they were teaching the most challenging pupils, like Yamilka, or gifted and talented students.

Berger gave me a tour of the prototype Wireless Generation designed that winter for the new ARIS dashboard, complete with fictional characters: teachers, administrators, and the like. He logged in as a math teacher called Jose. We saw a white screen cluttered with colorful links and charts. There was a small e-mail box at the top telling Jose he'd gotten fifteen messages and three alerts. Since Jose was said to be a math teacher, there was a box in the middle of the screen with folders for various math resources, such as a math discussion forum. On the right side of the screen, there was a list called My Networks. We could see Jose's friends, or contacts, with names and pictures of their faces, just like on Facebook.

The list included three principals, a teacher, an administrator, and a librarian.

Jose's contacts had all written reports called SoNo's. The term is shorthand for "So what? Now what?" Berger says these are the questions that are bound to arise whenever educators come across some new piece of data. It's not enough to know that scores went up among third-grade Hispanic pupils, for example. Teachers need to know why that matters, and then figure out how to use that information to help other students learn and close the achievement gap. We clicked on one of the people in Jose's network, described as a retired principal from Harlem. She had posted a SoNo. Next to the words "So what?" was a short summary. "Math scores for ELL students are always a bit tricky to interpret," she'd written. "Sometimes they are really just indicators of language issues." She included a link to an article. Beneath the "So what?" entry was a space called "Now what?" Here, the principal had written about her own suggestions for working with English Language Learners who lag behind in math. "In math it is always good to start from a child's strengths," she wrote. "If I have a student who can count successfully in Spanish, then I spend some time showing the close resemblances between some of the Spanish names for numbers and their English counterparts." There were also links to math sites, and reports that could be of interest to anyone reading the SoNo, the way Amazon.com tells you about a book you might enjoy based on others you've already bought.

Berger was planning to get a core set of users involved in writing and linking to SoNo's by the spring of 2008. But he told me Wireless got diverted by the sheer volume of work involved in other aspects of ARIS. "The decision in the fall was to get the core functionality of ARIS working," Berger explained. This meant "cleansing" the data for all 1.35 million students and ninety thousand teachers, principals, and other pedagogues. IBM was in charge of that aspect, but "it turned out to be a much more complex task than any of us thought, including to some extent the experts," said Liebman.

Liebman described it as different buckets of data. One contained "all the demographic data on kids, and who's special ed, and what courses they're in, and what grades they're getting in classes, and who their teacher is, and all of that." There were also state test scores and assessments. Sorting out all this student data was a headache. One system may have used percentiles while another had percentages. But that wasn't nearly as difficult as dealing with another bucket: the teachers. Unlike for the students, who have OSIS (Office of Student Information System) numbers, the city didn't have completely unique identifiers for determining which teachers were linked to which classrooms. Some teachers had full names, some had nicknames, and some had the same names as others. So linking the children in a class with a particular teacher "turned into a monumental task," said Liebman. Nor were all the different vendors, such as the test publisher CTB/McGraw-Hill, willing to change their formats to fit the city's needs for ARIS. Sorting out which administrators and teachers were allowed to see student information, because of federal privacy rules, also delayed the rollout of ARIS.

Other school districts were running into similar problems when they tried building new data systems. Andre Smith, the director of Florida's Education Data Warehouse, said low-paid secretaries were often charged with entering data. "Sometimes all the males at a school turn into females because a finger is still on the *f* key," he said, though he added that employees became more careful once the districts started using the data more and applying greater scrutiny. "We have a constant problem in education of dirty data," agreed Trevor Mahlum, the assessment data coordinator for Natrona County, Wyoming. In Casper, he said, student addresses weren't always up to date because the system relied on parents to come forward whenever they moved. He discovered the school bus companies had more reliable data. This was among the reasons why Natrona took the slow road and asked Jeff Wayman, now a professor at the University of Texas, to study what its people were already doing before building a new system. It took a couple of years. And Natrona had only 11,500 students—1 percent of New York City's enrollment.

New York's data wasn't completely "cleansed" until the spring of 2008, several months behind schedule. Educators wondered if IBM wasn't up to the task, and many questioned whether ARIS was a big waste of money. One parent group thought the funds should have been used to reduce class sizes. These frustrations only grew when Mayor Bloomberg ordered the school system to cut $100 million midyear—but the ARIS budget was spared. A website for parents parodied the situation with a faux news report about ARIS declaring "the computer upgrade will save huge personnel costs by rendering teachers 'obsolete.'"[5]

Some wondered if the city had bitten off more than it could chew. ARIS was extremely ambitious. Five companies had submitted proposals for the $80 million contract, three of which were seriously considered by the city.

One of those proposals came from SchoolNet. The New York City–based educational technology company makes information management systems with a suite of software products, somewhat like Microsoft Office. Districts can pick and choose which programs they want for charting individual student test scores, giving assessments, downloading attendance and demographic information, and designing a curriculum. SchoolNet also has a Web-based communication tool that can be used by teachers, parents, and students. In short, it's one of several technology companies making systems that are a lot like ARIS. As well as in Philadelphia, its products have been used in Atlanta; Columbus, Ohio; and Corpus Christi, Texas. Chicago also signed a contract with SchoolNet and was able to give teachers and parents more real-time access to student records, but other aspects of data management were not rolling out as smoothly.

SchoolNet was founded in 1998 by the education analyst-author Denis Doyle and Jonathan Harber, an entrepreneur who worked in investment banking and cofounded the multimedia software company Diva (which was later bought by the video-editing company Avid). Harber had attended the private and prestigious Dalton School in New York City. When the requests for proposals went out for ARIS, Harber figured he had the hometown advantage. But despite partnering with Deloitte, his company lost the bid to IBM. Though he concedes a bit of sour grapes, he was stunned that the city chose to design its own data management system from scratch instead of buying an existing product. "It's like saying, I'm going to have someone build me a spreadsheet instead of using Excel," he said. He claimed SchoolNet's products would have cost the city a quarter of the amount of building ARIS.

There were also questions about IBM's role in bringing public schools into the digital age. Two years earlier, the company had been named in the scandal surrounding E-rate, the federal program to hook up schools and libraries to the Internet. IBM was among several contractors accused of taking advantage of school districts to win lucrative government contracts. It was denied $250 million in federal E-rate funds after the FCC found the company helped steer Atlanta and seven other districts through what was supposed to be a competitive bidding process. IBM claimed the federal rules weren't clear.[6]

Jim Liebman defended IBM's work with New York City. The company had worked on data systems in fifty school districts, including Broward County, Florida—which Liebman considered a good model for parts of ARIS. He also said his team looked at SchoolNet and other companies with off-the-shelf data management systems, but they couldn't be customized to suit the city's complex needs. And Liebman claimed the increasingly dominant role of Wireless Generation in the ARIS project did not reflect any disappointment with IBM—despite complaints from insiders that the software giant wasn't up to the task and made a product more suited for a corporation than a school district. Rather, he said the shift made sense now that IBM had built the first version of ARIS. He also noted that the city awarded the $80 million ARIS contract to IBM precisely because it collaborated with Wireless on its bid. He vowed the system would be fully operational in the fall for all teachers and parents.

But ARIS had become a political football. A city councilman called for terminating the contract. And the teachers union was fighting what it perceived as an overreliance on test scores. Joel Klein was proposing to base teacher tenure on test-measured student achievement. Other districts were using test scores to evaluate teachers, and a few—including Houston—were using federal grants to give teachers performance bonuses for raising classroom scores. Tennessee's Value Added study had found the very best teachers could boost student performance. But as the Economic Policy Institute researcher Richard Rothstein noted, those effective teachers were already in the top 10 percent, and it would be difficult to get all teachers to that level. These top teachers also made a bigger difference in math scores than in reading scores.[7] Doug Wood says there were plans for Tennessee to use this data as part of a comprehensive way of measuring teacher quality, but they never got off the ground. This debate continues as the Obama administration encourages states to design ways of measuring "effective" teachers.

New York City's teachers didn't trust the chancellor and the mayor to rate them fairly. Their union fought the plan with television ads and persuaded state lawmakers to ban the mayor from linking test scores to tenure. United Federation of Teachers president Randi Weingarten said there was no way to accurately isolate the contributions of an individual classroom teacher, largely because the state tests are given in January and February. "So which teacher is that about?" she asked. "Is it about the teacher you had in fourth grade, fifth grade?" Weingarten agreed to let test scores be used informally in educating teachers about their strengths and weaknesses. Although she opposed merit pay, she also had agreed to an experiment that awarded money to schools with high concentrations of students in poverty if they raised their student's test scores. The extra funds would be distributed to staffers by compensation committees. Weingarten had a lot at stake politically. She was in the midst of her own (ultimately successful) campaign to lead the union's national umbrella organization, the American Federation of Teachers. Weingarten and some parent activists argued that the city should invest more in lowering average class sizes—which had been falling but were still in the mid-twenties for middle and high schools, larger than those in the suburbs.

Chancellor Klein and Mayor Bloomberg agreed that small classes were important in the early elementary grades. But they repeatedly referred to studies showing the best predictor of student achievement was teacher quality. That's why Klein was pushing for a way to measure effective teaching. He cited an example of two teachers with similar classroom demographics. "If I told you one moved [students] up from an average 2.5 in grade five to 2.6, and the other moved from 2.5 to 2.52, it wouldn't matter to me," he said. "But if one [teacher] moved to 2.9 and another to 2.2 it *would* matter to me, and I bet you it would matter to every parent in the city." When his plan died in Albany that spring, Klein declared its demise "one of the most ridiculous politically driven things I've seen."

Klein and the union continued fighting that winter and spring over midyear budget cuts. Teachers and principals also pressured the city to revise the formula for grading schools. The city had already eased the requirement that schools give five assessments each in math and reading, by allowing them to give four instead. The department said it wanted administrators to get more comfortable with the new system, but it was also worried about the costs.

The message was clear: schools might tinker around the edges, but the focus on testing was here to stay—at least as long as the city could afford to pay for the exams. But was this really the way to build a better teacher? Would Web-based computer networks and more frequent assessments force teachers, and principals, to pay more attention to struggling students like Yamilka, instead of sweeping them under the rug? Would they spend their precious spare time logging into a new computer network and reading about one another's classroom experiences? Or would they view the new ARIS website as just another mandate from the powers that be?

SPRING

Inputs and Outcomes

I see a movie in my head . . . I'm actually, like, seeing people when I'm reading.

—Antonio

Yamilka, Alejandro, and Antonio each make progress in their own way. Through good instruction, they're able to improve their reading. And with reading skills, these young adults are able to gain a little more confidence to keep pushing themselves.

The city's principals and teachers also rediscover why some children need more help than others, through their intensive use of data and by having teams in every school focus on struggling students. As the Bloomberg administration continues to roll out its reforms, the chancellor and his staff confront the challenges of measuring student progress. The roles of race, class, and family education can't be ignored. But neither can good teaching. This part of the book also explores what it means to be literate in today's society.

TWENTY

Back to School

In the middle of April 2008, Alejandro got a phone call from Hostos Community College informing him that he'd finally made it off the waiting list for its free pre-GED classes. He could enroll at the end of the month.

Though he was bored after studying at home for the past three months, Alejandro wasn't excited about going back to school. He was nervous about sitting in a room with other students. And while he'd kept on using the math and reading workbooks from his tutoring program, he still hadn't cracked open the GED book he had bought at Barnes & Noble. Its thickness was intimidating. "I think I've just been thinking about it too much, psyching myself out," he said quietly. Instead, he read magazines such as *Popular Science* and *Discover*, which had an article about Richard Branson's plan for Virgin Galactic to provide commercial space flights. Alejandro was still a reluctant subway rider, but he would have gladly accepted a ticket to space.

Reading the GED book probably wouldn't have mattered, though, as Alejandro discovered once he started his math and reading classes. They met on alternate days for three hours each. Alejandro found the math course way over his head. Most of the other students had taken math during the winter semester and were doing problems he had never been exposed to in his tutoring sessions. He'd only gotten through addition, subtraction, multiplication, division, and fractions and would need more personalized instruction to learn geometry and algebra. Meanwhile, the reading class wasn't about test preparation questions like those in the GED book.

Jacqueline Mason-Francis was teaching the reading course that spring semester. On a warm day in May, she arrived fifteen minutes late, at 9:45 a.m., and apologized to the seven students present that morning, explaining that there had been a police incident on her subway train. The tall, stylish young black woman wore a brown-and-green shirt, cropped pants, and a newsboy cap. Her teaching style was informal yet slightly theatrical. She looked around the room and asked which of the students hadn't yet read in front of the class. She wanted everyone to practice reading in public by the end of the course. She called on a Bangladeshi woman named Roma* who sat in the back of the room. Roma hadn't brought a book of her own to share with the class, so Mason-Francis handed her *How I Came to Be a Writer* by Phyllis Reynolds Naylor. Roma stepped to the front cautiously. She was dressed in black and read aloud softly, in a thick accent, "'The idea of being a writer never entered my mind . . .'"

"You must project," Mason-Francis interjected, telling Roma that she had a beautiful voice that sounded like a song. Roma started over and the rest of the students listened respectfully, though Mason-Francis shushed one man who checked his cell phone.

The class was held in a large trailer located one block west of the Hostos Community College campus on Grand Concourse and 149th Street, which is a few stops on the 4 train south of Alejandro's home. Adult education courses were held in trailers because the school had run out of space. Anyone walking by might have thought it was a construction site, except for a misspelled sign that said "Hostos Communiy College Trailer 5." A security guard was posted out front; inside, the trailer was strikingly clean, with polished floors and a tidy bathroom. But the classrooms were small and had security gates on their windows, making it hard to feel a breeze.

The students present on that hot sticky morning included a Dominican immigrant with cornrows named Juan, who was twenty-five but looked like a teenager. He sat behind an older man who translated into Spanish for him occasionally. Next to him sat an older woman, a man, and a couple of women in their twenties and thirties. There were plenty of empty seats between them. Mason-Francis stood by a desk and a chalkboard.

*The students in this class asked me to use their first names only.

At 9:55, the door creaked open and Alejandro cautiously entered. He smiled shyly and walked straight to the back row. Mason-Francis asked the students a few questions about the piece of writing Roma had just read. "What did you hear, Charles, besides zipping your zipper?" she asked an older black man from Guyana, who was fiddling with his bag. Another student entered the room and sat down in front; he was tall and lanky, with close-cropped hair, a black shirt, and a silver medallion necklace. Mason-Francis asked the class for feedback on Roma's reading. They discussed the content a little bit but the exercise was mostly about getting them more comfortable speaking in public. Charles encouraged Roma to keep on trying even though she was worried about her thick accent. Mason-Francis told her to speak louder and the class applauded her effort. Then it was Juan's turn to read a few pages of *Before We Were Free* by Julia Alvarez, which is about his native Dominican Republic. He said he moved to the United States when he was eighteen and didn't learn enough English to complete high school before aging out at twenty-one. He nervously held the paperback about a foot away from his face with both hands and read very slowly. Again, the eight other students applauded when he finished the section.

About forty students were accepted for the spring semester of this pre-GED class, which met through June. But Mason-Francis said only ten to fifteen showed up regularly. Hostos had an annual budget of $250,000 for its adult education classes, which are funded with state, city, and federal dollars. The program director, Zenobia Johnson, said the school admits more students than it expects will attend, because adults typically get caught up with work and family obligations. It also switched to offering three semesters of classes instead of two, in order to keep enrollment up and continue getting government funds. Going back to school is tough for high school dropouts who haven't been in a classroom in years. The average reading level is between fifth and eighth grade. This is why the classes don't involve any practice tests or GED books like the one Antonio purchased. The students all scored too low on a screening test to take the regular GED preparation class. "We find the GED is a reading exam, and in order to get through the exam you have to be a strong reader," Johnson said, explaining that the classes focused on basic reading and writing to help the students brush up on their skills.

Mason-Francis embraced that approach in her classroom. "Who's done some vocabulary work?" she asked. The students took out grammar worksheets about nouns and verbs and opened their notebooks. Mason-Francis was about to write something on the chalkboard, but then she stopped to tell the class a story. A student from another of her classes had told her, "Education is not important; it's just a piece of paper to get a job." She asked the class if they agreed and there was instant feedback. Shirley, a sixty-one-year-old woman in the front row, said she both agreed and disagreed. She was hoping to find a better job by finally earning her GED, but she said she also thought reading and writing were important for their own sake. Louis, the tall young man who walked in after Alejandro, said the statement was half right because some people go to college and still can't get a good job. Christine, a twenty-eight-year-old African-American mother with curly hair, seemed equally cynical when she said some jobs require only the right paperwork.

"I want you to write a statement about it," said Mason-Francis, suddenly inspired by her students. She wrote a phrase on the green chalkboard:

"An education is only important to help you acquire the needed certification."

She stepped back to look over the words. "You need to say, 'I agree with this because' or 'I disagree because,'" she told the students. She gave them fifteen minutes to write.

Alejandro held his pencil above his notebook, but the words didn't flow. He appeared to be concentrating hard. He wrote something and erased it. He held his head in his hand while staring down at the page. Around him, the other students were also writing and erasing but some filled a third or more of their page with several sentences. Alejandro was still working slowly on one sentence when the teacher asked them to stop.

"Who has a statement they're pressing to share?" she asked. Orlando, the older Hispanic man in front, stood before the class in his plaid shirt and jeans. He said he disagreed with the statement that education is only important to get the right certification. "In my opinion, it goes much farther than that," he read. "The GED certificate is needed when you apply for many different jobs, also a college education." Orlando told the class that his grandmother couldn't read or write, and that his mother was an immigrant who was too busy working to help him study.

Mason-Francis looked over at Alejandro. "Do you have a question?" she asked him. She might have seen a look of confusion cross his face. He smiled and muttered that he couldn't hear what was said, hoping to avert her gaze. The woman next to him, Yolanda, was called on next to share her statement. "It doesn't matter what kind of job you will earn after the GED, you still have to read and write," she read from her page. She elaborated more after she put down the paper.

Mason-Francis looked at Alejandro again. It was unavoidably his turn to read. "You haven't been up here in a long time," she said, playfully calling him to the front of the class. He stayed in his seat and tried to dodge the bullet. "I said the same thing," he said, referring to what Yolanda read. Reluctantly, Alejandro got up and walked stiffly to the front, standing before the other desks, holding up his notebook. He shifted uncomfortably and read in a quiet monotone:

"It's important to acquire your GED because it helps open doors and gives you more options in life."

Mason-Francis let the thought sit for a moment and then asked him for an example. Eager to return to the anonymity of his desk in the back of the classroom, Alejandro simply said that many jobs require a GED. Mason-Francis accepted that premise, then she encouraged him to write four more sentences about it for the next class. Then she told him that what he wrote today was "really well constructed." A few students clapped. Alejandro headed back to his seat, visibly relieved to have made it through the hazing.

Alejandro had panicked the first time he was called on to read aloud in class. They were going over an essay about American history. He said his heart was pounding when it was his turn, and he mistakenly started reading the wrong sentence. "Time slows down in those situations," he said. After class, he approached the teacher and told her that he had learned to read only two years ago. He thought that would spare him further humiliation. But he felt betrayed the next week when she "outed" him to the class, as he put it. "She's like, 'You know, guys, Alejandro told me he just learned how to read, and he wrote and spoke really eloquent.'" He knew the teacher intended it as a show of support. But he was horrified about everyone knowing he had been illiterate and he worried about being called on again.

The discussion about the importance of education revealed how insecure all the students were, in different ways. Roma said education can "increase your social status." Others said they didn't feel respected because they were high school dropouts. Shirley, the older woman, revealed how the accountants and lawyers at the office where she worked always acted surprised when she told them she didn't have a diploma. "It's like I shouldn't be there," she said. Then Louis spoke up and said people often think he's smart until he tells them he doesn't have a diploma.

Mason-Francis wrote some words on the chalkboard: "preparation," "professional," "social status," "society." She encouraged the students to use these words in their next essays so they could be more specific about the purpose of education. "Think of yourself talking to a child, so you want to make it as clear and simple as possible. Five or six sentences." She reminded them to use subjects and predicates in their sentences, steering them back to a recent grammar lesson.

Then she broke the class up into two groups. Alejandro stayed in the back, joining Shirley, Roma, and Yolanda in a circle. Shirley acted as the leader, maybe because of her age or the seriousness with which she approached the class. Her three-ring notebook was open to a handout about nouns, pronouns, and adjectives with various examples. They went around in a circle reading from the sheet. Mason-Francis stopped by to ask them to use each part of speech in a sentence, starting with proper nouns. Shirley's example was "I live in New York City." Mason-Francis queried whether she understood the difference between common and proper nouns. Shirley responded that if she said "The girl lives in New York City," then "girl" would be the common noun. "How can you change that sentence to make the city a common noun?" Mason-Francis asked. Shirley thought for a moment. "The girl lives in a large city." Then Alejandro jumped in with his own example. "The city is a place where the girl lives," he said.

In this small and more intimate grouping, Alejandro seemed much more comfortable speaking up. He didn't have to worry about being called upon; he could just speak when he had something to add. In the month that he'd been going to class, he learned he wasn't the only student having trouble with grammar and writing. As the students in his circle went over the rules for proper nouns, Shirley read from the page: "Proper nouns deal with more specific details," pronouncing "specific" as "pacific." Mason-Francis asked her to repeat the word; two more times she said it incorrectly. "Pacific," she said, oblivious to the mistake. "Specific," said the teacher. "Spe-ci-fic."

They moved on to pronouns and Alejandro asked a question. He wanted to know if the word "mine" is the same as "my." Mason-Francis had gone to work with the other group of students, and Shirley resumed the lead. She thought about an example that could help him. "This is *mine*," she said. Roma jumped in with another, "*My* name is Roma." Behind her, the students in the other group were also asking grammatical questions. Louis wanted to know if "I broke up with my girlfriend" was an example of a proper noun. "What is the noun?" asked Mason-Francis. "Broke up," he said. Orlando told him there were two nouns, "I" and "girlfriend."

The grammar lesson lasted only a few more minutes, and then the students moved back to their original seats. Mason-Francis wanted to review the difference between "pacific" and "specific," since other students had made the same mistake. She wrote some consonant blends on the board: "sp," "st," "sl," and "str." She had the class pronounce them all together, in a drill similar to Alejandro's tutoring classes.

The class was halfway through its three-hour meeting and Mason-Francis still had a lot of ground to cover. A few weeks ago she had assigned an essay topic and she was still waiting for everyone to turn in his or her homework. It was based on a handout they'd read in class about the creation of the U.S. Constitution, and the different views of the Founding Fathers. The handout was only two pages long, but it was challenging reading for students without much formal education. The piece often read like a section of *The Federalist Papers*. It discussed the social hierarchy of humans versus animals, and Samuel West's quote that "where licentiousness begins, liberty ends."

Alejandro was very interested in American history, and he'd just seen the HBO series *John Adams*, so these eighteenth-century arguments about the limitations of government were familiar. He could imagine Paul Giamatti as John Adams and Laura Linney as his wife, Abigail, and the vivid scenes of George Washington and Benjamin Franklin meeting in Philadelphia. He read the essay at his own slow pace, but he had trouble with some of the words. He didn't know "licentiousness." Nor was he familiar with "enshrined," though he figured it had something to do with a shrine. The essay was followed by discussion questions about the Constitutional Convention of 1787. One asked whether there's a contradiction between natural freedom and government.

Francis-Mason had told her students that they didn't need to write a formal essay in response to these questions. They could bring in newspaper stories that dealt with similar themes, or even bring in photographs. Alejandro could think of modern examples of the debate over the limits of freedom. The Patriot Act crackdown on Internet privacy after 9/11 came to mind. But when asked to come up with some combination of words or pictures to express his thoughts, he was stumped. When Mason-Francis optimistically asked if anyone had finished the homework, he sat at his desk hoping to be ignored.

Thankfully, Charles from Guyana had brought some newspaper clips to class. They had photos of cars parked on a sidewalk, taking up space. He said these illustrated licentiousness because the owners didn't care about affecting other people. Mason-Francis looked around the room, but nobody else offered anything to say, so she switched gears. Reaching into a bag, she pulled out a few prints of oil paintings that she'd shown the class for a lesson on visual composition. The GED has a section on the meaning of images, and they'd been discussing style, color, and lines by making comparisons between classic and contemporary art, and going over "informational" images such as "walk" and "don't walk" signs. Mason-Francis flipped through the art prints on her desk. They included a few still lifes and a yellow, swirling portrait of a man that she held up for the class to see. Alejandro was the only one who responded. "Van Gogh," he said with certainty.

The class was winding down and Mason-Francis had planned a group discussion about another topic. Since the handout she had given them a few weeks ago was about the birth of the U.S. Constitution, she selected a small paperback book from Children's Press on the Bill of Rights, which she intended to read to her students. It was written at an elementary level. Mason-Francis read a quote from James Madison about the U.S. Constitution: "'In framing a system which we wish to last for ages, we should not lose sight of the changes which ages will produce.'" She asked the class what that meant and looked to Louis, who tried to formulate a response about the system lasting forever, but he fumbled for the right words. Then she called on Alejandro as though she expected him to fill in the blanks. He did.

"We should think about what the future will bring," he said, explaining Madison's quote. "We should not lose sight of what time might bring, the future might change."

A few seats away, Charles asked him for examples. "New rights, new laws," Alejandro elaborated cautiously. "Like, Native Americans didn't have rights." The class discussed this a little and Mason-Francis finished by reading to them about the amendments that gave slaves and women the right to vote. It was almost twelve-thirty, and she reminded them of their homework assignment for the next class: writing a full paragraph on whether education is just about getting a certificate.

As the students trickled out, she asked Alejandro if he had a copy of a grammar assignment that was also given out a few sessions ago. The students were supposed to write sentences using different parts of speech. Alejandro told her he must have skipped that particular class. "For shame!" she said, in mock anger, handing him a new copy. He stuck it in his shoulder bag and took off.

Mason-Francis didn't know about the inner torture Alejandro was experiencing in class. When he pulled her aside that day to confide that he had learned to read only two years ago, she assumed he was a recent immigrant who had just learned to read *in English*. She had no idea that he had previously been illiterate. When I asked her to describe the different students in her class, without revealing that I knew Alejandro (he didn't want to draw attention to himself), she called him "the intellectual." She characterized him as "someone who does care about education, with the intention to go very far."

If Alejandro could have heard this, he probably would have thought she was talking about someone else. But Mason-Francis was impressed by the serious young man. "He has a different worldview," she said, explaining that he didn't seem "hindered" or "jaded" like other students who were beaten down or trapped by poverty or their lack of a formal education. She said her goal was "to move them beyond their issues." This was her first time teaching a GED class. She had studied teaching at Spelman College and taught in the Atlanta public schools before becoming a community organizer in Harlem. When she was hired by Hostos, she was told the average reading level was about fifth grade. She noticed several students who were really struggling to read, but when I asked her which ones, she never mentioned Alejandro. She didn't know that he'd spent more than two years training his brain to understand the sounds of the letters until he gradually worked himself up to high school–level reading. And she didn't know that he still sat in class each week fearing this truth would be discovered. When asked to describe Alejandro's reading abilities, she said he was "pretty good." But she didn't know why he hadn't brought in his written homework. "To me he shows such capacity, I've been letting him slide," she mused aloud. "I want to check in."

The adult education teachers at Hostos aren't given any transcripts. The director of the school's adult learning center, Zenobia Johnson, said it's up to individual students to tell their teachers about personal issues such as a learning disability. "We ask them on registration forms," she explained, adding that the program has a counselor who can help students with learning disabilities work with their instructors and get extra support. Students with disabilities are also given more time on the GED exam.

The GED exam was originally developed during World War II for returning veterans who hadn't completed high school before joining the military, but it's now seen as an alternative path for a variety of reasons. More than 400,000 people passed the GED exams in 2005. Critics complain that too many cities and states try to boost their high school graduation rates by failing to count students who don't make it to twelfth grade. The state of Mississippi, for example, reported a 2006 high school graduation rate of 87 percent, even though only 63 percent of entering ninth-graders earned their diplomas four years later. Researchers blamed lax federal standards for these different figures, and in 2008 they suspected the national four-year graduation rate was approximately 70 percent.[1]

It's widely believed that high schools "push out" teens who aren't likely to graduate. That's hard to prove, because the teens could have chosen to leave on their own, but there is some circumstantial evidence. One study of four urban GED programs in an anonymous northeast state reported a rising enrollment of younger students (between the ages of sixteen and twenty). It also found they were poorly educated. Between a third and 50 percent read *below* the fifth-grade level.[2] Zenobia Johnson of Hostos has seen a difference in the population since she started working there in 1999. Back then, she said, most of the students signing up for GED courses were in their twenties and thirties. But in the past few years "tons and tons of nineteen- and twenty-one-year olds are signing up for the program." The City University of New York won't take any students younger than nineteen for its adult basic education classes, steering them instead to its transitional high school programs.

Those teens who choose to leave high school because they think the GED is an easier alternative may be surprised. Many teachers say the test is harder than these students expect because of its five separate components, in math, science, social studies, reading, and writing. However, others believe the tests don't require any real academic knowledge and can be passed by anyone with as little as a fifth-grade reading level, so long as he or she takes the right type of test-prep class. In an article in the *City Journal* (published by the Manhattan Institute), Jay Greene wrote that armed forces recruiters have stopped treating the GED as the equivalent of a high school diploma. Greene cited figures showing GED holders were more likely to drop out of military training than applicants with diplomas.[3] It's hard to know if this was a reflection on the GED courses or the kinds of students who are drawn to them.

A month into the course, Alejandro was gradually loosening up—but he still dreaded being called upon in class. He could follow the reading at his own pace. And he knew he was not the only person struggling. He saw students with families to support, and older people who needed the GED to get better jobs. Most of all, he related to Juan, the young Dominican man who looked so nervous while reading aloud from the paperback English edition of *Before We Were Free*. "He's probably me when I was in high school," Alejandro said in sympathy. "Definitely junior high."

But Alejandro's biggest problem was writing, as demonstrated by his panic during the fifteen-minute exercise about the value of education. It was obviously an essay subject that he felt passionately about, since he had fought the city for his right to read. But he couldn't translate those feelings into a constructed sentence. "It's really tough, it takes me a long time," he acknowledged after the class. He said he was nervous about the time limit. "I was looking at the person in front of me, [thinking] this is not long enough!" Whenever he did write a word, he'd look at it twice, unsure of whether he was spelling it correctly. This is what he wrote in his notebook:

"Is important to acqiere your GED because it helps open dors and gives you more option in life."

The word "doors" was difficult because he kept asking himself, "How do I spell it?" He was also mentally preparing himself for the possibility of being called upon. "That's one of the things I do with anxiety," he explained. "I try to picture myself doing it." Alejandro visualized himself walking to the front of the classroom, reading to the students, concentrating on his notebook, and walking to his seat once he was done. This calmed him down a little, but he also worried about what the teacher would ask him.

Reading experts have published extensively about why reading and writing are such different mental activities. Speaking comes naturally because our brains are programmed to listen to and attach a meaning to sounds. Reading is much less natural because those sounds then have to be linked to the letters in the alphabet. But writing is even tougher. Sally Liberman Smith, who founded the Lab School in Washington, D.C., for students with learning disabilities, described it this way:

"To write something down means going into the mind, plucking out a series of visual symbols with sounds attached to them, putting them in the right order (going from left to right) to produce the word you want, then putting several words in the proper order (also going from left to right) to convey the message you want. It takes more organization, more differentiation, more remembering, more sequencing, and more integration than reading or many other skills. It is one of the most sophisticated activities devised by the human brain, and it clearly demands maturity."[4]

This is why writing is especially difficult for students who, like Alejandro, have dyslexia. Their brains can't easily connect those shapes with sounds, making it much harder to retrieve letters and words at will when they put the pen to the page. "Where you have difficulty with the reception, perhaps with the reading process, it's even harder to develop written language," explains JoAnne Simon, a disabilities rights lawyer and president of the International Dyslexia Association's New York branch. "It can be torturous, laborious, difficult; it's grinding; it's also sparked with a lot of failure."

Complicating that even further is the instability of dyslexia. Those with dyslexia are often riddled with doubts because they sometimes do spell a word correctly. They'll look at something they've written for a long time, not knowing whether they got it right or wrong. Simon calls this a form of intermittent reinforcement, which is actually the strongest type of enforcement because it keeps reminding people with dyslexia not to trust themselves. "If you can't remember the way the letters look, or the order in which those letters appear, or [if] the words look similar and you continually confuse them," then, Simon says, "you don't trust your system to recognize those in the future. And you don't trust the next hardest system—to replicate what those words look like."

My friend Karlis Rekevics, who's a sculptor, describes dyslexia as like "wearing a suit of armor, a blanket, or a leash." Even after overcoming his disability, graduating from college, and winning recognition for his art, he says he still feels an enormous sense of trepidation and doubt whenever he tries to write something. He uses a spell-check function when sending e-mail. But he still dreads composing a simple note. "You're stymied by doubt so strong that you have no confidence to move forward," he says. Karlis believes dyslexia has made him see the world in a different way, which is why he's an artist, but he says he'd still give anything to be able to write without agony, and he leans on others to proofread any applications for artists' grants and residencies.

Alejandro stayed in touch with his old tutors from Lindamood-Bell for encouragement. They warned him that writing would be the toughest portion of the GED class. He also knows that he's hard on himself. He diligently copied down everything on the chalkboard in his reading class. But his spelling still faltered at times. On one page, he wrote that the main idea for a story is "in the beginning, in the title or an the furst paragraph." Thankfully, there was no time limit. Students could take adult basic education classes until they were considered ready for a regular GED-prep class. Alejandro's tutors told him that it could take him a year or two, and Zenobia Johnson said that wouldn't be so unusual.

Alejandro admitted that he didn't feel comfortable reaching out for help. "I'm not that good at that," he said. But Alejandro wasn't one to let an opportunity pass. A few months earlier, his tutors at Lindamood-Bell had introduced him to Alison Bell, the daughter of one of the center's founders, Nanci Bell. She was touring the New York office and Alejandro jokingly asked her if he could have a name tag, just like the staff members, because he'd been there for two years. He got more than a name tag. Bell also runs a scholarship program called the Rhett Bell Foundation, which grants money to needy students, and Alejandro was encouraged to apply. His lawyer, Matthew Lenaghan, wrote a recommendation, explaining his academic history and his case against the city, calling him "incredibly hardworking, dedicated, gracious, and compassionate." At the end of April, Alejandro learned he was among twenty-one out of fifty-eight applicants who received a financial award that spring. It was worth five thousand dollars. He planned on using the money for a private tutor who could help him with the pre-GED classes. He didn't want to sit in another classroom next year, falling behind.

TWENTY-ONE

Unlocking Yamilka

The weather was getting warmer and Nancy Tarshis put on a pair of snazzy red sandals to match her red knit sweater. Yamilka noticed the shoes immediately when she sat down for her afternoon speech and language session, and complimented her teacher. "They might be too early to wear, but it's feeling like spring!" Tarshis responded.

Yamilka wasn't feeling the warmth yet. She was bundled up in a dark sweatshirt, a T-shirt, and jeans beneath a lightweight black jacket, and her hair was pulled back in a black headband. She was a little flustered. She wasn't sure if she had locked the door of her family's apartment correctly. At the age of twenty-four, she'd never had her own set of keys. She always relied on her father or a sibling to let her in, because there was usually someone around in a family of six keeping different hours. But her father had gone to the Dominican Republic for a funeral and had given her his keys. She couldn't recall whether she had turned all three locks the right way when she'd left that morning. Just the other day, she'd had so much trouble getting back into the apartment that she had to ask a neighbor for help.

Tarshis and the graduate student Melanie Leong were still drilling Yamilka each week in rhymes. Leong typically read a poem and had Yamilka identify which words sounded alike, or asked her to fill in the blanks. On this day, she'd chosen "Where the Sidewalk Ends" by Shel Silverstein. "Hopefully this will be more fun for you," she said. As usual, Yamilka was seated in the adult-sized chair next to the desk while Leong's knees jutted out from a little red children's chair. Leong read the first few lines aloud.

"So," she asked Yamilka, "which words do you think rhyme?"

Yamilka looked confused. She couldn't recall everything she had just heard. Tarshis suggested that Leong read fewer lines at once, because there was so much going on in the poem. Leong then read a single sentence, emphasizing the rhymes: "'And there the grass grows soft and *white*, and there the sun burns crimson *bright*.'"

"Brice," said Yamilka. Tarshis told her the word was actually "bright," but it was one of the two rhyming words.

Leong continued with a line about "peppermint wind" and "asphalt flowers" that "grow," concluding with a rhyme about a walk that is "slow." But she had already lost Yamilka by then. Yamilka would never have used the phrase "peppermint wind" or the word "asphalt" in daily speech. Leong reread the lines for her and Yamilka figured out that she was supposed to pick a word that rhymed with "slow," the last word in the rhyme.

"That's one of them," Leong said, offering to read the sentence once again.

"Uh-huh." Yamilka nodded.

Leong repeated the phrase about the asphalt flowers that grow, and Yamilka first said "flower," then corrected herself and said "grow."

They continued for a while and Yamilka nailed most of the rhymes. Then Leong moved on to another Silverstein poem called "Whatif" and asked Yamilka to fill in the blanks.

"'Last night, while I lay thinking here, some Whatifs crawled inside my . . .' blank," Leong read from the poem. "So we have the word 'here.' Think of a word that rhymes with 'here.'"

Yamilka asked to see the poem and Leong showed her the words and the blank spaces. "Ear," she replied, with more certainty than she had displayed in the other exercise.

"Right," said Leong. "'Last night, while I lay thinking here, some Whatifs crawled inside my ear.'" She kept on reading the poem.

Leong got to a line where Yamilka was supposed to fill in a blank to rhyme with the phrase "beat up." The clue was about pouring poison into something, obviously a "cup." But Yamilka drew a blank. Leong tried to help her by isolating the word "up" and asking her what would rhyme with it.

"Down?"

Leong reminded Yamilka that they were looking for rhymes, not opposites. "So what's something that rhymes with 'up'? Sometimes you drink out of it."

"Cup," said Yamilka, realizing her mistake.

Sometimes Yamilka's grammar got in the way of the rhyming exercises. When she heard the word "smaller," she said "tall," a sign of her difficulty grasping word endings. Tarshis thought her problem picking rhymes out of the longer sentences was related to her poor working memory. People with poor working memories can't hang on to as many words or numbers as other people. The therapists were using exercises like recipes and storytelling to help Yamilka improve her memory while training her ears with the rhymes. They moved on to a new exercise this day: alliteration.

Tarshis explained to Yamilka that understanding alliteration meant concentrating on how the front of a word sounds, not the back—which is what produces a rhyme. Leong uses her name as an example, saying "Marvelous Melanie." She asked Yamilka to choose which of four different words had the same beginning sound as "Melanie": "silly," "tall," "large," or "merry."

Yamilka hesitated and asked her to repeat the words. "The words are 'silly,' 'tall,' 'large,' and 'merry,'" said Leong. "Which one?"

"Can you break it down?" Yamilka asked. Tarshis jumped in to ask what she meant. "It's too long," she said, too many words. Tarshis told Leong to give Yamilka three options instead of four.

"Okay, so the words are 'Melanie,'" she began.

"Can you make the sound of the letter? Mmm," Yamilka asked.

"Mmm. Melanie." Leong nodded, catching on. "'Silly,' 'tall,' and 'mmm—merry.'"

Yamilka pursed her lips and made the "mmm" sound.

"Right," said Tarshis. "So it's merry Melanie."

Just as it was with rhyming, it was difficult for Yamilka to pick out the discrete parts, or phonemes, of a given word. The way her brain is wired made the sounds rush together. Tarshis and Leong could see her struggling and slowed their pace accordingly. When they gave her the name "Nancy" they emphasized the letter *n* before asking which of the words "neat," "clever," and "busy" had the same beginning sound. Yamilka repeated the *n* sound and settled on "neat."

"If only that were true," sighed Tarshis, pointing to a file folder and several papers scattered on top of her computer keyboard. "Look at my desk. Not neat!"

"Not so bad," Yamilka reassured her.

Then Tarshis asked Yamilka how to pronounce her own name. Unlike some words that start with a *y* that can sound like *j* in Dominican Spanish, Yamilka said her name is made with a "yah" sound in Spanish and in English. Leong gave her the words "friendly," "funny," and "young" and Yamilka said "young" starts with the same sound as her name.

Tarshis had been noting slow but consistent progress during her work with Yamilka over these past two months. She thought the young woman had had "tremendous success" with rhyming, which was why they were moving on to alliteration—the next stage for improving phonemic awareness. This session was her first attempt at working with the beginning sounds of words. Though it was bumpy, Tarshis was impressed by the way Yamilka was thinking about the sounds of speech. Yamilka had told her about the time she had been watching television and caught herself saying a "train" had crashed onto a building instead of a crane. That was the moment when Yamilka believed she really did have a language disorder.

"The truth is, there are a lot of people like you," Tarshis reassured Yamilka as they discussed the incident. "That's why there are methods for fixing it. 'Cause if there weren't a lot of people, nobody would spend a lot of time figuring out the method to fix it." When Yamilka had been going to public school, Tarshis said, there hadn't been as many people studying and teaching phonics.

But Yamilka still wished she could learn faster. She knew what the Shel Silverstein poems were about, but said she didn't know what to listen for. The rhyming words didn't jump out at her; they went right by and she couldn't catch them. When she heard the story, she said she felt the words "turning around"—gesturing with her hands like a rolling wheel. "I really have no idea what they want . . . to see in my head." Things got much easier when they said the words more slowly and read shorter sentences. With the longer sentences, she said, she sometimes couldn't remember the rhyming word, so she picked another word that was near the right one. I asked her if it was like throwing darts and she agreed. "Maybe I will get near because it's a lot of word I cannot keep it, in that moment, all the word in my head," she tried to explain in her choppy English. But it made perfect sense. If she couldn't remember the whole sentence, she compensated by recalling a word she could remember—hoping it might be correct, or close to the right one.

Yamilka had become a little more independent since starting her classes at Fisher Landau. Tarshis would sometimes go over recipes with her to improve her memory and to practice saying things in order. Yamilka would always have to recall each step in her own words. Sometimes they made the recipes together in class. One day in May, Tarshis brought in the ingredients for a salad with pecans, goat cheese, and dried cranberries. She asked Yamilka to read the recipe with her. She couldn't read the word "ounces" but recognized "goat cheese," which she had never eaten before but had seen on cooking shows. Tarshis helped her with the words "mix," "vinegar," "mustard," and "thyme." Yamilka also got "bowl" but had trouble with "large." It was an exercise geared at organizing her thoughts, but it was also something practical.

Yamilka had lost ten pounds since she had started weekly meetings with a nutritionist in February at Fisher Landau, and had become vigilant about her diet. There were other signs that she was gradually moving into new territory. Yamilka doesn't consider herself a materialistic person but her one big luxury is taking good care of her fingernails. She'd get her nails professionally wrapped every few weeks. They were long, but not outrageously so, and square. She favored pale colors and French tips. Yamilka's daily bus ride to and from the Fisher Landau clinic passed a salon on Morris Park Avenue called Sassy Nails. She thought the salon looked neater and cleaner than the places near home, so one day after class she walked over and treated herself to a manicure. "They did an excellent job, the place was very professional," she said. But when she got the bill afterward she cried. It cost much more than the salons in Morris Heights and she was embarrassed to admit she had spent thirty dollars before leaving a tip. She hadn't thought to inquire about the price before she asked for the service, and apparently didn't read the signs.

But Yamilka wasn't daunted by the experience. She went back to the salon several weeks later, deciding that an occasional splurge was worth it. She couldn't afford to buy a lot of clothes or shoes. She and her sisters shared a few of their nicer shirts and they all have a flair for accessorizing, favoring turquoise necklaces and hanging earrings. Yamilka believes nice fingernails make "a good impression."

When she got home from her speech class, on the day she'd read the

Shel Silverstein poems, the front door to the building was open as usual. A contractor was working in a ground-floor apartment across the hall that had been damaged during a fire. Yamilka pulled out her key chain as she approached her apartment, but Alejandro heard her and immediately opened the door. She didn't follow him inside. She stayed outside in the hallway and closed the door so she could practice locking and unlocking the three different locks. She was hesitant at first, unsure if she was turning each one in the right direction, and she forgot the order at one point. But her body memory took over and she moved from bottom to middle to top, then did it again and opened the door.

TWENTY-TWO

Antonio at Work

Adrian Martinez is standing behind the counter of the Route 46 Dry Cleaners in Little Ferry, New Jersey. It's a quiet morning, as usual, as he tries to get the new business up and running. A sign advertises a $2.50 special on shirts, if paid in advance, to attract customers. A few people just dropped off some clothes on their way to work.

Antonio emerges from the green curtains just behind Martinez. He's been working in the big main room where dirty clothes are sorted for cleaning and returned in plastic-covered hangers that are organized on revolving racks. He's wearing a brown leather jacket, a blue-and-white-striped sweater, and jeans. The clothes were a gift from Martinez, who's taken Antonio under his wing like a younger brother. "Just one of the perks," he jokes. "Got him shaven. Told him he gotta come clean-cut." Antonio smiles, looking bashful.

Martinez tries to set a good example. He's thirty-one years old, slim, and neatly groomed, wearing a sleek black leather jacket on this fine spring day. He moved to Washington Heights from the Dominican Republic when he was eight, and says he graduated from George Washington High School and then the Borough of Manhattan Community College. He now lives nearby in the New Jersey suburbs and has a wife and two young children. "You want a family, you want a backyard," he says, calling this a better life for his kids.

Martinez knows Antonio because he went to high school with the teen's older cousin Cesar. When he opened his first dry cleaning store in Washington Heights, years ago, Antonio helped him hand out flyers. This year, Cesar's mother—one of Antonio's many aunts—suggested that he "give the boy a hand." He hired him in February just as the New Jersey store was getting ready to open. Antonio has been with him ever since, sorting the clothes and assisting him part-time for $150 a week, though he often chooses to stay for the full day to avoid the boredom of his parents' house and to get a ride home. The store is only a few miles away from the house in Hackensack, but without a car he has to rely on two public buses.

Little Ferry is a small middle-class community with a traffic circle on its main drag. There are a few local businesses, and red tulips blooming outside a set of two-story apartment houses for the elderly. But the dry cleaning store isn't in the center of things. It's farther down Route 46, close to Teterboro Airport and right next to a car wash. The other businesses on this little strip include a Jeep dealer and a Burger King. This bleak location explains why the shop has been having trouble luring new customers, though Martinez remains optimistic because there aren't many other dry cleaners nearby. Antonio brings his PlayStation to work and listens to music when there's nothing to do. The first few weeks were rough, says Martinez. "We sat around, drove around, handed out flyers in malls," trying to spread the word. Once the clothes started coming, he says, Antonio caught on pretty quickly. "At the beginning I was kind of tough on him because I was like, 'This is the way things have to be.' And I kept repeating the same procedures. But now he's better than me at it, processing clothes, sorting."

"Thank you," says Antonio, happy for a rare moment of praise from somebody.

Sorting requires Antonio to match the number on each receipt with the ticket on every item of clothing. "We get all the numbers, he opens up the tickets, the clothes come in like this and then he basically sorts it all out," Martinez explains. "Then he double-checks it to make sure there's no mistakes. And then he bags them and puts the ticket on." It's a little complicated because there are two sets of clothes. Items from Martinez's other store, now in Harlem, also come here after they're cleaned. Antonio has to separate the green New Jersey tickets from the yellow Manhattan ones. "At the beginning he would make mistakes with the numbers," says Martinez. Antonio would sometimes look at a ticket and forget which item it went with, so he'd check the number twice. "I taught him to repeat the number in his mind," he says. "Like if he looks at the item, the piece, and it says three-eight-four, he would repeat it out loud. And it would be confusing for me because I'm right next to him with [other] numbers! So I said, 'Repeat it in your mind, three-eight-four, three-eight-four, and then look for the ticket.'"

Antonio didn't tell his boss that he has dyslexia, and Martinez never suspected it, attributing the occasional mistake to the learning curve of a new job. He knows Antonio had a tough time in school, but he's surprised to hear the teen didn't learn to read until he got private tutoring. Most of the work in the dry cleaning store involves matching numbers, but Martinez is also teaching Antonio how to use the cash register when he steps out for an errand. "Now it's evolved where I know he's doing such a good job with [sorting], that I've actually had him on a few occasions take care of customers and use the computer . . . Then he was excited because I told him the more you learn, the more you make. And he's handling money and giving people change."

The store's computerized cash register has a special program used by dry cleaners. It allows the user to select whether an incoming item is a sweater, skirt, blouse, jacket, or shirt, with accompanying icons and a color chart. It also breaks down some of the categories, for example listing short coats, wool coats, sport jackets, and down coats because they all have different prices. Antonio is gradually learning the different styles of clothing, says Martinez. He gives Antonio a quick review on the cash register by using a shirt. "You know how to click on it, right?" asks Martinez, while Antonio selects a box that says "Edit Drop" to launch the intake process. He types in $2.50 for the price because it's going to be a prepaid shirt, pausing to make sure he got the right number of zeros. He takes $2.50 from the counter and types the amount onto the touch screen to record the transaction. Martinez then gives him a pair of khaki pants and a sweater and acts as though he's a customer.

"Pay now or pay later, sir?" asks Antonio. "Pay now," says Martinez. Antonio clicks on the pants icon and chooses the color khaki, then moves on to the sweater icon and the color black. He could avoid having to read the words at this moment, letting the little images guide his way, but not for long. He has to know which other buttons to click as the intake process continues and how to input information from each customer. Antonio is familiar with keypads and computers because of MySpace, and the new Sidekick cell phone he finally bought—with a big keyboard for sending text messages. He also plays a lot of video games. All three seem to have made him much more comfortable with the written word.

Antonio's latest obsession is the new PlayStation Portable video game *Crisis Core: Final Fantasy VII*. He bought it over a month ago and he hasn't beaten it yet.

"I have to read a lot," says Antonio, referring to the directions that pop up repeatedly whenever he's about to compete in a fight. "You get into a lot of battles." He activates the combat mode and controls the movements of the main character, Zack, with the buttons, positioning him and firing from his sword as he confronts the enemy. Once he completes this battle, he can proceed to the next level. If he fails he goes back to the beginning. Occasionally, Antonio refers to the written instruction manual, which includes a backstory about the fictitious, powerful Shinra company. The game is rated for teenagers and the manual's vocabulary isn't so easy, with the words "monopoly," "burgeoning," and "prosperity," which Antonio mistakenly defines as "being poor." But he knows "aspires" and eventually figures out "situation" after sounding it out a few times until he recognizes the word. It's not *Anne Frank*, but it *is* a story that holds Antonio's attention and motivates him to read.

Parents may complain about their children spending too much time on video games, but some actually require real thinking skills. They have complicated story lines and problem-solving activities that make them good vehicles for teaching and learning, according to James Paul Gee, a reading professor at the University of Wisconsin–Madison. He's written books and articles about how video games mimic the best kinds of instruction because they're challenging, but not too difficult. The problems gradually get harder at the player's own pace. "Language acquisition itself works this way," he's written.[1] "However, schools frequently do not. They often demand that students gain competence through reading texts before they can perform in the domain that they were learning."

Antonio's mother, Noelia, sees him sitting on the couch with his PlayStation and says she wishes he would return to school. He never told her that he won more hours to continue his tutoring but hasn't yet made another appointment with Huntington Learning Center. He's still interested in learning test-taking skills so he can get his GED but says he also needs to make money to pay for his cell phone, meals, and travel. His parents are glad that at least he's holding down a job.

His parents own their three-family house on a suburban street in Hackensack. They rent out the basement and top-floor apartments, while they live in a two-bedroom unit on the ground floor and tend to a big garden out back. It's a huge improvement over their cramped apartment in Washington Heights. The living room is furnished with a gigantic, ornate white chair, a sofa, big lamps, and a flat-screen TV. There's a long table by the kitchen. By the television, there are framed pictures of Antonio and his sister as children, and a photo of the sister's high school graduation. She doesn't live here because she kept the apartment in Washington Heights. Antonio stays with her sometimes.

Antonio's parents bought him a laptop computer as a belated birthday present. Hector thought it would encourage him to read and write, and he has been more active on MySpace since getting the computer. He often hangs out in his stepfather's office in the back of the house, where he can plug the laptop into an Internet connection. Sometimes he uses Hector's desktop computer. There are colorful wooden parrots from the Dominican Republic on the window ledge in the office, and Hector's guitar is parked on the floor.

Antonio has been corresponding a lot lately with Theresa, the girl he had a huge crush on in high school. He looks at her MySpace profile and sees that she's just changed the song on the page to "I'm Not Okay (I Promise)" by My Chemical Romance. This makes him happy because he loves the song. Antonio's profile page has a picture of the George Washington Bridge lit up in white lights against a dark nighttime sky. He's also posted a cartoon of a skeleton pointing its two middle fingers with the words "For Tha Haters." A cousin about his age who lives in Washington Heights gave him the electronic images and showed him how to personalize his profile.

Antonio's relationship with his girlfriend Amy ended in March. This is how he announced the breakup on his MySpace page:

"amy left me so I move on with my life so, I won,t be here when she comes back"

Nonetheless, he listed his mood as "hopeful." He chose a song by John Legend to accompany his profile page.

Theresa had just had a baby, and her relationship with her boyfriend, whom Antonio calls "the Asshole," seemed to be on the rocks. He's been trying to get back in her good graces and sent this message:

"If you dont want to see me or be with me is ok because you think i propobly want to use you and thats not true, i am not trying to be made with you or anything . . . I know you have baby and is hard for you but stop listing to your don friends and follow what you think is best,i am someone thats like you alot and love you but i am someone that wants the best for in any way you want to go in life."

Sometimes Theresa thanks him for his sweet offers, but other times she tells him bluntly that she's not looking for a boyfriend. Unlike Antonio, she writes her messages in shorthand.

"wtf r u talking bout?" she replied after he said he loved her, adding "i dont want 2 b wit any1 right now."

Antonio wrote back two minutes later: "i am sorry i did not mean it like that." After a brief exchange in which she assured him everything was "koolz," he wrote this to her the next day:

"hey look what i was trying to say was how i feel and you talk it the wrong way so i am sorry about,and you need to know that i dont know how to write perfectly so sometimes i can muss up times,hey i am sorry if i hurt you."

Theresa knows about Antonio's reading problems and she told me in an e-mail message that she thinks his writing has improved. She left high school after she gave birth to her daughter and is planning on transferring to a GED program, to accommodate her child-care needs. She's seventeen years old and says school was sometimes hard because the classes at Graphics were crowded and she didn't like some of the people. Unlike Antonio, she said she was never in special ed.

In June he sent her a text message from his phone, asking, "How do you feel about me?"

She wrote back in text-speak, "idk [I don't know], u r a gd [good] friend." He reminded her of his offer to help take care of her baby: "I told you that I want to be the father of your child."

Theresa wrote back, "I HAVE 2 THINK OF WHAT GD 4 MY BAY" and then "I KNOW WHAT U WANT BUT I CAN'T THINK OF WHAT U WANT."

Antonio got worried and wrote back in four short sentences, "You said, that you know what I want. That's not true. I don't want sex. I want to be happy with someone."

• • •

It's a common refrain among teachers that student writing is suffering because of text messaging and e-mail. Even the students admit it's a problem. Almost two thirds of teenagers acknowledged these informal writing styles have seeped into their schoolwork, according to a 2008 report by the Pew Internet & American Life Project and the National Commission on Writing. Examples included shortcuts from instant messaging, such as lol (laughing out loud); leaving out capital letters; and using emoticons. But the students drew a distinction between what's appropriate online and what's expected in school—with 60 percent stating that text messaging is *not* real writing. And 86 percent of the seven hundred teens in the survey said good writing is important for success in life. Clearly, laments about the demise of the written word are greatly exaggerated.

According to a 2009 report by the National Endowment for the Arts, "Reading on the Rise," just over half of adults eighteen and over read some kind of literature in 2008.[2] That was up a few points from 46.7 percent in 2002, when the number had dropped by seven percentage points over the previous decade. The survey included online works and paper texts, and found reading rates increased for whites, blacks, and Hispanics, men and women. In fact, young adults (eighteen to twenty-four) showed the greatest rise in literary reading, as they gravitated toward short stories and novels. And 15 percent of adults read literature online in 2008. The NEA report was based on a sample of more than eighteen thousand adults.

But studies of younger readers' habits weren't as optimistic. Another National Endowment for the Arts survey, in 2004, found just over 20 percent of seventeen-year-olds reported reading almost every day for fun, compared to almost a third in 1984.[3] And a report by the Kaiser Family Foundation found that more than 60 percent of children between the ages of eight and eighteen go online on a typical day.[4] It's widely speculated that the Internet is contributing to a culture of distraction. The NEA's study found lower reading scores among the teens who don't read books for fun, while those who do are more likely to go to college. But the Web has its own intellectual challenges. Internet and text messaging have encouraged interactive forms of reading and writing. Teens flock to fan-fiction sites where they can write their own endings to a story. They keep blogs, post profiles on Facebook and MySpace, and surf websites that interest them. Many educators think these social media can be useful learning tools, especially for students like Antonio who have low reading skills, feel discouraged by years of failure, and aren't engaged in school.

Despite his frequent use of e-mail and text messaging, Antonio's writing and reading skills were obviously still not at a high school level. But since leaving school and getting a new cell phone and laptop, he was reading and writing much more frequently—which is how one succeeds in any subject. It's a case of practice makes better, if not necessarily perfect. "You cannot get better at writing unless you write," says the University of California at Berkeley education professor Richard Sterling, a former executive director of the National Writing Project. "I know that's simplistic, but that's how it is."

Sterling says e-mail provides an incentive to read and write because there's an audience. Antonio wanted to meet girls and to connect with other kids through the Internet. It's also a low-stakes environment. Teachers aren't judging his e-mail messages. There are no red marks when he spells a word wrong or uses shorthand. And there isn't a big blank sheet of paper daring him to fill all the lines. "Screen size is very important, because it doesn't take much to fill it up," says Dr. Kathleen Yancy, president of the National Council of Teachers of English and a Kellogg Hunt Professor of English at Florida State University. It's easier to feel like you've achieved something when you fill a small screen.

Yancy points out that the kids surveyed by the Pew Report said they preferred writing that had a genuine purpose and a genuine audience. "It's more motivating," she says, especially for students who struggle in school. "Would you rather write to someone who's only going to tell you what's wrong with your work, or someone who likes you and is going to do something with you?" That doesn't mean the same thing couldn't be done in print. The "Freedom Writers" in Erin Gruwell's Long Beach, California, high school classes had a purpose and an audience when they gave their teacher their diaries. But poor readers labor over the physical act of writing, which is why technology can help them. Alejandro was frozen with the fear of making a spelling error in his pre-GED class. It's easier to write with a computer because there are spell-check applications, and poor spelling is easily forgiven on a cell phone. There's also no fear about bad penmanship. "Reading has really changed in the move from print to digital," says Dr. David Rose, a cognitive scientist in the Harvard Graduate School of Education who's studied students with learning disabilities, including dyslexia. "A lot of the kids we have worked with are typically still not readers in print although they are readers digitally. They give themselves talking browsers and text to speech [programs]. The landscape has changed. One of the things that's interesting is now you have the capacity to, all by yourself, click on any word and to have it be read to you—which is a great way to learn to read. The kids are, in fact, in a completely different universe where the book reads itself to you."

Rose expects that students with reading problems will still need intensive instruction so they can learn to read on their own. But digital media could help them keep up in history, literature, and other courses with a heavy reading load. As founder of the Center for Applied Special Technology, Rose believes textbook publishers should make their materials more digitally accessible, and he's been working to develop a national standard.

But electronic communication isn't yet a replacement for reading, and swapping lots of jumbled text messages doesn't mean you're a good writer. These quick messages are too brief to make a difference in reading fluency, and they don't challenge the reader's vocabulary the way books do. However, an extended e-mail message, or a blog, requires more thoughtful composition than a text message. That's where new media can make the biggest impact on reading and writing skills, and teachers are trying to figure out how to use them. Cindi Rigsbee, a middle school teacher who was named the 2008/09 North Carolina Teacher of the Year, asked her students to translate lingo-based websites into standard English, and to translate classic literature to text-speak.[5] Other teachers have their students blog about the books they read. At Intermediate School 339 in the Bronx, an eighth-grader who identified herself as Francy created a blog to write about what she was reading in a school book club and the books she read on her own. She summarized *My Friend, My Hero*, which is about a teenage basketball star, and Sharon Flake's *Money Hungry*, which is about a girl from the projects named Raspberry. Each entry included a section with her own personal opinion. This is what she wrote after reading the first few pages of *Money Hungry*:

"I think that Raspberry is very ambitious and that when she sets her mind on a goal she does the impossible to complete it. I also think that Raspberry should pay more attention in school work than money."

Francy also had to write on her blog about what she learned from her reading assignments and classroom exercises. Here's what she wrote after reading *My Friend, My Hero*:

"I love this unit of study. The reason I love this unit of study is because we get to work in groups, when I need any help any one of my team mates are there to help. I get to be the character hunter, This is my favorite job because I get to keep track of the main character. My group has been performing pretty well even thought we are all in different pages. Two words I learned this week are 'Sanguine' (pg 43) which means when a person is happy, And 'Acquainted' which means knowledge's gained by personal experience's."

This entry was obviously filled with spelling errors and wasn't a great example of eighth-grade writing, though there was no way to know whether Francy was more careful with her other (paper) assignments. In the introduction to her blog, Francy wrote that reading is her favorite subject. She kept regular entries from January to June 2008.

But not all students are so motivated, and that's why some educators believe their reading and writing could improve through frequent assignments and intensive support, some of which they can access online. Inside Theodore Roosevelt High School in the Bronx, which Alejandro briefly attended, a handful of small new schools have taken root in the big old building. One of them, the Kappa International School, started using a Web-based program called eChalk to link students and faculty. The twenty-two-year-old global history teacher Laurel Schwartz puts notes from her lessons online so students can go over whatever they didn't fully comprehend in class. She mentions a boy who is fluent in English but writes so poorly that he needs a teacher to sit and coach him through an assignment. She thinks the website is helping him because she can see that he's going online to look at her lessons and PowerPoint charts, even though "he won't take notes in class."

The school has a college-prep emphasis, and the students are encouraged to write almost all their assignments with computers, the way they would as college students. Teachers say most students have computers at home, and they can use the school's own laptops during lunch and after class, and there's a library in the neighborhood. The students at Kappa International are from Harlem, the Bronx, and Washington Heights, and they're predominantly Latino and black. The school opened in the fall of 2007 with more than a hundred ninth-graders, who were reading between a sixth- and an eleventh-grade level. Like most of the small new schools, Kappa didn't take any special ed students in its first year.

During one of Schwartz's classes, she uses a SMART Board to show her students how to get on the new eChalk website and check their class pages. She's posted a list of resources, including the Modern Language Association's online guide to grammar and writing and an explanation of footnotes for Microsoft Word 2003. Schwartz looks a little like the singer Lisa Loeb, with long brown hair and rectangular glasses. Though she's not much older than her students, she confesses that she's not completely computer savvy. She doesn't know how to footnote in the latest version of Word. A boy shouts out, "I know," and she asks him to e-mail her the directions. "Will I get extra credit?" he asks. Schwartz also tells the students about a website on citations and they go over footnotes from different sources. "About.com, is that print or not print?" The students all shout, "Not print." "A book in the library?" she asks. "Print!"

Electronic communication is seen as a positive force in this school. There's a link on its site to a group called Goodreads for students to talk about books. The students can e-mail their teachers at any time, and they engage in online discussions about school issues. Fourteen-year-old Sharlette Velasquez says she recently contributed to an online forum about what should go in the school's new constitution. "It was nighttime and I was silly on sugar," she says, giggling, sitting down on a rust-colored couch in the school's main office, where she meets with her teachers during free periods. "I put, 'I would like it to be like the American Constitution with we the people, we want iPods in schools.'" The New York City schools have banned iPods and cell phones. Sharlette says she also posted to a discussion about the Byzantine emperor Justinian, whom the students have been reading about in global studies. "I responded he was emperor, he mixed races—Persian, Greek, Roman." The students were given writing assignments about the historical characters in this unit, which could be written as Facebook-style biographies, travel guides, or advertisements.

There are educators who believe teachers need to tap into these resources so they won't lose touch with their students. Will Richardson, a former English teacher who wrote the book *Blogs, Wikis, Podcasts, and Other Powerful Web Tools for Classrooms*, believes only 10 percent of educators know how to use Facebook, MySpace, and other Web 2.0 tools, based on his experiences giving workshops around the country. But most teens *do* use these resources. As students take charge of the new media and gravitate to the sites that interest them, Richardson says, this presents a huge challenge to traditional models of education. "Schools are having a horrible time because [new media] promotes individualized learning and we are not an individualized learning system," he says, noting that teachers may strive for differentiated instruction, but the standards movement forces them to give the same lessons and tests to everyone. This can alienate teenagers like Antonio, for whom school seems irrelevant or too difficult, but these students *can* be engaged by the Internet. Richardson cites his eleven-year-old daughter as an example of how education can be customized to a child's interests. "I'm totally convinced my daughter can learn much of what she needs to learn in the world in the context of horses," he says. "You can do science, math, history, and all sorts of things," he says. "It's not like every student has to do the same thing at the same time at the same place."

But that presents a big challenge to society's definition of what it means to be fully educated. Traditionalists strongly believe students still need to master a core curriculum of science, history, math, and literature to be "culturally literate."* Richardson isn't sure if today's students need to learn the basics the same way as previous generations. But he thinks blogs and wikis (where users can add information) are useful routes because they allow students to take ownership of their writing. He recalls teaching his high school journalism students the basics of good writing by encouraging them to become experts on whatever subjects they wanted, from wrestling to skateboarding, by using the Web. "What these tools allow is for people to connect to other people who share their passions," he says. "When you're in an environment like that, communities based around passions and collective interests, it changes the game in how you learn."

With students who have trouble reading, Richardson believes teachers need to work extra hard to engage their interest so they don't give up. "I don't think you teach a kid to read better by putting *Gulliver's Travels* in front of him," he says. "You teach a kid to read better by giving him things of interest, then that helps prepare him to read bigger books."

I asked Richardson what kind of Web lessons he'd design for a student like Antonio, who's passionate about wanting to join the military. Richardson acknowledged that he hasn't personally worked with many

*E. D. Hirsh is a proponent of the "Core Knowledge" curriculum and has written about this extensively.

students who have great difficulty reading, and thought it would be tough in a class of thirty pupils. But he suggested finding a teacher who could mentor Antonio and develop communities around his interests. He'd need help selecting legitimate blogs, discussion boards, and websites about the military, because there are so many cranks out there. "If you gave that kid to me, in six months I would probably first do that editing work for him, give him things to read, places to interact," said Richardson. "Then, over the course of that time, I'd slowly start to hand off that editing piece and then sit next to him as he finds his own places to engage. I might help him learn how to take his own ideas and publish in his own media. Not just writing in text, but writing in audio, video, games even. That kind of thing. I think there's a lot of different things you can do."

Antonio is afraid his reading isn't progressing. He's certainly able to communicate now by text messages and e-mail, even if his spelling and grammar aren't always correct. And his messages don't look all that different from those sent by other teens. Although Antonio worries when he struggles to spell a word, he doesn't let that fear stop him from writing, because he wants so badly to connect with others.

Antonio is also feeling overwhelmed at work and wonders if his dyslexia is getting in the way. There are so many new words for articles of clothing. "I don't know the difference between raincoats, top coats, long coats, car coats," he says as we're sitting in his downstairs neighbor's living room. He points to a landscape painting on the wall to demonstrate his point. "That's a painting," he tells me. "I would not know that's also a portrait." (It's not.) At work, there are differences between similar objects that he doesn't quite understand. "You know how you say that's just a shirt, you're wearing a shirt?" he says, explaining that he'd never heard the term "golf shirt" to describe a short-sleeved shirt with a collar.

"I did not know silk you cannot launder," he says, sounding ashamed that he charged someone only $1.75 for a silk shirt because he thought it could go to the store's laundry facility instead of being dry-cleaned. He offered to pay his boss the difference in price for cleaning the shirt, but Martinez told him it was all right.

Adrian Martinez never had Antonio's problems. After arriving in Washington Heights at the age of eight, he says, he continued speaking Spanish at home as he learned English in school. He was in a bilingual class for his first year. He thinks it took only about six months to speak fluently. He was already reading well in Spanish and recalls being skipped from second to third grade. He thinks it's because he attended a good school in La Romana, a city with a big tourism industry, in the Dominican Republic. "Comparatively speaking I can say that education over there was a lot harder than over here," he states.

As he takes Antonio under his wing, teaching him how to work in the store, he tells him that someday he could run his own business. "He wants to become a manager," he says. "He asks me the other day, 'Could I get to that position where I could be a manager?' I'm like, everything is possible. You want to do it, you can do it."

When Martinez hired Antonio's older cousin at his dry cleaning shop in Washington Heights a few years ago, the cousin apparently had very little education. "He didn't know how to read or write either." But Martinez says the young man got his driver's license, made deliveries, and ended up being able to open and close the store and do the books. Martinez says he paid him between $650 and $700 a week. But he says the cousin mismanaged his money and got into debt. When he became disrespectful, and the Washington Heights store was getting ready to close, Martinez says, he let him go.

Martinez sees this example as both a model and a warning for Antonio. It proves you *can* get ahead without a high school degree. "The most important thing is communication between me and my boss and my manager," Antonio agrees, adding that he thinks it would be easy to become a manager someday. But it also shows that advancement is no sure thing. "I wouldn't say easy. That's, you know, being a little cocky," Martinez tells him. "Everything is hard work. Just the same way you were learning that, struggling in the beginning. But you eventually got it."

At work, Antonio has a mentor in Martinez who can help him learn by doing. But it's not quite the same with his reading. He can explore the Internet and practice his reading and writing by sending messages. He may even learn new words on the job. But in the very wide world of the Web, he won't have someone telling him when he's right and wrong, or pushing him to a higher level. Without a school or tutors to guide his way, he'll have to keep learning to read by himself.

TWENTY-THREE

Upstairs, Downstairs

One of the biggest complaints about the city's new grading system for schools has to do with the way it measures progress. Schools that already had a lot of high-performing students claimed they had a difficult time getting A's because there wasn't much room for growth. On the other end, schools with a large percentage of special education pupils or English Language Learners thought they should get even more recognition for raising scores among these especially challenging students.

At Yamilka and Alejandro's old school, MS 232 in the Bronx, more than a quarter of its 511 students in the 2007/08 year were in transitional bilingual or English as a Second Language classes, and seventy-three students were receiving special education services. The eighth-grade teacher Hazel Brown was fiddling with her new SMART Board one morning in April as she got ready to teach a special education class. She had never used a laptop computer and a projector. Her students seemed much more familiar with the technology, and an enthusiastic boy with a ponytail sat at the keyboard, ready to type in the name of a social studies website she had been given by the Department of Education. Brown spelled it out for him, slowly saying the letters. "S-o-c-i-a-l s-t-u-d-i-e-s."

Only four of the fourteen students showed up for this eight a.m. class, an extra period that was added to the school day at MS 232 for students in need of intervention services. These students had mixed academic abilities. Brown nodded toward a black girl with a messy notebook, who she said was mentally retarded and got speech therapy. The girl seldom spoke and Brown had been giving her basic sight words to memorize, such as "am," "all," "brown," "but," "on," "please," and "pretty." Meanwhile, Brown said, the three boys in the room had learning disabilities, including a tall, hefty boy with a round face who had autism. He said he enjoyed *My Friend, My Hero*, which the class had just read. It happened to be the same book that Francy at IS 339 wrote about on her blog. This class wasn't doing any blogging, though. Its teacher was still getting used to her SMART Board and laptop.

The boy at the computer found a website with a video about the Dust Bowl, which was selected to accompany a lesson about the Great Depression the students read about in their history textbooks. Brown asked why the Dust Bowl happened and the autistic boy answered, "Farmers planted grass, the land turned dry, there was no period of rain." The girl seated across from him with the messy notebook giggled but didn't say anything. "The Dust Bowl was in the Plains," Brown added.

"In Oklahoma, so they went to California," said the big boy.

"What happened when they reached California?" the teacher asked him.

"Then they got rejected," he continued. "They thought they would take they jobs away." Brown asked him where the refugees lived and he told her "in tents." The other students were silent.

This boy was obviously reading the books. Brown said he was supposed to be mainstreamed to a regular eighth-grade class with extra support, but he didn't want to leave her class. Technically, she said, he wasn't even on her register, but he still came every day. "You can ask him about any subject," she said. But she added that he wasn't as good when it came to big-picture questions that tested comprehension more than facts, which is typical of autism.

Brown has been teaching special education classes for seven years, ever since she moved to New York from her native Jamaica. She started off as a paraprofessional, or classroom aide, and then got a degree and a license to teach special ed. She viewed her students as having "lots of abilities," and said that was confirmed whenever another one moved into mainstream classes. But she acknowledged it's often a big challenge getting them to pass a state exam. They all scored at level 1 or 2 on last year's math and English tests. And after giving them the new assessments from Acuity, she saw the same patterns other teachers noticed with low-performing pupils. "My kids have a problem when it comes to critical thinking," she said. They also often have emotional problems. "Control your impulses, please," she called out to a boy who started playing with the laptop.

Brown's class was following the school's English curriculum for the month of April. As the class ended, she geared up for a lesson on analyzing primary documents, such as the old Dust Bowl footage. The rest of her students wandered in for first period and the hallways were soon buzzing with the loud voices of adolescents.

Straight across the hall from Brown's special education class, the literacy coach Raedyn Rivera sat at her desk in the empty teacher resource room, blowing dry her long brown hair with the help of a round brush. There was a sign above her desk with the word "whining" in a circle with a red slash across it. The formerly dull walls of her office had been painted a deep rose color, another of her efforts to create a warmer and more professional atmosphere. The space was homey and inviting, with new furniture and neat rows of books for her teachers. The seventh-grade teacher John McDonald stopped by before class to grade a couple of papers. More students were completing their writing assignments, he reported, and he was finally able to apply some of the lessons he had learned from the AUSSIE consultant on how to question students about their work.

The school celebrates good examples of student writing. A few high-scoring eighth-grade papers were placed on a glass-covered bulletin board in the second-floor hallway. They were examples of "realistic fiction writing." It was impossible to read the full papers, because only their first pages were visible, but the teacher had posted her comments. Next to one called "Love at First Sight," which earned a 3 out of a possible 4, the teacher wrote: "Very romantic story," and "your plot was well-developed and I liked the writing. Next steps: 1) all essays should include five paragraphs 2) use more details to describe characters and settings 3) always check your spelling."

Rivera was noticing progress among her teachers. Despite the steep learning curve in managing his classroom, she thought McDonald had come a long way. "I know he cares, and that's half the battle," she said, adding that he had already committed to staying next year. And she pointed to a calendar for April that her teachers created together, as evidence that they could finally plan their lessons without her. The writer's workshop for eighth-graders that month was geared toward "document-based essays" and included a different theme for each week: immersion in the writing style, collecting seed ideas, drafting and revising, and editing and publishing. Rivera used to write the monthly pacing calendars by herself, but the teachers were meeting on Mondays about what they wanted to teach. "I'm weaning them off me," she joked.

Rivera was joined that morning by Ellen Padva, a specialist from the Center for Educational Innovation–Public Education Association. This is the outside group that was consulting with MS 232 and dozens of other schools after the chancellor eliminated regional offices. MS 232 was no longer tied to neighboring schools in the Bronx. Principals were free to join networks of like-minded supervisors that were supported by teams of consultants either inside or outside the Department of Education. Padva had been a Bronx special education teacher and a literacy coach before she took on her new position. She'd also worked for the old regional office that oversaw MS 232, so she knew the school very well. She was professionally dressed in a black pantsuit, her brown hair at chin length. She inquired about Rivera's efforts to start a book club.

"Give me your opinion," Rivera responded grimly. "Some teachers couldn't get the kids interested in a book. Should they drop it?"

"The whole class?" Padva asked, incredulous that not a single child would join a book club. She'd heard of individual students who fell behind when they didn't like the book that was assigned during class time, but this seemed a little extreme, since the students got to choose what they wanted to read for book clubs. Rivera's idea was to have groups of four to five students reading and discussing literature such as *To Kill a Mockingbird*, *A Raisin in the Sun*, or *The Outsiders*, and newer books. But she said the teachers didn't have enough control over their classrooms to manage twenty-eight or thirty teens reading several different books. A few had tried to get their students to rally behind a book but "some read it, others stopped," Rivera said, adding that students won't finish a novel they aren't enjoying. "They read slower than turtles." Last year, she recalled a teacher who couldn't get her students to read the late-nineteenth-century pirate-adventure novel *Treasure Island* by Robert Louis Stevenson. Padva told Rivera to give up on the book clubs. Forcing students to read books they don't like, on their own time, will not reinforce a love of literature, she said, "and you're not going to get meaningful work."

There was also an issue with teacher turnover. Seven of the school's twenty-one literacy teachers were new this year, and some hadn't taught before. Rivera said one woman from Florida left midyear because she couldn't handle her sixth-graders. It's not uncommon for new and inexperienced teachers to leave before the end of the school year; there are always plenty of unassigned teachers floating around the system who can replace them. At MS 232, the new teachers' classes tended to have the lowest scores on the weekly and monthly exams. The students scored mostly at or below 50 percent, and Rivera fretted that this was a sign of poor reading comprehension.

And yet she was certain the students could do better if their teachers could only figure out how to reach them. She had seen signs of intelligent life when she reviewed their weekly quizzes. Rivera deliberately alternated which textbooks the quizzes were drawn from. She used one book with long reading passages and another with short ones followed by short questions in big print, which Rivera called "baby work." A recent quiz from the more challenging book was based on an essay called "National Versus State Government," which was about the three branches of government and the powers of the states. It was a page long, single-spaced, followed by multiple-choice questions. Rivera noticed students were getting lower scores whenever they were given these longer essays. "They like short and sweet," she said, calling them lazy and reluctant to "think beyond the tip of their noses." She thought they needed to build more reading stamina. "It's stamina and motivation," the consultant, Padva, concurred. "It's a process over time. You have to build it in, and explain it's not an option." Padva suggested getting rid of the quizzes with the short passages and making the longer ones the norm, so the students would get used to reading more demanding material.

Rivera was glad when Mayor Bloomberg's proposal to base teacher tenure on classroom scores died in the state legislature that spring. "I used to teach the lowest-level third grade," she recalled of her old elementary school in the Bronx. "It was so hard and frustrating. My friend down the hall had a class reading on eighth-grade level . . . The top class will always succeed. It's not fair." At MS 232, Ms. Maley's eighth-grade class was consistently at the top, while John McDonald's seventh-graders were among the toughest and special education students were the most difficult of all.

Rivera kept a pile of pale pink cards on her desk, which she used for the school's word of the day. On this day it was "inept: without skill or aptitude for a particular assessment or task."

"Sometimes they're personal for me," she said with a sly smile.

• • •

Rosalinda Valenzuela was one staffer at MS 232 who didn't focus on test scores and essays. As a speech and language teacher, she concentrated on helping children who had problems reading and expressing themselves because they can't process information aurally, or because they have short- and long-term memory problems—students not unlike Yamilka.

Valenzuela is originally from Guatemala and she'd been assigned to work with thirty-four children who needed a bilingual speech teacher. Some schools have trouble getting enough speech teachers, especially bilingual ones, but she worked full-time at MS 232, which also had a part-time speech teacher and a part-time hearing teacher. Valenzuela's classes were determined by the students' Individualized Education Programs, and they were typically very small. The largest groups had three pupils, and some students required one-on-one services.

Back in September, Valenzuela said, six of her students came to middle school unable or barely able to read. In April three still weren't reading at all, she said, while two could read a little and one had just started. She gave them exercises in building phonemic awareness, comprehension, and vocabulary. They worked on prefixes, suffixes, words with multiple meanings, and synonyms. They started with phonics in September and by the spring they were reading short books and poetry. A few of her students read a small book called *Gloria Estefan: Cuban-American Singing Star*, which was written at a second- or third-grade level. "It is hard to imagine Gloria Estefan stopping—even for a moment," it began. They also used picture books. Valenzuela had a bachelor's degree in speech from Lehman College, and was finishing a master's degree in teaching English as a Second Language. But despite her schooling, and some extra professional development, she had never had a formal class in phonics and had to teach herself about it.

Valenzuela thought some of the reading problems she encountered among her mostly Dominican and Mexican students were related to economic and cultural factors. In Guatemala, her father had told her stories when she was a child, but she didn't read a book until she went to school. "Books in our countries are so expensive." She sighed. "We don't have libraries like here." While some Dominican immigrants recall going to good schools, others had little formal education and can't help their children when they struggle in school. She said there were also many failing special education students who continued to get passed to the next grade, despite Mayor Bloomberg's attempt to end social promotion.

Valenzuela's room resembled an elementary classroom, with bins of early reading books. A seventh-grade girl with a ponytail stopped by to ask a question about a recent assignment. The girl said Valenzuela helped her whenever she had a problem. "If we get stuck, she tells us to go back to look at what we read, highlight words you don't know." A few minutes later, a sixth-grade boy named Javier entered the classroom. He was still wearing a coat, although school had started more than an hour ago. It wasn't his day to meet with Valenzuela but he liked spending time with her. He pulled out a page from his folder—a short essay about Mother Teresa. He defined the word "charity" in his angular handwriting as "the giving of aid to the poor and suffering." He sat down at the small table and talked with Valenzuela about the Frederick Douglass biography he'd been reading. "He used to be a slavery," he told her. "Slave," Valenzuela corrected him.

Javier's parents were from the Dominican Republic and El Salvador, and he spoke Spanish at home. Valenzuela would give him puzzles to help improve his vocabulary whenever he read a new book. He pulled out a crossword puzzle with words and names from the Frederick Douglass book, such as "slavery," "escaped," and "Abraham Lincoln." Valenzuela worked with him twice a week. He also had a hearing teacher. Javier could speak English very well, but he said the hardest part of school was not understanding the words he sees in a book. His reading and writing were both improving, though. He'd written a little bit about Douglass: "In New Bedford, Douglass got married and joind a church. He was ability to spend more time reading books and education himself." Valenzuela went over the mistakes, explaining why he should have written "able" instead of "ability" and "educating" instead of "education."

Although Valenzuela was seeing progress among her pupils, she was quite concerned about an eighth-grade boy who hadn't progressed at all that year. She suspected he had dyslexia. "He can't recognize letters," she said, though she was able to teach him vowel sounds. She said his spoken English was good, despite coming from a Spanish-speaking home, and he had a normal IQ, but he forgot things easily. He was in a special education class with a ratio of twelve students to one teacher. Yet he was reading at a second-grade level. He'd been attending MS 232 since sixth grade, and she'd started working with him the previous year. "He didn't want to do his homework, any work," she recalled, even though she remembered him being very respectful. He also wouldn't work in his assigned speech and language class—which had a couple of other pupils—because he was too embarrassed. He'd only meet with her alone. Valenzuela was planning to speak to his classroom teacher about a one-to-one placement for speech class, though she knew that was unlikely because the school year was ending soon and the speech teachers were overloaded. Schools often ask them to take larger groups whenever possible to accommodate all the students who need their help.

One might wonder why, in April, Valenzuela hadn't spoken to the boy's classroom teacher earlier about getting more personalized attention. I was never able to pin down the details, but since the boy was moving on to high school, it seemed like Valenzuela was concentrating that spring on getting him appropriate ninth-grade services for the coming fall. Though she wasn't a reading specialist, she suspected that this was a child who could have benefited from an intensive decoding program like Wilson Reading, which was used in many of the city's public schools.

There was one big problem, though: there were no Wilson classes at MS 232. Principal Neifi Acosta said the majority of his school's struggling readers had comprehension problems, not decoding issues, and principals did have the right to pick and choose whatever programs they thought were best suited to their students. However, two floors up, in the very same building, there was another middle school that *did* offer Wilson Reading classes. But Valenzuela's eighth-grade student couldn't be transferred upstairs because the two schools were completely separate.

Intermediate School 303, or the Leadership and Community Service Academy, opened in 1999 just before the state shut down the old school that occupied the building, Community Intermediate School 82 (the name when Yamilka and Alejandro attended). IS 303 was started by its principal, Patricia Bentley, who was an assistant principal at the old school, and Monica Brady, who was a teacher there. They had help from the nonprofit group New Visions for Public Schools, which has played a critical role in developing smaller and more personalized high schools all over the city.

Bentley is a stylish, petite African-American woman with short hair and skin that's so smooth it's hard to believe she's worked in the city schools for twenty-six years. She recalled how CIS 82 was out of control during the 1990s. "There were kids having sex in the hallways and smoking pot," she said. "You couldn't park on the street because things were being thrown from the halls." Despite these lurid memories, Bentley and Brady, the assistant principal of IS 303, said CIS 82 had some good things going on, too, and wasn't all that dissimilar from other middle schools confounded by slumping test scores. "A lot of English teachers are literature majors," said Brady, echoing the complaints of so many other middle and high school teachers who don't feel prepared to help adolescents with low literacy skills. Neither Brady nor Bentley remembered Yamilka or Alejandro. But they were pleased to hear the former students fought the city for their right to learn how to read. Bentley said she once unsuccessfully tried to convince an illiterate sixth-grader to do something similar.

Brady and Bentley were working in a large, open room in the corner of the fifth floor. They sat at private cubicles surrounded by administrators who worked at desks positioned toward the front of the room. There were plants by the windows and books for the children. Three students who were on in-school suspension sat at a table working quietly. They wore white shirts and dark pants or skirts, the school's uniform. The school had an orderly feeling. In the hallway, there were banners that said "Believe and Succeed" and "Be someone you can be proud of: polite, understanding, caring, honest." IS 303 was smaller than MS 232 downstairs, with fewer than 350 students that year, all on the same floor, and a staff of thirty. It received an A on its progress report even though only 38 percent of students were reading at a proficient level. That was higher than the 25 percent at MS 232, which got a C, but the real reason for the better grade was student progress. IS 303 won praise from outside evaluators for doing a good job at using data to help low-performing pupils.

Those school report cards seemed to have aggravated tensions between the two schools. Teachers at MS 232 suspected their upstairs neighbor drew the cream of the crop from local schools. Some also believed the staff didn't reflect the neighborhood's diversity because many of its teachers were white. Principal Bentley and Assistant Principal Brady shrugged off such criticism. They'd seen a lot of turnover at MS 232, which went through five principals in five years. They maintained their school had the same type of students as the one downstairs and noted that 14 percent were receiving special education services in 2007/08. If anything explained their better scores, they said, it was a greater "sense of mission." Staffers at IS 303 held team meetings on a daily basis, where teachers also discussed which students were having trouble and whether to call their parents. Baseline tests were given in September, January, and June, well before the chancellor required new assessments. And teachers emphasized grammar because they didn't think it was getting enough attention in elementary school. They also used the Wilson Reading system because they'd found many of their English Language Learners didn't have a background in phonics. Bentley mentioned a sixth-grader from Africa who couldn't read at all and would not be promoted next fall. The teachers had to teach her the alphabet.

A few doors down from the main office, the seventh-grade teacher Tom Sullivan was working with his twenty-nine students on a writing assignment. Like Bentley and Brady, Sullivan had been in the building long enough to have taught at the old school. He's tall, balding, and fortyish. His students were reading one another's essays and looking for "powerful moments." Sullivan said some were reading well, but others were at a third-grade level. He keeps those differences in mind as he helps them select "a just-right book" for independent reading assignments. "Simply providing kids with books they can read is a big step," he explained, because suddenly students have an opportunity to read in every subject and stay engaged. He thought the baseline tests that are given three times a year, and the new assessments in math and reading, had changed his approach to teaching. "It made old-timers like me much more aware of the range of readers we have," he said. "Teaching one thing to everybody just is not cool."

Sullivan also considers his students' different reading and writing levels when dividing them up into groups for each activity. He doesn't want to be obvious about the groupings, but if you walk around and listen to their discussions, you can figure out which students are working at higher levels. At one table, four girls were discussing a story one of them had written about two characters comparing the young R&B singer Chris Brown with the rapper Bow Wow. It wasn't exactly Shakespeare, but Sullivan said these girls were reading and writing at grade level. They were eagerly searching for imagery as they discussed what made the essays memorable. One girl told an essay's author that her most memorable moment was when a character mentioned going to Red Lobster. "They said I said that with a lot of expression," the author exclaimed, with a touch of pride mixed with embarrassment. No one found any imagery in her story, but they suggested she read aloud more slowly.

A few more clusters of students were chatting and reviewing one another's work. Sullivan checked in with each and attended to two girls in the back of the room. "'I'm gonna get you Jimmy, she said as he shut the door,'" he read from one of their essays. "'The kid looked like he was going to pee in his pants.'

"There's your imagery!" he exclaimed, praising the girl's description.

Later, Sullivan said these two girls near the back had tested at a low fifth-grade reading level at the beginning of the school year. The one whose imagery he praised had since moved up to a high fifth-grade level. That might not sound like a huge difference, but Sullivan said her confidence and engagement in class both improved considerably. He credited the extra support she received in small "resource room" classes that offer reading interventions. There were two other clusters of students who, Sullivan said, were about two years below grade level. "Tomorrow it's second draft, we have a writing session," he told his students as the class wrapped up.

Assistant Principal Monica Brady called the Bloomberg administration's reforms "a stroke of genius," because they concentrated so heavily on the progress schools like hers were making instead of a school's overall reading level. But the principal, Patricia Bentley, argued that this measurement also led to confusion. She pointed out that 55 percent of the city's grade for any given school is based on student progress, which is markedly different than the state's system of using the percentage of students meeting standards. So while her school earned an A from the city, it technically didn't meet the state's definition of adequate yearly progress. She explained that that was because two special education students who performed very well were not included in the scoring system, since they lived outside the boundaries of the school's neighborhood. She was perplexed by that decision and said the state thankfully cut her a break with some kind of footnote to the test score. But she was fatigued by these requirements and the sheer volume of tests, which she called "absurd."

"Absurd" might be an apt term for a situation in which a struggling student isn't allowed to attend a reading class upstairs that might be able to help him, because the floors are controlled by two different principals. There's no way to know whether the eighth-grade boy in the speech class at MS 232 could have benefited from the intensive Wilson phonics classes offered on the fifth floor, at IS 303. But this is one of many consequences of a system that empowers principals to the degree that they can operate their schools as separate entities. In this five-story building on the corner of Macombs Road in the Bronx, two intermediate schools coexist without any collaboration. Their staffs are indifferent toward, and at other times suspicious of, each other. The schools use separate entrances and their students wear different uniforms.

This type of site-based leadership was popular in urban school systems during the 1990s. But the results weren't convincing, says Michael Casserly, executive director of the Council of the Great City Schools. That's partly why many cities like Los Angeles switched to a unified curriculum. "This is where the jury is still out," he said about New York City. Some critics said there was more consistency before the mayor's reforms—or at least opportunities for consistency. Carmen Farina, a former deputy chancellor for instruction, was a district superintendent in Brooklyn before Bloomberg's team consolidated the districts into regions. Farina then became one of the first regional superintendents before being promoted to deputy chancellor and has since retired, now serving as a consultant to Teachers College. She says there's a lack of coordination when principals are on their own, without any strong leadership. "You can't have some schools with interventions and some without," she says, referring to a situation such as IS 303 and MS 232. When she was a regional superintendent, she says, she encouraged schools to share resource-room teachers and guidance counselors, to get more bang for the buck. She was also able to tell a school that had extra seats to take students from another building that was overcrowded.

Some veterans of the system say that kind of help from above didn't always happen, though, and Chancellor Klein certainly agreed with them. "The superintendents weren't swapping kids from one school to another school, they were running school districts," he said. "And their performance was much worse . . . than it is now." As for children whose needs aren't being met, such as the eighth-grader at MS 232, Klein said principals should be turning to their networks for suggestions about the right services. And he stood by his belief that measuring student progress is a powerful incentive for principals to avoid letting any students fall through the cracks, though he conceded mistakes are bound to happen occasionally. "If we had each year only one kid in every elementary school that was written off it would be a dramatic change in the city," he said. "These kids, when I came here six years ago, the number of kids in high school who could not read—what happened to them in K through eight? Nothing."

This was the Bloomberg administration's view of principals as CEOs. Individual principals could build whatever type of school they thought was best, because the administration assumed they knew the needs of their students better than some regional superintendent in an off-site office. Annual progress report cards would tell the city if the principals were doing a good job, to provide accountability. But schools aren't insular systems. They exist within communities, and sometimes within the very same building. If, in the spirit of John Dewey, the schools were to learn from one another's experiences—as envisioned by the accountability architect Jim Liebman, with his plans to get everyone contributing to the same online system—they would need to develop a stronger sense of community in either the real or virtual world.

TWENTY-FOUR

Inputs and Outputs

Tourists walking through Lower Manhattan often mistakenly assume the Tweed Courthouse must be City Hall because of its imposing size.

The actual City Hall is located behind the Tweed, set back from the surrounding streets. The elegant French Renaissance–style white building has large arched windows and a graceful cupola capped with a sculpture of Justice. Its steps have served as the backdrop for countless press conferences and demonstrations. Inside, a dramatic rotunda sits between the two wings, which house the two branches of city government. Follow the stairs as they circle up one flight, beneath a domed ceiling, and the eastern side of the building is dominated by the City Council Chambers with its forty-five-by-twenty-three-foot oval ceiling mural of New York City receiving tributes from the nation, and a statue of Thomas Jefferson. The opposite end of the building is the mayor's wing. Bloomberg built his "bullpen," a big open room modeled after a trading floor, in a former government meeting room. It is protected by a small gate and a security guard.

On a chilly afternoon in May, Dennis Walcott, the deputy mayor for education and community development, convened the latest in a series of roundtables with about twenty representatives from community groups active in public education. Their meeting was held in a huge room directly across from the bullpen. The attendees sat on leather chairs around a stately round table. Sunlight streamed through the green draperies and dappled the round ceiling. An oil painting of James Monroe, who lived in New York City after his presidency, faced a tall grandfather clock on the opposite side of the room.

The representatives came from established organizations with an interest in the city's schools, including the Children's Aid Society, the After-School Corporation, and the JPMorgan Chase Foundation. Those who couldn't fit at the table sat on red leather chairs to the side. Walcott, a former head of the New York Urban League, is a tall, lanky African-American man with a formal bearing. He acknowledged the news of the day that was on everyone's minds: Chancellor Klein was in the process of cutting the education budget for the coming year. Walcott told the group that the chancellor was meeting with city principals about the economic downturn.

This roundtable discussion, however, wasn't about the budget. Jim Liebman was scheduled to brief the attendees on changes he planned for the next round of school report cards. Now that the system was up and running, the next progress reports—based heavily on the state test scores that would be coming out in June—were scheduled to be delivered in September. The first A–F letter grades had triggered an outcry the previous fall. Since then, Liebman had been meeting with principals, teachers, elected officials, and parents. He said he had taken their feedback into consideration as he modified the report cards' formula. Schools would still get one overall letter grade. But there would also be separate grades for school environment, student performance, and student progress. Schools where special education students made gains would also get more credits than they did in the previous year, to reflect their additional challenges.

The presentation was aimed at an audience of noneducators. Liebman's main goal was to help them understand how using data to measure student achievement marked a turning point in public education. He explained that teachers could glean a great deal from test scores because there's actually a huge spread within the state's four different levels of proficiency. For example, not all students who score a level 2 are in the same league. A third-grader at level 2, which the state defines as "partially meeting learning standards," could have gotten anywhere between a 615 and a 649 (out of a potential 800) on the English Language Arts exam. By studying this range, Liebman's team had drawn some conclusions. At the end of eighth grade, "if you are a low level one or below, the likelihood of graduation is less than twenty-five percent," he told them. "If you're a high level two or above [by then], that likelihood is fifty percent."

As Liebman went over these findings and his proposals for fine-tuning the report cards, the participants in the roundtable listened earnestly. He assured them that "every school *can* be an A," countering the widespread perception that a system based on progress penalized schools whose students were already high-performing. Schools would no longer lose credit for a student whose scores went down slightly if they maintained a level 4. Liebman also said the city would adjust the "peer groups," composed of forty similar schools, to ensure they're more demographically similar to whichever school is being rated.

When the presentation concluded, many of the attendees said they had a much better understanding of the scoring system, and that they wanted to help explain it to their communities. Liebman and Deputy Mayor Walcott looked pleased. This was the point of the meeting. Mayoral control would come up for state legislative review in 2009. Though Bloomberg hadn't yet decided to persuade the City Council to end term limits so he could to run for a third term, he needed to convince the public that his reforms were successful enough to continue letting *any* mayor run the schools. "We have not gotten true credit for the revolution that's taken place in using data," Walcott said, brimming with confidence.

The people at the roundtable did have a couple of tough questions for the city officials. A woman in the back of the room asked whether schools might be encouraged to "push out" failing students in order to get a better grade. Liebman assured her that wouldn't happen. "Every single student who starts in a school stays in the denominator," he said, referring to the way grades are calculated. Even the scores of students who transfer out of a school are counted. Walcott explained that this encouraged principals to take "ownership" of all their students—even those who were struggling. He also said giving schools more credit for raising the scores of special education students would encourage principals and teachers to work even harder. "This is a complicated system," Liebman said in his rational, quiet tone. "The only way we can make this clear is through people like you."

Warren "Pete" Moses was struck by that statement. Moses was executive director of the Children's Aid Society, which provides prenatal counseling, health care, and after-school programs for more than 150,000 children and their families in New York City. As he sat at the table facing Liebman, he thought about students in poor communities like the Bronx and Washington Heights, whose families often don't have health insurance. They might miss days or weeks of school because of asthma or an infected molar. Some students can't read well because of undetected vision problems. He'd met children who sleep on fire escapes to avoid domestic violence, and others who come to school hungry and rely on the city's free breakfast program. Moses raised his hand and congratulated Liebman on his work. Then he told Liebman about the children his organization serves, and described seeing a significant number of them who get stuck at level 2 and "don't move." He called these children "special ed with lowercase letters," because they don't advance even though they have no specific disabilities. To Moses these children were living, breathing proof that student achievement is also a product of a child's environment. "Not everything can get solved by teaching and curriculum," he said.

Liebman conceded this was a good point. But he told Moses that he was going to push back, nonetheless, and proceeded to do so with quiet force. "We believe it's not about inputs, it's about outcomes," he said. He agreed that the schools had challenging populations. Health care and family crises do contribute to school readiness, he said. But he argued that some schools with needy students nonetheless did a better job than others with similar demographics, and the report cards made that abundantly clear. Liebman said principals were free to partner with community-based organizations for health care and counseling services, and said he was open to creating a new structure for principals to share information about these organizations. But those efforts wouldn't be part of the report card.

Moses seemed impressed with this argument, but he said he would "push forever" to get everyone to focus on the external factors (or inputs) he mentioned, all of which affect a child's readiness for school. He also noted that many parents have complained about being left out of the Bloomberg administration's education reforms. But as the meeting ended, Moses acknowledged he couldn't think of a better system for weighing how much progress a school is making. "There are no pristine measures," he sighed.

The role of families and schools—or inputs and outputs—has been debated by educators and sociologists for decades. Who do we blame when our children are failing?

During the 2008 presidential election, education advocates split into two camps as they lobbied the candidates. One coalition, called the Broader Bolder Approach, argued that the No Child Left Behind law—and its testing and accountability measures—couldn't close the achievement gap until children were given greater access to health care, preschool, after-school, and summer programs. This coalition consisted of scholars, community groups, Rudy Crew (the former New York schools chancellor and Miami-Dade County superintendent), Diane Ravitch, and labor unions, including the American Federation of Teachers and its New York City chapter, the United Federation of Teachers.

Chancellor Klein preferred to focus more on the schools themselves. He joined with the Reverend Al Sharpton in starting another group aimed at closing the achievement gap between whites and students of color. Their coalition supported merit pay for teachers and changes in union rules that could make it easier to remove bad teachers. They were joined by the mayor and schools chancellor of Washington, D.C.; former Los Angeles schools superintendent and Colorado governor Roy Romer; Baltimore schools chief Andres Alonso; and Newark mayor Cory Booker, as well as a group called Democrats for Education Reform. Columnists portrayed the coalition as anti-labor.

Barack Obama's selection for U.S. education secretary, Chicago schools chief Arne Duncan, had supported both camps. The two sides had sound arguments. Obviously, the quality of teachers does play a role in the achievement gap. Schools located in poor neighborhoods—like MS 232—tend to have higher concentrations of inexperienced teachers, because those with more experience use their seniority and knowledge of the system to transfer to schools in better neighborhoods. This is why Klein wanted to make it easier for principals to fire bad teachers, and why he saw data as a powerful tool for figuring out which teachers are most effective. Schools in poor neighborhoods also often don't have as much money as schools in wealthy communities that have a bigger tax base from which they can draw additional funds to support public education; that's why the suburbs can lure the best teachers with higher salaries and provide more state-of-the-art materials. New York City pays for schools through its general fund, *not* dedicated property taxes; but parents in wealthier neighborhoods will often raise funds to hire extra teaching assistants and to buy school supplies. Education advocates all around the country have filed lawsuits over state school aid in an effort to level the playing field. Klein used the money New York City won from a state settlement to raise teacher salaries. He also gave more money to schools with lots of students in poverty and students with special needs, by assigning a greater weight to these students in the city's own funding formula. This angered parents at schools in wealthier neighborhoods because the principals would have to dip into their limited resources to keep more experienced and highly paid teachers.

The chancellor and the Broader Bolder folks weren't always in opposition, though. "I'd be the first guy to advocate much better prenatal care in America, the first guy to advocate much better early health care," Klein said. But he believed some schools were more successful than others in raising math and reading scores among disadvantaged pupils such as Yamilka or Antonio. Liebman argued that schools can't pass the buck and blame a child's upbringing. "If we do, we then blame the kids, not the schools, when kids don't learn." He said the city's policy was to assume kids can learn, despite environmental factors, and to hold the schools accountable for how well they help the students.

But the disadvantages that poor and minority children start off with before they ever enter the classroom do have lasting effects. In the 1960s, a major federal study known as the Coleman Report (named for the sociologist James Samuel Coleman) reached the then-controversial conclusion that a child's family background was a predictor of his or her academic success. Critics thought the report blamed the poor. But while there are always children who rise above their circumstances, volumes of research since then have bolstered the argument that socioeconomic status can play a decisive role in student achievement.

The developmental psychologists Betty Hart and Todd Risley concluded from their Kansas City study in the 1980s that by the age of three, children of professional families had heard more than thirty million words, while children from families receiving public assistance had heard ten million. They also declared that there was a link between early language exposure and IQ scores. And students from families in the bottom income group are four times more likely to drop out of high school than children from the top income group, according to the National Center for Education Statistics (2006), despite an overall improvement in graduation rates. Because blacks and Latinos are more likely to be poor than whites, that's resulted in a big difference in graduation rates. Fewer than 6 percent of whites between the ages of 16 and 24 were not enrolled in high school and lacked either a diploma or GED certificate in 2006. But that figure was almost twice as high for blacks, at 10.7 percent; and among Hispanic youths, more than 22 percent were out of school and without a degree. Minority students are also disproportionately assigned to special education classes; researchers believe this could have something to do with the role of poverty in a child's readiness for school, or cultural biases by teachers and the IQ tests.

"There are areas where you're never going to compensate for the advantage middle-class kids have," says Dr. Pedro Noguera, a sociologist at the Steinhardt School of Culture, Education, and Human Development at New York University. Like other researchers, he believes a parent's education is another predictor of student achievement. Neither Yamilka and Alejandro's parents nor Antonio's mother were college educated; they had very little formal education and their children have no memories of being read to, in Spanish or English.

Community-based organizations like the Children's Aid Society say this is why financially disadvantaged children need *more* services than middle-class ones if they're ever going to keep up. That was the federal government's goal with Head Start when it was founded in the 1960s to provide health, nutrition, and early learning activities for preschoolers. Numerous studies have concluded the program has had a positive impact on kindergarteners (though the jury is still out on its lasting effects). But educators and sociologists argue these extra services are *still* needed when the kids get older. A recent Brookings Institution report comparing health, economic, and educational statistics for white and black children and their families found an average gap of fifteen percentage points between the white and black statistics.[1] These inequalities are only compounded when children attend failing schools. Several studies have found that even when low-income students are successful in the early elementary years, their reading scores decline precipitously as they get older.

In 1988 a group of researchers in Massachusetts began a longitudinal study of low-income students in the Boston area to see how they fared in school. The Home-School Study began visiting eighty-three children and their families when the children were three years old and followed their literacy skills and grades through high school. The size of the group declined by the end of the study, but the results were considered valid because the demographics remained consistent—with the same mix of whites, Latinos, and blacks (and these studies are typically small). On the whole, the students were doing well enough in elementary school that the researchers expected only about 20 percent of them to encounter real academic difficulties later. But that figure ended up being much higher once they got older. When the students were located in the year they should have been twelfth-graders, 30 percent of them had dropped out of school or had been held back two years or more.[2]

The researchers concluded that reading problems alone weren't to blame, which is why their book was provocatively titled *Is Literacy Enough?* Several of the students who suffered academically had family or health problems, and others just weren't engaged in school. In fact, a few students with poor grades managed to get into college while some of the brightest teens dropped out. But literacy remained a huge factor—especially in the early years. The children's vocabulary in kindergarten—a reflection of family environment—was an accurate predictor of their reading comprehension in high school. That was the "scary" part of the findings, said one of the researchers, Dr. Catherine Snow, the Henry Lee Shattuck Professor of Education and chair of human development and psychology at Harvard's Graduate School of Education. "If the schools were really compensating by giving the strongest instruction to the lowest-vocabulary-level kids, it wouldn't be the case that kindergarten vocabulary would predict tenth-grade reading comprehension," she explained. "The kids who were the lowest in kindergarten would have been effectively instructed in ways that compensated for the fact they were low."

Snow had expected a correlation between kindergarten reading levels and those of third- and fourth-graders. A smaller study of low-income children by the reading researcher Jeanne Chall in the 1980s drew a similar conclusion. In second grade, the students scored at grade level or higher on five different tests of reading skills. By fourth grade, however, their scores began to slip on tests of word meaning, word recognition, and spelling—although the students were performing at grade level for their oral reading and silent reading comprehension. By sixth grade the students dropped even lower. They were two and a half years below where they should have been on a test of word meaning.[3] But Chall's work stopped there. Snow's group tracked its cohort through high school, where it could see the lingering effects of the word gap that was quantified so dramatically in the Hart and Risley study.

Snow and the other Massachusetts researchers looked at the home lives of their low-income children. Those who were reading well had more dinner-table conversations, and their families were more apt to read to them in ways that involved the children in storytelling and asking questions. "It was really the quality of talk in the home," Snow explained, noting that children who had more conversations at an early age improved their oral language skills, which led to better reading skills. Those who didn't were more likely to have the limited vocabulary skills that were a predictor of poor reading comprehension when they got older, succumbing to the Matthew Effect (the poor getting poorer). Snow's team called for the equivalent of Head Start in the middle grades, with teachers trained in adolescent literacy to support lagging teens and to engage the better readers, too, so they wouldn't slip away.

In Washington Heights, Middle School 324 is among three schools called the Mirabal Sisters Campus, named after the Dominican heroines Minerva, Patria, and Maria Teresa, who were killed for trying to overthrow the fascist government of Rafael Trujillo. MS 324 takes part in the community schools program run by the Children's Aid Society. The school's student body is entirely Latino or black, and almost all of its four hundred students are poor enough to qualify for free lunch. It has an on-site health clinic, which Principal Janet Heller credits for what she claims is the school's 100 percent immunization rate. Students can get dental and eye exams, too. And the building is open from 7:30 a.m. to 9:00 p.m. during the week and on Saturdays. Students sign up for after-school tutoring, academic workshops, and fun activities such as a bicycle repair lab. "Kids want to be here because they're supported," said Heller. The school's average daily attendance rate in 2008 was 97 percent, well above the citywide average for middle schools.

Test scores at MS 324 weren't stellar, but the school got an A on its report card because of steady improvements. More than 40 percent of seventh-graders were meeting state standards in 2007, roughly double the percentage of students who were making the mark when they entered as fifth-graders. The staff was trying new models for student engagement. Fifteen low-performing students who were at risk of failure were selected to read to local elementary students and to kids in a homeless shelter. Heller said all but one of them had improved enough to be promoted to the next grade. The school's social work supervisor, Michelle Kohut, was also finding ways to use literacy in her sessions with individual students. Like Erin Gruwell and her Freedom Writers, she encouraged them to keep journals and to read on their own. A bookshelf next to her desk was stacked with a few of her own favorites: *Yoga to the Rescue: Remedies for Real Girls*, *Gypsy Girl's Best Shoes*, *The Giving Tree*, *Yummers*, and *Who Moved My Cheese?* Last year she bought Hill Harper's *Letters to a Young Brother*, which she recommended for an eighth-grade boy. It was a challenging book, so they read it together. She also kept picture books, including *Where the Wild Things Are*, for students with trouble reading.

But as with the two middle schools in the same building that had different approaches to reading intervention, these community partnerships aren't consistent. Dr. Pedro Noguera, of NYU, credits the Bloomberg administration with reducing the number of failing schools and providing more choices through small new schools and charters. But in his visits to city schools he sees too much emphasis on testing and standards, and not enough attention to support structures like the community schools model. Noguera singled out PS 188 on the Lower East Side, where the principal, Barbara Slatin, was especially aggressive on behalf of her students. "She's got an Internet café, a partnership with St. Vincent's hospital, a dentist, her kids get a full range of services," he said. The school also pays for a program called Schools Attuned, which trains teachers to identify, and work with, different learning styles. PS 188 got an A on its progress report. But Noguera said another school across the street with a similar population doesn't get as many services because its principal isn't experienced enough to write grant applications and build partnerships. He suggested getting the health department and other city agencies more involved since the mayor controls the school system.

But community partnerships alone can't fix everything. The Harlem Children's Zone learned this the hard way when it opened two charter schools. The organization was already providing a "conveyor belt" of services in a hundred-block area for children from birth through high school.* A Baby College program for parents and expecting parents teaches everything from prenatal care to language and brain development, and there's a rigorous, full-day pre-kindergarten program called Harlem Gems as well as after-school tutoring. The president and co-founder of the Harlem Children's Zone, Geoffrey Canada, believed this neighborhood service model would lead to academic success when his two charter schools opened in 2004. But the first year's test scores were disappointing.

"We provided all of those services and supports, but we had lousy teachers and a weak administration," he says of the program's rough start. "And you know what? The kids were not learning on a pace that would prepare them to be on grade level." Canada says this doesn't change his belief that poor children are entitled to the same health care and academic services as middle-class students. But he realized they'd need even better teachers to close the achievement gap, and he made a series of personnel changes. In 2008, when there were two third-grade classes, 68 percent of one class and 81 percent of the other met state standards in English Language Arts. Middle school scores also went up, with 52 percent meeting state standards. In 2009, 72.5 percent made the mark.

Canada still believes he can get those middle-schoolers ready for college, but he acknowledges it's tougher to raise test scores with older students who have experienced years of failure. And he says too many principals don't spend enough time and energy on the early grades because they're so preoccupied with raising test scores. He sees this with the local schools in Harlem who work with his organization. "I always tell them, look in your kindergarten and you will see seventy-five percent of the children who are going to fail this test in three years and just fix it. Just fix it. Just stop it from that point on. Will you catch hell for two or three years? Yes. The scores are not going to be great, but guess what? They weren't going to be great anyhow."

Teachers at PS 157 in the South Bronx were learning about the importance of early intervention all over again. When the city schools were asked

*The *New York Times Magazine* editor Paul Tough wrote a book about the Harlem Children's Zone called *Whatever It Takes: Geoffrey Canada's Quest to Change Harlem and America* (Boston and New York: Houghton Mifflin, 2008).

to create inquiry teams to focus on their lowest-performing students, Principal Ramona Duran decided to choose fifteen English Language Learners in grades four and five. Her staff soon discovered these students were far behind grade level, largely because of their weak vocabulary.

Duran's school had made great strides—earning an A on its progress report—but it fell short of the state's NCLB target for its English Language Learners. The school had about six hundred students in grades pre-kindergarten to fifth grade, more than three quarters of them Latino. The fourth- and fifth-grade English Language Learners who were identified by the inquiry team were to receive intensive instruction for a couple of hours a day after school. The school called them TIGERS, an acronym for Talented Intelligent Gifted English Reading Scholars. Chris Lomot, a math coach and data specialist for the inquiry team, said the original plan was to work on comprehension skills by getting the pupils to "retell" a story and look at character development. "But what we were finding was the kids just didn't have the vocabulary to get to that point," he said. This wasn't just because they had grown up in households that didn't speak English. Principal Duran said these children of immigrants didn't always have enough exposure to words in their native language. Duran had worked in the city schools for thirty-seven years and is of Puerto Rican descent. She knew English Language Learners tended to have trouble in class, but she was surprised to rediscover the importance of vocabulary.

That spring, the school started doling out vocabulary words like vitamins to the TIGERS group. New words were introduced in regular doses each day after school, giving the students plenty of time to absorb the nutrients of every lesson. The third-grade teacher Laura Harrison, a willowy blonde, stayed after school from three-thirty to five-thirty to work with four fourth-graders. She'd taught English as a Second Language in Orange County, California, before moving to New York. One day in May, she sat at a small table with nine-year-old Mary, a chubby girl with pigtails dressed in the school's uniform of a navy skirt and blouse. To Mary's right sat Elisa, an eleven-year-old who was kept back a grade and who wasn't wearing the uniform. On Mary's other side sat ten-year-old Rosie, who wore a sweatshirt and jeans and had long brown hair. The one boy in the group was nine-year-old Jose.

The children had just read a book called *Alexander and the Wind-Up Mouse*, and they were going over some of its unfamiliar words. "Who can give me a summary?" asked Harrison. Jose and Mary discussed the real mouse who wanted to become a toy so people would love him. "Can I tell what happened before that?" Mary squealed. She had problems paying attention and she fidgeted frequently in her seat. Harrison gave Mary a moment to summarize the story and then announced their three new vocabulary words: "envy," "fond," and "adventure."

They began by all saying the word "adventure" together. Then Harrison read them the definition: something "exciting or dangerous." She gave them a few scenarios for which to decide whether "adventure" was a correct description.

"Riding a roller coaster?"

"Adventure," the students shouted.

"Taking a nap?"

The students went quiet. Then Mary said, "Your dream might be an adventure."

Harrison smiled. "Taking a trip to a new place?"

"Adventure," the students exclaimed.

Next, they had to use the new word. "If an astronaut wanted to go to outer space, how would you say that?" asked Harrison. Jose tried it first with no problem. "When the astronaut came back from space he wanted to tell people about his adventure." But when it was Elisa's turn, she seemed blocked. "What?" she asked. "My adventure . . . my adventure." She couldn't complete her thought. "I don't know."

"Yes, you do," said Harrison.

"Was fun?" asked Elisa. "My adventure was fun."

Harrison had them pull out their notebooks and write down the word's definition: "An adventure is an exciting time." Then she proceeded to the next words, "envy" and "fond." Most of the students could use the word "envy," but Rosie was stumped when it became an adjective. "I'm an envy person," she said. Elisa got stuck on "fond."

"If your favorite snack was fruit and yogurt, what would you say?" Harrison asked her.

"My favorite apple was fond?"

Harrison waited to see if she'd correct herself. The other students looked confused. Elisa laughed at herself, saying, "It doesn't even make sense to me!" They went over the word again and Harrison asked her how to use it if she wanted to say she likes playing with her friends. "I, I am . . ." Elisa hesitated, leaning into her elbow with her head in her hand. It seemed painful for her to find the right combination of words. Harrison stepped in. "I am fond," she suggested to the girl. " 'Fond' is a way you feel toward something. I am fond of playing with my friends."

After this exercise, the students drew pictures and sentences using their new words. They determined what each word meant and what it didn't mean by using a thesaurus to search for opposites. They talked freely in this group. None of them had an accent, so you wouldn't know they were English Language Learners. But Harrison said these fourth-graders didn't speak up during their regular classes, which have twenty-two to twenty-five students. They knew they're not good students. They'd look down frequently and were afraid of being called upon. The small after-school sessions helped them open up because slow readers aren't stigmatized and there's less pressure when they're asked to read aloud. Elisa, for example, "freaks out on assessments," said Harrison. But in this after-school class she'd become more confident. Elisa was sitting on a chair at the far end of the room doing her own reading after the vocabulary session drew to a close. She got up to tell Harrison about a character from another book who had envy. Harrison gave her a high five. "That's the stuff we're looking for and it's working," she said.

It takes time and money for teachers to nurture students like these outside of their regular classes. The city allocated each school about sixteen thousand dollars to fund the inquiry teams. Harrison said she was paid $320 a week, on top of her regular salary of $46,000 a year, to work eight extra hours with the TIGERS students. The other members of the inquiry team were also compensated for teaching or attending weekly meetings where they watched videotapes of the after-school sessions and brought in research they found about English Language Learners.

The woman Chancellor Klein put in charge of the inquiry teams, Irma Zadoya, was proud of the work they accomplished that year. "Our goal was to impact the lives of twenty-eight thousand students," said the veteran educator, referring to the total number of students in the intensive study. "Believe me, we have impacted twenty-eight thousand in the target population and many more." Zadoya attended several "share fairs" toward the end of the school year, where teams from all over the city displayed their findings. At one event in the Bronx, elementary school teachers brought in some of the games they had used to boost their students' vocabulary. They had folded a piece of paper into a star with four leaves. The top and bottom of each leaf had a different synonym for either "happy" or "sad." The words "joyful," "glad," "pleased," and "merry" went with "happy," while "woeful," "gloomy," "unhappy," and "sorrowful" were paired with "sad." This inquiry team also brought along a bingo-style vocabulary game based on a book its students were reading.

Zadoya said most inquiry teams focused on reading instead of math, with many of them looking at the role of vocabulary. She recalled one that looked at "social emotional" issues when it noticed their low-performing English Language Learners were extremely shy. Other schools looked at ways of getting their different classroom teachers to collaborate around the lowest-performing students, or concentrated on parent outreach and Saturday academies. But Zadoya said the goal was to influence regular classroom instruction. "This is obviously a change strategy," she said, one aimed at helping schools work with underperforming students. Teachers were encouraged to constantly assess their students and to use that data as they collaborated on ways to improve the curriculum and their instruction. "One of the problems had been low expectations," Zadoya conceded.

This was the change in culture the Bloomberg administration was trying to codify. "We're trying to make sure, as a system, as much as possible, that this really gets embedded," said Zadoya, acknowledging the resistance from some teachers and principals to giving their students more assessment tests. She figured the schools would eventually buy in, "because it's getting results."

Jim Liebman said the inquiry teams were doing what all good educators should do by looking for every factor that could be "treated" or "changed" to facilitate learning. In some schools, that could mean discovering environmental factors (or "inputs," in the words of the Children's Aid Society director), such as the connection between a child's vocabulary and family literacy. And a school's choice of intervention didn't have to be curricular, with Liebman suggesting some principals might focus on health care or hygiene. But he said the city would measure their effectiveness through "outcomes," or test scores. And he resisted any tendency to let the schools off the hook.

"If we instead wait for someone to come along and end poverty or end disparities in health care—conditions likely to persist for a long time—then we give up doing something that can make a huge difference now, while waiting for something else to occur that, whatever its potential effect in some Utopia down the road, is not likely to happen now."

TWENTY-FIVE

Yamilka's Progress

Nancy Tarshis and Mary Kelly had become Yamilka's own personal inquiry team since she had started her reading and language classes in early 2008. Together, they'd come to several conclusions.

This was a young woman with very serious language disabilities. She had enormous trouble discerning the different sounds, or phonemes, within a single word and transferring those sounds to the letters of the alphabet. She had memory problems. And because English wasn't her native language, and her education was so limited, she had poor grammar and vocabulary skills. She hadn't been exposed to a lot of words in her everyday conversations with her siblings, and didn't have to use formal English with them. She also didn't have an innate ability to pick up on the grammatical cues of spoken language. This made learning to read even more challenging because oral language comes first, and if that foundation is shaky, then it affects everything else.

In the SoNo parlance of Jim Liebman's inquiry team model, Tarshis and Kelly had identified the "So whats." They had also begun the "Now what" part of the equation with their teaching strategies. By the end of May, Kelly said, Yamilka was making nice progress in her reading classes.

On a bright Wednesday morning, Yamilka takes her seat across from Kelly's desk and pulls her homework out of her big black purse. "Why did I put stars on those three words?" Kelly asks, looking over a total of four vocabulary words at the top of the page.

"Those were the word that were really hard for me," Yamilka replies, sounding a little nervous. (She sometimes leaves out the *s* in a plural.)

Kelly holds out the sheet and asks her to read them. The first word is "adult."

"Any, b—about?" Yamilka says, searching for a word that resembles the combination of letters she's seeing on the page. She thinks there's a *b* in the word instead of a *d*.

"Adult," says Kelly, correcting her. "What is 'adult'? "

"A person," Yamilka replies. "A big person."

"Say this word again." Yamilka repeats "adult." Then she tries the next word on the page, "live," and says it correctly. But she can't get "place," saying something like "plint," which she knows is wrong. Kelly gently helps her and Yamilka moves on to the next two words. She reads "slow" and "that" successfully.

"Beautiful," says Kelly, doling out her usual term of praise. Then she taps her pen in front of each of the four words a few more times for review. Yamilka is tempted to put a *b* in adult again, but she catches herself. She also has a difficult time with "place."

Yamilka understands these words when they're spoken. But because her phonetic awareness is still weak, even after showing improvement in her language classes, she still can't always sound out written words—even the ones she knows. She has to remember them by sight. Each week, Kelly gives her about half a dozen new words with brief reading exercises so she can use them in context. One involves figuring out which word matches the blank space in a series of sentences. The blanks always include a clue. The first sentence is "Do you have a pl—— to go?"

Yamilka reads the sentence carefully. She knows the right word is "place" but she leaves off the ending, pronouncing it as "play." Kelly gets her to say the word correctly with the *s* sound. Yamilka reads a few more sentences perfectly: "I want to *live* in a big house," and "I will see *that* she goes to school." But she runs into trouble again with "adult" for a sentence that's supposed to read "The children mind an adult best." Again, Kelly corrects her. Then she asks her to repeat the words "adult" and "place," since they continue to give her a hard time. Yamilka looks at the words and reads them correctly a few times. They're now taking root in her memory. "Beautiful, Yamilka, that was really, really nice," says Kelly.

Yamilka also has had to read a short story with her words of the week. Kelly wants her to read these stories three times at home before reading them aloud in class. The assignments have gradually been getting longer.

They started with just a paragraph or two and this week's reading takes up almost a whole page. Yamilka reads the title, "Work Without Working." She uses a pencil with a bright green eraser to track each word slowly.

"'Pam is eighteen. She is in his—high school,'" she reads aloud in a careful staccato. "'She thinks about what she will do when she is nineteen. She wants to work. But she cannot think of any—dat—anything that she can be.'"

The word at the end of the sentence is "do," not "be." Yamilka often makes the common dyslexic mistake of confusing the *d* with the *b*, which is especially tempting in this case since "do" and "be" are both two-letter words. Kelly corrects her and then tests her comprehension by asking her why the character Pam in the story wants to find a job.

"She's gonna be getting older," Yamilka says.

"And what is she going to be finishing?"

"High school," Yamilka answers. "And maybe go to college."

Yamilka continues reading the story. Sometimes she drops the ending of a word because she isn't so good with tenses, but she gets almost everything right:

"'Pam talks to her friends. Many of her friends are going to be married. They tell her not to think about working. Them—'"

"They," says Kelly.

"'They tell her you are good-looking, you have a bay—boyfriend. You will not have to work. Pam thinks about being married. She like her boyfriend. She likes children and housework is okay. But she do not want to be married at—nineteen. She want to go places and see things.'"

Yamilka had substituted the word "do" for "does." This happens frequently. The word "does" simply isn't in her vocabulary because of her limited grammar, so it's harder for her to recognize the word when she's reading.

"Beautiful," says Kelly, apparently not wanting to stop the flow for too long to focus on the grammar just yet. "Now, what are Pam's friends telling her she can do when she finishes high school?"

"Get married," says Yamilka. She adds that this isn't what Pam wants to do. She keeps reading:

"'Pam talks to her dad. He tells her not to think about money. She can go on in school. Pam thinks school is okay. But she do—do not . . .'"

"Does not," Kelly says, gently correcting her this time.

"'Does not wan—want more school. Pam think about the thing that she likes to be.'" Again she's mixed up "do" with "be."

"Likes to do," Kelly tells her.

"'She likes to talk to people,'" Yamilka continues. "'She like to read and she lo—love to write. Pam want to make money. But she do not think money is all important. She thinks people are.'"

"So she thinks people are important?" Kelly asks. Yamilka agrees and keeps on reading. "'She like to be—to *do* things for other. Pam talk to some of her da—dad's friends. They tell her to look into working with old people. Pam do—'"

"Pam does," Kelly coaches her.

"'Pam does look into it. The money is not good but Pam want to be—'"

Again she mistakes "be" for "do" and again Kelly clarifies: "Wants to *do* it." Yamilka moves on.

"'From nine a.m. to five p.m. Pam talk to old people, reads to them and writes to them. Pam tells her friends that she works without working.'"

That's it. She's completed three quarters of a page of text, double-spaced. Aside from the "be/do" mix-ups and leaving off the *s* from some words, she's gotten almost all of it correct. This is the longest passage Yamilka has ever read aloud here.

Kelly tests her comprehension one more time with a follow-up question about why Pam's father's friends think she'd be good at working with old people. Yamilka tells her it's because she likes to talk to people and read and write for them. "Where does she work?" Kelly asks.

"Like a home or center, a home for old people?" Yamilka isn't sure because the location was never mentioned in the story. "Could be a nursing home or maybe a senior center during the day," Kelly suggests. "She works from nine a.m. to five p.m. What's 'a.m.' mean?"

"Morning," says Yamilka, going on to say that five p.m. is afternoon. Kelly then asks her what the "dots" on the page mean. "I have to stop and take a breath and maybe I understand the story better," Yamilka tells her. "Periods are important!" Kelly says, laughing.

Just like little children are told to speak in the voice of a character, and to stop reading when they come to a period, Yamilka's been learning that reading isn't just about getting the words on the page. She has to explain the stories in her own words and answer questions. And she has to use new words in context, like the English Language Learners in the TIGERS group at PS 157 in the Bronx. It takes a while to really own a new word.

Kelly's reading materials include short stories about things an adult can relate to, like getting a job or raising a family. One was about people who had trouble learning to read. The examples were Woodrow Wilson and Albert Einstein. Kelly asks Yamilka a few questions about that passage. Although Yamilka has trouble remembering Wilson's name, she knows he was a U.S. president and that he went to college, but she can't remember that it was Princeton. She has trouble recalling specific names but she usually gets the concept. When Kelly asks her about Einstein, she fumbles for his name and points to the bobblehead doll of Einstein on the shelf above Kelly's desk. She remembers that he was kicked out of school and went on to become "one of the most smartest men ever."

Kelly has been working on these memory problems by reviewing everything they do together multiple times. She also checks to make sure Yamilka knows the meaning of every word she's about to read and write. Kelly just discovered that Yamilka didn't know what "mat" meant, so she got her to visualize welcome mats and small rugs. Before the class ends today, she gives Yamilka seven new words to learn over the weekend: "women," "feel," "mother," "get," "ask," "afraid," and "first." She points to each word to see if Yamilka can read them on her own. For the first word, she says "woman" instead of "women." This leads to a short discussion of how English can be confusing when one letter changes a word. She also has trouble recognizing and sounding out the word "afraid." Kelly makes her repeat each word a few times and then they review the reading passage Yamilka will study over the weekend.

The title is "People Tell Why They Did Not Learn to Read." Kelly and Yamilka take turns reading from a series of quotes by illiterate adults.

"'Most of my teachers were women,'" Kelly begins.

"'I used to think reading was for girls and women,'" Yamilka continues.

Kelly: "'Reading used to make me feel sick.'"

Yamilka: "'I did not feel like being school work.'" She had mistaken "doing" for "being."

Kelly: "'My mother had ten kids.'"

Yamilka: "'My mother did not have time for me school work.'" The word was "my," not "me."

Kelly: "'I used to get out of reading.'"

Yamilka: "'I used to go my friend to read to me,'" substituting "go" for "get."

Kelly: "'I said I was sick when the teacher asked me to read.'"

Yamilka: "'Me teacher did not ask me to read.'" She jumps ahead and reads her new word "afraid" correctly, but it's Kelly's turn.

Kelly: "'I was afraid of the reading teacher.'"

Yamilka: "'I was afraid of school.'"

Kelly: "'My first teacher did not like me.'"

Yamilka: "'I did not like my first teacher.'"

At the end of the story, they review the words Yamilka misread and then switch parts. Kelly is impressed. Yamilka made even fewer mistakes the second time around. These new words will also appear in a longer story Yamilka will have to digest over the weekend, about adults like herself who are learning to read. Then Kelly wraps up today's lesson by asking Yamilka to read from one of three short passages. Yamilka declines to choose, leaving it up to her teacher. Kelly chooses an essay about positive thinking and Yamilka proceeds:

"'Know that you can be,'" she reads aloud. Kelly corrects her. Again, the word was "do." Yamilka gets it right in the next sentence.

"'Do not waste time thinking about the things you cannot do any—anything about,'" says Yamilka. She needed a prompt with "anything."

"'Do not—'" The next word is tricky. "Spend," says Kelly.

"'. . . spend time thinking about all the things you cannot do. Spend time thinking about the things you can do. Of—'"

"If," says Kelly, correcting her.

"'If you want some friends, think about going out more.'" Then she gets to the final line. "'If you believe you can learn something you will learn it.'"

Kelly asks her what it was all about. "You have to think positive," says Yamilka.

"You just summed it up."

Positive thinking was more than a cliché for Yamilka. There were many days when she wasn't sure if she'd make those two long bus rides to Fisher Landau, when she didn't want to get out of bed and face another hour trying to do something that's been a source of so much failure. She was jealous of teenagers who still had a chance to get a good education, and wished she could trade places with them. She got angry when she saw kids hanging out on the street instead of going to class; she thought they were "throwing away their knowledge." But whenever she wanted to "throw in the towel," she reminded herself that some people's lives were worse. She also wasn't ready to give up on her goal: to read a book by herself.

Fortunately, Yamilka had something so many failing students don't have: motivation to learn. Nancy Tarshis was immediately impressed by that quality when she met Yamilka. She had self-awareness, a sense of humor, and a strong desire to read. Her parents raised her to believe that education was the path to a better life. She longed to live in one of the nice houses in the middle-class neighborhood near the clinic, instead of her run-down apartment building with the broken front door and the leaky bathroom. And just as her brother, Alejandro, worried about being able to support his family someday, Yamilka, too, thought about what would happen after their mother retired in a few years and their parents moved back to the Dominican Republic. She wanted to go to a cooking school, and knew she couldn't do that without reading.

She was obviously still far away from that goal and would need some counseling about her job options. But Mary Kelly was genuinely pleased by Yamilka's slow but steady progress. "It could have gone either way," she conceded. People with learning disabilities often have problems with their working memory, and it could take Yamilka a couple of weeks for her to master reading and writing a new set of words. But she was gradually able to read longer and longer passages with more accuracy. She did her homework and rarely missed a class.

"She has a lot of positives—motivation, curiosity, and eagerness really do help," said Kelly. "She's really willing to work and her sister seems to help her at home in appropriate ways if she gets stuck." Yamilka was lucky to have a supportive family. Her sister Elizabeth had been reading to her at night. Elizabeth was engrossed in the "Twilight" vampire series by Stephenie Meyer. She told Yamilka that it was about a girl who doesn't know she's fallen in love with a vampire. "It's like a drug," she said, giggling. "I can't stop reading it!" Yamilka wished she could read the books, too, so Elizabeth began giving her updates and reading her sections of the series. That excitement encouraged Yamilka, too. Nobody read books to her when she was a child.

"You get to imagine things and you get to go to another dimension,"

Yamilka said about listening to the story. "That's the whole point about reading. That you get to use your mind, you get to re-create it."

Kelly sometimes read to Yamilka in class. She even played her sections of a Barack Obama speech from the Internet because she knew Yamilka was interested in the election. But again and again Kelly was confronted by Yamilka's deficits. Though the young woman followed the U.S. presidential election through television—and was intrigued by Spanish-language news programs about Latin America, or a segment on *Oprah* about rape in Africa—there was only so much she could learn from such a passive medium. "She doesn't have a lot of information, doesn't know history, geography, very much about the world," Kelly said. "So that has an effect on your reading because you don't know what you're reading about and it's hard to understand things when you don't know what they're talking about."

This is why, Kelly says, it's so hard for a student like Yamilka to improve her vocabulary. Students from low-income and poorly educated families rarely get enough reinforcement at home, picking up new words only in school. And it's easy to forget those words—and fall behind as the reading gets harder—without good and consistent instruction. "The dirty secret is nobody knows how to teach vocabulary," said Kelly, explaining that a student needs multiple exposures to a word in different contexts. The children in the inquiry team study at PS 157 had two hours a day of vocabulary lessons on top of their regular school day. Yamilka had only two hours a week of government-funded reading classes, plus an hour a week of speech and language therapy with Nancy Tarshis. It was too soon to say whether the rhyming exercises were making any impact on her reading, partly because Yamilka's limited vocabulary and grammar prevented her from recognizing enough printed words, like the difference between "do" and "does."

"It's really hard to get someone to read stuff that's not within their oral language," said Kelly. Likewise, "you can't repeat grammatical constructions that you haven't yet mastered yourself." In time, she hoped, the speech therapy would improve Yamilka's awareness of tenses and syntax. It was a big project. But Kelly was optimistic because Yamilka had developed a greater understanding of her language disability; she finally knew what was wrong, and had even caught herself messing up the words "crane" and "train" from the TV news. That recognition was a breakthrough.

This is what good teachers are supposed to do when they're told to "differentiate" or customize each lesson to meet the needs of their pupils. Kelly and Tarshis had figured out what was holding Yamilka behind and they were using every resource in their arsenal. "I used typical best practices," Tarshis explained of the rhyming exercises she used in their sessions. But those techniques are typical for small children. Yamilka was the first adult Tarshis had ever worked with, and she said there was little research on building phonemic awareness with adults—especially when they're learning a second language. She enjoyed getting to know Yamilka and had fun tailoring her classes for an older student and using recipes to improve her communication skills. "With any client you learn to think on your feet to adjust to the person in front of you," she said. "It confirmed for me that there's no one-size-fits-all."

Kelly and Tarshis were also "highly qualified teachers," a key goal of the standards movement. They had years of experience and multiple degrees. The tutors at Huntington Learning Center had less extensive academic backgrounds, though they were certified teachers. Dawn Helene, of Huntington's Manhattan office, thought it was "outstanding" that Fisher Landau had a language specialist working with Yamilka. Her center wasn't able to offer that kind of expertise. Yamilka had arrived at Huntington a nonreader in 2005 after she won her case against the city. She had to learn the alphabet and the sounds of the letters—which turned out to be trickier than expected because of the language disabilities that were diagnosed later at Fisher Landau. Helene knew Yamilka had memory problems. Things had to be "repeated and repeated and repeated," she said, by reviewing every new word and making flash cards. Huntington's tutors kept trying to improve Yamilka's "word attack" skills, or the ability to sound out letters, and they did make progress. Helene tested Yamilka before she left in July 2007 and determined she was reading at a first-grade level. She was able to read a few paragraphs at a time and occasionally a full page.

I told Helene about the short stories Yamilka was reading at Fisher Landau in the spring of 2008, to see if she thought there had been additional progress. She warned me that the length of a reading passage alone wasn't a fair gauge. Students in her tutoring program rarely read more than a page or two aloud during their sessions, regardless of reading level, because they have to finish the material and answer questions in a limited class period. But Helene said it sounded as though Yamilka was reading more complex words at Fisher Landau. The story about the character

Pam's decision to go to work, instead of marrying her boyfriend after high school, was a prime example. "There are words there she wouldn't have attempted, like 'boyfriend,'" Helene said. "Compound words were outside her reach at the time she was here." At Huntington Yamilka had mostly learned one-syllable words.

None of Yamilka's current or former teachers expected her continued progress to be quick or easy. It was hard to see her advancing to a third-grade level, and reading books independently, by the time she finished her year at Fisher Landau—though Kelly said she'd allow her to stay longer. But she couldn't predict how far Yamilka would advance in reading. "Over the years I have worked with adults, I have found that motivation is a key ingredient of progress, and she certainly has that," she said. "Progress will be circumscribed by her language problems. Lack of vocabulary and background knowledge limit her progress. All of us working with her feel she has come along. I don't think the sky's the limit, but certainly she will be more functional and more employable."

Kelly conceded that educators are faced with difficult choices when they encounter an older nonreader like Yamilka. "It is idealistic to think that all children will learn to read, given the very serious cognitive deficits some have," she explained. But there are very few people who can't learn to read. Less than 2 percent of the school-age population is mentally retarded, according to federal statistics, and Kelly says she's been successful with adults who have a "borderline" IQ. "Good instruction makes a difference, and research has shown that good, multisensory instruction yields changes in the way the brain is processing information. So if everyone got really good instruction from really good teachers at a pace they could handle, we would have a larger number of literate people."

Jacqueline Royster, an English professor at Ohio State University and a member of the Writing Advisory Board for the National Writing Commission, agrees that almost everyone can read, barring the most severe disabilities. "All children have the capacity to learn and to use their language abilities in keeping with the expectations of the society/communities in which they live and function," she said. "The real question is twofold: Does the society/community know how to recognize their capacities, [then] take positive advantage of these capacities and support the scope and range of learning needs?" She added that it shouldn't take a lawsuit to answer that question.

Though she often wished she could snap her fingers and become a fast learner, Yamilka knew she had accomplished more in her tutoring sessions than she ever learned in the public schools—and more than the city expected when she sought a "compensatory education" following graduation. That kept her going, and so did the feeling of accomplishment whenever she successfully read something new. "I feel pretty happy, more confident when I get it," she told me. "I give myself a pat on the shoulder."

Kelly viewed her success as a lesson for teachers as well as for students. "I think it says, work hard with everybody. Try different ways to teach. Don't give up even if you think the family is not supporting the schoolwork. We can never predict which kids will be the ones we really touch, and almost everyone can learn something."

But she acknowledged it's tough for teachers to keep their motivation when they don't feel supported; when they don't get enough time with their pupils; and when standardized tests become the be-all and end-all. "I heartily agree with those who say look at the inputs, too," she said, singling out early intervention and preschool programs like Head Start. "In fact, they are far more important than test scores. Changing the environmental factors would probably have far more positive consequences than giving tests."

If Yamilka could gradually learn how to read with the right support, then so could other students with far less serious reading problems. The New York City schools were on the verge of proving the same thing.

TWENTY-SIX

Scores and Soup

When politicians have good news to share, they call a press conference. They choose a site that's linked to their particular achievement. They make sure there are lots of good visuals for the cameras, such as enthusiastic crowds or colorful charts and graphs. And they surround themselves with supporters who can attest to their great works. If the news is *really* good, they'll even invite some skeptical community gadflies or labor leaders with whom they can generously share some of the credit, in the hopes of buying a little future cooperation.

Mayor Bloomberg made sure to follow all those steps when he announced the state's math and reading scores on June 23, 2008, because the news was really, really good. At least at first glance.

The event was held in the auditorium at PS 175 in Harlem, a neighborhood where test scores had gone up dramatically in the six years since Bloomberg took office. The mayor greeted Principal Cheryl McClendon with a kiss on the cheek and stood at a portable lectern with the city's seal. They were surrounded by the chancellor, the president of Medgar Evers College in Brooklyn, the head of a nonprofit that encourages children to volunteer, and the president of the principals union. The teachers union president was on her way. Staff members and students from PS 175 sat in the audience with members of the media. Television camera operators and photographers trained their lenses on two big charts, positioned on easels, showing test scores for the city's third- through eighth-graders. The columns for each grade were printed in bright colors and they were all trending upward.

Bloomberg wore a dark suit with flag and apple pins on the left side of his jacket. He was in an amiable mood. "When this administration came into office, we knew that we faced some big challenges in our public schools," he read from prepared remarks. "But over the past six years we've created the conditions necessary to transform schools and fundamentally change results for our kids. I don't think anyone standing up here with me ever accepted for a moment that the achievements of suburban districts were out of reach for New York City. And our students thankfully have proved them right."

The city's scores on the English Language Arts exams had gone up almost seven points over the previous year, with almost 58 percent of students in grades three through eight meeting the standards. Math scores had gone up nine points, with more than 74 percent of students in grades three through eight meeting or exceeding the standards. Bloomberg was right that the city was catching up to the state. Overall, 81 percent of students in New York State were proficient in math and 69 percent met or exceeded the standards in English. "There is no question. Our city students, relative to the suburbs, are doing better" than they had been, the mayor proclaimed.

Bloomberg called this part of "a dramatic upward trend over six years across all grade levels." He cited math scores that had doubled since he took office in 2002 and English scores that had gone up by eighteen percentage points in that same period. This claim wasn't completely accurate, since his school reforms hadn't started until 2003—meaning the progress in 2002 was really attributable to the Giuliani administration and the two previous chancellors of that era, Rudy Crew and Harold Levy. But the scores had continued to rise since then, giving Bloomberg the data he needed to argue that his reforms were working and that the state should renew the 2002 law granting mayoral control of the schools.

Bloomberg said little during the press conference about the numerous reforms of the previous year, leaving that to his chancellor. Klein pulled a folded sheet of paper out of his pocket as he took the microphone. "We dubbed this the year of achievement and achieve we did," he exclaimed. He said the overall gains in the past year represented more than fifty thousand students, many of whom went from performing below grade level to meeting the state standards. And the number of students testing at the lowest level had shrunk from 9 percent to 6 percent, or almost 25,000 students. In Klein's first year, the percentage had been three times higher. Eighteen percent of the city's students, nearly 80,000, had been reading at level 1 in 2003. That was a difference of about 55,000 students.

"We're moving the system toward a data-driven system with our teachers, assistant principals, and principals working together on inquiry teams," the chancellor said, referring to his new initiatives. "They all got a progress report this year and I can tell you a lot of principals called me and said to me, they said, 'You know, I don't think that progress report accurately reflects my grade. And I promise you this, it won't be that way next year.' And they delivered, they came through on this."

Principal McClendon of the host school, PS 175, told the audience how that new focus on student performance was paying off. She described how her inquiry team used data to find fifteen black and Hispanic boys in fourth and fifth grade who were having trouble in school. Her teachers worked with them intensely, "and seven of fifteen went from below standard to standard on the English Language Arts exam!" she said to applause. Overall, more than 76 percent of her students were proficient in math and 46 percent in English, gains of about ten and seven points, respectively, in the past year.

When test scores go down, union presidents often blame the policies of an administration. When scores go up, they say their members deserve some of the credit. This time, the presidents of the unions representing city teachers and principals praised the mayor—but they also focused on what they called an unprecedented investment in the public schools. They said the extra billion dollars the schools had received that year from the state and city had lowered class sizes in the early grades, improved teacher quality by giving them a raise, and allowed for an extra period of class time that benefited underperforming students.

"The mayor and I don't always agree," said Ernest Logan of the Council of School Supervisors and Administrators, cracking a smile. But "now what we have is sustainable achievement, and that's what we were looking for. If this thing really does work, then it's not just a one-year bump, but it's showing we're on the right track."

The significance of that "bump" was hotly debated, though. If the city's pupils were making so much progress under Bloomberg, why wasn't that reflected on their national NAEP scores? There had been little if any improvement on fourth-grade reading and eighth-grade math in New York

City on the 2007 exams, or in the rest of the state. Many educators and testing experts believe the NAEP tests are harder than state exams. But they also believe states deliberately set lower standards so their students can meet the proficiency targets under NCLB. That would explain why states like New York have seen their own test scores rise more than their NAEP scores.

Putting aside the difficulty in comparing state and national exams, there was evidence that the achievement gap between whites and minorities wasn't closing as much as Bloomberg optimistically pronounced. The *Education Week* blogger Eduwonkette (a Columbia University graduate student in sociology named Jennifer Jennings) broke down the NAEP scores and argued there was no statistically significant change in the achievement gap between 2003 and 2007. Nor was she convinced by the state scores, despite the higher percentage of black and Latino students scoring at level 3. Jennings looked at the average reading scale scores—not how many students made level 3—and determined the gap between whites and blacks and Latinos had *grown* among fourth-graders, though it declined among eighth-graders.[1]

It's hard to know whether this meant Bloomberg's gains weren't real. But the fact that test scores had gone up throughout the state did undercut some of his boasts. The state's education department credited greater funding, more certified teachers, a grade-by-grade curriculum with clear expectations, and the fact that it was the third year of testing in grades three through eight. In fact, the cities of Rochester, Buffalo, and Yonkers all saw even bigger gains than New York City on the English Language Arts exam—even though they continued to have lower scores overall. Under Jim Liebman's system, those districts could have gotten higher "progress reports" than New York City.

Bob Tobias, a professor and director of New York University's Center for Research on Teaching and Learning, was skeptical about the mayor's impact. Tobias ran the testing division for the city's old Board of Education, prior to the Bloomberg years. He wondered if the test had gotten easier. He looked at the way the questions were scored, and the cutoff for each level of proficiency, and determined that fifth- and seventh-graders didn't have to get as many correct answers on the ELA exam that year to meet the state's standards. This could have explained why the percentage of New York City seventh-graders performing at or above grade level in reading shot up to almost 60 percent—a gain of fourteen points—reflecting a similar spike throughout the state.

One high-level school official, who didn't want to be named for fear of retribution, was also deeply skeptical about the results. "We have become a test sophistication factory. We're using test-prep or interim assessments in lieu of curriculum and teaching." This official said there was no point in gathering so much data throughout the school year if teachers didn't have enough time to study it and learn how to improve their instruction. A survey that spring by the teachers union found 85 percent of respondents didn't believe the chancellor's emphasis on testing had improved education in their schools. The standards movement was a mixed bag, said Tobias. "The kids are becoming more familiar with the test format, more familiar with content being examined and with skills being examined. Part of this is not bad."

If the tests examined educational skills, knowledge, and basic comprehension, then those were things all pupils should learn anyway. "If the test is 'Can you read?' I hope they are [getting better at taking exams]," said Bloomberg. "Tests show what you know. You can't get better at taking a test that measures whether you can read unless you learn to read better. You can't get better at taking, doing math problems unless you know more math."

But were the scores really an accurate measurement? Tobias wasn't sure. "I think part of the gain is real changes in student learning," he agreed. But when asked if higher scores meant students were reading better, he called that "a tough question."

One thing was definitely clear from the state's ELA scores: there weren't as many horrible readers as there used to be. The drop from almost 18 percent at level 1 in 2003 to less than 6 percent in 2008 was a real change. Statewide, the percentage of students reading at level 1 had been pretty consistent in that same time period (4.8 percent in 2003, compared to 4 percent in 2008).*

Clearly, a large number of students who were reading very poorly had

*It's worth noting that the testing system changed after No Child Left Behind, and New York went from testing only grades four and eight to testing grades three through eight in that time period.

progressed enough to climb to the next level. The city had reached the low-hanging fruit, so to speak. And this wasn't at the expense of the stronger readers because there was no sudden surge at the next-lowest level. In fact, there was a slight decline in the percentage of pupils testing at level 2 (below state standards but usually good enough to be promoted to the next grade). Esther Friedman, the city's head of academic intervention services, pulled out a chart summarizing the breakdown for each grade. She had penciled tiny checkmarks next to the ones that showed a consistent reduction in the two lowest reading levels. "We reduced the ones and twos in most grades," she said with a smile.

There were also fewer special education students reading at the lowest level. Twenty percent were reading at level 1, half as many as in 2006. And 23.6 percent were reading at grade level—an increase of eight points in two years. That thrilled the head of special education services, Linda Wernikoff, who gave much of the credit to the Wilson Reading program. English Language Learners were also doing better, with more students meeting the standards and just over 19 percent reading at the lowest level—an improvement from nearly 31 percent the previous year.

Friedman believed the whole Toolkit of interventions made a difference, as did professional development and hardworking principals. But she warned that it's never easy to measure these factors, because schools are "messy" laboratories. There are no constants, no fixed control groups, in buildings where new students enroll at midterm and others leave, and where teachers change their approach from day to day to meet the needs of their pupils. Friedman called it a soup. "What I absolutely believe in education is it is really hard once you put that soup together, you really can't take those materials apart. You can't disaggregate and say, 'I'm sure this is one factor that did it.'"

So how much progress did the students really make, if tens of thousands had gone from level 1 to level 2? Level 2 was still below where they needed to be.

There's no easy answer because the standards are different for every grade. The ELA exams include both literary and informational passages, with multiple-choice questions that test the students' understanding of what they read. There are also short passages that are read aloud to them to test their listening comprehension. There's an additional written component in grades four, six, and eight. Children in grades three, five, and seven are given an editing task to assess their writing skills.

One third-grade reading passage from the January 2008 exam was about a girl named Abby who couldn't catch any fish on a fishing trip with her grandma. The story was about a page long and one of the questions afterward referred to a single sentence: "This time when she reeled in her line, an old tin can hung from her hook." Students were asked if the word "reeled" most likely meant Abby "cut her line," "found her line," "pulled in her line," or "fell on her line." They were also asked to draw conclusions about what Abby meant at the end when she said she'd have to go to a grocery store if her Grandma wanted her to catch some dinner.

The reading passages get progressively harder in the later grades, as students are asked about the meaning of a phrase in a poem, for example, or to edit out the mistakes in a grammatically incorrect story about a trip to the aquarium. The eighth-grade English Language Arts exam from 2008 included a passage with arguments for and against wolf restoration in Yellowstone Park. The students were asked to pick sentences that characterized each argument, and to decide whether describing wolves as the "dominant predators" in North America meant they were "major," "smartest," "most unusual," or "most demanding."

These tests are about understanding text and synthesizing information—the reading skills that are needed to get through high school. And those are tougher skills to teach than merely sounding out letters. "If your problem is skills—decoding and fluency—those are easy to fix," says Friedman, adding that a child could make good gains after about a year of steady assistance. Fluency is a combination of speed, accuracy, and prosody (using proper intonation when reading aloud). Decoding and fluency are what usually hold students back at level 1.

But Friedman says students who are stuck at level 2 usually have a limited vocabulary or knowledge base. These are deeper problems because they affect a child's comprehension. And, as the inquiry teams learned, vocabulary is notoriously hard to improve because it's tough to teach and because students often have little motivation. If they're not good readers to start with, they get frustrated as the material gets harder and lose their enthusiasm. This was the other lesson of the test scores. More than 60 percent of third- and fourth-graders were reading at grade level in 2008 but just 43 percent of eighth-graders were meeting state standards. As usual, reading levels decreased as the students got older. Educators have proposed solutions to this middle school slump, such as extending the school day and restructuring it to provide at least an hour and a half of reading time.[2] These solutions are getting even more attention following reports that teens are reading fewer books while spending more time on the Internet.

The consistent gap between math and reading scores in New York City also raised questions about the curriculum. Mayor Bloomberg had suggested that the city's reading scores were lower because 13 percent of the students were English Language Learners. (Nationally, math and reading scores on the NAEP exam are pretty close after years in which math scores were lower.) New York City's elementary schools use a program called Everyday Math, and middle schools use Impact Math. Both were introduced by the Bloomberg administration at the same time as balanced literacy. Just as opponents of the whole language approach derided balanced literacy, there were skeptics who labeled the math curriculum "fuzzy math" because of its nontraditional approaches to problem solving. The workbooks and lessons relied less on memorization and shortcuts and more on "activity based" experiments with students working in groups, playing with cubes and tiles (called manipulatives), and using real-life math examples based on the stock market or shopping in a grocery store. But the math curriculum was consistent and teachers became more comfortable with it over time. By contrast, balanced literacy is an approach, not a curriculum, and it can be interpreted in many different ways. Deputy Chancellor for Teaching and Learning Marcia Lyles acknowledged some schools and teachers did an excellent job of planning their lessons while others were more haphazard.

Lyles said the test scores didn't rattle her faith in balanced literacy because the results had improved over time. With more professional development and time, advocates of balanced literacy believed the city's teachers would become more comfortable and test scores would continue to rise. However, Lyles said the city would also encourage middle schools to integrate science and social studies into their reading periods so literacy isn't treated as a separate subject. And a handful of elementary schools were selected for a pilot program using E. D. Hirsch's Core Knowledge curriculum. The students would get a heavy dose of content and vocabulary starting in kindergarten. Hirsch is a University of Virginia education professor who has argued that teaching comprehension skills, such as summarizing a story or predicting what will happen next, is useless without giving students more of the factual knowledge they need to become better readers.[3]

But as the Children's Aid Society director noted in the meeting with Liebman at City Hall, curriculum can't fix everything. That's not just because children are products of their environment. The schools are also very different. Each one had its own recipe for soup, to use Friedman's phrase. Despite an overall upward trend, some schools still had much higher test scores than others.

Despite the best efforts of Raedyn Rivera, the reading scores at MS 232 in the Bronx remained exactly where they had been in 2007. Only 25 percent of the students were reading at grade level. Alejandro and Yamilka's old school would ultimately earn another C on its city report card.

The literacy coach had led approximately forty staff development workshops during the school year. There were a lot of new ELA teachers, and Rivera gave everyone ongoing resources, curriculum calendars, weekly newsletters, and demonstrations of different teaching methods. And she had succeeded in persuading the principal to bring in the Australian writing coach. But while the reading scores were flat, the school's math scores went up fifteen points—from 26.6 percent of the students performing at grade level to 41.4 percent. Math had been the target of the school's inquiry team, not reading, and these scores were enough to get MS 232 off the state's dreaded list of schools under registration review. One staffer, who didn't want to be identified, speculated that literacy is harder for students who have trouble concentrating because it requires sustained silence and stamina, "whereas with math your brain moves from one problem to another, switching frames."

But in a sign of progress, fewer pupils were reading at the lowest level. The school invited these students to come to summer classes. Assistant Principal Desiree Martinez was pleased to see the big gain in math scores. But she was also concerned about the stagnant reading scores. She said a close examination of the scale scores—instead of just how many students were reaching levels 3 and 4—revealed that a majority of students had made a year's worth of progress even though they were still behind grade level. And the seventh-grade reading scores, which rose statewide, went up sixteen points.

The seventh-grade teacher John McDonald said a lot of his students moved up from twos to threes. As a new teacher, McDonald said, he figured out the right balance of discipline and support, and "by the end of the year it became fun, I looked forward to being with them." Nobody was left back and none of his students scored a one. Even the boys who had been retained in previous years showed improvements. McDonald was planning to make more use of assessments during the next school year by going online and looking for trends, now that he understood the Acuity program. He also intended to focus more on grammar because he was surprised at his students' poor skills. "They received no grammar in elementary school," he said. "They actually asked for it; they want to know why their grammar is bad, and [their] punctuation."

Antonio's old junior high school in Washington Heights fared a little better. More than 27 percent of its students were reading at grade level, a 3.5 percentage point increase over the previous year. The sixth- and seventh-grade scores went up, but eighth-grade scores went down, with just one out of five pupils meeting state standards.

Gabriel Garcia was one of the students who did meet the standards. The thirteen-year-old scored a level 3 on his English Language Arts exam. Gabriel's mother, Carmen, said she paid for a tutor when he was doing poorly in elementary school. And because IS 143 was a "school in need of improvement," she also took advantage of federally funded Supplemental Educational Services, or after-school tutoring, offered to all students. She enrolled Gabriel in a program called Catapult that provided online tutoring every evening. When Gabriel was asked why he succeeded in a school where so many other students did not, his answer was simple. "Most of the kids in my school, they don't take education seriously. I know many kids that cut classes and stuff like that."

Gabriel was an example of how an "input" such as home environment can play a powerful role in student achievement. His mother is a Dominican immigrant who went to a community college, and his two older brothers were both in college. He grew up speaking English and Spanish and his mother hired tutors when he struggled with reading. Gabriel visited family in the Dominican Republic only during school vacations, never missing class. He also enjoyed reading. "I like books like 'Harry Potter,' mysteries, fantasy books," he said, naming some Japanese-style graphic novels.

The Manhattan elementary school that Chancellor Klein held up as a model when he announced the new report card system did not continue improving the way Principal Ivan Kushner had expected. Though it earned another B, its overall ELA scores were flat, with 56 percent of the third- through fifth-graders reading at grade level. Only the third-grade scores had gone up. By contrast, math scores went up a few points, with more than three quarters of the students at grade level. Kushner said he was disappointed with the reading scores, but he said the trend was still pretty consistent. "I was satisfied, I wasn't ecstatic," he said. There were no big dips and, as in the rest of the city, there were fewer students performing at the lowest level. If anything, he said, the school might have been experiencing the sort of holding pattern described in the *Breakthrough* book by Michael Fullan, Peter Hill, and Carmel Crévola, which said a school might need to consolidate for a couple of years before it can push to the next level. He was poring over the data to look for trends and had already ordered new vocabulary books and was planning to put more emphasis on grammar.

The extra attention to vocabulary could have helped drive the dramatic increase in reading scores at PS 157 in the Bronx, where the inquiry team had worked so hard with English Language Learners. Almost 53 percent of the students in this low-income immigrant community made grade level—a spike of eleven points over the previous year. And at PS 5 in Washington Heights, another poor immigrant community where the Wilson Reading program was widely used for children who had trouble sounding out letters, reading scores went up five points. Even more impressive was the decline in level 1 students, from 14.6 to 8.5 percent.

Sometimes progress seemed like the result of concentrated efforts; other times it just seemed random. At PS 59 in Midtown—a well-regarded school whose population included the sons and daughters of UN diplomats—the overall grade went from a B to a C, even though the numbers barely budged. In 2008, 85.3 percent of the students were reading at grade level, but was that really a change from 84.7 percent in 2007? What did it mean that 4.4 percent were reading at the lowest level compared to 1.8 percent the previous year, when it was a difference of just five students? Most of those poor readers were third-graders who had never been tested before. Assistant Principal Gabriel Feldberg studied the data and concluded that "broadly speaking, we probably are better at teaching reading than several years ago." But he also said it was tricky to make too many assumptions. He cited a fifth-grade boy who earned a perfect score and a girl who didn't do as well, even though she was reading higher-level material in class. "If we take their scores as a literal measure of being a better reader, we're in trouble," he said.

At MS 202 in Queens, seventh-grade reading scores went up seventeen points—with almost 69 percent of the students at grade level. That was the biggest gain of any grade in the school. The teacher Michelle Brier said she was "screaming as loud as some of the kids" who found out they wouldn't have to go to summer school. Was the seventh-grade test really easier, since scores went up throughout the state? Or did Brier and her colleagues make a difference by changing their instruction whenever they noticed trends on the assessments? "The ones I worried most about—the kids who had scored a one or a low two in the previous year—they did fairly well," Brier said, after digesting the numbers. "These were the kids who sent me slaving over those data binders, the ones I made individualized assignments for from the Acuity results. A lot of solid twos. No level ones even among my most struggling readers." She was disappointed that more of her higher-performing students didn't get fours on their tests, but that was also a citywide trend.

"So maybe what data mining does is help you target the [students] most in need, the ones who have the farthest climb to make," she speculated. "The kids already high up on the rock pile, did it help them as much that I could see in the data that every now and then they missed, say, an inference question, but other times blew points on author's purpose? I just don't think the data we were given was sharp enough, detailed enough, or just plain frequent enough to help all the kids."

Even though Jim Liebman believed it was possible to compare similar schools, this limited sample showed how difficult it could be to draw firm conclusions from the data. As Esther Friedman stated, they all made their own "soup," using variations on the city's literacy program and different interventions. Some schools had more new teachers and more challenging populations. Others had principals and teachers who were able to turn on a dime and figure out what wasn't working at the first sign of trouble. Despite all the focus on accountability measures and data-driven instruction, there was simply not a clear answer to why one school went up while another went down.

But Liebman didn't see that as a negative. If the city's public schools were to be a great laboratory for learning, as John Dewey envisioned, the answers weren't always going to come easily. "There is a difference between working out and testing a new truth or a new method, and applying it on a wide scale, making it available for the mass of men, making it commercial," Dewey wrote.[4] "A working model is not something to be copied; it is to afford a demonstration of the feasibility of the principle, and of the methods which make it feasible."

Liebman believed he was giving the schools the tools they needed to discover their own solutions. He also said the data would provide many more answers once the city had at least three years' worth of material.

If he were to write a screenplay about a turnaround at a failing school, his wouldn't be about one great teacher who saved the day—like *Stand and Deliver* or *Freedom Writers*. It would be about a school where the teachers are stuck until they realize they can't solve the problem alone. "And they can solve it by actually disclosing to each other where they're struggling and disclosing to each other—or discovering and then disclosing to each other—where they're succeeding pretty well," he explained. "And then realizing that by virtue of that kind of interaction, they can learn from each other. They can then put things in place. And the inspiring part is to watch what happens when you actually document what you're doing and see that suddenly kids are moving forward. Incrementally, yes, but the toughest kids in the school . . . they succeeded. And now they've demonstrated to themselves that they can have that effect. They do have the power to move them forward."

In Liebman's movie, that teamwork would enable the toughest students to succeed. Unfortunately, it was too late for Yamilka, Antonio, and Alejandro, because the schools had already failed them. They had to go elsewhere to prove they could learn.

TWENTY-SEVEN

Measuring Progress

When the crime rate fell during the Giuliani and Bloomberg years, Disney came to Times Square. Waves of gentrification swept through the five boroughs, with bank branches and Starbucks Coffee shops opening in previously destitute neighborhoods. The U.S. economy was also improving then, and the prosperity is widely believed to have lowered the national crime rate, so it's hard to say how great an impact mayoral policies had. We just know the city felt and looked safer.

It's even more difficult to see the effects of better public schools. Test scores may tell part of the story. But what would the city look like if more students were reading at grade level? Would we see young children reading to their parents in the grocery aisles of the South Bronx? Would the schools hold more spelling bees? Would students check more books out of their local libraries?

Yamilka and Alejandro's neighborhood library, across the street from MS 232, was filled with students after school let out for the summer. Most of them sat at computer terminals playing online video games and sending e-mail messages. A few of the younger children sat with parents reading picture books at small tables near the entrance. One day in August, Wahab Ashiru, a male nurse at Harlem Hospital, brought along his four-year-old daughter, Hannah, and his son, Daniel, who was about to turn six and would be entering first grade at PS 22 nearby. Ashiru said he checked out five books a week for his children, on average, and wouldn't let them watch television except on weekends. Daniel had just read *Silly Sally*, and Hannah was thumbing through the pages, unable to read them yet but excitedly retelling the plot, which she had obviously heard many times. Ashiru is a Nigerian immigrant, and he seemed happy that the teacher at PS 22 had given his son a lot of homework in kindergarten. When Daniel would ask him for help with writing, he'd say, "You have to spell it out."

The children's librarian Beverly Andrus said it was common for little ones and their parents to check out books, but that interest waned as the kids grew older. She walked through the children's section and pointed to the most popular items. The "Frog and Toad" series and *Don't Let the Pigeon Drive the Bus* were big hits with the rug rats. Those books were arranged at a circular reading section at the back of the small, plain room along with other picture books in Spanish and English. The "American Girl" and "Baby-sitter's Club" books were popular among third-to-fifth-grade girls, while boys liked the "Geronimo Stilton" series. But she said the nonfiction shelves with books about John F. Kennedy and slavery were used only for school assignments, and rarely. "They want the information online. We suggest a book and they don't want a book."

Andrus wore a green T-shirt that said "Catch the Reading Bug," a theme U.S. libraries were using for their summer reading clubs. She's a Jamaican immigrant who has worked in the library for eight years, a period that coincided almost perfectly with Mayor Bloomberg's tenure. Her job involved visiting public schools to read to children and get them interested in the library. She said the early elementary students seemed to be reading well, for the most part. Nine hundred had signed up for the summer reading program after intense recruitment, about 150 more than the previous year. But very few teens had joined, and she could see other signs that older students weren't reading for pleasure. "Our weakness is in our older books section," she said, meaning fifth-to-sixth-grade books. The "Harry Potter" series was an exception. Students that age, if they took out anything, preferred graphic novels. The popular ones were displayed near the front of the room: the sassy "Babymouse" series for girls, and graphic versions of "The Baby-sitter's Club" books and the "Redwall" fantasy series by Brian Jacques. Andrus went to her computer and saw that the original *Redwall* novel hadn't been checked out since 2005. The graphic version had been taken out six times in the past eight months.

Andrus blamed a combination of laziness and poor reading skills. "If a child is reading at [an appropriate] level . . . books like these shouldn't be so challenging," she added, referring to *Redwall* and *The Golden Com-*

pass. At about forty years old, Andus described herself as "old-fashioned" because she didn't think graphic novels were a good substitute for reading. "These kids won't be able to grasp the real content of the book, the real feel of the book, to me, because it's right there in ink. When you read a book you get so much depth in information from the book.

"I'm worried. It's very scary," she said. "We're losing our older kids."

The true assessment of the Bloomberg era's education reforms won't be determined by library use, or a single year's test scores. Even a few years' worth of scores won't tell very much. The real barometer will be high school graduation rates. If the city could get, say, 60 or 70 percent of its students graduating in four years, instead of a little more than half, according to the state, then that would indicate more young people were literate and prepared for the workforce. And if the dropout rate fell, simultaneously, skeptics would know failing students weren't being pushed out or encouraged to leave for GED programs. The graduation rate for special education students would also reveal over time whether more students were graduating with real diplomas instead of the Individualized Education Program certificate Yamilka had earned. Meanwhile, the city claimed it was completing 90 percent of all special ed evaluations within the thirty-day time limit, but it still faced a shortage of speech therapists and other specialists who could act on the recommendations. One Manhattan elementary teacher, who didn't want to be identified, described trying all year to get a third-grade boy evaluated for special education services but said the school's administrators were always too busy.

Because Yamilka, Alejandro, and Antonio had all left school by the end of the mayor's first term, Bloomberg's education department could technically blame their failure to get an appropriate education on the previous administration. The Department of Education could make a similar argument about any low-performing high school students, and even middle-schoolers—because they'd all started elementary school during the Giuliani years. Bloomberg and Klein often boasted of how the school system was now completely different. They'd brought in a new curriculum, encouraged more reading interventions, and introduced a different management structure. They raised the starting salaries for teachers by a total of 43 percent. New teachers were making $45,000 at the entry level, and top salaries hovered near $100,000. These salaries were much more competitive with schools in the suburbs and more attractive to high-quality applicants.

Early interventions have always had the biggest impact on reading scores. Eileen Reiter, the principal of PS 112 in East Harlem, which has been recognized by the state for its excellent reading program, said, "If you don't build a strong foundation in early childhood, when the kids move to third grade they're dead. It's really hard to catch up." Researchers have proven she's right. Dr. Joseph Torgesen of Florida State University compared the studies of six different early interventions in kindergarten through second grade. He concluded that if all students were exposed to them, only 1.6 to 6 percent of the population would be reading far below grade level (which he defined as beneath the thirtieth percentile).[1] By that standard, the city had done a good job by reducing level 1 readers to 6 percent. But Torgesen found reading interventions with older students weren't as successful.

The future of Mayor Bloomberg's initiatives was still uncertain in 2009. The economic downturn was forcing states to cut their education budgets. But the standards movement appeared here to stay. President Obama's stimulus package rewarded states that continued with school reforms such as high-tech data systems and frequent assessments. Even Lucy Calkins of Teachers College was working with a software developer so that her own brand of reading assessments could fit in with ARIS. At a conference for 130 principals who use her reading methods, held at the New York Botanical Garden in the Bronx, Calkins lamented that teacher morale was especially low because of the relentless focus on testing. But she went on to state: "The U.S. system of educating, and especially educating the poor, needs to ratchet itself up big-time. What will your teachers' relationship be to the mandates? To data-driven instruction?" Calkins urged the principals to involve their teachers in setting goals, so they'd feel empowered.

Obama's education secretary, Arne Duncan, supported national standards. But what does it mean to be literate in the early twenty-first century? Antonio's fourth-grade reading level might have been enough for him to get a good factory job in the early twentieth century. In 2008 he worked in the back room of a dry cleaner for a little more than minimum wage. Meanwhile, Alejandro had progressed to a high school reading level, but his dyslexia prevented him from speeding through the pages of a book or quickly scanning a computer screen. And Yamilka's language disabilities made it even harder for her to master basic reading, though she made progress with determination and good instruction.

In his book *Real Education*, the social scientist Charles Murray argues that the No Child Left Behind law and its belief in universal proficiency is a living lie. "The lie is that every child can be anything he or she wants to be," he flatly states.[2] Murray claims America's egalitarian philosophy sets the bar too high for most students. "Children in the lower half of the distribution are just not smart enough to read or calculate at a level of fluency that most of the rest of us take for granted," he argues.[3] He says it would make more sense to encourage the top 20 percent to go to college, while teaching the "forgotten half" who won't how to make a living. He proposes better career-development and technical-education high schools.

Murray is famous for coauthoring the controversial book *The Bell Curve*, which argued that the black-white achievement gap was partly genetic. His latest conclusion—that some students *should* be left behind—was viewed with disdain by much of the educational community. As in *The Bell Curve*, he put a premium on IQ and downplayed the powerful roles of class and family income in shaping a child's preparation for school (though he did say there should be further studies). Many European countries still track students at an early age for either career schools or universities. But Americans don't. The standards movement demanded more academically challenging schools in K–12, in a rejection of what President George W. Bush called the "soft bigotry of low expectations." The idea was to close the achievement gap. Traditionally, a disproportionate number of black and Hispanic boys and immigrants were sent to vocational high schools because their teachers and principals didn't believe they were capable of higher learning. That was still happening, according to Geoffrey Canada, founder of the Harlem Children's Zone. He sees the proof when he calls a meeting of his thousand-plus staff members. "I say raise your hand if someone in school tried to direct you away from college and you'll see seventy-five percent of the hands today, it's just shocking." Canada's charter schools and the Harlem Children's Zone's tutoring programs for teens encourage all students to go to college—and whether they do will determine his teachers' salaries.

Yet Murray does have a point in arguing that college isn't for everyone. There are plenty of jobs that don't require a bachelor's degree, or which can be obtained with professional certification. I've met parents of special education students who worry that the standards movement has made it too difficult for their children to earn a regular high school degree, and that the new generation of career-oriented and technical-education high schools are too academically demanding for some students with special needs. Like Antonio, these families don't want a special ed diploma. They want something more meaningful, and Murray correctly argues that a good education doesn't have to be narrowly defined as college readiness.

Is literacy defined by one's ability to pass tests? Does it mean reading the classics, and writing well-constructed essays about the symbolism in *Moby-Dick*? Or is it about reading a website and sending e-mail? Clay Shirky has thought about these issues at length, as a teacher in New York University's cutting-edge Interactive Telecommunications Program. Though he strongly disagrees with Murray's racially based arguments and his focus on IQ, he concedes the conservative scholar raises a valid question about the relentless push for college and postgraduate degrees. Decades ago, a high school degree was considered an accomplishment. "Now to be a high school dropout is only second to a career criminal," says Shirky (half in jest), adding that a two-year degree from a community college is just a step up from a GED. "Is there a point at which constantly altered baselines of intellectual attainment will always continue to make sense for the culture?" he asks. Shirky grew up in Columbia, Missouri, during the 1970s, when many students joined the Future Farmers and Future Homemakers of America. Although most of his classmates did not go to college, he says, "there was a pretty clear measure of what it meant to be a productive member of society. At least one trade you could practice, if you could also balance a budget, open a bank account, people knew what it meant to get on in the world."

Today, however, Shirky says, "it seems a significant part of getting on in the world means being able to read stuff on-screen and manipulate it." The National Assessment of Educational Progress is responding to this demand by adding an assessment of students' technological skills by 2012. But the shift to an interactive, screen-based culture has its challenges. Shirky recalls a 2008 essay in *The Atlantic* titled "Is Google Making Us Stupid?" The author quoted a blogger who admitted he can't read

War and Peace anymore because the Web has shortened his attention span.[4] But is *War and Peace* the standard? And was it ever, really?

We've heard these worries before about mass media dumbing down society. Back in the 1950s and '60s, television was called the "boob tube." Before that, the threat came from pulp fiction and comic books. The Internet is the next evolution in new media—making it an easy target for the cultural gatekeepers. As we revisit our standards, Shirky warns "it will freak people out" if reading and manipulating information on a screen becomes the baseline for educating productive citizens, or if the Great Books aren't valued as much as sending e-mail messages on MySpace. A similar culture war erupted almost a century ago when progressives argued that it made no sense to teach all the immigrants and poor children Latin if they'd be heading to factory jobs. Their goal was to make school more practical.

Today's students don't have good factory jobs waiting for them. With a struggling economy, President Obama declared that "dropping out of high school is no longer an option. It's not just quitting on yourself, it's quitting on your country—and this country needs and values the talents of every American." Our information-based society demands greater reading skills than it did when Shirky and I were kids in the seventies. Being functionally literate doesn't mean reading *War and Peace*, but it does mean navigating a world in which you're surrounded by text: job applications, street signs, maps, bus and subway timetables, and computers. Most newspapers are believed to be written at a sixth-grade level or higher. An eighth-grade reading level is required to obtain a driver's license in Oklahoma. New hires in fields ranging from human services to the insurance industry are expected to read technical manuals and to navigate the Internet. A survey of 120 major American corporations found writing is a "threshold skill" for professionals, because manufacturing documentation, operating procedures, and lab safety and waste disposal operations all need to be "crystal clear."[5] Antonio's best chance of joining the armed forces would be to enroll in a GED program with the army national guard, but he'd have to finish the ninth grade to be eligible. There's no getting around the need to read and write. We just need to agree on a baseline.

Business never picked up at the dry cleaning shop on Route 47. It shut down in the spring of 2008. Soon afterward, Antonio finally collected all his paperwork and got his state ID card. By June, someone he knew helped him get a new job loading trucks with UPS. He worked at a site in Maspeth, Queens, a trip that took about an hour and a half by bus and subway from his parents' house in New Jersey. The UPS facility on Fifty-fifth Avenue and Forty-eighth Street was a mile walk from the 7 train, in a bleak neighborhood that's also home to the police department's Fleet Services Division, a graveyard, and a sanitation department depot. An American flag flew over the brick UPS building, which was surrounded by brown trucks. The only other businesses on the street were auto repair shops and a deli.

During his first week at work, Antonio watched a training video and learned how to safely handle packages. He was going to load boxes onto a sixteen-wheeler bound for Long Island. "It's really crazy, the work in there!" he said, describing the busy scene. He said his mother was happy that he got the job. He carried a laminated photo ID and several papers from his training seminar, which he pulled from his pants pocket. "The ones with numbers is the truck numbers, zip codes," he explained. He also showed me the "2008 Depth of Knowledge Test" with questions and answers about different procedures. He read the first one aloud:

" 'What job methods do you'—sorry—'untilze, utilize to avoid injury for your job?' " He then answered, "Boots and gloves."

He read from the five steps to avoid slipping and falling. " 'Walk at brisk pace, don't run.' " I asked him what "brisk" meant, and he said, "Slow, like not slow but normal." Then he correctly read the rest of the safety tips: " 'Don't walk on conveyor rollers, shoots, slides, or unsecure belt.' " He had no difficulty with "conveyor" and correctly answered a question about how to properly secure a conveyor belt (you use the safety switch). "If I secure the belt I'm the only one that can unsecure it. The same person who secured it is the same person who has to unsecure it."

Antonio was enthusiastic about mastering a new set of rules. Though he was paid only $8.50 an hour for a part-time job loading boxes from about five to ten p.m. on weeknights, he saw it as a decent gig that would eventually give him health insurance.

In the new economy, Antonio's reading skills were good enough to navigate the Internet, send messages to girls on MySpace, and load boxes at UPS. He'd have a hard time climbing the ladder and becoming self-sufficient without a degree or a trade certificate, however. A UPS spokeswoman said truck driver is the highest-ranking position without a high school diploma or GED. But these employees, who typically make twenty-eight dollars an hour, have to pass an orientation program with detailed reading passages about safety policies and GPS technology. Antonio saw that as a possible goal. He also spoke about going back to tutoring so he could study for a GED, if he could fit it into his new work schedule. "I need a job, I just need to get myself stable," he said. He didn't yet have a bank account. But he'd certainly proven that he *could* learn to read once he got the right kind of assistance and motivation.

That spring, a friend of Antonio's gave him a book about a fictional marine named Patrick Seamus Flaherty who served in the Vietnam War. It was written in journal form, and was part of the history series by Scholastic called "My Name Is America." It's written at a sixth-grade level. Antonio had gotten to page 88, which was almost halfway through the book. He loved the character's description of his arrival in Vietnam. "I see a movie in my head," he said, using the phrase his tutors taught him when he first learned to read.

When Antonio reads comic books, he often skips to the last page because he wants to know what's going to happen. But he didn't do that with this book. "I'm actually, like, addicted to the book," he said. "I don't want to let go of the book."

The No Child Left Behind law has changed our expectations for all students, including those like Antonio. Previously, schools were judged by the overall percentage of students passing a test. It was okay to let a few slip through the cracks as long as the majority passed. Now schools have to break down how many students are passing by race, income, language, and special needs status. Schools face sanctions (and humiliation in the local press) if they fall short of their goals. Most educators I've met have embraced this principle, even as they criticize the tests themselves. They would never accept Charles Murray's argument that college is just for an elite 20 percent—though they concede there are always going to be some pupils who can't meet the high bar of college readiness.

But it's hard to argue for lowering the bar. We want everyone to read so they can reach their potential and contribute to society as active citizens and taxpayers. Yet studies have found U.S. reading levels are behind those of other developed nations. A 2005 survey of seven countries and regions by the Organization for Economic Cooperation and Development found 20 percent of American adults are *functionally illiterate*, ranking the U.S. fifth, behind Norway, Bermuda, Canada, and Switzerland—though ahead of Italy and a region of Mexico.* These adults have "difficulty making low-level text-based inferences," according to the OECD. The U.S. government conducted its own National Assessment of Adult Literacy in 2003, which found between 12 and 20 percent of respondents at the lowest of three different types of reading tests. People who scored this low would have a hard time summarizing a want ad or a magazine article, or determining whether their car has enough gas to get to the next station. This U.S. report also defined literacy as "using printed and written information to function in society, to achieve one's goals, and to develop one's knowledge and potential."[6]

That's one standard for literacy in the twenty-first century. Perhaps another can be found by looking at court rulings. In the past thirty-five years, forty-five lawsuits have been filed over levels of state education aid.[7] A suit brought by education groups and parents in New York City successfully proved the public schools had been starved of their fair share of funding, based on the state's constitutional guarantee of an "adequate education." In 2003 the Court of Appeals rejected a lower court ruling that found an eighth-grade education was constitutionally adequate. Instead, it said students deserved a "meaningful" education—which it defined as "one which prepares them to function productively as civic participants"[8] who can serve on a jury and get a good job. The city was ultimately rewarded an extra $5.6 billion in aid, based on what it would take to provide a meaningful education for everyone, factoring in the high percentage of immigrants and poor students. (These funds, however, were delayed afer the first installment because of the fiscal crisis.)

Michael Rebell, an attorney who represented the plaintiffs, says that's a good template as we grapple with the lessons of the No Child Left Behind law, and what we should demand from our schools. "If we provide the opportunities, we can push all kids to much higher levels than we've been achieving," he says. Rebell heads the Campaign for Educational Equity at Teachers College, which in 2005 concluded that the social costs to the United States of an inadequate education were $250 billion

*The report is based on the Adult Literacy and Lifeskills Survey, which is coordinated by Statistics Canada, the National Center for Education Statistics in the United States, and other agencies. The seven countries or regions in the report were the United States, Bermuda, Canada, Italy, Norway, Switzerland, and the Mexican state of Nuevo León.

annually, in terms of lost income, taxes, extra health costs, and crime. High school dropouts are more likely to be unemployed than people with more education, and they make a lot less money when they do get jobs. A 2004 study found dropouts made thirty-seven cents for every dollar earned by a high school graduate. The discrepancy wasn't anywhere near as great in 1964, when a dropout made sixty-seven cents for every dollar earned by a high school graduate.[9] Another study predicted that raising the graduation rate by just 1 percent among men could reduce the financial costs of crime by as much as $1.4 billion annually.[10]

Alejandro, Yamilka, and Antonio fought the city for the right to learn how to read. Cases like theirs were still being filed in 2008. At Advocates for Children, Matthew Lenaghan saw no noticeable decline in the number of calls from students seeking help with reading issues, "nor the number of people needing impartial hearings filed on their behalf." Advocates also won a class-action suit on behalf of parents of children like Antonio and Yamilka who had successfully challenged their special education services through impartial hearings, but claimed the orders weren't being enforced on a timely basis. A federal judge ordered the city to meet a series of benchmarks. And across the river in New Jersey, the attorney Elizabeth Athos, with the Education Law Center, represented a twenty-seven-year-old man who won up to five years of private tutoring at state expense, plus damages, because the Jersey City public schools didn't give him the right services for his dyslexia. He'd been kept in ninth grade until he was twenty years old and never advanced beyond a second-grade reading level.

On the bright side, in 2007 New York City reorganized its system for helping academically challenged older teens graduate from high school. The city opened a referral center in each of its five boroughs. These one-stop shopping centers could steer students without enough credits to graduate to either high schools or GED classes (if they wouldn't accumulate enough credits before turning twenty-two). Each center also offered on-site reading assessments and remedial classes with decoding, fluency, and comprehension exercises. Had Antonio or Alejandro brought their cases today, this could have been another option.

Alejandro continued working on his short essay about the importance of a formal education, right until his pre-GED class ended in June. He met with one of his old tutors, Andrew Plotkin, who helped him organize his thoughts, correct some spelling errors, and think about the right word choices. Eventually, Alejandro drafted several lines in his notebook, double-spaced, that he prepared to give his teacher:

"It is important to get an education because it helps open doors and gives you more options in life. The more education you have the more confidence you will have in your abilities to achieve all that you want. Without an education you wont be able to get the job that you want, the kind of job that will make you happy in life. If you get a job for necessity it could be one that won't provide you with enough money for you or your family. An education will help you fine purpose in somethig that is bigger than you and your family something that will add to the human condition. by taking responsibility for your education you will have shoor cuntrall of your life."

He still hadn't made the final spelling fixes. But he liked the phrase "human condition." He came up with it while talking to Plotkin. "I was trying to make it not too cheesy, not too big," he said. They threw around words like "society" and "responsibility," too.

"I was trying to talk about the responsibility people have to society, the world," Alejandro said, explaining that his tutor tried to steer him to simpler terms. "He was pulling me back, 'No, you shouldn't get too serious . . .'" But Alejandro kept the phrase "human condition" because "it makes you think."

Yamilka had been thinking about her own condition. Before, when she was illiterate, she said her mind "would wander around." She felt like her head was empty. Now she compared her head to a file cabinet filling up with words. She could read the sign for the library across the street; she could read the names of corn, lemons, and other foods in her supermarket; and her sisters caught her reading words on the TV screen. She still had a hard time reading her classwork alone, because she'd often stop at an unfamiliar word and type the letters into her speak-and-spell machine. It wasn't as smooth as listening to her sister read from the "Twilight" series. But she had images to go with the words she saw on the page. "My mind is not wandering," she said. "I can imagine things more, I can feel things more." Then, with a slight laugh, she said in all seriousness, "Hopefully I won't forget."

Epilogue

Based on statistics, 2009 was a good year for the New York City public schools. Math and reading scores for the city's students went up again from the previous year. Scores on the state's English Language Arts exam increased by eleven points, with 69 percent of students in grades three through eight meeting or exceeding the standards. But there was a statewide increase as well, and the Board of Regents said it was time to consider making the tests more challenging. Meanwhile, the city continued to reduce the number of students reading at the lowest level to just 3 percent, a 50 percent decrease from 2008. The city's graduation rate increased, too, according to the latest figures (for the class of 2008). Fifty-six percent of city students completed high school in four years.

The Bloomberg administration attributed all these positive signs to its school reforms, including the use of data to track student achievement. Jim Liebman stayed on at the Department of Education for an extra year. But he left in July of 2009, saying that Columbia Law School needed him back that fall. He also said he believed ARIS had helped educators figure out how to reach every child, and that this was a factor in the higher scores among students of all races and income levels. He planned to assist the city in its application for federal stimulus funds earmarked for innovative school reforms. The city's entire teaching force was trained in ARIS by late November. But while many teachers said they used the program, others said it still wasn't worth their time or that they relied on coaches and data specialists in their schools to print out the results. Few teachers were using the interactive Web 2.0 component of ARIS to communicate with teachers in other schools.

President Barack Obama's education secretary, Arne Duncan, praised the Bloomberg-Klein reforms. The federal stimulus package included $5 billion worth of grants that would be awarded to districts and states for setting up data systems, along with ways of measuring teacher effectiveness and turning around failing schools. Duncan also supported continued mayoral control of the city schools. Most state politicians agreed that the system had produced improvements, and legislators in Albany were poised to renew the 2002 law granting the mayor of New York control of the city's schools.

Antonio continued working at UPS. He got health-care benefits for the first time in his life and qualified for a raise after a year on the job, to $11 an hour. He flirted with the idea of enrolling in a GED program but worried that it would be too difficult. He said he was no longer interested in the military, explaining, "I want to figure out what I'm good at."

Alejandro resumed his pre-GED classes in the fall of 2008 at Hostos Community College. This time he told his English teacher about his reading problems. But he continued having a difficult time, and eventually left the program. His lawyer looked for other GED programs that might be better suited to his disabilities. In the meantime, Alejandro also enrolled in a state-funded vocational program to explore employment options. The family bought a laptop computer, which his sister Elizabeth used for her college classes. She showed Alejandro how to use it, and he got an e-mail account.

Yamilka's sight-word vocabulary—the number of words she could recognize in print—continued to grow. Mary Kelly discovered that by saying and writing new words many more times, Yamilka could improve her memory noticeably. Yamilka learned to recognize important words and phrases such as "poison," "flammable," "fire escape," and "do not enter." She was happy to know "wet paint," in particular, because she had occasionally gotten smudged by railings in subway stations. In the fall of 2008, Yamilka read a page-and-a-half-long story, from a beginning reader anthology for adults, about a couple's love life with reasonably good accuracy and comprehension. "She and I were both giddy when she finished," Kelly reported. But Kelly found it was still very difficult to teach Yamilka to sound out words on her own. Kelly said Yamilka's phonemic processing and memory, or the ability to recognize the sounds of letters, remained very poor. "This is a young woman who really needed earlier intervention," she said, referring to Yamilka's need for speech and language therapy when she was in the city schools. Now in her twenties, Yamilka couldn't make up for so much lost time without great difficulty. Fisher Landau persuaded Yamilka to try a bilingual speech class, after determining that her comprehension in Spanish was actually much higher than in English. But Yamilka found it difficult to switch back and forth from English to Spanish during her classes.

Kelly encouraged Yamilka to enroll in a vocational program. She thought Yamilka had a wonderful way with people and could envision her becoming an aide in a nursing home or working with preschoolers. Kelly had known that Yamilka's cognitive scores were deceptively low, but she had been more skeptical than the speech instructor, Nancy Tarshis, about "multiple intelligence" theories. "I never really believed in emotional intelligence," she confessed. "But [Yamilka] has really taught me something. I see this incredible understanding of emotion and empathy, and the ability to make inferences about emotions." But Yamilka had a negative impression of vocational programs and didn't want to enroll in one. She worried that her reading skills were too low, and that she would be exiled to terrible jobs. Kelly had seen other students who knew they'd never be able to read very much and were happy with menial jobs. But she said Yamilka was more distressed about her situation because she was so painfully cognizant.

Yamilka acknowledged she had trouble accepting her limitations. "Every time I close my eyes and go to sleep, I wish I could find myself in any place that I'm sitting down and be able to open a book and read," she said. Her goal was to accept herself as a person with learning disabilities. "It's hard to say to someone, 'This is who I am.'"

NOTES

BIBLIOGRAPHY

ACKNOWLEDGMENTS

Notes

All facts and statistics about New York City public schools came from the city's Department of Education and the New York State Education Department.

PROLOGUE: LOST

1. Beth Fertig,"Disabling Diplomas: How NYC Is Failing Its Special Education Students," WNYC Radio, June 5, 2006.
2. Karen Arenson, "SAT Scores Show Student Gains in Math," *The New York Times*, August 31, 2005.
3. M. Quinn, R. Rutherford, P. Leone, D. Osher, and J. Poirer, "Youth with Disabilities in Juvenile Corrections: A National Survey," *Exceptional Children* 71, no. 3 (2005): 339–45. Retrieved July 20, 2006, from journals.sped.org/EC/Articles/Quinn71-3.pdf.
4. Sally Shaywitz, *Overcoming Dyslexia* (New York: Vintage Books, 2005), 29–30.
5. National Institute for Literacy website, www.nifl.gov/nifl/facts/IALS.html.
6. Institute of Education Statistics, U.S. Department of Education, National Center for Education Statistics, nces.ed.gov/surveys/all/ib_overall.asp.
7. S. White and M. McCloskey, "Framework for the 2003 National Assessment of Adult Literacy" (NCES 2005-531). U.S. Department of Education, nces.ed.gov/NAAI/fr_definition.asp.

1: YAMILKA'S JOURNEY

1. Sarah Mondale and Sarah B. Patton, eds., *School: The Story of American Public Education* (Boston: Beacon Press, 2001), 21.
2. Ibid., 22.
3. Ibid., 48.
4. Ibid., 25.
5. Ibid., 31.
6. David Tyack and Thomas James, "Education for a Republic: Federal Influence on Public Schooling in the Nation's First Century," in *This Constitution: A Bicentennial Chronicle*, Project '87, a joint program of the American Political Science Association and American Historical Association (fall 1985).

7. Mondale and Patton, *School*, 58.
8. Ibid., 99.
9. Christopher B. Swanson, "Special Education in America: The State of Students with Disabilities in the Nation's High Schools" (Washington, D.C.: Editorial Projects in Education Research Center, November 8, 2008), 19.
10. Elissa Gootman, "In Special Education Cases, City Is Fighting Harder Before Paying for Private School," *The New York Times*, December 12, 2007.
11. Joseph Berger, "Fighting over When Public Should Pay Private Tuition for Disabled," *The New York Times*, March 21, 2007.
12. Dan Keating and V. Dion Haynes, "Special-Ed Tuition a Growing Drain on D.C.," *The Washington Post*, June 5, 2006.
13. Fertig, "Disabling Diplomas."

2: EDUCATION, INC.

1. Michael Grunwald, "The New Action Heroes," *Time*, June 14, 2007.
2. Text of Bloomberg's inauguration address, January 1, 2002.
3. Beth Fertig, "Neediest Students Crowd Worst Schools," WNYC Radio, March 14, 2005.
4. Joe Williams, *Cheating Our Kids: How Politics and Greed Ruin Education* (New York: Palgrave Macmillan, 2005), 39.

3: RENAISSANCE MAN

1. Shaywitz, *Overcoming Dyslexia*, 99.
2. "Remedial Instruction Rewires Dyslexic Brains, Provides Lasting Results, Study Shows," *ScienceDaily*, August 6, 2008.

4: BREAKTHROUGH MOMENT

1. Michael Fullan, Peter Hill, and Carmel Crévola, *Breakthrough* (Thousand Oaks, Calif.: Corwin Press, 2006), 37.
2. John Dewey, "My Pedagogic Creed," *The School Journal* 54, no. 3 (January 16, 1897): 77–80.
3. John Dewey, *Dewey on Education* (New York: Teachers College Press, 1959), 25.

6: A SCHOOL IN NEED OF IMPROVEMENT

1. Diane Ravitch, *The Great School Wars: New York City, 1805–1973; A History of the Public Schools as Battlefield of Social Change* (New York: Basic Books, 1974), 27.
2. Ibid., 168.
3. Ibid., 180.
4. Emanuel Tobier, "Schooling in New York City: The Socioeconomic Context," in *City Schools: Lessons from New York*, edited by Diane Ravitch and Joseph P. Viteritti (Baltimore: Johns Hopkins University Press, 2000), 24.
5. Ravitch, *The Great School Wars*, 244.
6. Tobier, "Schooling in New York City," 29.
7. Ibid., 32.

8. New York City Department of Planning, "The Newest New Yorkers 2000: Immigrant New York in the New Millennium" (2000), xi.
9. Sam Roberts, "City Growing More Diverse, Census Finds," *The New York Times*, December 9, 2008.
10. Ibid.

7: "DOUBLE WHAMMY"

1. Donald L. MacMillan, "Development of Operational Definitions in Mental Retardation: Similarities and Differences with the Field of Learning Disabilities," in *Better Understanding Learning Disabilities*, edited by G. Reid Lyon, David B. Gray, James F. Kavanagh, and Norman A. Krasnegor (Baltimore: Paul H. Brookes, 1993), 130.
2. Maryanne Wolf, *Proust and the Squid: The Story and Science of the Reading Brain* (New York: HarperCollins, 2007), 168–70.
3. Shaywitz, *Overcoming Dyslexia*, 78–85.

8: THE ARCHITECT MEETS THE PUBLIC

1. Yoav Gonen, "Topsy Turvy: Shock Marks in New Report Cards," *New York Post*, November 6, 2007.
2. Erin Einhorn and Carrie Melago, "City: Make the Grade or Else!" New York *Daily News*, November 6, 2007.
3. Jennifer Medina, "New York Schools Brace to Be Scored A to F," *The New York Times*, November 4, 2007.
4. Carrie Melago and Rachel Monahan, "Shocking Marks in Trendy B'klyn," New York *Daily News*, November 6, 2007.
5. Erin Einhorn with Bill Egbert, "State Sez F, But City Sez A!" New York *Daily News*, November 6, 2007.
6. Dan Brown, "New York City Schools Receive Misleading Report Cards," *The Huffington Post*, November 12, 2007, www.huffingtonpost.com/dan-brown/new-york-city-schools-rec_b_72238.html.
7. "Report Card Haiku: A Collection of 68 Haiku Responding to the New York City Department of Education's School Report Cards," compiled by Eduwonkette, November 16, 2007, blogs.edweek.org/edweek/eduwonkette.

11: AN ART AND A SCIENCE

1. Louisa Cook Moats, "Teaching Reading Is Rocket Science: What Expert Teachers Know and Should Be Able to Do" (Washington, D.C.: American Federation of Teachers, 1999), 11.
2. Marilyn Jager Adams, *Beginning to Read: Thinking and Learning About Print* (Cambridge, Mass.: Massachusetts Institute of Technology, 1990), 21.
3. Diane Ravitch, *Left Back: A Century of Battles over School Reform* (New York: Touchstone, 2000), 356.
4. Ibid., 354.
5. Ibid., 38–40.
6. Jeanne Chall, *Learning to Read: The Great Debate* (New York: McGraw-Hill, 1967), 7.

7. "Report of the National Reading Panel: Teaching Children to Read," summary report reprinted by the Partnership for Reading, a collaborative effort administered by the National Institute for Literacy (2000), 9.
8. Diana Jean Schemo, "In War over Reaching Reading, a U.S.-Local Clash," *The New York Times*, March 9, 2007.
9. Sol Stern, "Bloomberg and Klein Rush In: Under These Two, Mayoral Control of Gotham's Schools Threatens Disaster," *City Journal*, April 8, 2003.
10. Abby Goodnough, "Bush Advisor Casts Doubt on the Benefits of Phonics Program," *The New York Times*, January 24, 2003.
11. Louisa Cook Moats, "Whole Language Lives On: The Illusion of 'Balanced' Reading Instruction" (Washington, D.C.: Thomas B. Fordham Foundation, 2000), 15.
12. Betty Hart and Todd R. Risley, "The Early Catastrophe: The 30 Million Word Gap by Age 3," *American Educator*, Spring 2003.

14: LEARNING TO RHYME

1. Hugh W. Catts and Alan G. Kamhi, *Language and Reading Disabilities* (Needham Heights, Mass.: Allyn & Bacon, 1999), 61.

15: THE TOOLKIT

1. Frank R. Vellutino, Donna M. Scanlon, Sheila Small, and Diane P. Fanuele, "Response to Intervention as a Vehicle for Distinguishing Between Children with and Without Reading Disabilities: Evidence for the Role of Kindergarten and First-Grade Interventions," *Journal of Learning Disabilities* 39, no. 2 (March/April 2006), 158.

19: REALITY BYTES

1. Yoav Gonen, "Schools Computer an $80M 'Disaster,'" *New York Post*, February 27, 2008.
2. Lynn Olson, "Not All Teachers Keen on Periodic Tests," *Education Week*, November 30, 2005.
3. Richard Yeh, "High-Stakes Testing: Can Rapid Assessment Reduce the Pressure?" *Teachers College Record* 108, no. 3 (2006): 621–61.
4. Richard Rothstein, *Class and Schools: Using Social, Economic, and Educational Reform to Close the Black-White Achievement Gap* (Washington, D.C.: Economic Policy Institute, 2004), 64.
5. Posted on nycpublicschoolparents.blogspot.com/2008/02; accessed March 2008.
6. Paul Davidson, Greg Toppo, and Jayne O'Donnell, "Fraud, Waste Mar Plan to Wire Schools to Net," *USA Today*, June 9, 2004.
7. Rothstein, *Class and Schools*, 66–67.

20: BACK TO SCHOOL

1. Sam Dillon, "State's Data Obscure How Few Finish High School," *The New York Times*, March 20, 2008.
2. Dolores Perin, Bert Flugman, and Seymour Spiegel, "Last Chance Gulch: Youth Par-

ticipation in Urban Adult Basic Education Programs," *Adult Basic Education* 16, no. 3 (Fall 2006): 178.

3. Jay P. Greene, "GEDs Aren't Worth the Paper They're Printed On," *City Journal*, Winter 2002.
4. Sally Liberman Smith, *No Easy Answers* (Cambridge, Mass.: Winthrop Publishers, 1979), 80.

22: ANTONIO AT WORK

1. James Paul Gee, "Good Video Games and Good Learning," *Phi Kappa Phi Forum* 85, no. 2 (Summer 2005): 33–37.
2. National Endowment for the Arts, "Reading on the Rise," January 12, 2009.
3. National Endowment for the Arts, "Reading at Risk: A Survey of Literary Reading in America," Research Division Report #46, June 2004.
4. Kaiser Family Foundation, Program for the Study of Media and Health, "Children, the Digital Divide, and Federal Policy," September 16, 2004.
5. Sara Bernard, "Zero-Thumb Game: How to Tame Texting," www.edutopia.org, May 28, 2008.

24: INPUTS AND OUTPUTS

1. Clive R. Belfield and Henry M. Levin, eds., *The Price We Pay: Economic and Social Consequences of Inadequate Education* (Washington, D.C.: Brookings Institution Press, 2007), 44.
2. Catherine Snow, Michelle V. Porche, Patton O. Tabors, and Stephanie Ross Harris, *Is Literacy Enough? Pathways to Academic Success for Adolescents* (Baltimore: Paul H. Brookes, 2007), 52.
3. Jeanne S. Chall, Vicki A. Jacobs, and Luke E. Baldwin, *The Reading Crisis: Why Poor Children Fall Behind* (Cambridge, Mass: Harvard University Press, 1990), 30.

26: SCORES AND SOUP

1. "On New York State Tests, a Growing Achievement Gap Between White/Asian and Black/Hispanic Students," Eduwonkette blog, July 30, 2008, blogs.edweek.org/edweek/eduwonkette/2008/07/on_new_york_state_tests_a_grow.html.
2. Richard Allington, *What Really Matters for Struggling Readers* (New York: Addison Wesley Longman, 2001), 134.
3. E. D. Hirsch, Jr., *The Knowledge Deficit: Closing the Shocking Education Gap for American Children* (Boston and New York: Houghton Mifflin, 2006), 10.
4. Dewey, *Dewey on Education*, 90.

27: MEASURING PROGRESS

1. Joseph K. Torgesen, "Preventing Early Reading Failure," *American Educator*, Fall 2004.
2. Charles Murray, *Real Education: Four Simple Truths for Bringing America's Schools Back to Reality* (New York: Crown Forum, 2008), 11.

3. Ibid., 44.
4. Nicholas Carr, "Is Google Making Us Stupid?" *The Atlantic*, July-August 2008.
5. National Commission on Writing for America's Families, Schools and Colleges, "Writing: A Ticket to Work . . . Or a Ticket Out" (New York: College Board, September 2004).
6. National Assessment of Adult Literacy, sponsored by the National Center for Education Statistics, Washington, D.C., 2003, 2.
7. Michael A. Rebell and Jessica R. Wolff, *Moving Every Child Ahead: From NCLB Hype to Meaningful Educational Opportunity* (New York: Teachers College Press, 2008), 22.
8. *Campaign for Fiscal Equity v. State of New York* (2003), 332.
9. Cecilia Elena Rouse, "Consequences for the Labor Market," in Belfield and Levin, eds., *The Price We Pay*, 99.
10. Enrico Moretti, "Crime and the Costs of Criminal Justice," in ibid., 157.

Bibliography

Adams, Marilyn Jager. *Beginning to Read: Thinking and Learning About Print*. Cambridge, Mass.: Massachusetts Institute of Technology Press, 1990.

Adult Literacy and Lifeskills Survey. Washington, D.C.: Institute of Education Statistics, U.S. Department of Education, National Center for Education Statistics, 2003. nces.ed.gov/surveys/all/ib_overall.asp.

Advocates for Children. "Leaving School Empty Handed: A Report on Graduation Rates and Dropout Rates for Students Who Receive Special Education Services in New York City." New York: Advocates for Children, June 2005.

Allington, Richard L. *What Really Matters for Struggling Readers: Designing Research-Based Programs*. New York: Addison Wesley Longman, 2001.

Arenson, Karen. "SAT Scores Show Student Gains in Math." *The New York Times*, August 31, 2005.

Beers, Kylene. *When Kids Can't Read: What Teachers Can Do; A Guide for Teachers 6–12*. Portsmouth, N.H.: Heinemann, 2003.

Berger, Joseph. "Fighting over When Public Should Pay Private Tuition for Disabled." *The New York Times*, March 21, 2007.

Bernard, Sara. "Zero-Thumb Game: How to Tame Texting." www.edutopia.org, May 28, 2008.

Bloomberg, Michael. "I'm Not Running for President, But . . ." *The New York Times*, February 28, 2008.

———. Mayoral inauguration address, January 1, 2002.

Boudett, Kathryn Parker, Elizabeth A. City, and Richard J. Murname. *Data Wise: Step-by-Step Guide to Using Assessment Results to Improve Teaching and Learning*. Cambridge, Mass.: Harvard University Press, 2007.

Brown, Dan. "New York City Schools Receive Misleading Report Cards." *The Huffington Post*, November 12, 2007.

Calkins, Lucy McCormick. *The Art of Teaching Reading*. New York: Longman, 2001.

Carr, Nicholas. "Is Google Making Us Stupid?" *The Atlantic*, July-August 2008.

Catts, Hugh W., and Alan G. Kamhi. *Language and Reading Disabilities*. Needham Heights, Mass.: Allyn & Bacon, 1999.

Chall, Jeanne. *Learning to Read: The Great Debate*. New York: McGraw-Hill, 1967.

Chall, Jeanne S., Vicki A. Jacobs, and Luke E. Baldwin. *The Reading Crisis: Why Poor Children Fall Behind.* Cambridge, Mass.: Harvard University Press, 1990.

Davidson, Paul, Greg Toppo, and Jayne O'Donnell. "Fraud, Waste Mar Plan to Wire Schools to Net." *USA Today*, June 9, 2004.

Dewey, John. *Dewey on Education*. New York: Teachers College Press, 1959.

———. "My Pedagogic Creed." *The School Journal* 54, no. 3 (January 16, 1897): 77–80.

Dillon, Sam. "State's Data Obscure How Few Finish High School." *The New York Times*, March 20, 2008.

Doyle, Denis. "The Doyle Report." *School Business Affairs Magazine*, February 2003.

Einhorn, Erin, and Carrie Melago. "City: Make the Grade or Else!" New York *Daily News*, November 6, 2007.

Einhorn, Erin, with Bill Egbert. "State Sez F, but City Sez A!" New York *Daily News*, November 6, 2007.

Fertig, Beth. "Disabling Diplomas: How NYC Is Failing Its Special Education Students." WNYC Radio, June 5, 2006.

———. "Neediest Students Crowd Worst Schools." WNYC Radio, March 14, 2005.

Fullan, Michael, Peter Hill, and Carmel Crévola. *Breakthrough*. Thousand Oaks, Calif.: Corwin Press, 2006.

Gee, James Paul. "Good Video Games and Good Learning." *Phi Kappa Phi Forum* 85, no. 2 (Summer 2005): 34.

Gonen, Yoav. "Schools Computer at $80M 'Disaster.'" *New York Post*, February 27, 2008.

———. "Topsy Turvy: Shock Marks in New Report Cards." *New York Post*, November 6, 2007.

Goodnough, Abby. "Bush Advisor Casts Doubt on the Benefits of Phonics Program." *The New York Times*, January 24, 2003.

Gootman, Elissa. "In Special Education Cases, City Is Fighting Harder Before Paying for Private School." *The New York Times*, December 12, 2007.

Greene, Jay P. "GEDs Aren't Worth the Paper They're Printed On." *City Journal*, Winter 2002.

Grunwald, Michael. "The New Action Heroes." *Time*, June 14, 2007.

Hart, Betty, and Todd R. Risley. "The Early Catastrophe: The 30 Million Word Gap by Age 3." *American Educator*, Spring 2003.

Hehir, Thomas, Richard Figueroa, Sue Gamm, et al. "Comprehensive Management Review and Evaluation of Special Education." Submitted to the New York City Department of Education, September 20, 2005.

Hirsch, E. D. *The Knowledge Deficit: Closing the Shocking Education Gap for American Children*. New York: Houghton Mifflin, 2006.

International Adult Literacy Survey. Washington, D.C.: National Institute for Literacy, 1994–1998. www.nifl.gov/nifl/facts/IALS.html.

Kaiser Family Foundation. Program for the Study of Media and Health. "Children, the Digital Divide, and Federal Policy." September 16, 2004.

Keating, Dan, and V. Dion Haynes. "Special-Ed Tuition a Growing Drain on D.C." *The Washington Post*, June 5, 2006.

Kolker, Robert. "How Is a Hedge Fund Like a School?" *New York*, February 13, 2006.

Kutner, M., E. Greenberg, Y. Jin, B. Boyle, Y. Hsu, and E. Dunleavy. "Literacy in Everyday Life: Results from the 2003 National Assessment of Adult Literacy" (NCES2007-480). Washington, D.C.: National Center for Education Statistics, U.S. Department of Education, 2007.

Lenhart, Amanda, Sousan Arafeh, Aaron Smith, and Alexandra Rankin Macgill. "Writing,

Technology and Teens." Washington, D.C.: Pew Internet & American Life Project, April 24, 2008.

Liebman, James S., and Charles F. Sabel. "A Public Laboratory Dewey Barely Imagined: The Emerging Model of School Governance and Legal Reform." *New York University Journal of Law and Social Change* 28, no. 2 (2002–2003): 183–304.

MacMillan, Donald L. "Development of Operational Definitions in Mental Retardation: Similarities and Differences with the Field of Learning Disabilities." In *Better Understanding Learning Disabilities*, edited by G. Reid Lyon, David B. Gray, James F. Kavanagh, and Norman A. Krasnegor. Baltimore: Paul H. Brookes, 1993.

Martin, Michael O., Ina V. S. Mullis, and Ann M. Kennedy, eds. "Progress in International Reading Literacy Study (PIRLS) Technical Report." TIMSS & PIRLS International Study Center. Newton, Mass.: Lynch School of Education, Boston College, 2007.

McNeil, Michele. "Exit Scramble." *Education Week*, August 13, 2008.

Medina, Jennifer. "New York Schools Brace to Be Scored A to F." *The New York Times*, November 4, 2007.

Melago, Carrie, and Rachel Monahan. "Shocking Marks in Trendy B'klyn." New York *Daily News*, November 6, 2007.

Moats, Louisa Cook. "Teaching Reading Is Rocket Science: What Expert Teachers Should Know and Be Able to Do." Washington, D.C.: American Federation of Teachers, June 1999.

———. "Whole Language Lives On: The Illusion of 'Balanced' Reading Instruction." Washington, D.C.: Thomas B. Fordham Foundation, 2000.

Mondale, Sarah, and Sarah P. Patton, eds. *School: The Story of American Public Education*. Boston: Beacon Press, 2001.

Moretti, Enrico. "Crime and the Costs of Criminal Justice." In *The Price We Pay: Economic and Social Consequences of Inadequate Education*, edited by Clive R. Belfield and Henry R. Levin. Washington, D.C.: Brookings Institution Press, 2007.

Müller, Eve. "Juvenile Justice and Students with Disabilities: State Infrastructure and Initiatives." Project Forum at the National Association of State Directors of Special Education, Alexandria, Va., June 2006.

Murray, Charles. *Real Education: Four Simple Truths for Bringing America's Schools Back to Reality*. New York: Crown Forum, 2008.

National Assessment of Educational Progress. "The Nation's Report Card." September 25, 2007. Reading statistics at nationsreportcard.gov/reading_2007.

National Center for Education Statistics. "Fast Facts: Students with Disabilities." Washington, D.C.: U.S. Department of Education, 2006. nces.ed.gov/fastfacts/display.asp?id=64.

National Commission on Writing for America's Families, Schools and Colleges. "Writing: A Ticket to Work . . . Or a Ticket Out." New York: College Board, September 2004.

National Endowment for the Arts. "Reading at Risk: A Survey of Literary Reading in America." Research Report #46. Washington, D.C., June 2004.

———. "Reading on the Rise." Washington, D.C., January 12, 2009.

———. "To Read or Not to Read: A Question of National Consequence." Research Report #47. Washington, D.C., November 2007.

National Reading Panel. "Report of the National Reading Panel: Teaching Children to Read; An Evidence-Based Assessment of the Scientific Research Literature on Reading and Its Implications for Reading Instruction." Washington, D.C.: The Partnership for Reading, a collaborative effort administered by the National Institute for Literacy, 2000.

New York City Department of Planning. *The Newest New Yorkers 2000: Immigrant New York in the New Millennium*. New York, 2000.

Olson, Lynn. "Not All Teachers Keen on Periodic Tests." *Education Week*, November 30, 2005.

"On New York State Tests, A Growing Achievement Gap Between White/Asian and Black/Hispanic New York City Students." Eduwonkette blog, July 20, 2008. blogs.edweek.org/edweek/eduwonkette/2008/07/on_new_york_state_tests_a_grow.html.

Perin, Dolores, Bert Flugman, and Seymour Spiegel. "Last Chance Gulch: Youth Participation in Urban Adult Basic Education Programs." *Adult Basic Education* 16, no. 3 (Fall 2006): 171–88.

Pulliam, John D. *History of Education in America*. Fifth edition. New York: Merrill, 1991.

Quinn, M., R. Rutherford, P. Leone, D. Osher, and J. Poirer. "Youth with Disabilities in Juvenile Corrections: A National Survey." *Exceptional Children* 71, no. 3 (2005): 339–45.

Ravitch, Diane. *Left Back: A Century of Battles over School Reform*. New York: Touchstone, 2000.

———. *The Great School Wars: New York City, 1805–1973; A History of the Public Schools as Battlefield of Social Change*. New York: Basic Books, 1974.

Rebell, Michael A., and Jessica R. Wolff. *Moving Every Child Ahead: From NCLB Hype to Meaningful Educational Opportunity*. New York: Teachers College Press, 2008.

"Remedial Instruction Rewires Dyslexic Brains, Provides Lasting Results, Study Shows." Adapted from materials provided by Carnegie Mellon University. *ScienceDaily*, August 6, 2008.

"Report Card Haiku: A Collection of 68 Haiku Responding to the New York City Department of Education's School Report Cards." Compiled by Eduwonkette, November 16, 2007, blogs.edweek.org/edweek/eduwonkette.

Rogers, James. "North Carolina, IBM Lock Horns." *Byte and Switch*, February 10, 2006.

Rothstein, Richard. *Class and Schools: Using Social, Economic, and Educational Reform to Close the Black-White Achievement Gap*. Washington, D.C.: Economic Policy Institute, 2004.

Rothstein, Richard, and Tamara Wilder. "Beyond Educational Attainment: A Multifaceted Approach to Examining Economic Inequalities." In *The Price We Pay: Economic and Social Consequences of Inadequate Education*, edited by Clive R. Belfield and Henry M. Levin. Washington, D.C.: Brookings Institution Press, 2007.

Rouse, Cecilia Elena. "Consequences for the Labor Market." In *The Price We Pay: Economic and Social Consequences of Inadequate Education*, edited by Clive R. Belfield and Henry R. Levin. Washington, D.C.: Brookings Institution Press, 2007.

Saenz, Israel. "eChalk System Breaks Record." *Corpus Christi Caller-Times*, February 24, 2008.

Schemo, Diana Jean. "In War over Reaching Reading, a U.S.-Local Clash." *The New York Times*, March 9, 2007.

Shaywitz, Sally. *Overcoming Dyslexia*. New York: Vintage Books, 2005.

Smith, Sally Liberman. *No Easy Answers*. Cambridge, Mass.: Winthrop, 1979.

Snow, Catherine, Michelle V. Porche, Patton O. Tabors, and Stephanie Ross Harris. *Is Literacy Enough? Pathways to Academic Success for Adolescents*. Baltimore: Paul H. Brookes, 2007.

St. Onge, Peter. "State's School Network Stumbles." *Charlotte Observer*, May 18, 2006.

Stern, Sol. "Bloomberg and Klein Rush In: Under These Two, Mayoral Control of Gotham's Schools Threatens Disaster." *City Journal*, April 8, 2003.

Swanson, Christopher B. "Special Education in America: The State of Students with Disabilities in the Nation's High Schools." Washington, D.C.: Editorial Projects in Education Research Center, 2008.

Tobier, Emanuel. "Schooling in New York City: The Socioeconomic Context." In *City Schools: Lessons from New York*, edited by Diane Ravitch and Joseph P. Viteritti. Baltimore: Johns Hopkins University Press, 2000.

Torgesen, Joseph K. "Preventing Early Reading Failure." *American Educator*, 2004. Available at aft.org/pubs-reports/American_education/issues/fall04/reading.htm.

Tough, Paul. *Whatever It Takes: Geoffrey Canada's Quest to Change Harlem and America*. Boston and New York: Houghton Mifflin, 2008.

Tyack, David, and Thomas James. "Education for a Republic: Federal Influence on Public Schooling in the Nation's First Century." In *This Constitution: A Bicentennial Chronicle*. Project '87, a joint program of the American Political Science Association and the American Historical Association, Fall 1985.

Vellutino, Frank R., Donna M. Scanlon, Sheila Small, and Diane P. Fanuele. "Response to Intervention as a Vehicle for Distinguishing Between Children with and Without Reading Disabilities: Evidence for the Role of Kindergarten and First-Grade Interventions." *Journal of Learning Disabilities* 39, no. 2 (March/April 2006): 157–69.

Wagner, M., L. Newman, R. Cameto, and P. Levine. "Changes over Time in the Early Postschool Outcomes of Youth with Disabilities: A Report of Findings from the National Longitudinal Transition Study (NLTS) and the National Longitudinal Transition Study-2 (NLTS2)." Menlo Park, Calif.: SRI International, 2005.

Wayman, Jeffrey C., Vincent Cho, and Mary T. Johnson. "The Data-Informed District: A District-Wide Evaluation of Data Use in the Natrona County School District." Austin: University of Texas, August 2007.

Williams, Joe. *Cheating Our Kids: How Politics and Greed Ruin Education*. New York: Palgrave Macmillan, 2005.

Wilson, Barbara. "Instruction for Older Students Struggling with Reading," In *Multisensory Teaching of Basic Language Skills*, second edition, edited by Judith R. Birsh. Baltimore: Paul H. Brookes, 2006.

Wolf, Maryanne. *Proust and the Squid: The Story and Science of the Reading Brain*. New York: HarperCollins, 2007.

Yeh, Richard. "High-Stakes Testing: Can Rapid Assessment Reduce the Pressure?" *Teachers College Record* 108, no. 3 (2006): 621–61.

Acknowledgments

Yamilka, Alejandro, and Antonio agreed to tell their stories because they never want to see another student suffer the way they did in school.

It has been an honor getting to know them as individuals and writing about them. I am especially grateful to them for opening up to me because I know that it hasn't always been easy sharing the most difficult moments of their lives. They are tremendous human beings with reserves of great compassion and dedication.

I am thankful to my employer, WNYC Radio, for enabling me to take the time to complete this book. I'm proud to be part of an organization with such a strong dedication to news. In particular, my managing editor, Karen Frillmann, was the one who said Yamilka's story deserved more attention. My colleagues are wonderful, dedicated professionals who often seem like my second family.

The lawyers at Advocates for Children introduced me to Yamilka, Alejandro, and Antonio. These attorneys have spent countless hours with me explaining very complicated cases. Their dedication is extraordinary.

My agent, Tina Bennett of Janklow & Nesbit Associates, helped develop my book proposal. I had never done anything like this before, and would not have accomplished this without the faith she placed in me. Tina steered me to Paul Elie, my editor at Farrar, Straus and Giroux.

I cannot say enough about how much Paul has contributed to shaping this book. In an age when many news organizations are pulling back on coverage of weighty topics, Paul actually encouraged a greater focus on public policy. He has a rare combination of insight, intellectual rigor, passion for good storytelling, and kindness.

There are many individuals I'd like to acknowledge for sharing their time, whether that involved opening their classrooms or explaining their craft. I can't name them all, but you'll find them in these pages. I do want to single out my teacher friends Michelle Brier and Seth Flicker, as well as Jennifer Goldsmith and Rebecca Larkin, and Bill Robbins for his strong support. Esther Friedman, in particular, and the other academics and professionals I met in the course of writing this book were very generous and always knew which books and studies I should read.

Thank you to the City University of New York Graduate School of Journalism for the desk space. And to the New York Public Library's David Smith, and all the writers of the library's Frederick Lewis Allen Room, for giving me a place to work and to feel inspired.

I am also grateful to Liz Willen at the Hechinger Institute on Education and the Media, and to the Education Writers Association for all their recommendations. Thanks to my transcriber Michelle Starr, and to my friend and photographer Andi Schreiber for the picture on the book jacket. And to Maggie Robbins for helping me hustle.

Finally, I'd like to thank my wonderful family and friends. I can't name all of you here. But I must single out my cousin Dr. Nancy Prince-Cohen, who was always there for me as a professional educator and as a confidante. My cousins Barbara Chandler, Justin Leites, and Jessie Klein also deserve special acknowledgment for their guidance, as do my friends Lisa Magnino and David Feige. My uncle Robert Chandler always encouraged my work as a journalist and his high standards set the bar for me. I wish he had lived to see this.

This book is dedicated to the memories of Davie Fertig, the mother who gave me my childhood, and to Florence Reiff Fertig, the mother who helped me become the adult I am today.

It is also dedicated to my father, Sam Fertig, who is my rock of support.